W9-BVT-571
EAST MEADOW PUBLIC
3 1299 00602 9566

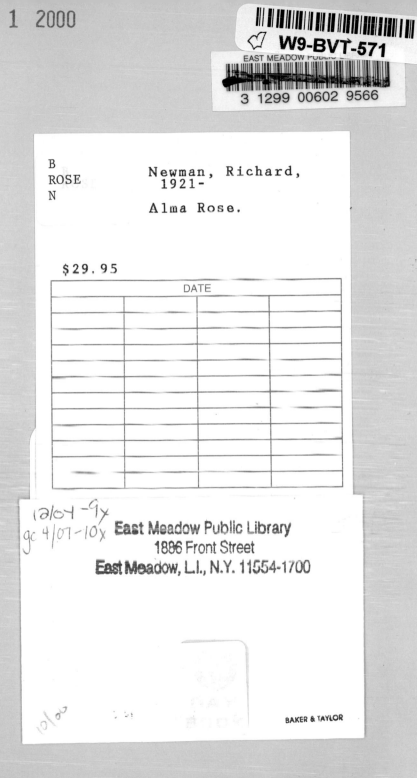

Alma Rosé

Fayer
Wien

Alma Rosé

VIENNA TO AUSCHWITZ

by Richard Newman
with Karen Kirtley

AMADEUS PRESS
Reinhard G. Pauly, General Editor
Portland, Oregon

The authors and publisher are indebted to Gina Alexander and Felix Pirani for permission to quote from *Letter to My Grandchildren,* the unpublished memoir of their mother, Leila Doubleday Pirani; to Henry Bulawko for permission to quote from his 1954 memoir *Les Jeux de la mort et de l'espoir;* to Anita Lasker-Wallfisch for permission to quote from her 1996 *Inherit the Truth;* and to Joy Puritz for permission to quote from her father's 1993 *Elisabeth Schumann: A Biography.*

We gratefully acknowledge the cooperation of the Auschwitz State Museum, which sent copies of documents pertaining to Alma's transport to Auschwitz and her death in the camp hospital, and a generous travel grant from the Social Sciences and Humanities Research Council of Canada. Maps of Auschwitz-Birkenau are reprinted with permission from Anna Pawełczyńska, *Values and Violence in Auschwitz: A Sociological Analysis,* ed. and trans. Catherine Leach, copyright © 1979 The Regents of the University of California. Photographs, documents, and letters from the Rosé family archive are reproduced with permission from the Mahler-Rosé Collection, the Gustav Mahler–Alfred Rosé Room, the Music Library, the University of Western Ontario.

ISBN 1-57467-051-4

Printed in Hong Kong

AMADEUS PRESS
The Haseltine Building
133 S.W. Second Avenue, Suite 450
Portland, Oregon 97204, U.S.A.

Library of Congress Cataloging-in-Publication Data

Newman, Richard.
Alma Rosé: Vienna to Auschwitz / by Richard Newman with Karen Kirtley.
p. cm.
Includes bibliographical references and index.
ISBN 1-57467-051-4
1. Rosé, Alma. 2. Violinists—Austria Biography. 3. Holocaust victims—Austria Biography. I. Kirtley, Karen. II. Title.
ML418.R76N48 2000
787.2'092—dc21
[B] 99-36000
CIP

If we don't play well, we'll go to the gas.

Alma Rosé, conductor of the
Auschwitz-Birkenau women's orchestra,
1943

Contents

Preface

This book began with an invitation to dinner in 1963. Professor Alfred Rosé of the music faculty of the University of Western Ontario in London, Canada, was planning a trip to Vienna, where he grew up, with his wife, Maria Caroline Rosé, also from Vienna. Alfred was making a will. On the recommendation of Renaissance scholar Dr. Wallace Ferguson, he asked me to serve as coexecutor, with his widow, in the event of his death. As a music critic with an interest in history and a personal friend of long standing, I gladly accepted the charge.

My wife, Jean, and I had known the Rosés since Alfred arrived at the university in 1946, although never so well as we came to know them over the next three decades. In Austria, where Alfred was a promising young conductor and composer before the Nazi takeover of 1938, he had been the protégé of Richard Strauss at the Vienna Opera. His uncle Gustav Mahler was known internationally, and his father, Arnold Rosé, was for many years the esteemed concertmaster of the Vienna Opera and Philharmonic Orchestras and leader of his own string quartet. Alfred had a sister, Alma, whom he rarely mentioned—one did not ask why. Yet among the Old World treasures that gave the Rosés' home on Cheapside Street the nickname "Little Vienna" were a photograph of Alma with her husband Váša Příhoda, the Czech violin virtuoso, and a beguiling picture of her playing the violin. These hung in Alfred's study, daily reminders of a shattering tragedy in his life.

A chance event in the 1970s, near the end of Alfred's life, stirred memories of Alma. One Saturday as he and Maria shopped in an outdoor market, a woman who overheard his name leaned across a vegetable cart and asked, "Are you related to the Alma Rosé who played the violin at Auschwitz?" Alfred stared in disbelief. "Yes," he said. "Alma Rosé was my sister. She led the women's orchestra."

"Your sister saved the lives of many Jewish girls," came the grave reply.

The woman at the market was one of three Jewish Slovak sisters who had helped one another to survive the death camp. They remembered Alma and her orchestra with gratitude—in those brutal circumstances, they said, each concert was an oasis of hope. They also remembered Alma's death in 1944, and the rumors that flew through the camp when the orchestra's conductor suddenly disappeared.

Alfred never recovered from the shock of his sister's death; he nursed his grief silently for more than three decades. In 1975, in his final weeks, he returned again and again to the consolation of the Slovak woman's words: *Your sister saved the lives of many Jewish girls.* Two days before he died, he spoke again of Alma. He had learned, he said, that she "saved many." In later years, many orchestra survivors would emotionally confirm her feat of courage.

From his father, Arnold Rosé, who survived the war in England, Alfred had inherited a treasure-trove of Mahler and Rosé memorabilia, which now passed to his estate. An entire bank vault, as well as the nooks and crannies of the Rosé home, was filled with autographed pictures of Gustav Mahler, Bruno Walter, Johannes Brahms, Johann Strauss Jr., Richard Strauss, Verdi, Toscanini, and other luminaries of the music world; personal letters from artists and musicians and testaments marking landmark anniversaries; paintings and etchings; precious programs, documents, autograph books, and photo albums; loose clippings in manila envelopes arranged approximately by date; family memorabilia such as gifts to Arnold from Emperor Franz Josef, locks of Mahler's hair and Mahler doodles on Hofoper stationery, exquisite pillow covers from Alma's handworked wedding trousseau. What to do with this vast, intensely personal archive?

Alfred expressly requested that the collection remain in Canada, where he and Maria had lived for thirty years. Maria decided to donate the archive to the Music Library of the University of Western Ontario, to be maintained in the Gustav Mahler–Alfred Rosé Room as a family memorial and resource for visiting scholars. During the long process of negotiation, transfer, and cataloging, I have had unlimited access to what is now known as the Mahler-Rosé Collection. Unless another source is explicitly named, all letters, documents, photographs, artwork, and memorabilia reproduced in the present book now reside in this superb collection.

The autumn after Alfred's death, French scholar Henry-Louis de La Grange called on Maria to offer condolences. In years past, as De La Grange prepared the first volume of his monumental Mahler biography, Alfred had led him through the family holdings. Later the Rosés were guests at the De La Grange villa in Corsica. Now De La Grange presented Maria with a copy of a newly published memoir, *Sursis pour l'orchestre* (published in English as *Playing for Time*) by Fania Fénelon, a singer in the Auschwitz-Birkenau camp orchestra. He had interviewed Fénelon on a radio program, he commented, and he had reason to question the book's reliability.

Anita Lasker-Wallfisch, cellist in the camp orchestra and later a well-known English musician, publicly protested the "fantasies" set forth in Fénelon's book. In particular, she and other members of the Auschwitz-Birkenau orchestra objected to its harsh portrayal of Alma Rosé. Fénelon's offensive portrait inspired Maria to search Alfred's estate for traces of the real Alma. I joined in the quest, which was immediately rewarded: in a corner of the cellar on Cheapside Street, we found a horsehide trunk marked "Philharmoniker" and decorated with labels from Europe's great hotels. It was filled with papers. The first envelope we opened contained a staggering seventeen letters from Alma to Alfred and Maria from Vienna and Nazi-occupied Holland, as well as letters from Arnold. We began to read, Maria renewing her sense of a much-mourned sister-in-law, I meeting the woman who would dominate the next many years of my life. In the end we uncovered more than sixty letters from Alma.

The woman who emerged from this correspondence was independent and strong-minded, sensitive, proud, witty, moody, refined, passionate about friends and family, uncompromising in pursuit of musical ideals. Father Rosé had declared Alma "possessed of Mahler's spirit," and so it seemed. I was charmed and intrigued.

Thus began a twenty-two-year journey that has led to the publication of this book. The search for Alma assumed a momentum of its own—it was as though her story had to be told. A pamphlet would fall on the floor just when it was needed, books would open to a pertinent passage, a chance encounter on a train or in a restaurant, a letter from a stranger, would answer a nagging question and point the way to discovery. Coincidences abounded. A German lecturer at the University of Western Ontario turned out to be the niece of the second wife of Alma's husband Váša and supplied valuable contacts in Czechoslovakia. The woman beside me at a Covent Garden performance shared her binoculars, and it came out that she was the wife of the violinist who replaced Alma in her father's quartet in England during World War II. An evening encounter with a baritone walking his dog in Vienna led to a meeting with an eighty-year-old violinist who had attended secondary school with Alma and studied privately with her father.

Friends and friends of friends helped with the scores of interviews at the core of this account. In Amsterdam Louis and Lotte Meijer, old friends of the Rosés', paved the way for research in Holland; in Poland, Helena Dunicz-Niwińska, a violinist in the camp orchestra, mentioned Alma to the staff of the Auschwitz Museum, obtained my name and address, and wrote offering to help, henceforth providing a vital contact with Eastern European orchestra survivors. A note posted at the 1987 Gathering of Survivors in Tel Aviv and Jerusalem resulted in a letter directing me to Helen Tichauer, an orchestra and camp office survivor in New York, and to her husband, the late scientist and former Auschwitz inmate Dr. Erwin Tichauer. The Tichauers mothered and fathered all subsequent research; their help has been invaluable.

Over the years, contacts in Austria, Canada, the United States, Belgium, Holland, Great Britain, France, Switzerland, Poland, Czechoslovakia, Australia, and Israel volunteered material that might have vanished, but by some mysterious force was preserved and made available at precisely the right moment. Among the many who helped to fill chinks in Alma's story are Terence C. Bacon; William Bush; Gladys Davis; Premsyl "Tom" Dolezal; Andrea Galland; Pietronella C. Gerritse; Hana Gregorova; Arthur Hudson; Jean Lassner; Alice and Philip Linden; Luba Pavlovicova-Bakova; Scott St. John and his mother, Shari, and sister, Lara; Hanna Spencer; Christian J. F. Stuhldreher; Guy van de Bon; Corinne Vandervelden; Jongkeer Jan Herman van Rooijen; Jongkeer van Sminia; Joy and Ernest Weiss; and Gerhard Wuensch.

For the English translations in the current volume (original to this book unless otherwise noted), I am grateful to William Bush, Irmgard Cayre, Sandford Goldstein, Jean Newman, Godrey Oelsner, Reinhard G. Pauly, Maria C. Rosé, Hanna Spencer, Florian Smieja, Abraham Smit, Fred and Lisl Ullman, Reuel Wilson, and Kurt Wreschner.

For research assistance, I especially thank Lisa Philpott and her colleagues at the Music Library of the University of Western Ontario. Alan Noon, the university's media specialist, photographed dozens of photographs and documents to provide the book's illustrations. Staff at the YIVO Center for Jewish Research in New York and the Austrian Documentation Center of the Resistance in Vienna have also given valued assistance.

Special thanks must go to Herta Blaukopf of the Internationale Gustav Mahler Gesellschaft in Vienna, to the University of Western Ontario medical research team, and to the staff of the Auschwitz-Birkenau State Museum, who have given generous support. Mahler scholars Kurt Blaukopf (d. 1999) and Gilbert Kaplan have been faithful resources. Kazimierz Smoleń, director of the Auschwitz-Birkenau State Museum from 1955 to 1990, and Louis de Jong, former director of the War History Documentation Center in Amsterdam, have also been helpful.

In a day when bureaucracy is under attack, I salute the cheerful and capable assistance of government officials and administrators on several continents. Even the European Union's personnel office in Brussels tracked down one of the key players in Alma's story.

I regret that space does not allow me to name all the individuals who have made important contributions to this biography—my debt of gratitude is overwhelming. For an alphabetical list of major interviews and sources, please turn to the back of the book.

A grant from the Social Sciences and Humanities Research Council of Canada made it possible for me to retrace Alma's path from Vienna to Auschwitz through seventeen cities. In three other research trips to Europe, I have visited the former Rosé family home in Vienna, met face to face with friends and loved ones from different segments of Alma's life, and stood shivering on the ground at Auschwitz-Birkenau where she and her fellow musicians made their brave stand.

The second-mile efforts of my coauthor and editor, Karen Kirtley, and the enthusiasm of Amadeus Press, especially general editor Reinhard G. Pauly and editorial director Eve Goodman, have brought this work to press in fitting form. Darcy Edgar Gross of Portland, Oregon, contributed valuable assistance on site.

I apologize in advance for any errors that might have crept into the account and will make every effort to correct them in later editions. Please send comments and suggestions to me in care of Amadeus Press.

Throughout the long gestation of this story, the greatest comfort and support have come from my wife and our three children, who allowed Alma to share—perhaps to dominate—our lives. Thank you Jean, Mary, Sara, and Scott.

Richard Newman
London, Canada

Editor's Note

The following pages offer interpretation but never invention. No incidents, scenes, or quotations stem from the imagination or attempts to improve the narrative through fictional polishing; all are based on documentary evidence and the testimony of witnesses. Even firsthand testimony, however—particularly on a subject so fraught with emotion—is sometimes baffling in its contradictions. Where facts cannot be established due to meager evidence or conflicting positions taken, we have reported on what is likely. Such speculation is clearly labeled.

Throughout we have made a scrupulous effort to give precise source information. In some cases, press clippings preserved in the family archive were unidentified, letters undated, memories vague. Although occasional gaps remain, this reconstruction of the life of Alma Rosé represents the best knowledge to be had in our time.

Alma's life story divides naturally into two parts: before and after Adolf Hitler's rise to power, when because of her Jewish ancestry Alma became a hunted person. Her own voice animates the early chapters. But after her arrest by the Nazis she is silent, and we rely on the testimony of those who remember her, including some two dozen of her Auschwitz-Birkenau "orchestra girls." Richard Newman has made a determined effort to record the orchestra survivors' memories while they are vivid; many of the camp musicians have died or become infirm since his first round of interviews in the 1980s. Insofar as this book is their testament as well as Alma's, its publication has been a race against time.

Some facts and figures related to Auschwitz and the Holocaust are disputed by reliable authorities. In supplying background information we have made considered choices; for the sake of brevity we do not recapitulate scholarly debates.

In tribute to the surviving members of the orchestra, and in the hope of making their recollections, in their own words (often in translation), widely available, we begin the Auschwitz section of the book with individual stories. Chapters 16 and 17 trace the evolution of the women's ensemble in personal accounts that overlap and occasionally collide. Chapter 18, "The Music Block," presents the larger picture, weaving the threads of the survivors' narratives into a description of daily life within the orchestra. An orchestra roster at the back of the book shows the composition of this unlikely group, a multiethnic, polyglot, peculiar musical ensemble like no other before or since.

Names used for the orchestra members follow no prescribed scheme but conform to usage in the camp—thus some women are called by their surnames, some by given names, and some by nicknames, as the orchestra survivors still speak of them. Similarly, the special vocabulary of the death camp appears throughout the later chapters; the "Camp Glossary" at book's end provides a guide.

Richard Newman's phenomenal achievement has been to meet and talk with more than a hundred people able to provide firsthand information about Alma Rosé, a remarkable woman musician who died more than half a century ago. Unless otherwise stated, he personally conducted every interview listed in the notes to the text and the following sourcelist. It has been a privilege to work with him in bringing this passionately felt book to fruition. We share the belief that in its pages, history and personal truth converge.

It is hard to take in the incredible aspects of Alma's saga—the very idea of playing a violin at Auschwitz-Birkenau and leading an orchestra of concentration camp inmates who never knew whether they would be alive the next day. Like so many indisputable facts of the Holocaust, Alma's story is a lingering horror. It is also a tale of pride and courage that leaves an indelible impression.

Karen Kirtley
Portland, Oregon

Prologue: Alma Maria Rosé

Alma Maria Rosé: honor her name. She was born to musical royalty in Vienna when the imperial city was a center of the musical world. Her father was Arnold Rosé, violinist and concertmaster of the Vienna Opera and Philharmonic Orchestras and leader for six decades of the Rosé Quartet; her mother was Justine Mahler, Gustav Mahler's devoted younger sister. She was the namesake and godchild of Alma Mahler, her Uncle Gustav's talented young wife; and "Uncle Bruno" Walter was a lifelong family friend. Alma's husband, violinist Váša Příhoda, was the Czech master of pyrotechnics, revered in Central Europe as the Paganini of his day. Her girlhood friends were Erica Morini, who became an internationally known virtuoso violinist, and Margarete (Gretl) Slezak (the daughter of heldentenor Leo Slezak). Margarete, a singer and film star, became the intimate friend of a rising young German politician, Adolf Hitler.

Alma—ardent, impetuous, steeped in musical tradition—embraced music as some embrace religion. She was independent of mind and ahead of her time. In the 1930s, she founded and led a women's touring orchestra that personified the froth as well as the musical acumen of Old Vienna. Smiling, swaying in unison in graceful waltz gowns, the young players charmed with their music and calculated feminine appeal. In the years of economic depression between the wars, Alma's orchestra ate when others went hungry, a pattern that would repeat itself grotesquely.

Like many other prosperous and assimilated Viennese Jews who did not practice the religion of their ancestors, the Rosé family were caught off guard by Nazism. When Hitler seized power in Austria and Alma's brother and his wife fled to America, Alma took responsibility for her aging father's welfare. She arranged her father's flight and her own to London; then, alone, she went to Holland to continue her musical career. Caught in the Nazi vise, she was arrested in France, held in Drancy outside Paris, then deported to Auschwitz-Birkenau.

There Alma again led a women's orchestra—the only female musical ensemble in the Nazi camps. With violin and baton, steely will, and dauntless spirit, she molded a terrified collection of young musicians into an orchestra that became their sole hope of survival. The orchestra women played to please their Nazi captors; in exchange they remained alive.

By trusting in music for salvation, by insisting on standards that seemed absurd against the backdrop of the gas chambers and the smoking chimneys of the crematoria, Alma saved the lives of some four dozen members of the orchestra. Most members of the Auschwitz-Birkenau women's orchestra survived the war—not one was sent to the gas. Tragically, Alma died in the camp of sudden illness. Josef Mengele himself, who loved music, tried to save the orchestra leader.

Alma's true story has never before been told in full. In the telling and remembering, we honor her and the prisoner-musicians who played at Auschwitz-Birkenau by her side, that valiant band for whom music meant life.

1

Musical Royalty: The Background

We never felt any different from anyone else.
—Alfred Rosé, on childhood in Vienna

Alma Rosé was born in Vienna, the bustling capital of the thousand-year-old Habsburg empire. She arrived on Saturday, 3 November 1906, a cloudy day in the imperial city. Her parents, Arnold and Justine Rosé, celebrated with music.

Justine's pregnancy had been troubled. She was often sick and exhausted by the demands of running the commodious household and looking after rambunctious "Alfi," the Rosés' precocious, almost four-year-old son Alfred. With her usual sense of decorum, Justine carried on with a curtailed social schedule. In 1906, invitations to her musical teas and Sunday dinners were rare and highly prized.

From concern for his wife, Arnold spent the year close to home, canceling an appearance with the Philharmonic in Salzburg as principal soloist in the Beethoven Violin Concerto in D. When Justine delivered a healthy baby girl, he immediately sent word to the Vienna Opera.

Justine's brother, Gustav Mahler, was at the opera the night the baby was born, conducting a new production of Hermann Götz's *Der Widerspenstigen Zähmung* (The Taming of the Shrew). He and his wife Alma Mahler were the devoted parents of two little daughters. Maria Anna, their dear "Putzi," was four years old to the day when little Alma arrived—the cousins would share their November birthday. Anna Justine, named for her maternal grandmother and her Aunt Justine but called "Gucki" for her blue eyes, was a year old. In honor of Gustav's beautiful young wife, the Rosés named their baby Alma Maria.

Bruno Walter was also at the opera when Arnold's happy announcement arrived. Like the Mahlers, he and his wife Elsa, the Rosés' closest musical friends, had two young daughters. They made haste to visit the proud parents and saw Alma the day she first surveyed the world. Years later, they remembered the joy and promise of her birth.[1]

The new arrival was heralded far beyond the family circle, for the Rosés lived in the public eye. Justine bore two of the most illustrious names in Austrian music: her brother Gustav was the brilliant director of the Vienna Opera and a composer of growing renown, and her husband was Arnold Rosé, the venerated orchestra leader. Six months earlier, Arnold had celebrated his twenty-fifth year as first violinist of the Vienna Philharmonic and Opera Orchestras; for twenty-three years, he had led the Rosé Quartet, among Europe's most distinguished chamber music groups.

In the cosmopolitan city that was home to Beethoven and Brahms as well as Schubert and the famous Strausses, the Mahler-Rosé family were musical royals. The Viennese adored the celebrities from what they called "*our* Burgtheater" and "*our* opera." Some said that only the Habsburg emperor Franz Josef and Vienna's mayor Karl Lueger were more revered by the public than the city's reigning artists, who were everywhere recognized and deferred to.

The Viennese zest for life and passion for art were legendary. As Stefan Zweig wrote of the city in the first years of the century, "It was sweet to live here."[2] The autumn of Alma's birth, chestnuts roasted as always in the street-vendors' carts, filling the air with enticement. Fiacre drivers whistled tunes from *Die lustige Witwe* (The Merry Widow), the operetta by Franz Lehár that had opened the previous December in the Theater an der Wien.[3] Lehár's "Velia" echoed from the carriages along with the traditional songs of *Gemütlichkeit,* the easy-going manner of the streets.

The drivers lectured passengers as they toured the Ringstrasse, Vienna's grand six-mile-long boulevard, pointing to musicians, singers, dancers, painters, poets, professors, and distinguished doctors and surgeons as national treasures. Pedestrians sometimes stopped to applaud their favorites. Regulars of the Ringstrasse boasted they could set their clocks by the punctilious "Der Mahler" as he emerged from the opera at noon to walk briskly home for lunch. Max Graf, the Viennese music historian, remembered his daily glimpses of the "Opera Director of the Emperor":

> This man always carried his soft hat in his hand, and walked with a strange, stamping gait, limping with his right leg from time to time. His dark face, framed by long hair, had a sharp profile and eyes which shot out dark looks through his glasses. It was the ascetic face of a medieval monk. In this man the nerves pulled tensely and from him a spiritual strength streamed forth. It could be either a good or bad spirit flashing from the high forehead and the eyes.[4]

With disdain for appearances, Gustav Mahler made it a point to wear shabby hats and coats with torn linings. Arnold, in contrast, dressed with panache. Among Alma's earliest memories was her handsome father in his flowing opera cape, mounting a court carriage with royal crests and liveried attendants, on his way to perform at the opera or at Vienna's majestic Hofburg, the imperial palace of the Habsburgs.

ALMA'S FOREBEARS on both sides were Jewish. Her mother's father, Bernhard Mahler, was a businessman who began his career as a village peddler and rose to own a small distillery in Kalischt (Kalište) in Bohemia and finally an inn in Iglau (Jihlava) in Moravia, in what later became Czechoslovakia. He and his wife, the former Marie Hermann, had fourteen children, seven of whom died in infancy and one, Ernst, at the age of thirteen. When both parents as well as the eldest sister, Leopoldine, died in 1889, five of the Mahler children were still living: Gustav, born in 1860; his younger brothers Alois and Otto; and two younger sisters, Justine, born in 1868, and Emma, seven years younger. Gustav became the Mahler patriarch and undertook the maintenance of the family.[5] From that time until their marriages, Gustav and his two sisters lived and traveled together. Justine dedicated herself to giving her brother the support he needed: she ran his household, corresponded on his behalf, copied reviews and programs, attended important rehearsals, planned vacations at Easter, Christmas, and summer break, and did her best to surround him with quiet when he composed.

Alma's father was born Arnold Josef Rosenblum on 24 October 1863. He was one of four sons in a family that came from Jassy, in what is now Romania. The musical potential of the two younger sons—Eduard, born in 1859, and Arnold, four years his junior—inspired the family's move to Vienna. Taking advantage of a new freedom of movement granted Jews in the Austro-Hungarian empire after 1867, when a new constitution lifted anti-Semitic restrictions, they left Romania for Vienna when Arnold was four years old.

In Vienna Arnold's father, Hermann, was a prosperous carriage builder. French tutors taught the children, and they were educated in literature and the arts as well as history and the sciences. Arnold's mother, Marie, was intent on fostering her sons' talents and found the best musical contacts for them, not hesitating to write to such an eminence as Ferruccio Busoni[6] to inquire about a concert at which Arnold was to play. Eduard was a fine developing cellist, and Arnold an extraordinarily perceptive violinist. Karl Heissler, at the Vienna Conservatory, was among Arnold's teachers.

In 1879, when Arnold was sixteen, he made his professional debut as Arnold Rosenblum in the Leipzig Gewandhaus. On 10 April 1881, still as Arnold Rosenblum, he gave the first Viennese performance of Karl Goldmark's Violin Concerto, opus 28, under conductor Hans Richter. Wilhelm Jahn, newly appointed director of the Vienna Court Opera or Hofoper (later the State Opera or Staatsoper), immediately appointed him first concertmaster of the Vienna Court Opera Orchestra. The Vienna Opera Orchestra, traditionally the parent of the Vienna Philharmonic, doubles in the pit of the opera house and on the concert stage in an arrangement unique to Vienna. Thus from the tender age of seventeen, Arnold led two venerable orchestras from the first chair, later to become the first playing member of the orchestra to receive honorary membership in the Philharmonic. After 1893, he also taught at the Vienna Conservatory, where he remained more than three decades.

Arnold's musicianship and talent for leadership were well recognized. At the opera, patrons would peer into the orchestra pit before the opening curtain, seeking out the young concertmaster whose presence ensured the finest performances. Stars of the opera were reassured when they learned that Arnold Rosé would occupy the first chair at a performance in which they would appear. Young conductors making their first appearances in Vienna felt honored if Arnold were their concertmaster, while more established conductors expected no less. Looking back, the esteemed English conductor Sir Adrian Boult proclaimed Rosé Europe's most famous orchestra leader of his time.[7]

In 1882, eighteen months after his debut, Arnold adopted the stage name Arnold Rosé and founded the Rosé Quartet with his brother Eduard (who also took the name Rosé) as cellist and Julius Egghard and Anton Loh as second violinist and violist. For more than fifty-five years, with various other members, the Vienna-based ensemble maintained a reputation for excellence.[8]

In 1897 the Rosé Quartet gave its hundredth Viennese performance, at which the eminent Dutch pianist Julius Röntgen—friend to Johannes Brahms and Edvard Grieg—was special guest. The great Brahms himself turned to the Rosé Quartet to premiere some of his late chamber works, including the revised String Quintet in G major, opus 111. With Brahms at the piano, between 1890 and 1895 the ensemble performed from manuscript the premieres of four compositions: the revised 1854 Piano Trio in B major, opus 8; the Clarinet Quintet in B minor, opus 115, with Franz Steiner, clarinetist; and the Piano and Clarinet Sonatas in F minor and E-flat major, opus 120, nos. 1 and 2, with Richard Mühlfeld as clarinetist. So enduring was Brahms' spirit in the Rosé household that young Alma referred to him as "Uncle Brahms" although he had died almost a decade before she was born.

Eduard Rosé played with the quartet for only a season. In 1898 Eduard married Emma, the youngest Mahler sister. (Thus two Rosé brothers married two Mahler sisters, causing untold confusion for future biographers.) The couple emigrated to the United States, where Eduard joined the Boston Symphony Orchestra and their first son, Ernst (later Ernest), was born. Because Emma sorely missed her sister and brothers, the family returned to Europe after only two years. Eduard continued his career at Weimar, where he was first cellist at the Weimar Theater and taught at the Conservatory. Wolfgang, a second son, was born in Europe in 1907 and was the Rosé cousin closest in age to Alma.[9]

Arnold's two older brothers also carved out niches in the arts. Alexander was a Viennese impresario, bookseller, and stationer. Berthold, an actor who had been a favorite of German Kaiser Wilhelm II at the Royal Theater in Wiesbaden, became almost a court jester for the king. His nephew Ernest described him as completely different from his brothers—a *fresser* whose huge appetites led to an early death in his mid-fifties.[10]

In 1889, Arnold appeared as concertmaster of the Vienna Opera Orchestra at the Bayreuth Festival; Mahler was in the audience attending *Die Walküre.* During the performance, the orchestra had difficulty. Arnold stood up and with strong, emphatic registration on his violin, set the orchestra back on track in both pitch and tempo. Mahler, who admired the bold gesture, is said to have exclaimed, "Now, there IS a concertmaster!"[11] The admirable Rosé would become a trusted friend and colleague as well as Mahler's brother-in-law.

In 1890, Arnold was honored by Ludwig II of Bavaria with the presentation of the Grosse Goldene Verdienstkreuz. This was the first of more than thirty-five awards he received from the Habsburg, Spanish, and Italian courts, the republic of Austria, and the city of Vienna.[12] As a member of the royal musical establishment with the rank of *k. u. k. Hofmusiker* (Royal and Imperial Court Musician), he enjoyed the privilege of a court carriage to carry him in state to the opera. A carriage of his own, with a fine livery, took him to concert appearances in other venues.

Joseph Joachim, the revered leader of the Joachim Quartet, was in his seventies at the turn of the century and noticeably losing his power. At the 1899 Beethovenhaus celebrations in Bonn, Joachim was the chief musical attraction. Arnold, his heir apparent, received second billing.

Like Joachim, Arnold was known as the exponent of a tradition that went back to Beethoven; he was considered conservative and above all, correct. Yet he embraced contemporary challenges, "breaking lances," as critic Paul Bechert wrote, on behalf of aspiring young musicians whose talents he quickly recognized.[13] For his quartet's performances in the 588-seat Bösendorfer-Saal, Arnold charted an adventuresome course. Although he opened every season with the credo "I believe in Haydn, Mozart, and Beethoven,"[14] he gave new and recent music a hearing and was sought out for the premieres of works by Erich Korngold, Hans Pfitzner, and Max Reger. Over the years, scores of young composers were accorded Rosé premieres.[15] Arnold Schoenberg, in particular, benefitted from Arnold's unwavering support.

As a young man about town, Arnold was fond of modish clothing, gambling parties at the Hotel Sacher, and fashionable women, but he did not hide his serious side. He shared with Gustav Mahler the conviction that slavish adherence to traditional performance practices could result in *Schlamperei* (slovenliness) at the expense of deeper insight into a musical work and fidelity to the composer's intentions.

ROSÉ AND MAHLER had been musical acquaintances for several years before Gustav won the directorate of the Vienna Opera in 1897 and moved from

Hamburg to Vienna. At first Gustav lived in furnished rooms, served only by his cook, as Justine and Emma remained in Hamburg to settle family affairs. In August 1898, he moved to an apartment on the Bartensteingasse, where his sisters joined him. The same month, Emma married Eduard. In the fall, Gustav and Justine moved to a large apartment at Auenbruggergasse 2, where Justine again assumed the role of household mistress.

In his new position Gustav was besieged with social demands. Justine soon put her foot down: never was he to bring home unannounced visitors from the theater. Shortly after this ultimatum, Gustav appeared for lunch with Arnold Rosé, the popular concertmaster. Arnold, a bachelor in his mid-thirties, was so witty and charming that Justine instantly forgave the trespass.

Arnold liked to boast that he saw Justine every day thereafter. This was gallant exaggeration, since his touring schedule took him away from Vienna many weeks each year. It is true that from that time forward, Arnold was virtually a member of the family, lunching with Gustav at noon at the opera, playing music with friends at the Mahler or Rosé home into the night, spending vacations at rented summer houses with Gustav and Justine and their friend Natalie Bauer-Lechner.[16]

Although the attraction between Arnold and Justine was immediate, their courtship lasted nearly five years. At first they kept their romance a secret from the volatile Mahler, but Viennese gossip-mongers delighted in the fact that the opera's dashing concertmaster was courting the sister of the director. Justine was in love; but Gustav relied on her, and she would not desert him until he too found the person he wanted to marry.[17]

For Gustav, love struck in November 1901. At the home of Berta Szeps Zuckerkandl, an art critic and well-known hostess who entertained intellectuals and artists in her salon every Sunday, Gustav met Alma Maria Schindler. The child of her mother's first marriage to landscape artist Emil Jakob Schindler, Alma Schindler was a society beauty and a budding pianist with ambitions of becoming a composer. Her beloved father died when she was thirteen. Her mother, Anna Schindler, then married Carl Moll, a well-known painter and member of the outspoken Secessionist group of turn-of-the-century Vienna.[18] Alexander von Zemlinsky, a young composer who would gain considerable distinction, taught Alma composition and was himself deeply in love with his pupil.

Gustav was powerfully smitten, but he was forty-one years old, and Alma Schindler only twenty-two. She had grown up amidst extravagant luxury in the company of Vienna's most provocative visual artists, and she showed the marks: she was outspoken, capricious, vain, demanding, rebellious. She was also delightfully intelligent and original. Gustav's conservative colleagues and some of his closest friends were scandalized by his infatuation as well as by Alma's impudent behavior. (For instance, she did not hesitate to say about Gustav's music, "I know very little of it and the little I do know I don't like."[19])

Bruno Walter was concerned for Mahler's sake. Alma Schindler was "the most beautiful girl in Vienna," he wrote, "accustomed to a glittering life in society, while [Gustav] is so unworldly and fond of solitude; and there are plenty of other problems one could mention."[20]

Justine encouraged Gustav in the romance, assuring him that Alma would return his love. A month after they met, Alma and Gustav became secretly engaged; Gustav told Justine the next day.[21] Two wedding dates were set. Justine would marry Arnold and leave the house on Auenbruggergasse for an apartment at Salesianergasse 8, a few blocks away, and Gustav's bride would move into the Mahler apartment.

The two couples were married in ceremonies one day apart, the Mahlers on 9 March 1902 in the sacristy of the Catholic Karlskirche, and the Rosés on 10 March at the Evangelical church on Dorotheergasse.[22] They announced their weddings with simple ivory cards of matching design.

THE YEAR Arnold and Justine were married, the Rosé Quartet, augmented to a sextet and encouraged by Mahler, gave the first performance of Arnold Schoenberg's *Verklärte Nacht* (Transfigured Night). The Viennese audience hissed loudly, and fistfights erupted in the theater. A second performance scheduled for March 1904 was canceled by the authorities because of the riot generated by the premiere; yet Arnold had enough faith in Schoenberg's genius to perform the piece at a later concert. Heedless of catcalls from the audience, the ensemble played it through, rose and bowed, then repeated it from beginning to end as if it had won an ovation.

Alma was two months old in 1907 when the quartet performed Schoenberg's Quartet in D minor, opus 7—music so complex it took forty rehearsals to master it—again from manuscript. In 1908 in Vienna, with Vienna Opera's great Carmen and later Salome, Marie Gutheil-Schoder,[23] the quartet premiered Schoenberg's Second String Quartet in F-sharp minor with soprano voice from manuscript. This revolutionary work coincided with the sixtieth-anniversary jubilee marking Emperor Franz Josef's ascendancy in 1848 to the Habsburg throne.

As Schoenberg worked on the quartet, he and Rosé exchanged letters, the composer urging Arnold to persuade Gutheil-Schoder to sing the first performance. To his dying day, Arnold Rosé kept the more than thirty letters in Schoenberg's hand.[24]

ARNOLD ROSÉ's discipline and charm were well known; so too were his bouts with despair. Justine, accustomed to her brother's mercurial moods, coped admirably, but Arnold's periods of melancholy weighed on the family and on his professional associates. Friedrich Buxbaum, principal cellist in the Vienna Philharmonic and a member of the Rosé Quartet for more than twenty years, was grateful for Justine's vigilance and tact. When Arnold was in one of his "deep brown" moods, his wife would greet the quartet before rehearsal with a word of warning. All knew that at such a time, a careless quip could turn a rehearsal into a disaster.[25]

ALMA'S BIRTH YEAR, 1906, was the "Mozart Year," the 150th anniversary of the composer's birth, when Mahler conducted thirty-seven performances of new productions of Mozart's operas. In August, Salzburg celebrated the Mozart anniversary. During the festival, the two dominant personalities on the podium were Mahler and Felix Mottl, a former rival for the directorate of the Vienna Opera. Mahler conducted an historic *Don Giovanni,* and composer-pianist Camille Saint-Saëns was the festival's special guest.

The year 1906 was also distinguished by the Dresden premiere of Richard Strauss's opera *Salome,* based on Oscar Wilde's classic horror play and banned by the censor in Vienna. In Cologne, in a later production, the opera would receive fifty curtain calls.

Just two weeks before Alma's birth, Parisian friends of the family—all former champions of Alfred Dreyfus—arrived in Vienna for what Mahler called a "secret festival" in their honor. In the group were Sophie Szeps Clemenceau (Berta Szeps Zuckerkandl's sister); her husband Paul (brother of Georges Clemenceau, the prime minister of France from 1906 to 1909 and again from 1917 to 1920); and Colonel Georges Picquart.[26] Every day Mahler conducted and Arnold took his place in the first chair—*Figaro, Don Giovanni, Tristan,* a week of opera that left mouths agape.

CLOSELY ALLIED to the Mahler-Rosé dynasty was Bruno Walter—Alma's beloved "Uncle Bruno." As a young conductor in Hamburg, Berlin-born Bruno Walter Schlesinger became Mahler's protégé. In 1901 he joined Mahler at the Vienna Opera, where as Mahler's close associate and obvious favorite, he inherited the director's enemies among the singers and musicians. The press accused him of slavishly imitating Mahler's conducting technique and even his personal mannerisms. The anti-Semitic press was especially virulent, with its usual references to "Jewish rogues" and "Jewish filth" sullying the German or "Aryan" artistic tradition. As a beleaguered twenty-four-year-old, Walter found solace in the warmth of the Mahler-Rosé circle.[27]

Walter performed with Arnold Rosé in what he called "sonata evenings" and made various appearances with members of the Rosé Quartet. When Alma was two months old, on 8 January 1907, Walter, Rosé, and Buxbaum performed Walter's own Piano Trio in F major from manuscript in the Bösendorfer-Saal. Audiences greeted chamber-music recitals played with Arnold with such enthusiasm that Walter and Rosé made them an important sideline over fifteen years. Their duo performances became a much-loved Viennese musical tradition.

THE MAHLERS and Rosés appeared to live charmed lives. But for Jews anywhere in Europe at the turn of the century, tensions could suddenly erupt. In Vienna, where Sigmund Freud, Hugo von Hofmannsthal, Max Reinhardt, and many other eminent Jews made profound cultural contributions, anti-Semitism was a steady undercurrent.

In theory the rights of Jews in Austria-Hungary were protected by law, since the constitution had guaranteed "freedom of religion and conscience" since 1867, reflecting the tolerant attitude of Emperor Franz Josef. The emperor himself was disgusted by anti-Semitism: on one occasion, when a theater audience began chanting an anti-Jewish rhyme, he rose and scornfully left the hall.[28] But Catholicism was the official religion of the empire, and a vocal anti-Semitic minority made its presence felt, anticipating Hitler's obsessive hatred of the Jews.

The popular mayor of Vienna since 1897, Karl Lueger, was an avowed anti-Semite and one of the founders of the Christian Socialist political party, a forerunner of Nazism. Anti-Semitic newspapers protested the appointment of Jews to high positions, especially in the arts, which they were accused of monopolizing. Theodor Herzl (born in Budapest the same year as Gustav Mahler), the prominent journalist who led the Zionist movement to create a Jewish state, attracted the support of fewer than half the Jews of Austria and perhaps no more than a quarter. Most Austrian Jews rejected Zionism and aimed instead at assimilation. Acceptance by the mainstream population was a widely shared ideal.[29]

The Mahler-Rosé family made little of their Jewish ancestry. German was their language, and they had less in common with the Yiddish-speaking Jews of Eastern Europe than with their fellow Austrians and Germans, particularly the educated classes. Like many other European intellectuals of their time, they considered the notion of Judaism as a race ridiculous and found it impossible to believe that a brutish, close-minded few posed any real threat to society.

Shortly before Alma's birth, Anton (Toni) Schittenhelm, a tenor at the opera, expressed concern at Arnold's refusal to consider job offers from the United States. Vienna might not repay the loyalty he gave it, the singer cautioned.[30] Arnold brushed off the warning. He was Viennese above all, a servant of the city's music.

A DECADE before, in the winter of 1896–97, Justine and Gustav Mahler had confronted the impact of their Jewish ancestry. Wilhelm Jahn, director of the Vienna Court Opera, was ailing and faced a cataract operation. Jahn's impending leave set off a behind-the-scenes search for a replacement. Mahler, after six years as first Kapellmeister at the Hamburg Opera, was ready to leave and eagerly sought the post.

Mahler was a superb candidate. His energy and high musical ideals were a matter of record, and he had shown a rare ability to achieve discipline in a milieu rife with artistic temperament. As a conductor he had won international recognition, although fame as a composer continued to elude him. (In despondent moods, he referred to his compositions—almost four of his own symphonies and three cycles of art songs—as mere additions to his library because they were performed so rarely.[31])

Despite his credentials, Mahler's Jewish heritage technically barred him from a Habsburg court appointment; the Spanish ceremonial, traditionally observed by the court, stipulated that only the baptized could hold major court positions. Enforcing strict protocol, Prince Alfred Montenuovo (the acting opera administrator) opposed a Jew for the post.[32]

Cosima Wagner, widow of the composer, also opposed Mahler because of his ancestry. As high priestess of the Bayreuth shrine to Richard Wagner, Cosima let her opinion be known from Wahnfried, the Wagner home. Her lack of support was ironic, since Mahler had often proclaimed his ardent admiration of her husband.[33] During earlier pilgrimages to Bayreuth, Mahler had manifested pride and gratitude at being accepted within the Wagner family circle. Justine, who had long distrusted Cosima, was not surprised by her opposition. The Wagners' sly malevolence toward Gustav had already led to bitter brother-sister debates. Each time, Gustav ended the discussion by declaring himself so devoted to the genius of Wagner that he would beat the kettledrum at Bayreuth if only he were asked.

Gustav enlisted influential supporters to press his case, but to no avail. Woefully he told his friend Dr. Arnold Berliner in January 1897, "Everywhere, things fall through at the last moment on account of my race. . . . Under the present circumstances, it is impossible to engage a Jew for Vienna."[34]

Siegfried Lipiner, a member of the Mahler-Rosé circle and a parliamentary librarian as well a classical scholar and poet, wrote to Gustav that despite his own considerable influence at the court, attempts to support Gustav's appointment were thus far in vain. Everything began to point in the direction of Christian baptism. It would be a crucial decision for all the family.

Late in 1896, Justine wrote from Hamburg to a friend in Vienna, Ernestine Löhr, describing what she considered a hateful and hypocritical process.

> We all continue to take instruction, and the priest said yesterday we might not finish until February. Emma and I are really doing it only to make the whole thing easier for Gustav, as the position in Vienna at the opera (a secret) depends on it. . . .
>
> The first priest asked why we are doing it. I did not have the heart to pretend it is out of conviction, and he seemed to have little enthusiasm for it. Now I have gone to another priest, who by the way is Austrian—very liberal and such a fine fellow that we invited him to dinner next week. The whole affair is play-acting for me, since I don't believe a thing and could refute whatever he says. I memorize whole sections like poems in a foreign language.[35]

In mid-February 1897, Justine wrote again to Ernestine:

> Our baptism has still not taken place, should now be definitely on the twenty-eighth. I always postpone it. It is too loathsome and makes me quite melancholy. . . . I don't know what I would give if we did not have to do it. . . . We don't want to let Gustav jump into it alone. I have such an antipathy towards the priest that I can barely shake his hand. In Vienna, the story goes around that we are already baptized, so please keep this secret.[36]

In conclusion, Justine wrote that she could do this for "only one person," her brother.

According to Henry-Louis de La Grange, Mahler said that he converted to Catholicism shortly after leaving Budapest. At any rate, De La Grange tells us, his baptism took place in Hamburg in the Kleine Michaeliskirche on 23 February 1897.[37] It accomplished its purpose. In April of that year Mahler was named deputy director, under Jahn, of the Vienna Opera; in October 1897 Jahn was forced out, and Mahler became his successor.

Arnold Rosé, too, had chosen the route to acceptability taken by many Jewish members of the Vienna Philharmonic and Opera Orchestras. He had been baptized *Evangelisch*—Protestant—at the Evangelical church on Dorotheergasse well before his marriage to Justine in the same sanctuary. For him, as for Justine, the conversion was merely expedient.

Thus, when Alma Rosé was born in 1906 and for almost a decade before, both her parents were formally Christian Austrians—her mother Catholic like her Uncle Gustav, her father Protestant. Both Alma and her brother Alfred were baptized Protestant Christians as infants. Emma and Eduard Rosé became Alfred's godparents. Alma Maria Schindler Mahler stood for her namesake, Alma Maria Rosé.

LITTLE ALMA entered a world of social and political unease. The poor of Vienna were oppressed and restless, and stirrings of Balkan nationalism strained the claims of the House of Habsburg. In response to a Russian popular uprising of 1905 and against the advice of his noble advisers, on 1 January 1907 Emperor Franz Josef signed a universal male suffrage bill, giving virtually all Austrian males, four and a half million voters, a say in the choice of deputies for the 516 seats in parliament. The vote reflected the diversity of the multinational empire: 233 seats went to Germans, 107 to Czechs, 82 to Poles, 33 to Ruthenians, 24 to Slovenes, 19 to Italians, 13 to Serbo-Croats, and 5 to Romanians. For the time being, the results stalled the momentum of a growing pan-German movement for political union of all so-called German peoples. Nonetheless the election produced gains for the Christian Socialists led by the anti-Semitic Lueger and for the Social Democrats, champions of the laboring classes.

Trouble was also brewing at the opera. Jabbing his baton at wrongdoers, preaching, shouting, stamping his feet, Mahler worked furiously and ceaselessly and demanded the same striving from his colleagues. His certainty of his own genius and the rightness of his approach gave him an imperious manner that some considered inhumanly strict, even brutal. He was accused of ruining voices and putting his own fussy stamp on the works of the masters.

Hugo Burghauser, a former president of the Philharmonic, recalled hearing how Mahler, when displeased during a rehearsal, would turn to Rosé in the first chair and ask in a loud whisper how soon the offending musician would qualify for pension. (A premature retirement of course resulted in a smaller pension.)[38] Never guided by others' opinions of him, he paid scant heed to his colleagues' delicate feelings. Art, for him, was a realm apart, and perfection the only possible goal. The inevitable resentments multiplied, and individual artists and coalitions joined in intrigues to undermine their leader.

GUSTAV AND Alma Mahler suffered a terrible blow in the summer of 1907, when their eldest daughter, Maria Anna, died of scarlet fever. Mahler was devastated; he had lost the one person whose visits he could tolerate while he was composing. Following the trauma of Putzi's death, his health began to fail. Doctors diagnosed a heart condition similar to the one that had killed his mother eighteen years earlier.

The Mahler decade at the Vienna Opera was coming to a close. In 1907, hoping to devote more time to composing, Mahler accepted an offer from the Metropolitan Opera in New York. His resignation was accepted with extreme reluctance. Now Vienna's *Neue Freie Presse,* which had often lambasted Mahler and his works, lamented the city's failure to nurture its artistic giants.

Mahler left the Vienna Opera painfully divided over his legacy. His parting message to the "Honored Members of the Court Opera," a farewell posted at the opera house, was an emotional defense of his policies:

> Instead of the whole, the consummated, of which I dreamed, I leave patchwork, the incomplete, as man is fated to do. . . . I meant well and aimed at high goals. Not always could my efforts be crowned with success. . . . But I have always given my all, have subordinated my person to the cause, my inclinations to my duty. I did not spare myself and was therefore justified in demanding that others, too, exert their strength to the utmost.[39]

It is said that a day later, Mahler's letter was found crumpled and torn on the floor.

Debate has long raged over the anti-Semitic factor in pressures leading to Mahler's departure. In any case, a large and loyal Mahler following remained in Vienna after Gustav and Alma Mahler sailed for New York in December

1907, leaving their youngest daughter Gucki in Vienna with Frau Moll for the season.

Young Alma was a little over a year old when the Rosé family joined in a tearful farewell at Vienna's Westbahnhof. During the next three years Mahler found fertile ground for his work in New York City, where he made lasting contributions to the American symphonic tradition. Each summer he returned to Vienna to family and Austrian roots.

During the final year of Mahler's reign in Vienna, in Alma's birth year 1906, Vienna's splendid buildings and Mahler's artistry with the works of Richard Wagner captivated a sixteen-year-old visitor from Linz. He could frequently be seen in the standing-room section at the Court Opera, where tickets were a mere two crowns, his dark eyes blazing under the crop of black hair he combed to one side when he made the effort. This was Adolf Hitler, an aimless young man on his first two-month visit to Vienna, where he sought a place as an art student. He returned a year later to spend "five and a half years [until May 1913] loving and hating the glamorous capital of the Habsburgs," as he later wrote in "The School of My Life."[40]

By the end of Hitler's Vienna years, the Academy of Fine Arts had rejected him twice. He had lived in cheap rented rooms and hostels, selling sketches and watercolors, making posters, and reading voraciously. Those who knew him in Vienna remembered his daring, his relentless tirades, his wild fantasies and sudden rages. At every opportunity he immersed himself in Wagner's music dramas at the opera. In those years, it is said, he never missed a performance of *Tristan und Isolde,* in which Arnold's third-act violin solo was unforgettably magical.[41]

A non-smoker, non-drinker, and too shy to become involved with women, the young Austrian became passionately interested in the pan-German ideology at the heart of Austrian political unrest. Later he wrote in *Mein Kampf* (My Struggle) that he had found a prototype for his anti-Jewish program in the policies of Karl Lueger and the mayor's gift for propaganda.

At this distance, it is difficult to reconcile conflicting views of the Lueger years in Vienna. Stefan Zweig wrote that despite his anti-Semitic policies, Lueger was "just" and "helpful and friendly to his former Jewish friends."[42] In contrast, pianist Artur Schnabel wrote that in Lueger's Vienna, as a Jewish youth of thirteen, he "learned the meaning of fear," although his childhood was otherwise very happy and he was molested only once.[43] "Encouraged by Lueger," wrote Schnabel's biographer, "it was a favorite sport of patriotic male adolescents to bully and beat, with a jolly brutality, children whom they thought to be Jewish."[44]

2

A Fine Musical Nursery

To those who give generously to art, art is generous in return.
To little Alma.—Selma Halban-Kurz

Little Alma—"Almschi," as her family called her—suited the role of celebrity child. With her huge dark eyes and kewpie doll beauty, her hair curled in perfect ringlets, she never failed to make an impression. Within the family she was known for her apple cheeks. Justine dressed her in lace-collared frocks with puffed sleeves and hand-sewn rosettes and taught her the traditional Austrian girl's "Knicks," or curtsy. Visitors to the Rosé home met Alma briefly. Her face aglow, she would make a graceful bow that drew a smile or a courtly kiss on the back of a dimpled hand, then a governess or nanny would whisk her away. Visitors remembered the willfulness on her small face, and perhaps the trace of a pout.

By 1909 Alfred was a vigorous seven-year-old; Alma, at three, was often in his shadow. Alfi did his best to be domineering, barking out orders and demanding to be heard. Using charm instead of bravura, Alma soon learned how to make her presence felt.

The Rosés lived within easy walking distance of Vienna's inner city in the fourth district, known as Wieden—first at Taubstummengasse 4, then at Strohgasse 3. These were the neighborhoods favored by the dynasties of the Habsburgs' golden days, nobility and gentry from the far reaches of the empire who preferred cosmopolitan Vienna to their holdings in the provinces. Each year, after the autumn hunts at their splendid rural castles, the aristocracy returned to the capital.

Leila Doubleday (later Leila Pirani), a young Australian living in Vienna, recalled her first visit to the Rosés' comfortable apartment.[1] A violin and piano student, she had arranged an audition with the eminent Professor Rosé. Her heart pounding with excitement, she climbed past three levels of apartments belonging to counts and barons to the Rosés' on the fourth floor. A maid answered the door. Leila, waiting to be announced, studied the large prints of Michelangelo's Vatican frescoes that hung in the square front hall.

Justine, a handsome woman although "considerably heavier than was healthy," greeted her with a warm smile. Arnold kept a dignified distance until he decided the young musician was sufficiently *musikalisch* to take as a student. He was imposing, with a "finely trimmed black beard and perfectly tailored clothes," yet something in his eyes allayed fear. Leila made a good impression and became not merely a favorite Rosé student, but a beloved family friend. The Rosés, she wrote in recollection, were a family distinguished by their "vitality, talent, and devotion to others."[2]

The Rosé children were close to their cousins Ernest, Wolfgang, and Gucki and to the children of their parents' friends from the opera. When their governess took them to Schwarzenberg Park near the Ringstrasse, their playmates included Gretel and Lotte Walter, Bruno Walter's daughters, and Walter and Gretl Slezak, the children of Leo Slezak.[3]

In 1910, needing more room for the family and household staff, the Rosés moved from Wieden to Döbling, which would become Vienna's upper-middle-class nineteenth district. Here they occupied the first two floors at Pyrkergasse 23 and had the luxury of a flower garden. The music room, reserved for making music and entertaining, was on the ground level, together with a traditional dining room and a kitchen skillfully managed by the family's Czech cook, Marie (Manina) Jelinek-Klose. Manina's rich Central European creations added to the special reputation of Rosé hospitality. Justine, too, deserved credit for the specialties of the kitchen. As a hobby she collected the recipes of Viennese musicians, including the favorites of singer-critic Ludwig Karpath, a highly regarded cook.[4] Over the years Justine perfected the family's favorite dishes, including her brother Gustav's favorite dessert, the Viennese *Marillenknödel,* sumptuous apricot dumplings. The children always knew when Uncle Gustav was coming to dinner, since his favorite Danish butter would appear on the table.

On the second floor at Pyrkergasse, reached by a massive spiral staircase, were two large bedrooms and other smaller rooms, one of which served as an extra bedroom. A second servant looked after their upkeep. The twisting staircase appealed to little Alma, who loved to race up and down the steps, her long curls flying behind her.[5]

Returning from an afternoon in the park, Alfi and Almschi sometimes found their mother in the Rosé music room presiding over one of her popular afternoon teas. Justine never lacked company, although Arnold was often away from Vienna.[6] To maintain her currency as a fashionable hostess and to stay abreast of the latest *Skandal,* Justine read avidly and made weekly book-hunting and gossip-gathering tours of Vienna's inner-city bookshops.

Sundays were especially festive for the Rosés. The noon Philharmonic concerts were followed by a family dinner, often with visiting friends and relatives.

Stories abound about the liveliness of the Rosé music room, where Uncle Gustav and Uncle Bruno at the piano indulged in playful renditions of four-hand Viennese waltzes, and young Alma sat spellbound as her father played the violin. Alma idolized Arnold, whom the family called "Vati," and was always happiest when he was home.

Arnold's busy schedule set the pattern of the days. In addition to his duties at the opera and the Philharmonic, he served repeatedly as concertmaster of the Bayreuth Festival Orchestra between 1888 and 1896, led the Rosé Quartet, gave private lessons, taught at the Vienna Conservatory, and frequently conducted concerts with pickup orchestras he engaged.[7] Justine managed the household and looked after Alfi and Alma.

It was fashionable in Vienna to engage English governesses for the children. This led to complications in the Rosé family because in their early years, both Alma and Alfred became more fluent in English than in German. They sometimes had difficulty communicating with Arnold, who never learned English.

Their first governess was Elly Burger, a cheerful young Viennese who lived nearby and became a lifelong friend. When Elly left, to the children's dismay, a "proper" English teacher they called "Miss Jessie" (Jessie Thompson) became their governess. Even Justine sometimes found her overbearing.

Miss Jessie was joined by an English au pair girl and piano student named Dorothy (Dory) Beswick (later Dorothy Hetherington). Dory, like Elly before her, grew to love the Rosés and remained close to the family. Decades later she smiled at memories of "those days in Vienna and all the glorious music."[8]

Occasionally Alma and Alfi attended Anglican services with their nannies, but the church played an insignificant role in the Rosés' cerebral world. Their parents never hid their ancestry, yet the children had no reason to feel Jewish. The innocence of youth and the artistic cocoon around them insulated them completely from the stings of anti-Semitism, which scarcely seemed to concern them.

Their mother's attitude toward questions of race, like their Uncle Gustav's, could have been influenced by the writings of Arthur Schnitzler, Vienna's reigning playwright and novelist. In *The Road into the Open,* a novel first published in Berlin in 1908, Heinrich, the intellectual Jew, is accused of anti-Semitism. He replies: "Every race as such is naturally repulsive. Only the individual is able sometimes, through personal strengths, to reconcile himself to the repulsiveness of his race. But that I am particularly sensitive to the failings of the Jews, I will not at all deny."[9] Similarly, with a remarkable disdain for "racial" consciousness, Justine was capable of complaining that certain Jews vacationing at a resort she and Arnold visited early in their marriage had disturbed her summer.

ALMA'S CHILDHOOD summers were glorious days beside the blue lakes around Bad Aussee, bordered by the sheltering mountains. In the early years the

Rosé family came together in a rented house that sometimes bulged with twelve or fourteen people. Emma and Eduard Rosé visited with Ernest and Wolfgang, and friends on holiday came and went. One memorable visitor was the sixty-year-old musicologist Guido Adler, who sought refuge with the Rosés after a bicycle accident.[10]

Reliving the happy summers of the 1890s when she ran Gustav's household at Mitterach am Attersee while her brother retreated to compose, Justine loved to organize day-long outings with family and guests. Now it was she who set the pace. The group would wander among the hills and to neighboring lakes and villages, stopping for picnics or lunches at picturesque inns.

The summer of 1910, when Alma was three and a half, Arnold's quartet mate Friedrich Buxbaum, his wife Käthe, and sons Walter and Erich joined the Bad Aussee holiday community, renting a small house near the Rosés'. Leila Doubleday and her family—mother, grandmother, and brother Kingsley—also joined the Rosé entourage, taking rooms at a neighboring inn. "Kings" and the other boys soon became fast friends. Alma was left on the sidelines, the only girl among six rough-and-tumble boys. In their hard-wearing lederhosen of country menfolk, they teased her about her peasant-style dirndl skirts, part of her impeccable holiday wardrobe, and made fun of her "broken" German.

Justine came to the rescue. She had a girl's version of lederhosen made especially for her daughter, complete with a leather jacket and hat. To further turn the tables in Alma's favor, she called her doll-like daughter "Tommy" for the rest of the summer. Now Alma could hold her own among the boys, and her bright smiles returned. A photo from the family album shows she could not really have been mistaken for a "Tommy."

Leila recalled the rules of the household that summer—Arnold's decrees, which Justine faithfully enforced. Alfred, Wolfgang, and Leila, all serious piano students, were not permitted to practice within earshot of the Professor. Even on vacation, he could not tolerate wrong notes.[11] Of the men and boys in the Rosé circle, only Arnold did not wear lederhosen, nor did he have his hair cut almost to the skull in the fashion of the others. The Professor's air of authority was always with him.

For Arnold the summer was overshadowed by preparations for the Munich premiere of Mahler's Eighth Symphony, the vast synthesis known as the "Symphony of a Thousand." Mahler had asked his brother-in-law to serve as concertmaster for the first production of this ambitious work, which would be performed by a chorus of 858 members (including 350 children), 8 solo singers selected and prepared by Bruno Walter, and 171 instrumentalists. The date was set for 12 September 1910.

Arnold had questioned Gustav's request that he lead an orchestra which had a concertmaster of its own. When Gustav insisted, Arnold agreed on condition that the orchestra be told of the arrangement in advance. But when Arnold arrived in Munich and took his place in the first chair for the opening rehearsal, he was faced with the most embarrassing moment of his professional life. The Munich orchestra had not been forewarned of his coming and refused to play unless their own concertmaster were given the important part. Rosé withdrew chivalrously, rising from his seat and leaving the platform with his violin. As Alma Mahler commented in her *Memories and Letters,* "This would have covered him with shame if his dignified forbearance had not at once shifted the blame to the other side." Apparently Gustav had trusted the concert manager to inform the orchestra of his decision, but the manager had been afraid to do so.[12]

IN NEW YORK in the spring of 1911, Gustav Mahler became desperately ill. When doctors judged his condition hopeless, his wife brought him home to Vienna to expire in the city he loved. He spent his last days in a sanatorium, drifting in and out of a feverish haze. Justine joined Alma Mahler and the Molls at Gustav's bedside, where they attended to his minutest needs, but the battle was lost. On 18 May, he drew his last breath.

Alfi was eight and a half years old, Gucki not yet seven, and Alma four and a half the night Mahler died. Both Alfred and Dory, the Rosés' nanny, recalled the scene. As thunder crashed outside, the three children sat in a room with Dory. Behind a closed door, Justine and Alma Mahler were with Gustav. The atmosphere was tense, and it was all Dory could do to keep the children calm. At last Justine emerged from the door sobbing, and Alfred soberly announced, "It is because of Uncle Gustav." Dory took Justine in her arms to comfort her.

Seventeen years later, in 1923, Leila Doubleday visited the Professor and his family in Vienna. In a quiet moment Justine took her aside and opened a drawer. There lay the death mask of her brother taken by Carl Moll, the icon of her continued mourning.[13] Justine grieved for her brother to the end of her life. In the years to come, her sense of loss was only amplified by bitterness toward Gustav's young widow.

The tensions between the proper Justine and the headstrong young woman who supplanted her as head of her brother's household have been the source of endless speculation. Ernest Rosé described the relationship between Justine and Alma Mahler as "love-hate," the feeling that might exist "between the wife of the Pope and the sister of the Pope. . . . Alma [Mahler] was very jealous of Justine, and Justine very jealous of her." In later years, Anna Mahler, who had her own difficulties with her strong-willed mother, commented only that Justine too was a "woman of temperament."[14]

In Gustav's lifetime the ill feeling between his wife and his sister was never allowed to flare in the open, as neither woman wanted to feed the Viennese rumor mill. Justine and Arnold appeared at all the expected events, and Arnold and Gustav maintained their friendly collegiality. Gustav and Justine continued to exchange affectionate letters, yet the paths of their lives diverged inexorably with their marriages.

There were peace initiatives as late as spring 1909, when the Mahlers returned from New York by way of Paris so that Gustav could sit for the sculptor Rodin, who was preparing his famous bronze bust. Alma Mahler wrote to Justine to announce their imminent arrival in Vienna. In the large purple scrawl that was her trademark, she wrote:

> Dearest Justine—
> I received your letter. And I only want to tell you quickly that it is also my warmest wish that we understand each other when we return.[15]

The incident that inspired the letter is not explained, but it is obvious that both women had staked their dominions.

In her memoirs Alma Mahler complained that Justine's "wild extravagance" had left Mahler debt-ridden, and that her chief task in the early years of marriage was to restore order to Gustav's finances.[16] In Justine's view, the charge was self-serving and unjust: Alma Mahler came on the scene after Gustav had made a name for himself in the music world, when life was substantially easier for him than in the years when Justine looked after his affairs.

Mahler's widow did not languish long after his death. In the spring of 1912, the thirty-three-year-old Alma Mahler lived in a garden apartment near the Molls' elegant home on the Hohe Warte. Oskar Kokoschka, a twenty-six-year-old expressionist painter with a reputation for audacity, was engaged to paint Carl Moll and began frequenting the household. Alma asked to meet him; at their first encounter, he found her "young and strikingly beautiful in her mourning."[17] Afterwards, each claimed the other fell in love at first sight. Thus began a tempestuous three year affair that ended only when Alma Mahler turned her attentions to the architect Walter Gropius, with whom she had enjoyed a passionate idyll the year before Mahler's death.[18]

Alma Mahler became famous for her alliances with men of genius and remained in the public eye through her love affair with and marriage to Gropius of Bauhaus fame, an assortment of amorous adventures, and finally, her love affair with and marriage to the poet, novelist, and playwright Franz Werfel.[19] Werfel, eleven years Alma Mahler's junior, was a good-natured partner who remained her faithful companion until his death in 1945 in California.

IN THE MONTHS after Mahler's death, Arnold took Justine and the children—with Dory to look after them—to the Tyrol, hoping that a vacation would prove cheering. As late as September 1911, a postcard from Dory cautioned her mother in Penrith, England: "Whatever you do, don't write Mrs. R. I should be unhappy if you did."[20] Justine was still extremely emotional, and any word, however well meant, could set off paroxysms of mourning. Still on the road the following month, Dory wrote to her mother: "We should like a pinafore dress for Alma very much! The coat No. 1010 is very nice, but don't you think the one at £4 14s. and with a skunk collar better value?" Dory loved little Alma and stepped in to help as best she could when Justine withdrew behind her veil of pain.

By March 1912, the Rosés were motoring in style around Vienna, and Alma and Alfi, both excellent students, were attending primary school in Gymnasiumstrasse. Dory gleefully wrote to her mother: "This morning, the Professor, Mrs. Rosé, and I went to town in an auto, then called at the opera and called for the children at school."

The next summer brought more travels, and Dory's sporadic reports to her mother continued. In July 1912, Dory had each of her companions sign a card from the Tyrol. In an uneven hand, Alma, who was not quite six, printed her name and enclosed it in a three-sided box, giving it a striking prominence. This is the first record of Alma's own hand.

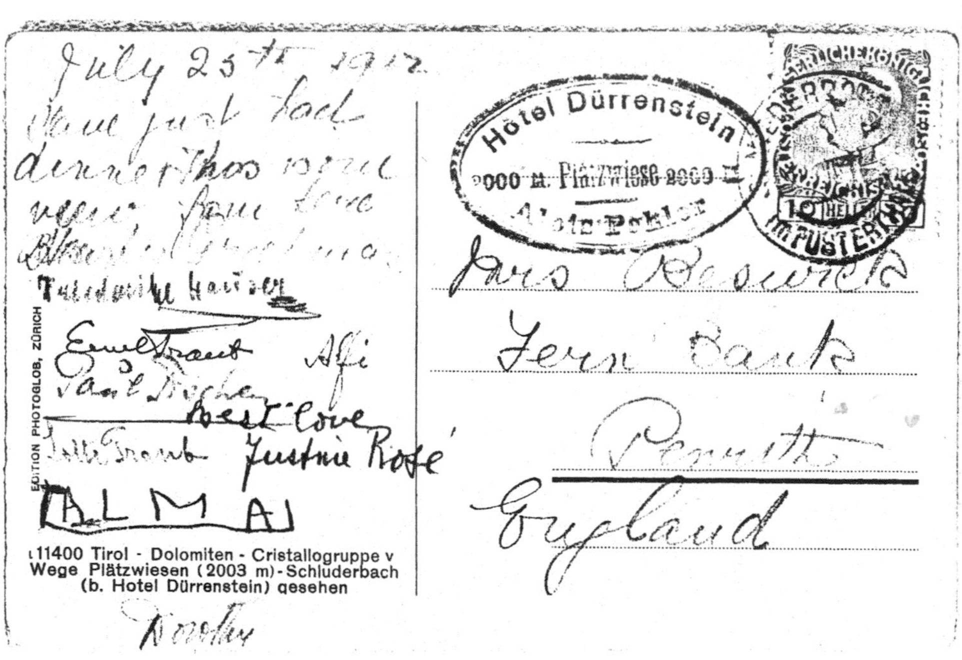

Little Alma's signature on a July 1912 postcard from the Tyrol.

Another postcard from that summer mentions that both Alfi and Alma had severe cases of whooping cough. Dory wrote to her mother: "Alma is particularly bad in the night. Could you send the prescription that you had for our chests?"

In November 1912, Dory's mother visited Vienna while Dory was in England. After a visit to the Rosé home, she too was enamored of Dory's young charges. She wrote to her daughter: "Alma sends a kiss and love to you. She plays games so well! I will tell you about her when I arrive home."

For all its rigors, the Rosé household was not immune to fads. For a time every portion served to adults at the table was weighed to conform with a certain Dr. Norbert's diet, with Father Rosé presiding over the kitchen scales. During another period, Arnold dipped his hands in warm wax before each meal, conditioning his priceless tools.

Before she was six, Alma knew that she wanted to follow in her father's footsteps. Each morning when he was home, Vati gave her a violin lesson in the music room before breakfast. To the amazement of all the family, she eagerly passed up her morning chocolate until after her lessons, in complete contrast to Alfred.

Alfi too studied violin with his father. But Vati occasionally exploded during Alfi's lessons, which more than once ended with a stupendous crash. In a moment of temper, Arnold would lift the piano with his knees and allow the instrument to bang on the floor. The crescendo of voices from the music room and the impact that shook the rafters told the family that Alfi's lesson was over for the day.

Eventually Alfi and Vati made a truce, but Alfred abandoned the violin and took up clarinet and piano. From that time onward, encouraged by Justine, Alfred patterned his musical ambitions on his Uncle Gustav, hoping to become a composer and conductor.

With Arnold so often away from Vienna, Alfred became the "man of the house." When Arnold returned, father and son sometimes clashed. Alma's older cousin Eleanor[21] remembered one dinner when ten-year-old Alfred began talking about the momentous medical discovery of the day, Paul Ehrlich's discovery of a treatment for syphilis with salvarsan, which became known as "606." Said Eleanor: "The topic was on everybody's lips, and Arnold was cruel in telling Alfred in front of everyone that it was not a subject for a ten-year-old to mention at the table."

No such outbursts were directed at Arnold's Almschi, who sweetly and intently devoted herself to learning the violin. She had a gift for music, and Arnold was pleased with her progress. Taking piano lessons as well, Alma became proficient enough to play four-hands with Alfred, whom she loved almost as much her dear Vati. Someone was always making music in what one Viennese critic called the "fine musical nursery at Pyrkergasse."[22] From a young age, Alma aimed at a single goal: she would be a violinist worthy of her father.

At school Alma abstained from playground games. Like all Arnold's students, she was forbidden to play games that might injure her hands. Skating, Vienna's popular wintertime pastime, was not allowed. As for tennis, Arnold believed it developed the wrong arm muscles for a violinist. He trained Alma to protect her hands at all costs. Later friends would be amazed at the disciplines imposed on her even as a child. Alma sometimes commented that her dedication to music meant she had missed "many beautiful days" in her youth, but for Alma such hints of regret were always tinged with pride.

By the time Alma entered the Cottage Lyzeum in Döbling, a girls' school, she was studious and preoccupied with her music. Like Alfi she was a talented linguist, and she became fluent in French as well as in English and German. She was intensely proud of her father and struck some as aloof; one fellow student described her as "cautious about people she didn't know." Walter Strauss, a friend from her school years in Vienna, mentioned that Alma was near-sighted, which gave an impression of distance. "She always seemed to be looking at something hard to see. She therefore conveyed the feeling she was having difficulty concentrating on the person with whom she was talking."[23]

The Rosés withdrew Alma from the Döbling school one spring before she was thirteen, preferring to prepare her for a musical career through studies at the Vienna Conservatory and later the Vienna State Academy. Within a fortnight, another student, Anita Ast, also left the school to study violin.[24] The headmistress told Anita's mother that within two weeks, she lost her two best students to music.

To help them pass the Conservatory entrance test, Arnold coached both Alma and Anita (who was a year older than Alma) on one page of the Goldmark Violin Concerto, the prodigiously difficult piece he had introduced to Vienna in 1881. At one time, Arnold confided to Anita that he hoped Alma would devote her talents to chamber music instead of choosing the precarious route to a virtuoso career.

Violinist Erica Morini was another of Alma's childhood friends and fellow music students. Erica remembers a close threesome who were like "peas in a pod": herself, Alma, and Gretl Slezak. Carl Bamberger, the noted conductor, also recalled the girls—all violin students—as a happy trio.[25] All three studied piano as well as violin and hailed from distinguished musical families. Erica's father headed an important music academy in Vienna, and Gretl's father was Leo Slezak of the Vienna Opera.

It was Erica, two years older than Alma, who showed the easy flair of a virtuoso. She was a star of the Viennese concert stage before she was twelve, and she would become a favorite of Arturo Toscanini and Bruno Walter. Those who remember her debut in Vienna in 1916 retain a picture of a diminutive marvel, hair flying as she displayed her innate musicality.[26] Arnold was especially proud: he had coached young Erica in the Beethoven Violin Concerto at a time when he was considered its greatest living interpreter. Once, Erica recalled, he offered her a reward if she could teach Alma how to master a staccato. "I did it, too," Morini said years later, although she could no longer recall the reward.[27]

The third member of the trio, pretty Gretl Slezak, was confident and high-spirited, less hard-working and dedicated than Alma, and less prodigiously gifted than Erica. She would become a singer and a glamorous soubrette at the opera, and she would also make her mark in the film industry.[28] While studying violin in Munich a few years later, she became a friend of the young street politician Adolf Hitler, an association that survived her admission that she had a Jewish grandmother. Still later, the friendship with Hitler placed Gretl on the periphery of the Nazis' inner circle, an experience diametrically opposed to Alma's.

In their early years, Gretl, Alma, and Erica shared a privileged cosmopolitan world, a love of music, and a zest for fun. Erica confessed their childish pranks: they would press doorbells and hide, delighting in the resulting confusion. Like young girls everywhere, they loved "the parks, the birds, and the flowers." Sunday afternoons, after dinner at the Rosés', good music, and girl talk in Alma's room, Erica and Gretl often returned home with bouquets of flowers from the garden.

In her youth Alma sometimes complained to her cousin Eleanor that her parents were too caught up in their own intellectual lives to tell her anything. It is true that in those days, parent-child communication among the upper bourgeoisie often took place at a formal level. But more than that, Alma's parents were isolated in their elevated spheres and had little understanding of political realities. They were convinced that music could erase all difficulties, that it was bulwark enough against the political extremists around them. Like many other members of Vienna's artistic elite, they could do little to prepare their children for the world that awaited them.

3

War

You are only as rich as your richness in tears. You are only as free as your success in surpassing yourself.—Franz Werfel

In 1913 excitement pervaded the Rosé apartment in Pyrkergasse. On 18 March, the Rosé Quartet would give the last concert in the soon-to-be-demolished Bösendorfer-Saal, the Viennese home of the quartet for more than thirty years. The hall, the converted riding academy of the Prince of Liechtenstein, had become famous for acoustics with "the resonance of an old violin."[1] Viennese music-lovers were sentimentally attached to it. It was fitting that their famous quartet should have the honor of the last performance in the grand old hall.

The program was the last of a series of six Rosé performances of Beethoven quartets. Included were the Quartets in E-flat, opus 74; C-sharp minor, opus 131; and A major, opus 18, no. 5. Stefan Zweig reported:

> When the last measures of the Beethoven, played more beautifully than ever by the Rosé Quartet, had died away, no one left his seat. We called and applauded, several women sobbed with emotion, no one wished to believe this was farewell. The lights were put out to make us leave. Not one of the four or five hundred enthusiasts left his seat. A half hour, a full hour, we remained as if our presence could save the old hallowed place.[2]

THE SUMMER holidays of 1913 ended as usual when the Rosé family returned to Vienna for the annual reopening of the opera on the emperor's birthday, 18 August. Arnold would be fifty years old on 24 October—ten days before Alma's seventh birthday—and a gala mood was blossoming. There were calls and gifts, plans for dinners and concerts, new dresses and fittings. Letters and telegrams arrived from every corner of Europe.

The Countess Mysa Wydenbruck Esterházy, friend and confidante of the Mahler-Rosé circle and with Princess Pauline Metternich the organizer of many arts-related events, was planning an extraordinary celebration. The countess belonged to one of Austria-Hungary's most influential noble families, whose patronage of Josef Haydn had enshrined the Esterházy name in musical history. The daughter of Count Franz Esterházy, married to art patron Count Wilhelm Wydenbruck, she had followed Arnold's career from the beginning, visiting Bayreuth in the summer and attending myriad performances of the Rosé Quartet. Among her personal gifts to Arnold was a delicately fretted silver bowl commemorating his twenty-fifth year as concertmaster of the Vienna Philharmonic. Engraved with the Wydenbruck crest, the bowl bore the simple message "*1881–1906: Der süssesten herrlichsten Violine*" (1881–1906: To the sweetest, most glorious violinist).

The countess began by secretly rallying Vienna's wealthy music-lovers to her plan for the occasion: to give their faithful Arnold a violinist's highest prize, a Stradivarius violin. A fund was established under the name of the Rosé Society, and contributions poured in. Even Viennese who were pressed to buy tickets for the opera's standing-room section joined in the spirit and made contributions.

All Europe was searched for the instrument. Finally a 1718 Stradivarius played by G. B. Viotti (1755–1824) was located in the collection of the English Earl of Crawford and authenticated by violin experts in the Hill family's venerable London shop. In the autumn of 1913 the instrument was presented to Arnold at a testimonial to which Vienna's most elite society subscribed. In gratitude to the countess and with his typical gallantry, Arnold immediately christened the violin the "Mysa," the name he used for the precious instrument from that day forward.

Trouble was brewing in the distant reaches of the empire. In 1912 and 1913, war raged in the Balkan Peninsula, with Serbia, Bulgaria, Greece, and later Montenegro opposing Turkey. Serbia emerged from the Balkan Wars with new territories gained at the expense of Bulgaria and Turkey, and with designs on Austria-Hungary's Bosnia and Herzegovina. Russia backed Serbia's nationalist aggressions, as Austrian politicians fumed and ranted. Every newspaper carried accounts of the mounting tension between Russia and Austria-Hungary, and confrontation over the situation in the Balkans seemed inevitable.

On Sunday, 28 June 1914, all Vienna was in the parks. Suddenly the music from the bandstands stopped, and stunned conductors announced that Archduke Franz Ferdinand, the emperor's nephew and heir to the throne, had been assassinated in Sarajevo, the Bosnian capital, by a Serbian nationalist. A month later, on 28 July 1914, Emperor Franz Josef declared war on Serbia, precipitating World War I. In quick succession, Russia mobilized in support of the Serbians; Germany, Austria's ally, declared war on Russia and France and advanced through Belgium into France; and Great Britain declared war on Germany. In September, after the ferocious Battle of the Marne, the Germans were blocked a few miles outside Paris, and opposing lines settled into four years of bloody trench warfare. Although the imperial forces were mired in conflict in the East, Austrians firmly believed the war would be over by Christmas.

A patriotic fervor swept through Vienna. Schoolchildren learned war songs, and the Austrian imperial anthem boomed from every bandstand as onlookers stood and sang. English and French were stripped from Vienna restaurant menus. The philosopher Elias Canetti, remembering Vienna in the war years, wrote of the beating he and his young brothers received in a crowded park when they innocently sang the English words "God Save the King" to the strains of a German anthem set to the same melody.[3]

With winter came more havoc. Throughout Austria food and fuel were short. Soldiers' songs lost their vigor as casualty lists grew longer and the realities of war came home in trainloads of the wounded and uprooted.

For the Rosés, 2 January 1915 held sad significance: Karl Goldmark, whose Violin Concerto had propelled young Arnold into musical prominence, died at eighty-three at his home on Josef-Gall-Gasse. The Rosés joined a throng of black-hatted mourners at his funeral. Elias Canetti, a child of nine who lived above the esteemed composer, watched the scene from a third-floor window with Paula, his nanny. "Where do they all come from?" he asked. "That's the way it is when a famous man dies," Paula replied. "They want to pay their last respects, they like his music so much."[4]

Lack of coal did not keep music lovers at home. Through the winter audiences huddled in their overcoats in opera houses, theaters, and concert halls, as the city's artists valiantly sought to offset the chill. "We swam in a sea of free tickets," Buxbaum's son Walter remembered. The Rosé Quartet repeated several popular Beethoven concerts and never failed to complete a season.

Like a magician's helper, Alma attended performances by her father and the quartet. The players, who still used gut strings, needed a supply at the ready in case a string should break, so Alma was on hand with replacement strings for all four instruments. Long before she herself began to perform, she was at home in the gilded concert venues of Vienna.

As food became scarce, bakers mixed corn with flour in Viennese bread, making it distinctly yellow. Elias Canetti recalled that the bread was often spotted with black as well, due to less wholesome additions.[5] For a time the Rosés sent Alfred, with his cousins Wolfgang and Ernest, to the country home of Marie Gutheil-Schoder in Thuringia, where food was more plentiful. Alma was deemed too young to leave home; nor would she have wanted to leave her father, whose touring was limited because of wartime restrictions. Now it was Justine who was frequently away from home, volunteering for duty as a Red Cross nurse for the returning wounded.

In November 1916, Emperor Franz Josef died at the age of eighty-six. It seemed that the entire city turned out to honor the end of his sixty-eight-year reign, the longest in history. His remains were deposited in the Capuchin monastery with those of his forebears. His successor, the Emperor Karl, tried vainly to negotiate a separate peace with the French in 1917. Deposed in 1918, Karl went into exile, and the new Austrian republic was formed. With the collapse of the empire, Hungary became an independent state, and the former Austrian crown lands were dispersed among neighboring nations.

The United States entered the war in April 1917; and in 1918 Russia, beset by civil war, signed the Treaty of Brest-Litovsk with Germany, giving up many territories and ending Russian participation in the war. Also in 1918, British and Italian forces defeated the Austrians in Italy; and following a fierce battle at Amiens in France, Allied forces launched a victorious offensive against Germany. After uprisings in the major German cities and the abdication of Kaiser Wilhelm II, Germany too capitulated, and an armistice effectively ended World War I. Officially the war ended 28 June 1919, when Germany and the Allies (excluding Russia) signed the peace treaty of Versailles. (The United States would conclude a separate peace with Austria and Germany in 1921.) German dissatisfaction with the terms of the treaty, particularly the required reparations payments, combined with postwar inflation, hunger, and crushing depression in Germany, would contribute to the rise of National Socialism, the Nazi movement.

Austria emerged an impoverished island in newly republican Central Europe, which it had once ruled. Now reminders that Austria had depended on Germany in fighting the war gave new weight to pressures for union with Germany. The two nations had long shared a language; now they also shared the memory of a humiliating military defeat.

In the aftermath of war, the Rosés and many fellow artists were spared the worst hardships, the spreading hunger and disease. The quartet, playing across the frontier in newly independent Hungary, returned home with provisions. Hungarian music students, who could pay for lessons with meat, flour, and root vegetables, were suddenly in demand.

All over Vienna people lined up outside food shops. Children were often dispatched to stand in the queues, sometimes in relay. Alma and Erica Morini joined the lines to buy bread and other precious commodities. Even in the worst of times, Justine could arrange for a choice cut of meat, and the Rosé kitchen was better supplied than most.

Arnold's musical life continued to flourish. German writer Thomas Mann, meeting Rosé in December 1919 before a Walter-Rosé performance of three Beethoven sonatas, noted that "he looks like a distinguished professor." Mann pronounced the ensemble playing perfect, adding that "Walter and Rosé gave an extremely beautiful performance of [Beethoven's] 'Spring' Sonata. The audience of about a thousand was moved."[6]

By war's end, when Alma was thirteen, she was playing violin and piano up to six hours a day. For a time she and Erica Morini shared a teacher at the Vienna Conservatory, the influential Czech violinist Otakar Ševčík, known for his stress on perfection of detail.[7] They were among his first female violin pupils.

Alma and Erica remained fast friends. One summer when they were in their early teens, Alma joined the Morinis on vacation in Bad Gastein, and they had a riotous time. The elder Morinis believed the girls should be in bed early; but with a hotel room of their own they were able to lead a secret night life. "We would go down to a local inn and stay until well after midnight. When we appeared so tired in the mornings, my father could not understand why young girls needed so much sleep!" Erica recalled.

The girls had discovered the fascination of young men, but they still had their taste for pranks. "On our way back to our room," Erica said, "with the halls quiet, seeing shoes outside the rooms, we would change the shoes and boots around. It was great fun!" Soon afterward, at home in Vienna, Alma and Erica shared a suitor. According to Erica, "a young Bulgarian medical student fell in love with both of us. One day he would send flowers to me, the next he would send them to Alma." The girls compared notes in long daily telephone calls.

Alma could have envied Erica's triumphs on stage; in January 1921, when Erica appeared in New York at Carnegie Hall and her international career was assured, Alma had yet to make her local stage debut. Yet Alma never showed jealousy. She admired excellence and believed, as her Uncle Gustav had said, that "the best cannot harm the good, but only enhance it and prepare its way."[8]

The young musicians' friendship was deep and enduring, but it could also be taxing. Erica recalled that in their lengthy conversations, Alma would question her devotion, and Erica would try to be reassuring. Mixed with Alma's love of life and sense of fun, Erica believed, were a deep sensitivity and fear of rejection.

In 1921, when Alma was fourteen and Alfred eighteen, the Rosés spent the summer holiday at Weissenbach am Attersee. Among their fellow vacationers were the family of Margit and Yella Pessl, young Viennese musicians who befriended the legendary Trapp family.[9] Margit had vivid memories of the summer. Alfred would sit by the hour on the railing of the veranda with baton and music scores, playfully conducting an invisible orchestra. The only young man in a group of eight girls, he was often enlisted as teacher in games of "school." He was far more sociable than his sister, with her big brown eyes and brooding expression, who remained aloof from games the other young people enjoyed. Alma is missing altogether in the only snapshot from that summer. She was hiding, Margit explained, because she did not want to pose "in a cluster of girls."

In Vienna in the autumn of 1921, Justine invited the Pessl sisters to an afternoon tea. Both Alma and Alfred were present, and Erica Morini played a dazzling solo. Justine and Alfred were warm and hospitable, but Alma remained distant.

Kurt Herbert Adler belonged to a set of young people who lived near Döbling and liked to meet at concerts and local cafés. He described Alma as lively and forthright, but with "a sadness always about her."[10] Adler, who was shorter than Alma, remembered the fun of dancing with her. She loved to dance, he recalled. "She enjoyed the tango, which had become popular among those attending the Elmayer dance studio in the Rotenturm area." Adler was friendly with Alfred too. Once, he remembered, Alfred was to lead a school orchestra in a performance at Der Wilde Mann, a popular restaurant near the Volksoper (People's Opera) with a large hall that was used for balls and concerts. To his dismay, he found himself without any brasses for the concert. In his resourceful way, he made the occasion a success by having two pianos play the brass lines.

Adler too was eager for conducting experience. On one occasion he was selected to conduct the Döblinger Gymnasium student orchestra in a performance at Der Wilde Mann. When he confided to Alfred that he did not have a concertmaster, Alfred proposed Alma. She was not even a student at the school, and she would be the youngest member of the orchestra. All the same, Adler invited her to fill the key position. She accepted and performed with a pleasure that took him by surprise. Her aura of sadness vanished, he said, as she threw herself into the work. Adler was extremely happy with the result and pleased that Professor Rosé himself attended the performance. Afterwards, Arnold was elated and told Adler that he predicted Alma would one day become a gifted conductor.

"It was more than a father's pride in his daughter," Adler remembered. "In conservative Vienna, where women hardly received the time of day as serious musicians, this was startling." Every time Alma's name came up in conversation after that student performance, Adler remembered Arnold's comment. "After all," he said, "by that time Rosé had played for forty years under almost every great conductor." His professional judgment was not to be taken lightly.

Walter Strauss, another member of the Döbling set, had fond memories of parties at Pyrkergasse 23 and especially of Justine, who relished the company of young people. Walter, his sister, and Alma and Alfred grew up in the same circle and often went out as a foursome. Although Walter found Father Rosé stiff when he visited at Pyrkergasse, his opinion changed after he attended a Rosé Quartet concert near Baden-Baden and joined the musicians afterwards, as Rosé, Buxbaum, and Anton Ruzitska shared a flood of anecdotes and roared with laughter. It was impossible, in the future, to forget Arnold's great good humor.

Alma was increasingly in the public eye and beginning to make her mark. Was she beautiful? Walter was not smitten. As he put it, "she had a face that projected considerable personality."[11]

In 1916, during a wartime tour to Switzerland, Arnold bought two small autograph books, which he presented as Christmas gifts to Alma and Alfred. Alma's book, a faithful record of memorable encounters over twelve years, mirrors the musical, theatrical, and literary history of the period.[12]

First to sign were the members of the Rosé Quartet in 1916: Arnold (first violin and leader), Paul Fischer (second violin), Anton Ruzitska (viola), and Anton Walter (cello). Conductors Franz Schalk and Felix Weingartner signed the same year, along with Elise Elizza, dramatic coloratura soprano of the Vienna Opera, and William Miller, American Wagnerian tenor. The next year, eleven-year-old Erica Morini pledged her "undying friendship," and revered German soprano Lotte Lehmann wrote encouragingly that "Art speaks to all youth in one language."[13] Alfred Grünfeld, jack of all musical trades and guest pianist with the Rosé Quartet on a score of occasions, charmingly added a "*Kleine* Serenade of my own composition."

Milestones were commemorated in Alma's slender autograph book. On 25 March 1917, at a performance of his Quartet in D minor, opus 7 (a work the Rosé Quartet performed from manuscript a decade earlier), Arnold Schoenberg drew a few notes on two staves and wrote above them, "For the beginners and . . . for the advanced." On 2 May 1917, Erich Wolfgang Korngold testified to "the unbelievably masterful first performance of my sextet [Sextet for strings in D major, opus 10] by the Rosé Quartet." The composer Hans Pfitzner signed in 1919 on the occasion of a performance with Arnold Rosé of his Sonata for piano and violin in E minor, opus 27.[14]

In 1921 Wilhelm Furtwängler (Arnold's friend "Furzi"), one of the century's greatest conductors, added his autograph. Arturo Toscanini signed in his bold script. A thrilling entry in 1922 was the scrawled signature of violinist Eugène Ysaÿe, commemorating a solo recital and a joint appearance in a Philharmonic concert with Arnold on viola, playing the Mozart *Sinfonia Concertante.*

In 1917 eminent Dutch conductor and Mahler enthusiast Willem Mengelberg penciled the last three bars of Mahler's *Das Lied von der Erde* (Song of the Earth) with its whispered ending, "*ewig . . . ewig*" (forever . . . forever). Richard Strauss, the mustachioed blond giant born in Bavaria who was a Viennese favorite and a frequent visitor at the Rosé home, signed in 1918, and soprano Maria Jeritza, the first Ariadne in Strauss's opera *Ariadne auf Naxos,* in 1926. In 1917 soprano Selma Halban-Kurz, a favorite of Mahler's, wrote: "To those who give generously to art, art is generous in return. To little Alma." Halban-Kurz signed a second time in 1926, on the occasion of her farewell performance at the Vienna Opera.

Rabindranath Tagore signed in 1921, the year he won the Nobel prize for poetry, together with Anton Wildgans, the Viennese poet and philosopher. Playwright Ferenc Molnar signed at Salzburg in 1926.[15] Actor Alexander Moissi signed the same year at Salzburg. Jakob Wassermann, the German-born novelist who lived in Vienna and wrote a number of bestsellers, added a signature so crimped it could be read only under a magnifying glass.

Close family friends also signed Alma's book, including Bruno Walter, Marie Gutheil-Schoder, and Leo Slezak. Ever the jokester, Slezak quoted the contradictory counsel of his neighbor and friend from Rottach-Egern am Tegernsee, the writer Ludwig Thoma: "I give you good advice—Do everything I didn't do. Especially leave out what I haven't done."

A page from 1927 bears the signature of Váša Příhoda, the Czech violinist of such dazzling virtuosity that he was compared with Paganini. The youthful Příhoda added the inscription "*Meiner lieben jungen Kollegin zur Erinnerung*" (Remembering my dear young colleague). The poet Franz Werfel signed in 1923, when he was already well established in Viennese society as the lover of Alma's godmother, Alma Mahler. Quoting his 1917 poem "Secret," he offered this inspiration: "Dear Alma—You are only as deeply wondrous as the depth of wonder you see."[16]

The final entry in Alma's book, offered in 1928 with a musical fragment by pianist Wilhelm Backhaus, was a portentous message written three weeks after Alma's twenty-second birthday: "The dignity of man is in your hands. Preserve it, Alma Rosé. With best wishes for the future."

THE SUMMER of her fifteenth birthday, Alma made her debut as a soloist at the Kurhaus in Bad Ischl, a resort popular among the wealthy nobility and the Austrian cultural elite for more than a century. The date was 29 July 1922. Countess Mysa Wydenbruck Esterházy watched over proceedings like a nervous aunt. Alma played Svendsen's popular "Romanza," Dvořák's "Humoreske," and Kreisler's "Alt-Wien Tanzweise." The program was appealing, designed to showcase expressive violin playing, and Alma was warmly received. Commemorating the event on the back of the program, the countess pronounced Alma's debut performance a "major success."

The event was a family affair. Arnold also appeared on the program, with Alfred at the piano playing Beethoven's "Spring" Sonata in F major, opus 24. Singer Franz Steiner, with pianist Franz Mittler, performed songs by Franz Schubert, Richard Strauss, Hugo Wolf, and Karl Loewe, as well as Mahler's serenely beautiful "Ich bin der Welt abhanden gekommen" (I Am Lost to the World).

The most enraptured review of Alma's debut performance came years later from Gerd Puritz, who as a boy spent his summer holiday at St. Wolfgang in the Salzkammergut with his mother, Elisabeth Schumann.[17] Writing in the third person, Gerd (whom his mother affectionately called "Schnuck") gave this account:

> One day they crossed the lake to Bad Ischl, the elegant spa resort where the Emperor Franz Josef had often stayed. As they were walking through

> the town Elisabeth suddenly cried: "But that's Rosé!" It was indeed Arnold Rosé, the leader of the Vienna Philharmonic Orchestra, and well known for his string quartet. Schnuck could hardly greet the gentleman properly; his eyes were fixed on the girl standing behind him—his daughter Alma. She certainly was the loveliest sight: brown hair framed an unusually animated face in which shone big dark eyes, so warm and friendly that one felt immediately drawn to her. The eighteen-year-old girl [in fact Alma was fifteen] began a conversation with Schnuck, and he was simply enchanted by her personality. Elisabeth observed this with delighted astonishment, and at once she knew what he was feeling. She promised him that they would go to Alma's afternoon concert in [St.] Wolfgang in a few days' time.
>
> They had seats in the front row so that he could see Alma well. She looked charming in her white dress, playing the violin so gracefully and beautifully. Schnuck wandered about in a dream afterwards, even on the next day too. He was in love! It was just as well that he was now off to Salzburg. They set off on August 5.[18]

"Talented and very pretty" were the words another admirer used to describe Alma at that time. Rudy Karter and his family spent the summer holiday at Mitterach am Attersee enjoying a "nice concentration of old Austrian culture."[19] Maria Jeritza and Franz Lehár were among the celebrities from the Vienna Opera who joined the vacation community. Alma, at nearby Weissenbach am Attersee, was Rudy's "flirt." Automobiles were a luxury, so he would pedal on his bicycle over hill and vale for twenty-five minutes to visit Alma. The two would then bicycle on short trips—short because the ever-watchful Justine insisted on it. Karter was to conclude that "Alma's mother was tough and didn't like my visits very much."

Alma was soon to be sixteen, an age when proper young women of Viennese society began to think about courtship and marriage. She had no lack of admirers, but Justine was particular about the man Alma would marry, to the point that her vigilance became a staple of local gossip. Her coolness curtailed Alma's romance with young Rudy.

Leila Doubleday, visiting the Rosé family in Vienna that autumn, was pleased to see what a lovely young woman Alma had become. Yet Leila still sensed the inner sadness that had been with Alma since childhood. "It seemed to me that she had no joy in life to express," Leila wrote.[20]

On Arnold's sixtieth birthday in 1923, the Viennese republic honored him with yet another medal, and the city gave him the honorary title "Hofrat," or Court Counselor, a professional rank above "Professor." "Herr Hofrath" continued to encourage his children in musical pursuits and took increasing pride in their accomplishments.

Alfred's career was well under way by his twentieth year. By 1922 he had gained considerable stature as an accompanist for such singers as soprano Elisabeth Schumann and mezzo-soprano Maria Olszewska. As the protégé of Richard Strauss at the Vienna Opera he garnered rich experience. In 1922, he hosted Giacomo Puccini for several weeks in preparation for the first Vienna performance of Puccini's opera *Manon Lescaut.* Alfred, who spoke Italian fluently, had the job of relaying the composer's thoughts to German-speaking conductor Franz Schalk,[21] as well as ministering to every need and whim of the Italian master. Evidently Puccini was well pleased: later in the year he wrote to Julius Korngold: "I would like to live in Vienna, where one breathes in the true essence of art."[22]

Alfred's first compositions were performed in 1922. The same year he managed the second Rosé Quartet tour of Spain and played the piano part in Schubert's "Trout" Quintet in many cities. The highlight of the tour was a command performance before the queen of Spain.

In October 1924 Alfred made his long-anticipated operatic conducting debut, leading the third performance of Richard Strauss's music for *Der Bürger als Edelmann (Le Bourgeois Gentilhomme)* in the Redoutensaal.[23] Friends penciled congratulations on the back of the program. Alma addressed her dear "Alferle" as "Herr Bürgermeister," a pun referring to *Der Bürger* or "mayor," and a title she would use in future letters to show confidence in his worldly wisdom.

By 1925 Alfred had conducted at the opera fifty times, including first performances in Vienna of Stravinsky's ballet *Pulcinella.* Now Arnold and Alfred made news together. In his excitement at the close of one concert, Alfred forgot the traditional handshake with his father in the first chair, prompting one Viennese writer to surmise, erroneously, that a schism had developed between father and son.

Alma too was adventurous and embraced every opportunity for her music. A photograph in her album labeled "Prague–Vienna, 3 June 1925," shows eighteen-year-old Alma wearing an aviator's helmet topped by a heavy woolen toque. She sits in the open cockpit of a Nero A-22 built in Czechoslovakia, a commercial version of a Czech Army Air Service reconnaissance biplane.[24] The purpose of the flight remains a mystery. Perhaps Alma had been to Prague for lessons from Otakar Ševčík in preparation for a Vienna concert, or she may have given a performance in Prague.

The Rosés enjoyed more security than most Austrian families, for the nation was still struggling to recover from World War I. In 1922 Austria appealed to the League of Nations to save it from national bankruptcy.

A symbol of the Austrian will to survive was a gifted young pianist who had studied with the Polish teacher Theodor Leschetizky. This was Paul Wittgenstein, who lost his right arm on the Russian front in 1914, a year after his debut as a soloist in Vienna. Subsequently he developed a remarkable technique for the left hand, commissioning works from Maurice Ravel, Richard Strauss, Benjamin Britten, and Serge Prokofiev.[25] Each time Wittgenstein appeared on stage, he summoned up the harsh world outside the music hall. As he became an international hero of the concert stage, he was also a reminder that an empire had been dismembered in a war the empire itself ignited. Tragically, that war had killed over eight million men, wounded over twenty million, and claimed as many as five million more through hunger and disease.

4

Double-Edged Sword

I did possess certainty, but I lost it again; and I'll find it again tomorrow and will lose it again the next day.—Gustav Mahler

In a city where even the valet of a celebrity was a celebrity, the Viennese debut of Alma Rosé was a major occasion. Alma's premiere performance was set for 16 December 1926, six weeks after her twentieth birthday, in the Grosser Musikvereins-Saal. Father Rosé would conduct a chamber orchestra composed of musicians from the Philharmonic and would step down from the podium, passing the baton to his frequent colleague Adolf Busch,[1] to play the Bach Double Violin Concerto with his daughter.

Alma was under intense pressure. To appear with Vati in Vienna was to fulfill a dream, and to disappoint him was unthinkable. Yet the "made in the musical nursery" label would work for her as well as against her.

Richard Strauss was among the notables who attended the Thursday concert. Alma was nervous, and her playing tentative. The audience had expected the fiery abandon of the popular Erica Morini, but Alma was schooled in a quieter musicianship and did not throw herself into her playing. Audience reaction and reviews were lukewarm. Alma's talent was unripe, the critics judged. A Polish writer concluded that Alma was not yet able to release "the song within her."[2]

Music critic Paul Bechert, in the prestigious New York–based *Musical Courier,* devoted a column to Alma's "auspicious debut at Vienna." His judicious comments, with an accompanying picture, appeared under the headline "Enter the Young Generation."

> Something of an event was the debut concert of Alma Rosé. She is loved in Vienna for her father's sake, and as the niece of Gustav Mahler. Such descent sufficed to ensure a full house—but it is a sword that cuts both ways, for expectations in such cases are far higher than usual. Young

KONZERTDIREKTION GUTMANN (Hugo Knepler)

III., Lothringerstraße 20 (Konzerthaus). — Telephon Nr. 96-1-79, 96-1-80
Kassa: I., Kärntnerring 3 (10 bis 1, 3 bis 5 Uhr). Telephon Nr. 72-0-54.

GROSSER MUSIKVEREINS-SAAL
Donnerstag, den 16. Dezember 1926

KONZERT

ALMA ROSÉ

Begleitung:

Mitglieder des Wiener Staatsopernorchesters

Dirigent und Mitwirkender:

ARNOLD ROSÉ

PROGRAMM:

Beethoven . . . . Romanze F-dur.

Bach . . . . Konzert D-moll für zwei Violinen und Orchester.
Vivace.
Largo ma non tanto.
Allegro.
Alma Rosé — Arnold Rosé.

Tschaikowsky . . Violinkonzert D-dur op. 35.
Allegro moderato.
Canzonetta.
Allegro vivacissimo.

Preis 30 **Groschen** (inkl. Steuer).

Stern & Steiner, Wien

Program from Alma's debut concert in Vienna, 1926.

> Miss Rosé was visibly conscious of the difficult situation, and to some extent hampered by it. The Beethoven Romance [in F] suffered from such "inhibitions," and to some extent also the Bach Double Concerto, which her father played with her. Only in the Tchaikovsky Concerto did the young artist attain that freedom both of technique and expression which is the criterion of the true artist and no doubt latent in her. She has all the fundamentals—a solid technique and a musicianship inherited from and cultivated by her illustrious father. What she still lacks—the assurance to place such merits in the right light—can be acquired only by routine and experience, which is merely a question of time.[3]

A later performance of the Bach Double Concerto by Alma and her father is the only known recording of Alma playing the violin.[4] Comparing this recording with those of Arnold Rosé's solo pieces, experts agree that Alma plays the second violin part, which begins each movement. In liner notes for the historic recording (part of the Archive Performances series produced by a subsidiary of Peter Biddulph Violins in London), Tully Potter proclaims the Rosés' recording of the Bach Double Concerto "one of the best ever made, in spite of the dubious insertion into the Finale of a splendidly written cadenza by Joseph Hellmesberger the Elder."[5] Noting that Alma, "in spite of her reputation as a mediocre player, . . . gives a good account of herself in the Bach," he adds that "the close understanding between the soloists is noticeable, with Alma no doubt coached assiduously by her father." Even decades later, credit for the quality of Alma's performance went primarily to Arnold.

Perhaps the memory of Alma's lackluster debut informed the opinion of another Viennese violinist, Dea Gombrich (later Lady Forsdyke), a much-praised young contemporary who remarked many years later: "[Alma Rosé] studied with Ševčík and probably also with her father. She was a beautiful girl, a very nice girl, but she was not a very good violinist—in fact she was a very bad one."[6] Even Erica Morini confided after sixty years that the sheltered Alma she knew in her youth "did not have the big gift."

Alma took the disappointment in stride. Importantly, her adored Vati's faith in her musicianship never wavered.

Kinder, Küche, und Kirche, "children, kitchen, and church"—bywords of the women's world in old Austria—had as little meaning for Alma as they did for young Erica, who by 1926 had a following on two continents. A Berlin newspaper reported Morini's engagement to a certain Lord Douglas, who, "according to the tradition of young lords, wanted her to abandon her career." Morini admitted that she had been pleasantly entertained by a charming aristocrat at a party at Lady Astor's but said that she had no intention of being unfaithful to her "only and favorite life companion until further notice, her Stradivarius."[7]

Pretty Gretl Slezak (now known as Margarete), the third member of Alma's girlhood threesome, also made a debut appearance in Vienna in the 1926–27 season. While continuing her violin studies, she had secretly taken up a singing career. (Erich Korngold, who was well acquainted with both Alma and Gretl, teasingly pretended to confuse them. Inscribing a copy of his song cycle *Abschied* in 1921, he addressed Alma as "*Sängerin, Geigerin*" [singer, violinist], as if she could be either.) Margarete came by her vocal talent honestly: her mother, the former Elsa Wertheim, had been an actress and singer before she married tenor Leo Slezak. Unbeknownst to her parents, Margarete had been training at the Theater an der Wien under Hubert Marischka, the reigning tenor and entrepreneur of Viennese operetta.[8] Her father wrote in *Mein lieber Bub* that he and his wife knew nothing of Gretl's secret coaching until they read a newspaper announcement of her debut in 1927—an event they hastened to attend.

With her parents' blessing, Alma held to her ambition: independence as a virtuoso violinist. Fellow Viennese violinist Anita Ast, a well-known chamber music player by the time of Alma's debut and later the founder of the Ast Quartet, recalled with pride that the eminent Adolf Busch offered both Alma and herself a chance to play in his quartet, but both women politely declined.

SPRING 1927 was a rush of activity. In March Arnold and Justine celebrated their twenty-fifth wedding anniversary. In April Vienna observed the centenary of the death of Beethoven, an anniversary that took Arnold and the quartet on a tour of European capitals. On 27 March 1927, Arnold played the violin solo in Beethoven's sublime Mass, the *Missa Solemnis,* opus 123, under Franz Schalk in the Konzerthaus. The same night Pavlova and her Russian dance company opened in the Volksoper for a two-night stand. The bustling Währingerstrasse was compared with the Bayreuth *Auffahrt*—the fabled "arrival" in coaches of society's upper crust before performances.

The Vienna Opera was abuzz because general director Franz Schneiderhan had arranged the return of Richard Strauss, who agreed to interrupt his international conducting career for the unprecedented nightly fee of $500 (in U.S. currency at 1927 values) for twenty nights each season for five seasons. Strauss had left the opera in 1924, vowing not to return as long as Franz Schalk remained at the company's helm, but material enticements proved persuasive. Strauss's first return engagement at the opera was conducting his own *Elektra.* In the same season he prepared the Viennese premiere of his autobiographical opera, *Intermezzo.*

Arnold Rosé made headlines at Beethovenhaus celebrations in Bonn, the birthplace of the composer. Vienna's Beethoven Festival attracted official delegations from dozens of nations, including statesman and Beethoven biographer Édouard Herriot, the French minister of education.

Lotte Lehmann's first Leonora and Alfred Piccaver's first Florestan, together with distinguished appearances by Elisabeth Schumann, Hermann Gallos, and Richard Mayr, made Beethoven's opera *Fidelio* the festival's crowning event under Schalk. The *Fidelio* had such impact that by year's end, the French government had completed negotiations for repeating the production the following year in Paris.

Another festival tour de force was the Rosé Quartet's coupling of opus 130 with the "Great Fugue" of opus 133, originally written as the last movement of opus 130 but subsequently replaced. Paul Bechert found the quartet's performance more harmonious than that of a prestigious chamber trio formed for the Viennese celebrations by pianist Ignaz Friedman, violinist Bronisław Huberman, and cellist Pablo Casals, remarking in the *Musical Courier* that their performance fell short of "ensemble of the ideal kind, say of the type the Rosés gave."[9]

In Budapest, Arnold's quartet played all the major Beethoven quartets in four evening concerts. In Berlin, "the celebrated Viennese artists" played the three quartets from Beethoven's opus 59 with "all the rare perfection and admirable spiritual elevation at their command."[10]

Musically the spring of 1927 was Beethoven's, but historically it belonged to American aviator Charles Lindbergh. On 20 and 21 May in his monoplane *The Spirit of St. Louis,* Lindbergh made the first trans-Atlantic solo flight, from Roosevelt Field, New York, to Le Bourget Air Field, Paris, in thirty three hours and twenty-nine minutes. The Rosés were in Paris at the height of the excitement. Alfred joined the throngs at Le Bourget and saw the young hero touch down.

In Paris Alma and Alfred sampled the jazz scene. Josephine Baker, the black American exotic dancer who performed in a skirt of satin bananas, was the belle of the city's nightlife, and Alfred eagerly acquired her autograph.

The French capital was home to a staunch coterie of Mahlerites, including the Parisians treated to Mahler's "secret festival" in Vienna shortly before Alma's birth. To strengthen the cultural links between Paris and Vienna and to honor the Viennese contingent attending the Beethoven Festival, Madame Blanche Rebatel Herriot, the wife of Édouard Herriot, held a luncheon on 24 May 1927 at the ministry of education. The Rosés were special guests. For Justine the occasion was a welcome reunion with her brother's Parisian admirers, including Georges and Paul Clemenceau and Paul's wife Sophie, the sister of Vienna's Berta Szeps Zuckerkandl.

Alma's souvenir menu card bears the signatures of sixteen men and two women. Among the guests was the German conductor Oskar Fried,[11] who had conducted Beethoven's Ninth Symphony in a concert that drew complaints for its length when it also included Stravinsky's *Rite of Spring.* Officially, Franz Schalk and his wife were the guests of honor. But as the luncheon came to an end, Herriot presented the flowers from the table to young Alma instead of to Frau Schalk, paying Alma the supreme compliment of the day. On her menu card the admiring M. Herriot wrote, "With respectful compliments to the daughter of the illustrious Rosé."

The following evening, Alfred and Arnold performed sonatas at a soirée given by Paul and Sophie Clemenceau. Before they left Paris, the Rosés spent a pleasant evening with Eleanor Rosé, who lived in the French capital with her daughter Farouel.

BEHIND THE scenes, the Rosés spun a mystery that remained a family secret for many years. After the Beethoven celebrations in Paris in May 1927, they vanished from the scene until August.

Father Rosé had been visited by the demon that haunts string players and pianists: the ring finger on his left hand was losing its power and dexterity on the fingerboard. His left-hand technique was a Rosé hallmark (the legend persists that a contemporary composition was written especially for him to capitalize on this exceptional prowess). Arnold hoped to correct the problem under conditions of the utmost privacy. If the music world learned that Hofrat Professor Rosé was undergoing surgery due to difficulty with his finger, a scandal would erupt in Vienna, and hereafter audiences would view his playing in a suspicious light.

No one in the Rosé family remained behind to answer prying questions. Alfred took a leave from the State Opera, where he had been conducting and coaching in ballet and opera; Justine and Alma cleared their schedules. Through the summer, Arnold and the quartet were unavailable. The Rosés had celebrated their twenty-fifth wedding anniversary in the spring, and Alma would be twenty-one the following autumn—reason enough for a summer of family travels.

In Freiburg im Breisgau, Germany, Arnold had contacted Dr. Erich Lexer, who became famous for his surgical skills during World War I. Instead of checking into facilities in Freiburg, which would have become public knowledge, the family accepted an offer of accommodations at the luxurious Black Forest spa Hotel Römerbad at Badenweiler, a few miles south of Freiburg. The owner, Louis Joner, an amateur violinist and Rosé admirer, assured the Rosés of as much privacy as possible among the hotel's illustrious clientele. The stage was set for a painful treatment: for a month Arnold suffered a pin through the nail of his important left-hand finger, stretching the muscle and ligament.

Alma, too, had a secret operation that summer: cosmetic surgery on her nose. Ever the perfectionist, Alma was eager to correct what she saw as a flaw in her appearance, a nose too large in proportion to her other features. Dr. Lexer encouraged her to profit from his skills. An inscription by Lexer in Alma's autograph book dated 29 July 1927 reflects the surgeon's confident approach: "Surgery is knowledge, craft and art."

Alma's decision to undergo nose surgery was not an attempt to obscure her Jewish heritage, since the Rosés were thoroughly assimilated into Austrian society and blind to the threat the growing anti-Semitism could pose to their comfortable lives. Alma's hopes were firmly fixed on a career that would keep her in the spotlight, and if she saw in herself a blemish she believed to be correctable, corrected it would be. Her mother and father gave their support. As Ernest Rosé recalled simply, within the bosom of the Rosé family "nothing was too good for Alma."

Dr. Lexer plied his art with skill, and Alma and her family were pleased with the result. Only Alma's cousin Anna Mahler saw the matter differently. "Alma was prettier before she had her nose cut," she candidly declared sixty years later.

The summer at Badenweiler gave birth to a friendship between the Joners and the Rosés that lasted until the German political upheavals of the 1930s. The Rosés became regular visitors to the Hotel Römerbad in the summers, when Arnold gave lessons to Louis Joner and the quartet played frequently at the hotel. In the winters, the Joners visited Vienna for two or three weeks. A photograph records one summer when the entire Joner family, the Rosés, and the family of Artur Bodanzky, the Metropolitan Opera conductor specializing in the Wagnerian and German repertoire, were on holiday at the same time.[12] Snapshots in Alma's album recall motorcycle rides, country jaunts, and gay outings to the Black Forest.

Elisabeth Joner Fellmann, the daughter of Louis Joner—in the 1980s still an elegant hostess presiding over the Hotel Römerbad—remembered Alma across the years. Alma was "a very soft person," she said. "She even told me stories. Her father said she was lazy, but I don't think he could have been serious, for she was always working."[13]

As a child, Elisabeth Marum Lunau of New York was also a guest at the Römerbad. Her father, Ludwig Marum, a Karlsruhe lawyer and member of the Reichstag who later died in a concentration camp, pointed out the Rosés at their table. Elisabeth remembers that she was captivated by the strains of music that floated into the hallway as the Rosés practiced in their rooms.[14]

On 11 August 1927, Alma played in a morning concert in the Badenweiler Kurhaus with Alfred at the piano. Her program included an air from a Goldmark concerto and a lively mazurka by Henryk Wieniawski.

The family of a young Dutchman named Theo Bakker also regularly visited Badenweiler during the summer holidays. Although Alma was taller than Theo, he was her favorite dancing partner. "We were very close friends during those summers in Badenweiler," Theo recalled. "I know she enjoyed me. She seemed to pick me out from others around us, even though I was younger than she was. I could never understand why. When Alma finished her practicing, we could take off for walks through the picture-postcard green beauties of the Black Forest."[15]

The Golden Book of the Römerbad records the long list of important guests before 1932, when the book ends abruptly. One of the last pages, dated 16 November 1931, is signed by the members of the Rosé Quartet, writers Thomas Mann and René Schickele (Schickele lived in Badenweiler), the Adolf

Busch family, and pianist Rudolf Serkin. To Louis Joner, Arnold wrote, "Sincerest gratitude for your true friendship." The last signature, dated 1932, is that of Winifred Wagner, widow of Siegfried Wagner and heiress to his legacy at Bayreuth. Later pages were ripped from the book, testimony to shame over the Nazi past, since after Hitler came to power the hotel became a retreat for high-ranking Nazi officials.

The summer of 1927, young Czech violin virtuoso Váša Příhoda appeared at Badenweiler. At twenty-seven, he was already the talk of Europe. His was a sensuous playing style, and he had the mesmerizing intensity of a matinée idol. With his short, powerful fingers, he drew distinctively sweet sounds from the strings of a violin. Alma was a dark-eyed beauty of twenty, a serious violinist, and Arnold Rosé's daughter. The attraction was immediate.

Příhoda was confident and smooth, and he paid Alma a kind of attention quite different from that of her young hiking and dancing partners. Gallantly, vividly, he courted Arnold and Justine as well as their daughter. Photographs show Příhoda taking the three Rosés for drives in his sleek black car.

It was hard to say whether Alma or Arnold was more smitten with the charming Váša. Only Justine did not warm to him completely. She found his manner crude, and despite his success and obvious talent, she judged that he was not the proper marriage partner for her daughter.[16]

Viennese *Tratsch* (gossip concerning the city's celebrities and their families) had linked Alma romantically with several young men before the summer when she met Příhoda. She was often seen dashing about town with Walter Slezak. She and Alfred had grown up with the Slezak children, and she and Walter remained close friends.

Another name associated with Alma's was that of Rudolf Bing. A tall, handsome Viennese four years older than Alma, Bing was an employee of the influential Alexander Guttmann concert management agency, a department of the Gilhofer and Ranschburg bookshop in Vienna. He was also a regular visitor to the Rosé home in Pyrkergasse, where rumor had it that Justine's literary luncheons were not the chief attraction. "There was hardly a week that I didn't spend at least one luncheon at their attractive little house in Döbling," Bing wrote in *A Knight at the Opera.*[17] In his later years, Bing warmly recalled both Alma and Justine and professed to enjoy the company of mother and daughter alike.[18] Alma's cousin Eleanor recalled that Justine was fond of the young Bing but considered him unsuitable as a marriage prospect. At the time, his connections with the music world were peripheral, and his bookstore jobs could have seemed menial. When it came to Alma's associations with young men, Justine was notoriously on her guard.

VÁŠA PŘÍHODA was born into humble circumstances in Czechoslovakia in 1900. It is said that he showed his talent early: as a five-year-old, he picked up a toy violin and played it without a lesson. His father was his first teacher. On

Christmas Day 1919, playing for his supper in a Milan café, the penniless violinist was heard by a newspaperman who spoke of him to Toscanini. The ever-generous conductor arranged an audition and was touched by Váša's seemingly spontaneous outpourings of music. The enthusiastic Toscanini helped to launch young Váša's career.

By 1923 Příhoda had made his American debut and first tour, and his Viennese concerts were consistently sold out. Two years later, by the time Příhoda was twenty-five, he had earned a significant reputation internationally. In Genoa in a series of highly publicized appearances, he had played Paganini's violin; like Paganini, he was famous for his trill and dazzling technical display. Father Rosé admired the young Czech's daring approach to the violin.

Váša had worked his way to fame through a tougher school than the young Rosés could imagine. Although some critics found weaknesses in his interpretive capacities, it was clear that on stage and off, Váša Příhoda generated excitement.

SOCIALLY AND politically the summer of 1927 was a harbinger of turmoil in Vienna, and the Rosés were fortunate to have been away. Even the city's well-insulated artistic community had been roused to political action. In the "Manifesto of Thirty-nine Intellectuals" published on behalf of the Socialist Party during campaigns for May 1927 Austrian elections, several dozen of Vienna's cultural elite showed their concern. Among those signing the manifesto were composers Alban Berg, Wilhelm Kienzl, Franz Salmhofer, and Anton Webern; poet Franz Werfel; Alma Mahler and her stepfather, Carl Moll; fellow artists Gustav Klimt and Oskar Kokoschka; and Professor Sigmund Freud.

Violence erupted in the streets on one of the hottest days of the summer. Writer and philosopher Elias Canetti described the events of 15 July 1927 in his autobiographical *Torch in My Ear:*

> Today, I can still feel my indignation when I took hold of *Die Reichspost:* the giant headline said: "A JUST VERDICT." There had been shootings in Burgenland [an Austrian province bordering Hungary]; workers had been killed. The court had declared the murderers not guilty. This verdict had been termed, nay, trumpeted, as a "just verdict" in the organ of the government party. It was this mockery of any sense of justice rather than the verdict itself that triggered an enormous agitation among the workers of Vienna. From all districts of the city, the workers marched in tight formations to the Palace of Justice, whose sheer name embodied the unjust verdict for them. It was a totally spontaneous reaction: I could tell how spontaneous it was just by my own conduct. I quickly biked into the center of town and joined one of these processions.
>
> The workers . . . were acting *without* their leaders on this day. When they set fire to the Palace of Justice, Mayor Seitz mounted a fire engine and raised his right hand high, trying to block their way. His gesture had

> no effect: the Palace of Justice was *burning*. The police were ordered to shoot; there were ninety deaths.
>
> Fifty-three years have passed, and the agitation of that day is still in my bones.[19]

THE ROSÉS returned to Vienna in August 1927. Richard Strauss was stirring things up at the opera with his usual zest. Adding to the excitement was the Viennese debut of Russian bass-baritone Fyodor Chaliapin, considered by many the greatest singing actor of his time.

At the Philharmonic, change was in the air. Felix Weingartner, director of the opera for four years after Mahler's departure for New York, had conducted the Vienna Philharmonic concerts since 1908. Now he was leaving for London to join the Royal Philharmonic Society and London Symphony Orchestra.[20] Furtwängler would succeed him as conductor of the Philharmonic concerts from 1927 to 1930, and Clemens Krauss from 1930 to 1933.

A highlight of the 1927–28 chamber music season was the appearance of an American patron who summoned up memories of Haydn's Esterházys and Beethoven's Razumovskys. Elizabeth Sprague Coolidge, the wife of U.S. President Calvin Coolidge, toured Europe and sponsored concerts of contemporary chamber music. Her visit to Vienna and two by-invitation evening programs in the Mittlerer Konzerthaus-Saal in September coincided with the announcement that the following spring, in April 1928, she would present the Rosé Quartet in its first North American tour.

The *Musical Courier* underlined the importance of Arnold's coming tour, which would open at the Library of Congress Chamber Music Festival in Washington, D.C., then take the quartet to Baltimore, Chicago, Cincinnati, and New York.[21] Arnold's ensemble would have the signal honor of giving the first performance of a quartet by American composer John Alden Carpenter.[22] The Washington performances, social highlights of the season in the U.S. capital, would take place in the acoustically superb recital hall personally donated to the Library of Congress by the U.S. First Lady in 1925.[23]

Patronage from abroad was especially welcome in this time of economic strain. Even the eminent firm of Bösendorfer, long established as piano makers in Vienna, was suffering. The Viennese were too poor to buy pianos, a spokesman complained, and the company sold more instruments in Portugal than in Vienna.

ALMA PLUNGED into public performance in the autumn of 1927. Billed as a virtuoso, she performed Henri Vieuxtemps' *Ballade et Polonaise* with Alfred at the piano in the showcase of entertainment preceding a gala ball sponsored by the Concordia organization of journalists and writers. The long program in the Grosser Musikvereins-Saal on Saturday, 26 November 1927, featured such stars as tenor Alfred Piccaver and soprano Vera Schwarz from the opera, tenor

Hubert Marischka from the Theater an der Wien, ballerina Anny Coty, the Vienna Choirboys, and French chanteuse Yvette Guilbert.

That season the Sedlak-Winkler Quartet gave the first performance of Alfred's Second String Quartet in an evening concert devoted to contemporary music; the Rosé Quartet would perform the work a few weeks later. Alfred's decision to entrust the premiere of his work to a quartet other than his father's reflected the fact that by the end of 1927, Viennese music-watchers described the Rosé Quartet as the leading ensemble of the "right wing" of chamber music. No longer seen as champions of the avant garde, the quartet had settled into a solid reputation as masters of the classic repertoire.

Perhaps Alfred also hoped to avoid the trials of the young Erich Korngold, a musical genius among the younger generation of Vienna's musical society, whose successes were all too often ascribed to his father's influence. Korngold's opera *Das Wunder der Heliane* (The Miracle of Heliane)—an unqualified success outside Vienna—was sharply attacked in his home city. In the international *Musical Courier,* Bechert spoke disparagingly of the role the young Korngold's father, *Neue Freie Presse* critic Julius Korngold, may have played in furthering his son's career. Ironically, Julius Korngold, who was aware of the powers of his position and eager to avoid this accusation, insisted that the works of his gifted son receive their premieres outside Vienna.[24]

Another gifted young composer in the Rosés' inner circle was Ernst Křenek, whose 1926 opera *Jonny spielt auf* (Jonny Strikes Up), incorporating elements of jazz, was a spectacular success. The multi-talented Křenek was briefly married to Anna Mahler after 1923.[25]

Alban Berg and Anton Webern, students and close associates of Schoenberg's, also figured prominently in Vienna's musical scene and in the Rosé orbit.[26] Berg's controversial *Wozzeck,* which had its premiere in Berlin in 1925, was shakily accepted at first but soon recognized as a milestone in twentieth-century opera. Both Berg and Webern were regulars at the music room in Pyrkergasse and also at the Molls' patrician home on the Hohe Warte, a district favored by the city's affluent bourgeoisie. Here Alma Mahler presided over musical salons until she and her third husband, Franz Werfel, moved into their own mansion on the Hohe Warte in 1931.[27]

Pages from Alma's photograph album show a range of activities in 1928. In May she enjoyed a tour she described as the "Marischka Tournée"—perhaps a sampling of talents organized by the Theater an der Wien's busy Hubert Marischka. A layout of snapshots shows a happy company of some two score young people on a river cruise. Vienna remained the capital of operetta with Oscar Straus's unbroken string of successes at the Theater an der Wien. *The Queen,* mounted extravagantly with the comedic genius of Hans Moser and starring Fritzi Massary and Max Pallenberg, was Straus's latest. Pallenberg signed Alma's autograph book in 1927 with the inscription, "Only for Alma."[28]

The singer Maria Asti, writing in Alma's book in spring of 1928, addressed her words "to my darling 'unruly' Alma: *L'Art est long. La vie est brève.*" (Art is long. Life is short.) "Unruly" would scarcely have applied to the serious, disciplined Alma in the years before she met Příhoda, but it was fitting now. In art as in life, she had begun to reveal her passionate nature.

Alma appeared as a soloist in varied venues. Early in 1928, she and Alfred played Sarasate's "Zigeunerweisen" (Gypsy Airs) at a cultural evening sponsored by the Vienna Hungarian Club. Wherever she performed, she was in good company. In Warsaw, *Music* magazine announced for the 1928–29 season: "Among [the many instrumentalists on the circuit] will be Huberman, Flesch, Szigeti, and Alma Rosé."

A performance in Vienna on 22 October 1928 was reviewed in the *Neue Freie Presse.* The critic "L. R." expressed enthusiasm over Alma's progress but made the inevitable comparisons with her father, saying that her performance fell short of her father's celebrated excellence. According to him, the "graceful girl gained from her father the big, constant tone of a man, the vigorous attack, at the same time maintaining a tranquil outward appearance." He compared her public playing (less fiery) with her playing in private (freely youthful) and remarked that she should take more of the license allowed to young performers.

Her bowing, the critic wrote, had the energy characteristic of her father, and her steadiness was reminiscent of his iron-clad control, "with the phrasing and the musical fire showing through." Although he noted a diffidence in her playing, Alma's critic lauded the way she brought the marble elegance of Alfredo d'Ambrosio's concerto to life. Along with her "technical bravado and fervor," he reported, she brought to the virtuoso pieces of Sarasate and Wieniawski a piquant tastefulness. She received an ovation.

Within two weeks of Alma's Viennese performance, Příhoda gave a concert at the Urania. Alma sat raptly in the audience. She was now a slender young woman with her dark hair cut in a fashionable bob. She and Váša met after the concert.

Arnold continued to promote their interest in each other. As a potential son-in-law, Váša Příhoda seemed ideal, and he and Arnold regularly crossed paths. On 10 and 11 November, the Rosé Quartet and Váša Příhoda performed at Munich's Odeon on successive days.

The Rosé Quartet's April 1928 U.S. tour had been immensely successful. Because the other members of the quartet did not speak English and Alfred had proven himself as a linguist as well as an admirable chamber music player, he participated in the tour, piloting the elder musicians, writing articles for Viennese newspapers, and stepping in as pianist for quintet performances. The quartet, who made a side trip to Niagara Falls, proved so popular that an extra concert was given in Steinway Hall in New York. In the autumn, Alfred continued to appear frequently with the quartet when the program required a pianist. Memorably, at a single concert the quartet performed Schubert's "Death and the Maiden" Quartet and "Trout" Quintet.

Franz Schubert zum Gedächtnis

ODEON Sonntag, den 11. November 1928, abends 7½ Uhr

III. KONZERT Einziger Kammermusikabend

Rosé-Quartett

Arnold Rosé / P. Fischer / Anton Ruzitska / Anton Walter

unter Mitwirkung:

Alfred Rosé (Klavier) **Ludwig Jäger** (Kontrabaß)

Franz Schubert:

1. Streichquartett d-moll „Der Tod und das Mädchen" op. posth.
   Allegro / Andante con moto / Scherzo. Allegro molto / Presto
2. Quintett A-dur op. 114 für Klavier, Violine, Bratsche, Cello, Kontrabaß „Forellenquintett"
   Allegro vivace / Andante / Scherzo, Presto / Andantino mit Variationen / Finale. Allegro giusto

Konzertflügel: Blüthner aus dem Magazin J. Reißmann, Wittelsbacherplatz 2.

ODEON Samstag, den 10. November 1928, abends 7½ Uhr

Violin-Konzert

Vasa Prihoda

Am Flügel: **Charles Cerné**

1. Sonate A-dur . . . . Cesar Franck
   Allegretto ben moderato — Allegro — Recitativo fantasia — Allegretto poco mosso
2. La Folia . . . . Corelli
3. Violin-Konzert D-dur . . . . Paganini
4. Serenade melancholique . . . . Tschaikowsky
   La Capricieuse . . . . Elgar
   Chant d'automne . . . . Tschaikowsky-Cerné
   Walzer aus Rosenkavalier . . . . R. Strauß-Prihoda
   Jota Navarra . . . . Sarasate

Karten v. 9—1 u. 3—½6 b. d. Vorverkaufsstellen: Bauer, Halbreiter, Schmid u. Amtl. Bayer. Reisebüro

Program announcements for back-to-back concerts by the Rosé Quartet and Váša Příhoda, November 1928.

In 1929 Alma made her first tour of Poland. Martin Glinski, a Warsaw critic, was less enthusiastic about Alma's performance than the Viennese critic of a few months before. Sniffed Glinski: "Alma Rosé should have given a better interpretation of the d'Ambrosio concerto."

In 1929, to no one's surprise, Alma and Váša announced their engagement. The brilliant Příhoda so outshone every other man she encountered that from the day Alma first met him, she had no interest in anyone else. Arnold steadfastly encouraged the romance. In the family it was no secret that Justine was less fond of Příhoda, but her willful daughter had made her decision, and Justine accepted it.

On 20 January 1930, Alma and her father were guest soloists with the Vienna Chamber Music Society, playing the Bach Double Concerto (which they had recorded two years earlier) under Otto Steinbauer. By 6 February 1930, when the Rosé Quartet appeared in an all-Beethoven concert in Berlin, the program listed two Electrola recordings to the ensemble's credit. Alfred, in Berlin at the invitation of Max Reinhardt,[29] was studying with Schoenberg, conducting the productions of the Komische Oper, and playing in jazz ensembles. By 1931 he was working with singing-actresses of the rank of Marlene Dietrich, whom he coached in her masterpiece *The Blue Angel.*

In March 1930 Alma was again in Poland. In the Lwów (Lemberg) monthly music and literary publication *Lwowskie Wiadomosci Muzyczne i Literackie,* Władysław Golabiowski reviewed her performance with little enthusiasm:

> The musician herself knows she has long years of study ahead of her which will surely compensate for the technical and intellectual shortcomings of her playing today. . . . It is not a clean sound. . . . She gave significant musicality to the Brahms G major [sonata], but she could have been more animated in the first part. In the Wieniawski G minor [sonata] she brought a good deal of virtuoso zest and in the Tchaikovsky and shorter encore pieces showed considerable freedom and grace. Hilde Loewe accompanied her very well on the piano.

As the decade of the thirties began, the biggest bank in Austria, the Credit Anstalt, was bankrupt, and unemployment and hunger were rampant. The Rosés felt the menace, but Arnold's and Alma's performance schedules and preparations for Alma's marriage kept them in a spin throughout the traditional year of engagement. Justine painstakingly copied out a handwritten book of recipes for Alma, a cookbook she dedicated to her daughter.[30] Alma's wedding dress was designed by a couturier, along with many outfits for her trousseau. Every piece of the delicate bed linen she would take into the marriage was elegantly hand-embroidered with the initials "AR" or "AP."[31] Alma's great names were multiplying: soon she would become Alma Příhoda-Rosé.

On 16 September 1930, Alma and Váša were married at the Vienna Rathaus. Alma was almost twenty-four, a socialite and aspiring violin virtuoso; Váša, at thirty, was a star of the concert stage. Franz Werfel and Arnold Rosé officially witnessed the civil ceremony. Both the bride and the groom signed the marriage certificate as "*konfessionslos*"—without religion.

Příhoda's concert income could finally support his taste for grand gestures, and he had built a villa for their new life together at Zariby on the banks of the River Elbe, in a resort area a few miles from Prague.[32] The mansion had five or six guest bedrooms, a living room, dining room, and billiards room, a spacious music room, and a garden. Váša's parents and brother occupied two rooms in the villa but often stayed in a small hotel nearby. Like all Váša's homes over the years, the villa was beside good fishing waters to satisfy his enthusiasm for angling.

Váša's wealth allowed him not only to support his parents in lavish style, but also to indulge in expensive hobbies of his own. He was a keen model railroader; eventually he had numerous railroad layouts in his homes. According to his biographer Jan Vratislavský, he was fascinated by mechanical gadgets and enjoyed tinkering on the cars in his collection, which grew to thirty vehicles. Whenever possible he traveled by car in the 1930s in a huge white touring-model Mercedes-Benz—driving at breakneck speed.

Váša was generous and spontaneous. An Egyptian student later described him as carefree and affectionate with his family. A man of phenomenal appetite, he would consume two heaping plates of spaghetti, a chicken, and a half-liter of wine at a sitting. Offstage, he cared little about his dress (attested by the worn underclothing that appeared on the villa clothesline on washday). For the young Egyptian as for countless others, Váša played the violin the way one "imagined Chopin had played the piano."[33]

When Alma was with Váša at the Zariby villa, she was happy. She sang a lot, their housekeeper recalled. One picture in Alma's photograph album shows her in the unlikely act of feeding chickens. She and Váša made day-trips into the surrounding countryside but rarely visited with their Czech neighbors.

Alma did not cook, for she did not know how to; Justine's handwritten recipe book went unused. According to the housekeeper, Alma's only culinary skill was hardboiling eggs then deviling them to make a dish she especially liked. Her favorite treat was a deep-fried Emmenthaler cheese—called by many Wenceslas Cheese—with a crispy crust and creamy interior.

Alma's mother-in-law continued to do most of the cooking and baking and presided over the household in Zariby, whether Alma and Váša were at home or away. From the beginning, communication with Váša's mother was difficult because Alma did not speak Czech, her mother-in-law's only language.

Both Alma and Váša continued to tour. Váša was particularly in demand and was often away. When the couple were in Vienna, Arnold and Justine welcomed them to the house in Pyrkergasse, but Justine soon resurrected her complaint that Váša's manners were abysmal, whatever his talent for the violin. She was horrified when at least once, he wore his shoes to bed.

Arnold remained enchanted with his son-in-law. He was delighted to have a third professional violinist in the family and gave Váša professional as well as personal support. At one stage, Příhoda played Arnold's Stradivarius, the famous Mysa.[34] Alma often played the Rosés' other precious instrument, a 1757 Guadagnini Arnold had purchased in Holland in 1924. At the time Arnold would tell colleagues that it did not matter what he played: "I can play any fiddle," he boasted. This was quite different from the attitude he had shown Leila Doubleday a few years earlier, when he looked disparagingly at her violin and called it a *Holzschachtel*—a wooden box.[35]

5

Waltzing

Alma was a tremendous rarity. Women simply did not do what Alma was doing in those days.—Ingeborg Tonneyck-Müller

Alma was ecstatic when she and Váša were able to travel together. Soon after their marriage they toured Poland, and the following spring they were on the French Riviera. In Nice Alma visited Louis Gutmann, formerly Bruno Walter's secretary and a family friend who had moved from Vienna to the south of France. On a postcard to Dory Hetherington dated March 1931, Gutmann wrote: "Imagine the fun to meet our dear little Alma. Her husband met with tremendous success." Alma also scrawled a bright greeting: "I'm traveling all the time, touring with my husband, and my head is filled up as you can imagine."

After one Italian engagement, a critic wrote of Váša, "What technique!" and of Alma, "What sensitivity!" More than once, reviewers noted the unusually sweet sound Příhoda could produce and commented that Alma's playing was "more manly" than her husband's. Alma was not displeased by the comment but found it puzzling. Was Arnold's technique "manly"? If so, she was proud of the description.

On a solo excursion to Regensburg, Alma gave a concert on 8 November 1931, playing a Sunday matinée at the Stadttheater. One reviewer began with a familiar comment:

> Alma Příhoda-Rosé bears a heavy load of great names, and only if you relieve her of this burden and keep an open mind can you do her justice. . . . In which case you will encounter a violinist highly trained to master her instrument who gives its tone a softly feminine charm and who, moreover, is equipped with an amazing technique.
>
> Her great strength lies in a certain carefree musicianship, and for this reason, she is most successful with those works which lend them-

selves to this unproblematic way of playing, such as Wieniawski's Concerto in D minor—the first allegro movement particularly successful—or Dvořák's Slavonic Dance. But in more demanding pieces one cannot help noting a lack of fullness of sound and of shaping. This was the case in the Handel Sonata in D. Nor, on the other hand, does she as yet command the surpassing technique of pure virtuosity.

Furthermore her *Rosenkavalier* Waltzes by Strauss-Příhoda [Váša's violinistic adaptation of music from the Richard Strauss opera] lacked the melting sweetness which his adaptation definitely demands.

The applause of the loyal but sparse audience of this morning concert—unfortunately all too sparse—was friendly but not enthusiastic.[1]

Another critic added a third "great name"—Gustav Mahler's—to a description of Alma's "burden,"commenting that Alma was "very capable and plies the strings very energetically, yet this cannot make up for the lack of temperament or profound understanding of the masters whom she has chosen." The same critic remarked acerbically that the *Rosenkavalier* Waltzes "enabled us to recognize the limits of her artistic personality."

A third critic noted Alma's "rich artistry," "dazzling verve," and "faultless technique," elaborating that she "captivates by her energetic strength of playing, truly masculine tone which is free of sentimental whispering, and phenomenal rhythm such as I have seldom heard from a woman violinist."

A fourth, moved to write a feuilleton on the concert, said:

Alma Příhoda is the slave of her flaming temperament, in whose red-hot emotional heat of artistic feeling the tonal element seems to dissolve; purity of style and nobility of artistic feeling are sacrificed to more subjective tendencies, and the essential musical happening is obscured by excessive stress on the personal and on tonal volume. . . . But even [in the choice of Wieniawski, Dvořák, Tchaikovsky, and Sarasate, here considered more suitable for her program than other selections], a better balance, a calming of the towering waves of emotion, might have contributed to a better, more deliberate artistic effect.

However, we happily acknowledge that Alma Příhoda is an artist who possesses considerable professional capability and great musical capacity. With her immaculate and assured technique, she masters all grades of difficulty to the point of virtuosity. Her excited and stimulating emotionalism communicates and shapes powerfully, and her expressive ability betokens a great performing potential. We hope she will also succeed in cultivating a noble concept.

All four reviewers contrasted Alma to Příhoda and more or less grudgingly attributed to her playing "wondrous" tone and rhythm and "freedom from all material and personal impediments." Obviously Alma had shed the reserve earlier reviewers criticized.

In 1932 an appearance in Lwów (Lemberg), Poland, was billed as a "Concert by Váša Příhoda with the collaboration of Alma Rosé." Dr. Severyn Barbag reviewed the concert in the magazine *Chopin:*

> Váša Příhoda is more a violin player than a musician. . . . The dexterity of the fingers and bowing is in contrast with the tone he develops. . . . We can feel this contrast when we hear the Bach D minor Concerto for two violins, in which Alma Příhoda-Rosé was better than her husband. She played in a more profound and more musical way.[2]

ALMA AND VÁŠA were settling into a pattern that left Alma more and more often alone. Váša was in demand in Europe and the Middle East, where his concert tours consistently sold out. Although Alma sometimes joined him in the spotlight, Váša often toured without her, and his remained the greater name.

When her husband was away for long periods, Alma returned to Vienna. At Zariby her relations with her mother-in-law were strained, and she missed the warmth of her own family and the comfortable routines of the Rosé household.

Concerns about her mother's health also drew Alma back to Vienna. Justine had become severely diabetic and suffered from a heart ailment. As her health deteriorated, she refused to leave the house unless she was accompanied by Dr. Alfred Fritsch, the doctor on call for the Vienna Opera. The Rosé home at Pyrkergasse became a daily call for Dr. Fritsch, who warned the family that Justine might not have long to live.

Alma also missed the family pets, Pepsi and Arno. Pepsi, a white lapdog, was Justine's constant companion. Arno, a black German shepherd, was especially devoted to Alma and begged to go with her whenever she went out in her sporty convertible, a red Czech-built Aero Váša had given her. Alma and Arno in the Aero, Arno perched in the back seat with his head as high as Alma's, became a familiar sight around Vienna. Soon Alma began taking Arno back and forth to Zariby, where he slept in the bedroom she shared with Váša.

Justine confided to her sister Emma that Alma began early to fear for her marriage. When Váša was away tongues wagged, and Alma was sensitive to teasing as to how her husband might be amusing himself. The gossip was especially disturbing when Příhoda was in Italy filming *The White Wife of the Maharajah,* and rumor had it that his relations with his glamorous co-star Isa Miranda went beyond the professional. Such innuendo, coupled with Váša's long absences, cast Alma into melancholy moods that could last for days. Many nights Justine heard her daughter sobbing in the next room and sat with her for hours to offer comfort. Alma's frequent visits to Vienna and her subdued spirits gave rise to a false rumor that Alma could not physically fulfill the marriage. Nothing was farther from the truth of her passionate nature.

The Rosés began to feel that Váša was taking advantage of their generosity, since despite his considerable concert income, he did not support Alma as a wife. He gave her expensive gifts, including the sportscar and a diamond solitaire, yet she had little to live on and was always short of cash.

Even Arnold was less enchanted with Příhoda. Although he continued to admire Váša's technical brilliance, he complained to fellow Philharmoniker Otto Strasser: "I cannot play chamber music with my son-in-law." As Váša's relations with the Rosés eroded, his own visits to Vienna became few and far between.

Inevitably, as tensions mounted, Alma was jealous of her husband's professional triumphs. The fame and adulation heaped upon Váša continued to elude her, and after their marriage he showed little interest in her own aspirations to a career as a virtuoso violinist. Anny Kux, a young violinist who became Alma's closest friend during the years of her marriage, put it succinctly: "Although she didn't show it, Alma remained jealous of everything Příhoda did and everyone he was with."[3]

Two years into her lonely marriage, in 1932, Alma had an idea that propelled her into action. Vienna had a tradition of all-girl salon orchestras—frothy, costumed ensembles that played in cafés and in the Prater, the four-mile-long park on the south bank of the Danube that was studded with restaurants and beer gardens. Building on this light-hearted model, Alma decided to create a chamber orchestra that would recruit talented women musicians, espouse high musical ideals, and guarantee a measure of independence and a musical career for everyone in the ensemble. Perhaps she also sought to make money to support herself.

Capitalizing on the romantic appeal of Old Vienna, Alma would call her orchestra the "Wiener Walzermädeln," the Vienna Waltzing Girls. The ensemble would include singers as well as instrumentalists, and its repertoire would be varied and distinctive. It would tour extensively: all Europe—not merely Vienna—was Alma's target.

Arnold gave his blessing. More than anyone else, Alma was aware of her legacy as Rosé's daughter and Mahler's niece. As long as her standards for the orchestra met his expectations, Arnold approved. His daughter's adventurous plan reflected his own belief that music well played and performed with conviction justified itself.

Alma knew many talented women music students whose families were struggling in the postwar depression. She sought the help of friends and colleagues and called on all the conservatories in Vienna to recruit the best who were prepared to play and tour with her. Ablaze with purpose, she arranged competitions at the music schools and auditions at Pyrkergasse. At each audition, Arnold sat behind a curtain listening and evaluating, as he so often reviewed candidates for the Vienna Opera and Philharmonic Orchestras. Alfred too lent support, helping his sister to scout for vocal talent and creating musical arrangements for the orchestra, which would include from nine to fifteen players.[4]

Alma's recruitment efforts sometimes met with disappointment. She pleaded with Anita Ast to join her as concertmistress, but the young violinist was aware that Alma's plans called for touring. Anita was soon to be married and did not want to leave Vienna for long periods. Violinist Dea Gombrich also turned down Alma's invitation, disdaining the repertoire of light music she imagined for the ensemble and preferring to continue in her own blossoming career.

More often, the women Alma invited to join the orchestra were thrilled at the prospect. Anny Kux, a diminutive violinist from a prominent Viennese banking family, became Alma's concertmistress, recruiting officer for the orchestra, and close friend and confidante. When Alma founded the group, Anny said, only two other touring women's orchestras existed in Europe, one based in Germany and the other in Hungary. Neither had the advantage of being able to conjure up an authentic vision of gay Vienna.

Alma ordered floor-length blue gowns from Ella Bay, one of the city's best-known designers. A second set of gowns, white with a blue print, were created by Gerdago. Custom-made orchestra stationery bore an elegant motif linking the scrolls atop instrument fingerboards to the sinuous curves of a female violinist.

Drawing on her connections in the music world, Alma shaped her Waltzing Girls into a uniquely polished ensemble. She enlisted Professor Michal Karin to help build and arrange repertoire and to work with her in coaching the orchestra. Karin said they worked together harmoniously, consulting about particular musical effects and the keys and tempi best suited to the ensemble. Alma asserted her rights as music director with the final say in every decision.

"It was her concept. I contacted her for the job," Karin remembered. "She knew that I knew how it had to sound. The orchestra varied from time to time when she had weaker or stronger players. I had to arrange the music to accommodate these changes. She knew what she wanted—one, two, or three violins and so on. Thanks to her, I became known."[5]

The Wiener Walzermädeln made their first appearances in Vienna early in 1933, playing waltzes, polkas, and popular operetta music. Their debut was described as an "explosion" sparkling of Old Vienna. "No one disparaged the orchestra," Anny wrote; "its debut in Vienna was a great hit." With the orchestra, Alma's career was reborn.

Through the years the composition of the orchestra would vary, but as a rule there were one or two harpists, a pianist, and a singer, and the remainder of the ensemble played stringed instruments. Every program included at least one solo by Alma. She cast a spell with her violin, and she often stole the show. Her successes redoubled her desire for perfection, Anny recalled. In a matter of months, the Vienna Waltzing Girls won a large following at the Zirkus Busch, which played in the Prater in summer and in the recently renovated Ronacher theater, a center for high-caliber cabaret, in winter.

Alma's Walzermädeln recruits understood that their leader's language was independence. Caroline Rostal, the former wife of eminent violinist Max Rostal,[6] was an early member of the ensemble. Remembering her first appearance with the group, in Vienna at the Apollo movie theater, Madame Rostal described the rigors of being a Wiener Walzermädel:

> As the third violin, I had to memorize—like the great Mannheim orchestra. I had the difficult third-violin part that moved all alone in harmony with, and yet in opposition to, other strings. It was like chamber music. At the same time we had to become part of a choreography that would respond and move with the music. It was very demanding. Anny worked with me for two and a half months before I took part in a performance.
>
> Even then, the conditions were difficult. During the engagement at the Apollo, we were made up and in our costume at noon and had to stay backstage or in our dressing room almost the whole day waiting for our place in the program.[7]

Madame Rostal recalled the Wiener Walzermädeln programs as models of musical taste.

The young Caroline's association with the orchestra typified the problems Alma encountered in an era when marriage frequently ended a woman's career. Caroline was barely trained when she announced to Alma that she and Rostal had become engaged and she intended to leave the orchestra. Alma was no doubt disappointed—now she would need to train another *Mädel*—but she responded with a warm wish for happiness, which Caroline remembered gratefully. Anny, too, recalled that "Alma was very popular with the girls and treated them with great generosity."

Another former Walzermädel, violinist Ingeborg Tonneyck-Müller, was still in her teens when she joined Alma's orchestra. For her it meant an opportunity to have money for herself and to buy her own clothes. Of Alma she said, "the Wiener Walzermädeln was her way to make money too, and she wanted to make the most of it. She was glad to find me. She told me I was a good violin player, and she appeared to be as pleased as I was when I played well."[8] Looking back over her association with the orchestra, Tonneyck-Müller concluded admiringly that "Alma was a tremendous rarity. Women simply did not do what Alma was doing in those days."

Alma might have given up after the orchestra's first out-of-town engagement, in Munich in March 1933. Only a few weeks earlier, on 30 January 1933, Adolf Hitler had risen to power in Berlin and declared the birth of the Third Reich. With Hitler as chancellor, Nazi pressures multiplied. Alma's concert date coincided with the height of a Nazi putsch in Munich, when militants took over the police and staged anti-Semitic demonstrations that attracted huge throngs. In the state Hitler now controlled, brown-shirted gangs of thugs roamed the streets with impunity, robbing, beating, and killing members of the despised and separate Jewish "race."

Alma's orchestra arrived in Munich in good spirits, but the evening show was canceled just hours before curtain time. Financially the blow was devastating, as Alma had used all the money she had been able to raise to get the orchestra to Munich in the first place. She and her Waltzing Girls were stranded and penniless.

A desperate Alma telephoned Příhoda. Quick and generous in his response, he paid the expenses for the troupe's return to Vienna. Later Váša even appeared with the orchestra; yet his enthusiasm for his wife's endeavor, like his monetary support, was sporadic and unreliable. After Alma's career achieved an impetus of its own, the couple toured separately most of the time. Alma made Vienna her home base and spent less and less time at Zariby. At first she used the stage name "Alma Příhoda-Rosé," then it was "Alma Rosé-Příhoda," then—as early as 1934—merely "Alma Rosé."

Significantly, by 1937, after Alma's orchestra had toured for several years, its promotional brochure did not quote a Munich newspaper. After that first disastrous snub, Alma refused to play in Munich.

The laudatory quotations selected for the brochure—an elegantly designed two-color folder with a calligraphed "AR" on the cover—offer glimpses of the impressions the orchestra made in Vienna and beyond. Even the Nazi party organ, the *Völkischer Beobachter*, had praise for the Waltzing Girls, who headlined a 1933 variety program at Berlin's Winter Garten.

> BERLIN. The high point of the program . . . An intoxicating attraction from sweetness to a hurricane.—*Völkischer Beobachter*
>
> Her instrument and ensemble a wonder . . . Injected the public with happiness.—*8 Uhr Abendblatt*
>
> Chamber music of the highest fulfillment.—*B. Z. am Mittag*
>
> VIENNA. A high cultural achievement . . . Alma Rosé's magic violin has overwhelming enchantment.—*Neue Freie Presse*
>
> PARIS. A select ensemble . . . One cannot resist the rapture inspired by these nine girls.
>
> PRAGUE. A complete conquest . . . Unbelievable rhythm, technique, and fluidity . . . An ideal image of the Waltz Dream era for the public to take home.
>
> WARSAW. A symphony in blue full of wonder . . . Conquers and enchants . . . From sweet to hurricane force.
>
> ZURICH. Height of charm and femininity . . . Cultivated and natural musicality creates a melodious and fascinating atmosphere with sustained passion.

GENEVA. Exact and precise.

THE HAGUE. Violinistic sex appeal . . . the blue pyramid of the ensemble combining refinement and temperament.

COPENHAGEN. This sweet, happy, bittersweet music melts hearts . . . Hearts left beating in waltz time.

STOCKHOLM. The best orchestra of the genre that we have heard . . . at the peak of musical culture.

Alma reveled in the life of a conductor. For engagements within range, she drove as Příhoda did—fast. Concertmistress Anny was her companion on car trips, as the other members of the orchestra traveled by train.

Once, Anny recalled, she, Alma, and Arno were driving to Zariby for the weekend in the red Aero. A few miles from the Příhoda villa, something went wrong with a wheel. Alma called Příhoda, who had no patience for repairs and told her to go to a dealer and pick up a new car. The second Aero was white, a match for Příhoda's own big white Mercedes. This was to become Alma's Viennese trademark. When parked outside the Rosé apartment at Pyrkergasse, the car was a distinct attraction, admired as much for its rarity as for its styling.

Alma was riding high. She was one of the celebrities in the city center encircled by the Ringstrasse, the boulevard that replaced the ramparts of the ancient city. In a traditional gesture of recognition, policemen controlling the intersections would halt traffic to permit the famous to cross to the Hotel Imperial or the Bristol. When the traffic policemen saw Alma approaching, they waved her through.

"We frequently stopped at the Hotel Bristol, where Alma loved the very black coffee," Anny recalled. Some mornings the pair would drop in for coffee at the Café Herrenhof and chat with the guests. "We would go into a café and in our happiness greet strangers. We felt so free in those beautiful days."

Although Alma did not like alcoholic drinks, she and Anny sometimes drove to nearby Grinzing or to outlying villages for a *Heuriger* or "new wine" celebration (a tradition of drinking young wine from the local vineyards that Ralph Benatzky celebrated in his "Grinzing Song"). More than once they were followed by another car whose driver found the stylish Aero with its Czech license and pretty female passengers irresistible.

When the orchestra was on tour, many of its programs included a carefully staged "schrammel"—a Viennese-style musical free-for-all in the mood of the "new wine" celebrations. For the schrammel, four musicians—two violinists, a guitarist, and an accordionist—took part in a seemingly freewheeling musical spree.[9]

Sometimes the orchestra provided the musical fare in variety shows. On various touring engagements, the Waltzing Girls shared the bill with French folk-singer Yvette Guilbert; opera singers Vera Schwarz and Joseph Schmidt;

the "equilibrists" the Myrons, American aerial star Eddy Clark, and other acrobats and trapeze artists; and French clowns, stunt cyclists, and cowboys. On holidays performances were especially festive, and Alma and the orchestra had their pick of engagements.

The programs Alma liked best were the orchestra's alone, when the ensemble would play selections from Chopin, Schubert, Fritz Kreisler, and Rimsky-Korsakov as well as the more familiar Johann Strauss, Dvořák, and Franz Lehár. Alma's programmatic selections were never haphazard. In Poland she gave Wieniawski his due; in Czechoslovakia she featured Dvořák or another native composer. Příhoda's virtuoso adaptation of music from Richard Strauss's *Rosenkavalier* was a regular, together with the popular "Zigeunerweisen" by Sarasate.

Photographs from the era show smiling young women in a succession of matching gowns, each more graceful and feminine than the last. Sometimes they pose in perky hats with armloads of flowers, their instruments on display; other times they are captured in the midst of music-making. Alma is always at the center, the orchestra's radiant leader.

Ernst Křenek, a discerning critic, judged that the orchestra's performances, and the programmatic content, greatly surpassed the workaday popular fare of "*Gebrauchsmusik.*" Frilly gowns and calculated girlish appeal notwithstanding, in Křenek's view Alma and her orchestra brought high musical values to every performance. Alma had long ago adopted the musical doctrine of her Uncle Gustav: in music at least, she would maintain her standards.

Alma was an exacting music director, and orchestra rehearsals were frequent and businesslike. She intensely attacked each problem and was unwilling to compromise. As Anny Kux put it, "Alma was the most modest person imaginable, in her dress and in her general behavior; but she tolerated no compromises in artistic matters. She demanded a great deal of the girls. Playing this huge repertoire from memory was no small accomplishment."

Lisl Aufricht (later Lisl Anders Ullman) was only sixteen when she was recruited at the last minute to replace the orchestra's singer, who was ill, for a Berne casino engagement. Fortunately, Alfred Rosé had heard the teenager sing in one of the small cellar theaters that had mushroomed in Vienna, and he recommended her to Alma. Lisl had no passport of her own, nor had she ever been on a train alone. Her father took her to the passport office to acquire the necessary documents, and she borrowed a suitcase from an aunt as she left for her first big engagement. Lisl recalled:

> I was fine in rehearsal. Alma was non-committal but seemed satisfied. With her standards, she never would have let me perform if she had thought otherwise. On stage for the opening show, I froze in front of the crowded casino. The orchestra played my introduction a second time, but it was useless. I couldn't sing a note until a third try.

> Alma was furious. Fuming backstage at the break between sections, she exclaimed: "What are they sending me? Amateurs!" In tears, I begged her for another chance, and I became a success with the very next vocal number.[10]

Thus began a career in cabaret and operetta that took the young singer, under the name of Lisl Anders, to many parts of the world.

Despite the odds against success for young women musicians, several members of Alma's orchestra continued in musical careers. Violist Adele Pribyl joined the faculty at the Vienna State Academy. Soprano Mady Meth gained a considerable reputation as an operetta singer in Holland. Anny Kux played first violin in the Slovak Philharmonic after she and her non-Jewish German husband, Eduard Polak, sought refuge in Bratislava (then called Pressburg). Polak, a cellist, also played in the Slovak Philharmonic and toured with a string quartet during World War II.

In 1933 Arturo Toscanini arrived in Vienna to conduct the Philharmonic. On Arnold's seventieth birthday, 24 October, Toscanini brought a bouquet of flowers to a dress rehearsal and embraced the concertmaster as he presented them. The Viennese press heralded the incident with a photograph bearing the large headline "Toscanini Kisses Rosé."

That autumn the big event in the Rosé family was Alfred's marriage to Maria Caroline Schmutzer, daughter of well-known Viennese etcher Ferdinand Schmutzer. Maria was Roman Catholic, and in preparation for their marriage Alfred took instruction in the faith. He was baptized Catholic in May 1933 by Johann Hollnsteiner, who also officiated at the wedding.

Hollnsteiner, a professor of moral theology and one of the foremost Catholic scholars of his day, was close to the Rosés, Bruno Walter, and Thomas Mann and particularly close to Alma Mahler-Werfel. Both he and the elder Alma encouraged everyone in the Mahler-Rosé family to be baptized Catholic in the hope that this would protect them from the Nazi threat. When Justine urged the same course, young Alma allowed herself to be persuaded. Along with her brother, she was baptized Catholic in May 1933. Hollnsteiner, although he later married and left the priesthood, had been considered a likely successor to Cardinal Innitzer of Vienna. Later Alma jokingly maintained that the cardinal himself baptized her into the faith.

After their marriage Alfred and Maria took an apartment in the spacious family villa Maria's father had built in Sternwartestrasse, a half hour's walk from the Rosé home at Pyrkergasse. Alfred's career again flourished. He conducted at the Vienna Volksoper and various provincial opera houses, performed frequently with the Rosé Quartet, and continued to be a sought-after piano accompanist. Although he accepted a teaching post with the Volkskonservatorium in Vienna, he did not cease to weigh his options. Aware that Germany, and possibly the Austria of the future, no longer held rich opportunities for him, Alfred joined the many European musicians who sought positions elsewhere.

England was the logical target. Fortuitously, British conductor Adrian Boult had made a guest appearance at the Vienna Philharmonic on 2 March 1933, and Arnold and Boult remained in touch. Arnold wrote to the conductor in England inquiring about prospects for Alfred. Boult replied in June, offering introductions to various contacts who might be able to help and confiding that four or five well-known musicians from Austria and Germany had already appealed for his help.

During this period many Viennese Jews in the arts began to leave for the United States—another option Alfred and Maria considered—or for other safe havens such as Palestine. In this they followed the example of their German neighbors. Officially Nazi policy was to encourage emigration, and in the first panicked reactions of 1933, some thirty-seven thousand Jews fled Germany alone.[11] Among the Jews who thought of themselves as German above all, suicide rates rose markedly. Remarkably, every organized Jewish group within Germany—Zionist or not, orthodox or not—initially responded to Nazi policies with emotional proclamations of their right to remain loyal Germans living in their "fatherland."[12]

In the first year of his marriage, Alfred received considerable attention when on 28 November 1934 he conducted the first performance of the Waldmärchen movement Mahler himself had cut from his youthful cantata *Das klagende Lied* (The Song of Lament). Justine had preserved the manuscript despite her brother's orders to destroy it. Alfred and Maria worked day and night to copy out the parts for a first performance in Czech on Brno radio (translated by a friend, Frantisek Kozik) and a second performance six months later in German for Vienna radio (RAVAG).[13]

The newlyweds had other interests as well. Maria was an excellent cook and Alfred a devotee of the culinary arts. Eventually they supplied a meticulously prepared newspaper column giving a week's menu of Viennese dishes with ingredients priced to the last *groschen,* a feature widely appreciated in these pinched economic times. The couple's practicality stood in stark contrast to the extravagances of Alma and Váša, who refused to acknowledge economic restraints.

In the early 1930s political tensions were unremitting and explosive. With Hitler firmly in power in Germany and German Nazis supplying their Austrian cohorts with dynamite and weapons, street riots and bombings in Vienna approached the proportions of civil war. In 1933 Chancellor Engelbert Dollfuss dissolved the Austrian Parliament and abolished the freedoms of speech, press, and assembly: there would be no more open elections. His new nationalist government, dedicated to maintaining Austrian independence, established the *Vaterländische* Front (Patriotic Front) as the official ruling party and banned the swastika and the Nazi uniform. The fascist-style government aimed to avoid the excesses of Mussolini's Italy as well as the Nazi terror in Germany. On the surface Austria was now a one-party state ruled by a government that put all its stakes on loyalty to the Austrian state and opposition to Hitler's goal of uniting Austria and Germany, an aim set forth in the very first paragraph of Hitler's 1925 *Mein Kampf.* Inevitably, open warfare broke out among the various Austrian factions.

For three days in February 1934, Vienna became an armed camp after a workers' uprising led to a general strike and street fighting quelled only when twenty thousand government troops and right-wing militia bombarded the workers' quarters with howitzers, killing a thousand men, women, and children and wounding many more. On May Day Chancellor Dollfuss addressed an audience of forty to fifty thousand boys and girls in Vienna Stadium, reaffirming his resistance to the Nazis. On 25 July 1934 he was dead, murdered in a failed coup when a hundred and fifty members of the Nazi SS Standarte 89, in Austrian military uniform, broke into the chancellery at noon and shot him at close range. Hitler, in Bayreuth attending the opera, received the news by telephone during a performance of *Das Rheingold.* In Vienna, the memorial to the slain chancellor was a performance of Verdi's Requiem with Toscanini conducting on 7 August, simultaneously with riots in the Heldenplatz.

On 28 October 1934 Prince Ernst Rüdiger von Starhemberg and his forty-thousand-strong right-wing army the Heimwehr—ostensibly opposing the Nazis but chiefly targeting the Austrian Social Democrats who opposed the one-party government—marched into Vienna to cure Austria's ills. By November violence flared again. The successor to Dolfuss, Chancellor Kurt von Schuschnigg, openly bemoaned the flow of material support for Austrian Nazis, which had progressed from "paper bags which burst with little else than acoustic effect" to bombs and explosives of the deadliest sort.

Waltzing around Europe in the 1934–35 season, Alma and the Wiener Walzermädeln toured Czechoslovakia, Hungary, and Poland. When the orchestra played in Prague, a young music student, Oskar Morawetz, looked longingly at the posters advertising their performance. The young musicians were all beautiful, visions from a world beyond his reach. Across the years, he remembered the yearnings awakened by Alma's Waltzing Girls.[14]

On New Year's Eve 1934, the orchestra appeared in Warsaw at the Staniewski Circus, known the world over as a showcase that ranked with Berlin's Winter Garten. In February 1935, they were back in Poland for a performance at the Old Theater in Cracow. The *Illustrowanny Kurier Codzienny* (Illustrated Daily Courier) of Cracow welcomed the Wiener Walzermädeln with the following notice:

> The announcement of the forthcoming appearance of the famous Alma Rosé orchestra of ladies from Vienna will be of special interest to the Cracow public.
>
> Under the direction of the excellent violinist, with the collaboration of the singer Karla Kohler and harpist Lisl Löffler, the orchestra will present a performance under the title "On the Danube in Vienna: The City of My Dreams."
>
> Waltzes, marches, and tunes from Grinzing. The members of the orchestra have generated a great deal of admiration for the special feeling they put into their performances. Very clean intonation. All these qualities fully guarantee that today's concert will be received with great enthusiasm.[15]

One of the Wiener Walzermädeln programs preserved remarkably through the years records this concert in Cracow. "Alma Rosé and her orchestra of twelve virtuosos of the waltz" performed the following selections:

1. Johann Strauss	Tales from the Vienna Woods (full orchestra)
2. Rimsky-Korsakov	Song of India (Karla Kohler, soprano)
3. Dvořák	Slavonic Dance (full orchestra)
4. Schubert	Fantasy (Lisl Löffler, harp)
5. Johann Strauss	Emperor Waltz (full orchestra)
6. Wieniawski	Oberek, Polish Dance (Alma Rosé, violin)
7. H. May	The Harp Wants Love (full orchestra)
8. Johann Strauss	Wine, Women, and Song (full orchestra)
	Intermission
9. Lehár	Gold and Silver Waltz (full orchestra)
10. Sieczyński	Vienna, City of My Dreams (Karla Kohler, soprano)
11. Johann Strauss	Wiener Blut (full orchestra)
12. Chopin	Fantaisie Impromptu (Nusy von Molnar, pianist)
13. Leopold	Hungarian Melodies (full orchestra)
14. Benatzky	Grinzing Song (full orchestra)
15. Benatzky–Alfred Rosé	Without Women and Songs (full orchestra)
16. Waldteufel	España (full orchestra)

A Polish critic, Dr. Apte, reviewed the performance in the *Nowy Przegląd* (New Newspaper) published for the Jewish colony in Cracow. Singling Alma out for praise, he wrote:

> Alma Rosé's orchestra is an ensemble of outstanding women musicians in the real meaning of the word. This is my first impression of these very happy, elegant, and tastefully dressed ladies in blue—their pleated and frilled dresses with a décolleté top. They sat in perfect order facing the public. On both sides were pianists. In the center of the stage in the first row were three violinists, one viola, a harp; between them, slightly raised, were two cellos and one bass.
>
> For us it was an outstanding impression in blue, made more startling by the presence of a lady in blue playing the huge bass. At one side the young woman singer waited for her entrance and her performance.
>
> As they played, they swayed with the music and laughed in tempo. From time to time, emphasizing the lyrical and melodic moments, one or two of the women rose and approached the director as soloists. It made a beautiful living picture as they stood near the director, who is at the same time the principal soloist.
>
> Of course when they play there is movement and gaiety, as well as very fast music, happy and lively. They showed great energy and revealed an ensemble of great virtuosity. . . .
>
> The soul of everything this ensemble offers is Alma Rosé, the daughter of a great father, Arnold Rosé, and the wife of a great husband, Váša Příhoda.[16]

This engagement in historic Cracow was less than forty kilometers from Oświęcim, where Alma was to die nine years later in the death camp Auschwitz-Birkenau.

W NIEDZIELĘ DNIA 3 LUTEGO 1935 ROKU O GODZINIE 8[1] WIECZÓR

WIECZÓR WALCÓW WIEDEŃSKICH

WYKONAWCY:

ALMA ROSÉ

ORAZ JEJ

ORKIESTRA

ZŁOŻONA Z 12 WIEDENEK-WIRTUOZEK

W PROGRAMIE:

1. J. STRAUSS-UHER:	Opowieści wiedeńskiego lasu
2. RIMSKY-KORSAKOW:	Pieśń hinduska
3. DVORAK:	Słowiański taniec
4. SCHUBERT:	Fantazja
5. J. STRAUSS:	Cesarski walc
6. WIENIAWSKI.	Oberek
7. H. MAY UHER:	Serce, które rwie się do miłości
8. J. STRAUSS-UHER:	Kobieta — Wino — Śpiew
	PRZERWA
9. LEHAR:	Złoto i srebro (walc)
10. SIECZYŃSKI:	Wiedniu, miasto moich marzeń
11. J. STRAUSS UHER:	Wiedeńska krew (walc)
12. CHOPIN:	Fantazja Impromptu
13. LEOPOLD:	Hungaria — Węgierskie melodje
14. BENATZKY:	Pieśń o Grinzigu
15. BENATZKY-ALFRED ROSÉ:	Bez kobiet i pieśni...
16. WALDTEUFEL:	Espagna

Nr. 1, 3, 5, 7, 8, 9, 11, 13, 14, 15, 16 — wykona *Orkiestra Almy Rosé*, Nr. 2 i 10 — odśpiewa *Karla Kohler*, Nr. 4 — solo harfowe: *Lisl Löffler*, Nr. 6 — solo skrzypcowe: *Alma Rosé*. Nr. 12 — solo fortepianowe: *Nusy v. Molnar*

Fortepian koncertowy August Förster Georgswalde Č. S. R.

Program for the Waltzing Girls' Cracow performance in February 1935.

6

Blood and Honor

Who feels art with his whole soul and love can never be unhappy.
—Bruno Frank

The "Nuremberg Laws for the Protection of German Blood and German Honor" were decreed in Germany on 15 September 1935. Marriages between Jews and "citizens of German or related blood" were forbidden. Any such marriages would henceforth be considered invalid, even if they took place outside Germany. Extramarital relations between Jews and non-Jews were outlawed. Jews were forbidden to employ German females under the age of forty-five in their households and forbidden to fly the Reich flag or display the Reich colors. The new laws were announced at the Reich Party Congress of Freedom by Führer and Reich Chancellor Adolf Hitler. Except for the provision regarding German household employees, they went into effect immediately.

An attachment to the laws on 14 November 1935 described a Jew as "a person descended from at least three grandparents who are full Jews by race" and defined another category of state subjects, the *Mischlinge,* as Jews if descended from two full Jewish grandparents, if practicing the Jewish religion at the time the Nuremberg Laws were effected, if married to a Jew at that time or subsequently, if born from an "illegal" marriage between a Reich citizen and a Jew that took place after 15 September 1935, or if born illegitimately after 31 July 1936 as the result of "illegal" extramarital intercourse with a Jew.

In a speech delivered in the Reichstag in September 1935, Hitler stressed that the new race laws were "an attempt to regulate by law [the Jewish] problem, which, should this attempt fail, must then be handed over by law to the National Socialist Party for a final solution."[1] The relentless defamation, disenfranchisement, and impoverishment of the Jews went forward in full view. By 1934 German Jews were barred from careers in civil service, public office, agriculture, theater and film, broadcasting, journalism, and stock exchanges. Signs in hotels, movie houses, and eating places, even pharmacies, groceries, and butcher shops, proclaimed "*Juden unerwünscht*" (Jews Not Welcome). Increasingly the Jews of Germany were denied access even to such essentials as lodging, food, and medications. By 1936, at least half the German Jewish population had no means of livelihood.[2]

Alma knew that under the German race laws, she was considered a Jew. The message came home in 1935 when her cousin Ernest, caught in the anti-Jewish purge of a theatrical company in Berlin, arrived in Vienna to stay with the Rosés. In the past he had been highly successful in Berlin; now only Vienna held opportunities for a German-speaking actor.[3]

Against the backdrop of Nazi insult and attack, the marriage of Alma and Váša was ending. Outwardly Příhoda's lavish gifts to Alma indicated that all was smooth in the marriage, and until 1935 Alma kept up what Anny called "the charade." When both Alma and Váša were in Zariby, the weekends were usually quiet, Anny remembered. The couple had few guests and did not mix with their neighbors, and Váša's parents, who considered Alma remote and aloof, made it a point to stay away. When Anny visited, the three violinists spent happy evenings making music, with Alma often playing the piano. But even in the good times, Anny said, Váša began to treat Alma "more like a friend than a wife." Alma sadly confided to Anny that "she wanted his children, but he did not want hers."

Both Váša and Alma were accustomed to the spotlight. When they were together, even small disagreements could rage out of control, and the quarrels escalated. Anny would never forget one night when Váša railed against Alma for hours after they came home from a party. Instead of insisting on a courtly kiss on the back of her hand, Alma had allowed a man to kiss her palm in front of a hundred other guests. Váša in his raving accused her of being wanton.

Michal Karin, who continued to work with Alma and her Wiener Walzermädeln and also accompanied Příhoda on the piano, had become a close friend to the couple. In one troubled time, Váša complained to Karin that he and Alma had argued bitterly over an offer Příhoda received to live and work in the United States. Alma was adamant that she did not want to leave Vienna and Prague; in both places, as Váša put it, she could have everything she wanted. Besides, her career was built on the European scene, and she was devoted to her parents in Vienna. Karin also confided that he once heard Příhoda say unkindly, "Sometimes I wonder if I married Alma or her father."

The surviving members of Váša's family blame the collapse of his marriage to Alma on the fact that she was always "larger than life and on tour." They say she did not live up to Váša's ideal of a caring homemaker who could devote herself to being his wife and the mother of his children. Some say that Arnold pushed the marriage even though problems were apparent from the beginning, and that three such demanding and gifted violinists—Váša, Alma, and her father—simply combined too much temperament in a single family. In any case, it was clear to all that Váša's passion for Alma had dimmed. As for Alma herself, Anna Mahler said she remained "insanely in love" with Váša through all their quarrels and reconciliations. Anny, who knew Alma as an adult better than anyone else did, agreed with Anna's assessment. Toward the end, Anny said, only Alma's feeling for Příhoda kept the illusion of marriage alive.

On 9 March 1935, a month after Alma's orchestra played in Cracow and six months before the Nuremberg Race Laws became doctrine, Příhoda filed divorce papers at Brandeis an der Elbe in Czechoslovakia. According to Anny, in persuading Alma to agree to the divorce, Váša promised her that everything would remain the same between them; he said he just did not want to feel tied down. "Alma loved Příhoda so much," said Anny, "that she accepted the divorce because he wanted it. She wanted to do everything to preserve the relationship, with or without marriage. Things changed totally later, and it was an ugly divorce."

Alma was devastated. She told friends there had been a lull in Váša's concert schedule prior to the divorce, perhaps implying that like many prominent musicians with Jewish wives at precisely that place and time, Příhoda sought the divorce for the sake of his career.

The Czech document that finalized the divorce, dated 30 October 1936, stated that the two parties seeking the final decree had not been together since the divorce application at Brandeis an der Elbe in March 1935. The decree gave "Pyrkerstrasse 23" in Vienna as Alma's address, and the Zariby villa as Váša's. A German translation of this document cites "*unüberwindliche Abneigung*" as the reason for the divorce, a phrase that could be translated as "insurmountable aversion." Was this language as standard in its time as today's vague "irreconcilable differences," or was it borrowed from the anti-Semitic rantings more and more publicly aired throughout Europe? Did it reflect the attitudes behind the harsh new race laws?

The suggestion that Váša wanted to end the marriage to a Jewess in order to further his concert career is vehemently denied by his surviving family and friends, and even by his former tailor in Prague. In Váša's defense, a member of the Příhoda family pointed out that two years after divorcing Alma, Příhoda married the Jewish lawyer Dr. Jetti Kreuz in Prague, and during the war he went through many difficult times in order to protect her. (He later divorced her and married a third time; Jetti Kreuz died in 1982.)

Nonetheless it is a fact that during the war Příhoda was active in Germany, Austria, and Czechoslovakia (sometimes touring with Michal Karin as his pianist), which made him suspect of Nazi sympathies. In 1940 Příhoda was among a group of thirty-four Czech artists and journalists invited by the Reich's Kultus Ministerium on a ten-day tour of Germany and Holland. His biographer Jan Vratislavský notes that in answer to a journalist's question, Příhoda reportedly said he was grateful to the Reich for enabling him to make the tour. The biographer says the quotation was unfair and out of context.

Příhoda taught at the Salzburg Mozarteum after 1936 and at the Munich Academy of Music in 1944. After the war he was condemned by Czech authorities for collaboration with the Nazis, sentenced to pay a fine, and forbidden to concertize in Czechoslovakia. He moved to Rapallo, Italy, in 1946 and continued to give concerts in Italy, Istanbul, Ankara, and Alexandria. In 1948 he obtained Turkish citizenship, and the next year he played a last engagement in the United States. In 1950 he moved to St. Gilgen, on the Wolfgangsee in Austria, where in the last decade of his life he taught at the Vienna State Academy. Finally rehabilitated and allowed to perform again in his native land, he returned to Prague for his first appearance in ten years during the Spring Festival of May 1956 and was greeted with a thirty-minute standing ovation.

Recordings made during Váša's long career captured the rapturous expressiveness of his playing and remain collectors' treasures. Příhoda died in Vienna on 26 July 1960, assured of a place in the history of the violin as a romantic virtuoso exemplary in his time.

Perhaps by acceding to Váša's wishes in the divorce, Alma hoped to give Příhoda's career and his spirits a boost and thus to revive their faded romance. But despite his assurances to the contrary, the divorce changed everything between them. Alma, not quite thirty when her divorce became final, returned to Vienna with the white Aero (part of the settlement) and little joy in life. It seemed to her friends that the pleasure she found in music was all that remained to her. Although Alma pretended she was happy to be free again, Justine heard her crying softly in her room at night.

In March 1936 Justine wrote Alfred the following note, revealing her deep concern:

> My beloved Alfi,
>
> I feel the need to give you an explanation for the change in my will which I made after careful consideration and many sleepless nights. And I beg you to accept this without any rancor. . . .
>
> We cannot leave you any capital, only what we own in material possessions, and it seems a matter of course to divide these according to my better judgment between you and Alma. That is, you will receive Father's personal possessions, and Alma mine. After Alma's divorce from Příhoda, Father willed to you all the things that had been meant for Příhoda, while in changing my original intentions, I assign all my jewelry to Alma.
>
> Your wife, who has brought you the happiness which I so passionately hoped for you, and for which I am thankful every day of my life, will after all inherit very beautiful jewelry from her mother, which is natural. Thus it would seem to me an injustice to take away from my daughter anything that could possibly help her in great need.
>
> The knowledge that I am following my innermost feelings, which I am sure are correct, diminishes somewhat the worry I would otherwise

> have about her future. I am not worried about you, since I was able to see you happy in your marriage, and safe from the worst material considerations.
>
> This worry I still have in Alma's case, and therefore, as I am convinced you will understand, I will do everything I can to make her future easier.

Ernest Rosé recalled that one day some time after her divorce, Alma came charging down the spiral staircase to the Rosé music room. Her face was flushed, and she ordered Ernest and Alfred to stop talking because the radio was broadcasting a Příhoda performance of a concerto. She had missed the announcement but insisted that she recognized Váša's playing. When the piece ended and the announcer identified the violinist as Zino Francescatti, not Příhoda, Alma was stricken with an "unreasonable remorse" because she had been unable to detect the difference—even her connection to Váša through his music was slipping away. What seemed a small incident to Ernest and Alfred assumed tragic proportions for Alma.

INGEBORG TONNEYCK-MÜLLER, a Wiener Walzermädeln violinist, remembered Alma on tour with the orchestra in 1936:

> Even as a teenager not very conscious of the complexities of maturity, I was aware of a pressure behind Alma. Perhaps it was the virtuosity of Příhoda, or her father's great name. You had the feeling she wanted to run from one place to another, prodded by a haunted restlessness. She was not in her right mind.
>
> That year after her divorce, I felt Alma could never find peace. When I think of her, I think of a thirty-year-old woman never laughing.
>
> Alma's technique was well-honed, and she had an inner musical sense, although there were times when she couldn't reach the heart of an audience. So much was expected of Alma because of her lofty inheritance that she could not be free, nor be herself. I don't think the public fully appreciated her.

Alma avoided the subject of Příhoda, Tonneyck-Müller continued. "It was as though she were always unconsciously asking, 'What are all these men expecting of me?'"

In the wake of her divorce, Alma found consolation in chamber music, which she played with her father and brother. Occasionally she took the part of second violin when the Rosé Quartet performed in Vienna. Arnold praised her chamber-music skills and welcomed opportunities for joint performances. Notably, during the Vienna Festival programs of June 1936, "Rosé's highly talented daughter" (as the press persisted in describing her) was second violinist to her father in Brahms' String Quintet in G, opus 111. The composition's wide contrasts between the carefree and the solemn, uncharacteristic of

Brahms' works, pose one of the major challenges in the chamber music repertory. The performance was a success for father and daughter alike.

Alma led her orchestra on their final visit to Scandinavia in 1936. In Stockholm the orchestra stayed in the same hotel as tenor Richard Tauber, an old friend of the Rosés' and one of many singers who continued to call at the Rosé home whenever they performed in Vienna, to inquire whether Arnold would be in the first chair in the Opera Orchestra. After Tauber finished his concert and the Walzermädeln gave their last performance of the evening, they joined forces for an impromptu session in the hotel lobby. Alma's singer, Mady Meth, remembered her soaring duets with Tauber as a highlight of her career.

HOWEVER LOW Alma's spirits sank, however impossible consolation may have seemed, she carried on with the same unshakable dignity her father had always shown. Alma could get things done, and she did not hesitate to use her strength in the service of others.

Peter Gorlinsky, editor of the *Argentinisches Tageblatt* (the only German-language newspaper in Argentina), said in a 1991 interview that he "came across Alma Rosé . . . in Paris,"[4] no doubt during a Walzermädeln tour. She needed a secretary, and he was an obvious choice given his wide journalistic and show business experience. He had no visa for France, however, so he was unable to accept Alma's offer. He proceeded to Vienna, where he went underground but was discovered and deported to Germany. The Gestapo interrogated him for three harrowing weeks. At last he was freed—he did not know how this came about—and he stayed for a time in Berlin.

Ernest recalled that during his prolonged stay with the Rosés at Pykergasse, Alma made determined manipulations on behalf of a journalist and theatrical promoter who had fallen into Nazi hands. The time period and description coincide exactly with Gorlinsky's story.

Michal Karin told a similar tale about Alma. He recalled that in 1937, still recovering from her personal trauma, Alma found an opportunity to arrange escape to Holland for a German Jewish concert manager she had come to know. Neither Alma's methods nor the identity of the concert manager can be discovered now, but Karin was certain that Alma orchestrated the escape.

Sometimes Alma's friends caught glimpses of her old exuberance. Ernest recalled a dash with Alma around Vienna's elegant Ring in the white Aero. At the Café Herrenhof they stopped to talk with Walter Slezak, by this time a prominent actor in the United States,[5] who was visiting Vienna. Friends since childhood and perhaps old flames, Alma and Walter were delighted to see each other and launched into excited conversation. Soon they were laughing gaily.

Walter was accompanied by his English bulldog, who despite a sinfully ugly, slobbering countenance, bore the name Angel Face. Alma took the admiring Slezak for a drive around the Ring, leaving Angel Face to maul Ernest affectionately.

7

Anschluss

A man is happy, I maintain, when no circumstance can reduce him; he keeps to the heights and uses no buttress but himself.—Seneca

The winter of 1936–37 was stressful in the Rosé household, for Justine's health was failing. After the Scandinavian expedition of 1936, Alma was less far-ranging in her tours, limiting her appearances to neighboring Switzerland and Czechoslovakia.

With her divorce Alma's world had come apart, and she was not easy to live with. She had moods of intense melancholy punctuated by irritable outbursts. At times she could hardly suppress her impatience with her mother, whose prolonged illness seemed to consume the lives of all the family. Seeking to restore her own equilibrium, Alma began to read philosophy—particularly the works of the Stoic Roman philosopher Seneca. Self-sufficiency became her aim.

She was quarrelsome and imperious with Justine's chambermaid and practical nurse, Mitzi, who administered the hypodermic injections that brought Justine relief on days when Dr. Fritsch could not attend her. More than once Alma fired the all-important nursemaid, and Alfred hastened over to Pyrkergasse to restore peace and to hire Mitzi back.

During the 1937–38 season Alma's orchestra again stayed close to home, playing in Switzerland and northern Italy. Continuing what had become a Wiener Walzermädeln tradition, on New Year's Eve 1937 Alma and her orchestra played at the Ronacher theater in central Vienna.

Because of Justine's condition, Arnold withdrew from a Vienna Philharmonic tour to England in the 1937–38 season, but he continued his chamber music performances in Vienna. The Rosé Quartet had played its first "farewell" program in 1936; they continued to draw large audiences, and again and again they decided to play one last season, one final concert. For its fifty-fourth season, the quartet presented a Brahms cycle commemorating the fortieth anniversary of its performing the Brahms String Quintet in G major from manuscript.

At seventy-four, Arnold was feeling pressure in both the Opera and the Philharmonic Orchestras to find a concertmaster who could succeed him. Although he was still authoritative in the first chair, he was aware that some of the younger men were eager for him to depart.

ALMA WAS briefly cheered by the attentions of a Czech journalist, Karel von Klaudy, from Zlinwhich (now Gottwaldov). After attending a Walzermädeln performance in Brno, Czechoslovakia, Von Klaudy began following Alma's tours and professed to have fallen in love with her. He fervently pressed his suit, and Anny, for one, wished that Alma could return his love. But Alma was not ready for new attachments, she told her suitor and her friends; she still grieved for Váša.

Then, during a train trip with the orchestra, Alma met a tall blond man, a Viennese eight years her junior, and suddenly she was passionately in love again. He was Heinrich (Heini) Salzer, younger son of the Viennese owner of the centuries-old Carl Ueberreuter paper and publishing conglomerate. Heini struck a chord in Alma, although he was not musical and thus stood apart from every other influential man in her life. Alma enjoyed taunting him for his lack of musical knowledge and was no doubt relieved that he expected nothing from her artistically.

Heini was a quiet personality and a stark contrast to the gregarious Příhoda. Unlike Alma, who stood out in a crowd, Heini remained in the background. His attitude was kind, and he was quietly sympathetic toward her enthusiasms. A young engineer destined to inherit part of the family empire, Heini returned Alma's ardent feelings, and the two began to spend as much time together as possible. At least once, Heini went on tour with Alma and the orchestra, neglecting to explain his disappearance to his family. According to his older brother Thomas, Heini was a "loner" even within the family circle. "As a brother," Thomas said, "he was a very good friend, but he rarely spoke about himself." It was his way to act on his own, without consulting or confiding in even those closest to him.[1]

Although Heini knew that his future lay with the family company, he was sometimes diffident, even antagonistic, toward the enterprise that provided for his support. He had created something of a sensation with his doctoral thesis, a penetrating study of the Austrian paper-making, printing, and publishing industry. The thoroughness of his work left no one in the industry unscathed, including the members of his own family. According to Thomas, although times have changed, Heini's well-made thesis is still an authoritative source for any study of the Austrian industry.

Alma's Waltzing Girls did not think the relationship with Heini could last. The ever-loyal Anny Kux—whom Father Rosé by this time described as

"Alma's only true friend"—admitted that she "didn't like it from the start." Neither she nor the other players in the orchestra dared to tell Alma so.

Inexorably Hitler tightened the vise on Austria. Under intense pressure from the German Führer, Chancellor Schuschnigg agreed in 1936 to allow Austrian National Socialists into the inner circles of government. In return for his compliance, the Nazis continued to pay lip service to Austria's constitutional definition of the nation, under the Patriotic Front, as a one-party independent state.

On the surface, 1938 began with promise of better times in Austria. Unemployment was down by nearly a third from 1934, and Mussolini's adventures in Africa and the Japanese invasion of China seemed far away. Writer Fritz Molden estimated that of the two hundred thousand Jews in Vienna, most were intellectually and culturally active. The Jewish community was split definitively between Zionists and assimilationists. According to Molden, regardless of their political or religious views, whether they had become Protestants, Catholics, or agnostics or remained practicing orthodox Jews, the great majority of Viennese Jews still saw themselves above all as Austrians or Germans. Most viewed the so-called Aryanization of German public life and dispossession of the German Jews as a passing aberration of Hitler's Germany.[2] Arnold, like many others, was convinced that "Hitler and his gang" would not remain in power, a sentiment he expressed to Michal Karin.

In Vienna, outbreaks of street fighting continued in 1938. Nazi students openly demonstrated at Vienna University. On 11 February, Chancellor Schuschnigg met Hitler at Berchtesgaden and capitulated to an ultimatum that he lift his government's ban against the Nazi party in Austria, grant amnesty to Nazis in jail (including the murderers of Dollfuss), and give five key positions in the Austrian government to pro-Nazis of Hitler's choice. The alternative was armed invasion of Austria by German forces. The most important cabinet post, as "minister of security" in charge of the police and the military, was given to Viennese lawyer Arthur Seyss-Inquart, who came from Iglau (Jihlava) in Moravia, the childhood home of Gustav and Justine Mahler. In a speech delivered to the Reichstag on 20 February 1938 and broadcast on Austrian radio, Hitler left no doubt that he considered the more than ten million "German peoples" of Austria and Czechoslovakia to be "racial comrades" linked by destiny to the Third Reich.

Schuschnigg knew that he had signed away Austrian independence, yet in desperation he called for a plebiscite on the joining of Austria with Nazi Germany, a vote of the Austrian people to take place on 13 March 1938. In protest the headquarters of the Patriotic Front was besieged on 11 March, when two hundred brown-shirted Nazi SA (the *Sturmabteilungen,* "brown-shirts" and storm troopers founded in 1921 as a private army of the Nazi party under Ernst Röhm) showed up in full uniform outside the city hall. The same day, Hitler sent peremptory orders to Schuschnigg giving him nine hours in which to call off the vote to determine Austria's future. If he declined, German troops would invade. Schuschnigg knew from experience that it would be useless to appeal for support from Great Britain, France, and Italy—three nations that had previously guaranteed Austrian independence.

Schuschnigg called off the plebiscite and resigned as Hitler demanded. In a moving farewell broadcast on 11 March 1938, he told the Austrian people that the government had yielded to German force since it was not prepared for bloodshed. "*Heil Hitler*" soon replaced "*Grüss Gott*" (the simple "good day") as the standard Viennese greeting. Seyss-Inquart took over the powers of both chancellor and president.

In the opera that fateful Friday, on the evening of 11 March 1938, Karl Alwin conducted Tchaikovsky's *Eugene Onegin.* The noise from the Opernring outside penetrated into the house. At intermission the audience went out to a frightening show of chaos: a torchlight demonstration swelled out of Kärntnerstrasse into the Opernring; Nazi slogans and swastikas dominated, amidst shouting and brawling. Many music lovers did not return to the opera, the last in free Austria.

That night Arnold was in the first chair as usual when Alwin conducted. (Alwin and his wife, soprano Elisabeth Schumann, were intimate friends of all the Rosés.) After the performance, daringly wearing the Patriotic Front's red and white ribbon in his lapel, Arnold took one of the last trams still running through streets that echoed with cries of "*Sieg Heil,*" "*Heil Hitler,*" and "*Ein Volk, Ein Reich.*" At Pyrkergasse, Alma, Justine, and Lotte Anninger Zuber, a family friend, were frantic by the time Arnold reached home. They scolded him for the risk he took, for Jews were being victimized in the frenzy of the night.

Maria Rosé remembered in detail how she and Alfred spent that evening. They were invited to dinner at the apartment of dental surgeon Richard Fürst and his wife Gretel. Alfred arrived later than Maria, when crowds were already gathering in the streets. The din from a throng in the plaza in front of the Votivkirche created a storm outside the Fürst apartment: it was difficult to separate the sounds of gunfire from fireworks. Fürst dramatically smashed an empty wine bottle against the fireplace and gave each person in the room a piece of glass—to be put back together when the four might meet again. The pieces of glass have remained scattered. Alfred and Maria walked home via Währingerstrasse late in the night, avoiding the rioters still milling in the streets.

At daybreak on Saturday, 12 March 1938, Germans troops poured across the border, meeting no resistance. Hitler himself visited his birthplace, Braunau am Inn in Upper Austria, ostensibly to visit his mother's grave at nearby Leonding. Most importantly, his short journey was to test the waters, and he was touched by the reception he met. Wherever he went he was cheered. All day leaflets rained on Vienna from German aircraft. By nightfall, a phalanx of German tanks had rolled into Vienna, and Hitler was in Linz drafting the Anschluss (annexation) law that would abolish a nation.

On Saturday night, the opera was *Tristan und Isolde* under the baton of Hans Knappertsbusch. According to Philharmonic archivist and historian Otto Strasser, Arnold Rosé played the sensuous third-act violin solo for which he was famous. It was his last appearance in the pit of the opera house that had been his second home for fifty-seven years.

On Sunday, 13 March 1938—the very day of the canceled plebiscite—the Anschluss law was proclaimed in Vienna to a newly formed Austrian government. On Monday, 14 March, Hitler triumphantly returned to the city that had rejected him as a student, arriving at Vienna's Hotel Imperial at five in the afternoon amidst a tumultuous welcome.

Wilhelm Jerger, composer and contra-bass player of the Philharmonic and Opera Orchestras, was named Commissar (*Leiter*) of the Opera Orchestra. With due courtesy, Arnold, Friedrich Buxbaum, and other Jewish musicians were pensioned off. The service each had rendered the organization was acknowledged; but under the new order, Jewish players were no longer on the roster.

Former Philharmonic president Hugo Burghauser recalled that as Hitler's oratory was charging a crowd of two hundred thousand in the Heldenplatz, Arnold went to pick up his personal belongings at the Philharmonic. A boisterous young violinist wearing Nazi insignia appeared on the scene. In front of the other musicians he said contemptuously to the silver-haired Rosé: "Herr Hofrat, your days here are numbered."

Burghauser, a bassoonist, had been a guest with the Rosé Quartet and was the first to admit that he and "the great Rosé" occasionally had differences. All the same, more than forty years later, he trembled as he recalled the shame that swept through the ranks of musicians who heard this "insult to the broken seventy-five-year-old concertmaster."

Michal Karin recalled a second professional insult to Rosé the same day. Arnold knew that the Führer would attend the hastily prepared gala performance of Eugen d'Albert's opera *Tiefland* in the evening. D'Albert, too, was Arnold's personal friend, and his exclusion from the orchestra was incomprehensible to him. Although Arnold considered Hitler a scoundrel, he recognized the importance of the operatic event and expected to perform with the orchestra. "He asked, 'Why can't I play with them? I belong. I am the concertmaster!'" Karin remembered sadly. "Such an old and noble man, Professor Rosé didn't understand, although he had been advised in the most delicate way that he should not appear at the opera that evening. That he couldn't play in the opera was beyond him."

If Arnold had been in the first chair that night, how would he have reacted when he saw Hans Knappertsbusch on the podium bow to Hitler—now seated in royal splendor far from the standing-room section of his youth—and give the Nazi salute?

THE NAZIS wasted no time in enforcing their racial laws. Less than a week after the Nazi conquest of Austria, the Gestapo was in charge of the nation. By the end of May 1938 the Nuremberg Laws were the law of Austria as well as Germany, and Austria was officially a province of the Reich—the Ostmark, or "eastern frontier": even the name of the once-proud nation had disappeared. Hermann Goering announced the Nazis' four-year plan to make the Ostmark *Judenrein*—"purified" of Jews. The exodus of Vienna's artistic and intellectual elite began immediately. Those who would leave Vienna included Freud, Ernst Křenek, Franz Werfel and Alma Mahler-Werfel, Bruno Walter, Arnold Schoenberg, Lotte Lehmann, and Alexander Zemlinsky.

The music world was stunned. Arturo Toscanini was the first to boycott the Salzburg Festival. In the month before the Anschluss, after Hitler's speech of 20 February and during the subsequent frenzy of Nazi rioting, he cabled from New York to cancel his scheduled appearance. (In previous seasons he had defied the Nazis by canceling appearances at Bayreuth.) Cancellations by other artists soon followed. The Salzburg programs were rearranged to accommodate blanks in the slate. Bruno Walter, whose association with the Salzburg Festival dated from 1925, resigned a few weeks after he had signed a new three-year contract with the Vienna Opera, whose orchestra traditionally appeared in the pit at Salzburg. Toscanini and fellow conductors announced the establishment of the Lucerne Festival in Switzerland as a show of opposition to political developments in the former Austrian nation.

Some artists could not comprehend the enormity of what was happening. Lotte Lehmann initially said that she expected to appear at Salzburg because she was "not a politician in mind or deed." She hoped, she said, to "devote my art as a singer to Salzburg."[3]

Ironically, the 1 May 1938 edition of the *Musical Courier* carried a German Railroads promotional article headlined "Germany—Happy Land of Music." The article singled out Vienna's Opera and the Salzburg Festival for glowing praise.

FOR ALMA, the race laws after the Anschluss posed insurmountable problems. She and Heini were deeply in love, but marriage with a non-Jew was now impossible for her in their homeland. Heini's family did not object to Alma on the grounds of "race," Thomas Salzer recalled. Indeed, Johann (Hans) A. Salzer—Heini's father and the fifth generation of Salzers to head the paper and publishing empire—helped Jews in these difficult times, personally escorting one of the company's managers to safety in Paris. Thomas later spoke warmly of Alma, saying that he had met her several times and "was always very much impressed by her beauty, her intelligence, and her very agreeable character." Still it is doubtful that the Salzers were enthusiastic about the match at a time when non-Jewish men were under pressure to divorce their Jewish wives to save jobs and position.

To make matters worse, Alma, Alfred, and Arnold found their careers and means of livelihood suddenly cut off. The old Rosé friend Richard Strauss obligingly became head of the State Music Bureau, the Reich Kulturkammer, licensing authority for performers in the arts. As Jewish artists, the Rosés were barred from public performance. Strauss apparently did nothing to help them, although Max Graf wrote that the composer told him he had sent three memorandums to the Nazi government "asking that its attitude on the race question be made more mild in the music field." Graf further said that by allying himself with National Socialism, Strauss "placed himself in a difficult position; because not only were his best friends Jews and his librettist Hugo von Hofmannsthal a half-Jew, but his daughter-in-law was Jewish and his grandchild, therefore, a half-Jew."[4] Stefan Zweig, Strauss's Jewish librettist, was barred from working with him. By cooperating with the Nazis, perhaps Strauss sought to protect his daughter-in-law and his grandchild. His advocates have insisted that he was literally blackmailed to take the post in order to protect his family. Whatever the explanation, his compliant behavior during the Nazi years earned him disrepute after the war.[5]

Hitler's regime quickly formalized its division of the music world according to "biological musicology," into Jews and non-Jews. Arnold, who kept a bust of Beethoven in the Rosé dining room and referred to the composer as "mein Beethoven," was appalled that the new race laws prohibited Jews from playing Beethoven. By June 1938 Arnold received word that his pension would be cut by a quarter because he was officially designated a Jew. In a weighty tome entitled the *Lexikon der Juden in der Musik* (Dictionary of Jews in Music), first published in 1940 under the sponsorship of the Nazi party, all three Rosés were listed as Jewish musicians regardless of their religious affiliations. As Ernest Rosé said of these years: "The real horror to me was that it was the blood in our veins that categorized us—not any other basis."

Alfred too had reached an impasse. Before the Anschluss, his hopes for a career as a composer were high. The German conductor Hermann Scherchen, a resident of Switzerland since 1933, began rehearsals on Alfred's *Triptychon,* a major work for orchestra and baritone voice, for performance in Vienna in May 1938. But suddenly Alfred's works were banned along with those of other Jewish composers. Through "de-judification" of musical activity, the Nazis intended to eradicate Jewish influence on the nation's musical life. Henceforth the party would rule on music acceptable in the Reich. The most fanatical anti-Semites went so far as to demand that the standard repertory be "Aryanized" to eliminate any traces of "mixed racial collaboration." For instance, Mozart's librettist, baptised Jew Lorenzo Da Ponte, had collaborated in the creation of *Cosí fan tutte, Le Nozze di Figaro,* and *Don Giovanni;* these librettos now required new "Aryan" translations into German. Performers, too, must change their practices. For example, violinists must desist from performing Beethoven's Violin Concerto with cadenzas written by Jewish musicians Joachim, Kreisler, and Flesch.[6]

Within a few weeks of the Nazi takeover, seventy-nine thousand "unreliables" were arrested in Vienna alone. Word spread that Alfred was on a special list to be arrested; yet he dared to go in person, literally dodging Nazis in the lobby, to retrieve the manuscript score of his composition at the Hotel Bristol, where Scherchen had left it before returning to Switzerland.

Alfred was of military age and could have been arrested. When his racial background was affirmed, he would have been sent with other Viennese Jews to Dachau or another concentration camp or forced into service in the Wehrmacht. He was incriminated in advance for having appeared in a Patriotic Front program.

As early as May 1938, Alfred contacted his friend Louis Meijer, an influential Dutch journalist, music critic, and political correspondent who had often joined in revelries in the Rosé music room. Immediately Louis began to explore means for Alfred and Maria to escape from Austria.

On Sunday, 10 July 1938, Meijer could scarcely disguise his enthusiasm for the news he had to impart. Two days out of Stockholm on a car trip around Scandinavia, he sent Alfred a six-page letter from Rättvik, Sweden. The previous Friday, Louis and his wife Lotte had lunched at the Grand Hotel in Stockholm. Passing through the dining room, they made an exciting discovery:

> Almost hidden in a corner I noticed three guests having lunch at the only occupied table. There, sitting with an unknown gentleman . . . Greta Garbo and Stokowski!! I met him ten years ago when we sat in a box together listening to a Mengelberg concert in Salle Pleyel in Paris.
>
> I did not want to disturb Garbo, but sent in a closed envelope my card with the wish to refresh the acquaintance and so forth.
>
> Afterward he sat at our table for about ten minutes, and we had a nice talk. After that we saw him driving away alone in a taxi, his face hidden behind a paper to avoid the journalists.
>
> By the way, he told me that as an exception he would maybe be able to do something in Hollywood for the musical friend you know about. Of course, it is also important that he [the friend] have his affidavit for entry there. As a whole, he is rather optimistic about the case, but it is almost too good to be true. So the friend ought to be moderately optimistic about the case with the normal skepticism that Stokowski might forget it—which I doubt—or not be able to do it.
>
> We decided that as soon as we are back in Holland at the beginning of August, I will send him in Hollywood all the further information, which he will find at the end of August after his return to America. . . . Normally I should have an answer from him before the second half of September.[7]

"The musical friend you know about" was obviously Alfred himself; such code references were necessary to protect the people concerned. Louis also mentioned that he had contacted the Russian-born Serge Koussevitzky, conductor of the Boston Symphony Orchestra, concerning the case of Alfred's "musical friend."

Alfred's hopes were revived by Louis's letter and bolstered by the memory of an incident in 1930 in Berlin when Stokowski was denied entrance to a Toscanini rehearsal until Alfred made special arrangements for his admittance. In a thank-you note to Alfred dated 3 August 1930, Stokowski had said that he hoped to call on Alfred the following year, when he would again be in Berlin, and had added a handwritten postscript: "Can I be of service to you in America?" Perhaps the great Stokowski remembered him.

ARNOLD WAS well aware that Jews of his age had been forced to wash away the slogans left from Schuschnigg's aborted plebiscite. Nazi mobs were a plague; even non-Jews avoided the parks now reserved for "Aryans," fearing attack by roving gangs. Nazis appointed to take over Jewish businesses so abused their power, pocketing huge sums at every opportunity, that even the Nazi administration challenged their practices.

Immediately after the Anschluss, Bruno and Elsa Walter fled to Lugano then on to Montecatini, Italy.[8] Soon after the couple's flight from Vienna, Elsa wrote the Rosés that non-Jewish lawyers they had trusted to look after their possessions and affairs had treated them unfairly, and they had lost everything. Their daughter Gretel, who had married a Prussian and remained in Vienna, had been arrested and held overnight for being seen in a place barred to Jews.

Alma's Czech passport from her marriage to Příhoda provided some protection, but the Nazis warned that "foreign Jews" were in Austria under sufferance. Too well known to move quietly about the city, Alma did not dare to venture where Jews were not allowed.

Alfred was in danger in Vienna and needed to leave as soon as possible, but with Justine growing weaker by the day and Arnold more and more dependent on help, Alma could not consider flight. Every aspect of the family's future was now in jeopardy, and marriage to Heini was increasingly doubtful. For Alma, it seemed that every avenue of escape was blocked.

In retrospect it is difficult to believe that the consequences of the Anschluss were not immediately understood. Colleagues of Příhoda's at the Vienna State Academy after the war said they had pleaded with Váša to help Alma, who had been a student at the academy. His standard reply was that Alma was safe because she was Catholic.

IN JUNE 1938, Alma, Arnold, Heini, his father, and his brother Thomas convened to discuss Alma's future. The plan of action involved a trip to Berlin taken by both Heini and Alma. It remains a mystery whom they saw there, but one of the stops could have been a visit with Margarete (Gretl) Slezak, who appeared to remember Heini a few years later. Margarete, whose friendship with Adolf Hitler had survived the years, was now a star with the Charlottenburg Opera in Berlin and a leading lady in German and Austrian films.[9] For a time she was an acknowledged favorite of the all-powerful Führer.[10]

One of Hitler's adjutants, Ernst Hanfstängl, suggests that Margarete was at one time Hitler's mistress.[11] Reinforcing the suggestion, film director Leni Riefenstahl, chronicler of the monumental 1935 Nuremberg rally in the film *Triumph of the Will,* reported seeing Hitler and Margarete together at the Olympus of the Nazi hierarchy, the Hotel Kaiserhof in Berlin.[12]

In his rare excursions into portrait painting in the 1930s, Hitler is reputed to have painted Margarete twice—in a 1931 portrait verified by Hitler deputy Rudolf Hess, and in a costume portrait of 1932 that bears the signature "Adolf Hitler." A note attributed to Hitler says that he modeled the painting in costume after a photograph by Heinrich Hoffmann, Hitler's friend and official photographer. In the costume, as Hitler reputedly wrote in imitation Viennese dialect, the mischievous, outspoken Gretl—known for asking embarrassing questions and making pointed remarks—personified a "*Weaner Tschaperl,*" a charming Viennese "scatterbrain."[13] Among the tales that persist is a legend that when Eva Braun saw Hitler with Margarete in Hoffmann's studio, she was so distressed that she attempted suicide.

Another story still circulating in Vienna is that sometime between 1936 and 1938, Alma was slated to appear on Breslau radio in Germany. When her racial heritage became known, the appearance was canceled. Hermann Goering, the Nazi controller of all things Prussian who famously remarked "I decide who is a Jew," is said to have ordered that Alma's program be reinstated. There are unverifiable clues that Margarete may have pleaded Alma's case.

Leo Slezak's memoirs do not address the subject directly, but they include references to the Führer. As one story had it, Hitler sent an adjutant to facilitate Gretl's 1939 divorce from her first husband "within ten minutes."

Whatever the extent of Margarete's influence with the Nazi hierarchy, it is safe to assume that her relationship with the Führer—together with her father's eminence in the music world—helped to provide for her family's security in what was known as the "Slezak compound" at Rottach-Egern am Tegernsee in Bavaria during the Second World War. Throughout this period Margarete starred in opera in Berlin and performed in Nazi-held Europe, entertaining troops and concertizing. Her mother's mother, who was Jewish, lived with the family in safety.

Although Margarete apparently enjoyed Hitler's protection, she did not help Alma. The summer of 1938, Alma and Heini returned from Berlin with no solution to their problems. Except for the emotional support that Alma received from Heini, Vienna held nothing more for her.

ALSO IN the summer of 1938, on his annual visit to Vienna, a former student of Arnold's called at Pyrkergasse. This was Felix Eyle, a Romania-born violinist enjoying a successful career with the Cleveland Symphony Orchestra in the United States. The previous summer he had driven his mentor around Salzburg, but in 1938 Arnold was not permitted to take part in the festival.

When Eyle arrived at the Rosé apartment, the Professor himself answered the door. "He looked so old—he was stooped," Eyle recalled. Justine, who had lost weight, sat on the sofa drawing breath with difficulty. "She looked so much like Mahler that I was stunned."[14] After a short visit, Eyle was accompanied to the door by Arnold, who told him that his wife did not have long to live.

Justine Rosé died on 22 August 1938 in the home she loved, surrounded by her family. Leila Doubleday Pirani, married and living in London by then, had remained close to the Rosés. Aware that Arnold depended on a reduced pension and that Justine was ill, she had sent the few pounds she could spare to help buy drugs for Justine in her last weeks. It was to Leila that Alfred poured out his heart, in a letter written in English soon after his mother's death:

> Dearest Friend,
>
> Your friendship and sympathy and your everlasting kindness are comfort for us, as far as comfort is possible in our sadness. You are quite right that my relationship with my mother was similar to yours, and therefore you are able to feel what I feel.
>
> Mother knew about your kind letters, which I read to her until the last week, and was so pleased to know that you will help us. On Thursday, the 19th, she felt very weak, and Thursday night I said good night to her for the last time and kissed her to sleep.
>
> She stayed unconscious until Monday, the 22nd. Of course, I was there the whole time and we stayed up in turn all those nights. In the night from Sunday to Monday, Father and Alma watched at her bed with me. But she never recovered consciousness but slept on till Monday morning at 11 o'clock, when she softly passed away.
>
> I took Father and Alma up to my flat, where they stayed until Thursday. On Wednesday the 24th, we put her to rest in Grinzing, quite near the place where Uncle Gustav lies. The whole week was terrible weather, just as if Heaven and Earth were angry. I am doing all the formalities that are necessary for Father, who is broken down.
>
> You are so right in saying that the delay in my leaving Vienna has its reasons. I am so glad I could help Father in this saddest time of our life. And I believe I did everything quite as Mother would have wished me to.
>
> Thank you so much for your present, that has been announced to me by the Dresdner Bank. I am to receive it in a fortnight's time. I will use it to help Father with the expenses that have arisen now. . . . I will surely bring you a thing that belonged to Mother, and we will all be thankful if you will keep it as a remembrance.

When Alma returned home the day after her mother's funeral, she thanked Alfred with a gift. Inside a copy of a collection of Seneca essays entitled *The Happy Life,* she wrote, "May this book help you as much as you have helped us live through this our worst time. I am, in the truest sense, your sister." This book would be on Alfred's bedside table to the end of his life.

A black-edged newspaper advertisement announced Justine's death. Defiantly centered at the top of the two-inch announcement was a Christian cross.

Alfred and Maria continued to pursue every possibility for emigration. Louis Meijer's May account of his visit with Leopold Stokowski was almost forgotten by the time a second letter, dated 22 September 1938, arrived in Vienna. Not only was the letter an official invitation to visit the Meijers in Scheveningen, but Louis quoted the following from "my Swedish-American friend": "I have just arrived in Hollywood and have spoken to several people about your friend. Would you mind asking him to let me know as soon as he arrives in this country in October. I shall hope to have something for him by then."

8

Black Wednesday

The dignity of man is in your hands. Preserve it, Alma Rosé.
—Wilhelm Backhaus

Arnold was devastated by Justine's death and his expulsion from the orchestras he had served so faithfully. He had a crushing sense of isolation as many of his old friends fled the city and others he had considered friends kept their distance (Richard Strauss, for one, no longer came to Pyrkergasse to play skat). Arnold despaired at the thought that fellow musicians were prevented from playing music with him in his own home. Now his "deep brown" moods were black, and Alma became alarmed at his despondency.

She confided her worries in a letter to the Walters. Bruno Walter promptly wrote to Arnold from Montecatini, trying to boost his old friend's spirits:

> In my mind I am with you. What is binding us together, the love towards Gustav, all the things we did together, the decades of this wonderful music-making with you, dear Arnold—everything that is good has a connection with you. Many evenings at the opera and middays at the Musikverein! Your quartet! Our sonata evenings!
>
> And the decades of personal friendship. That is, and remains, and cannot be erased.[1]

Elsa added that her husband had written on Alma's behalf to Monte Carlo and on Alfred's behalf to conductors Artur Bodanzky and Walter Damrosch in New York.

After the Anschluss, non-German Europeans were shocked at the wave of terror in Viennese streets. Police ignored even the most sadistic displays of anti-Semitism. Brown-shirt rowdies could pluck Jews from the streets and force them to clean gutters or scrub SS toilets or public latrines. Jewish businesses were confiscated and homes looted. Thousands were incarcerated at Dachau,

Buchenwald, and a new concentration camp built at Mauthausen on the banks of the Danube.[2]

Karl Adolf Eichmann, an Austrian Nazi from Hitler's hometown of Linz who was born the same year as Alma, offered the Jews of Austria the only alternative to the terror of the streets: emigration spurred on by administrative terror. Eichmann's creation the Zentralstelle für jüdische Auswanderung (Central Office for Jewish Emigration) became the only agency with the authority to issue exit permits to Jews. Obliging the persecuted to assist with their persecution, the Nazis placed Jewish community leaders at the agency's head. Centralized processing expedited the removal of some forty-five thousand Austrian Jews in the six months following the Anschluss.[3] Eichmann's Zentralstelle was so efficient that it became the model for similar agencies in Germany and in other Nazi-occupied territories.

Ostensibly the Zentralstelle cleared Jews for emigration and served as liaison between the German state and the Jewish people. In practice its activities were more sinister, for the same agency later ran the bureaucracy of mass murder. A witness at the Eichmann trial after the war bluntly summarized the Zentralstelle process:

> A Jew is fed in, with all he possesses, at one end, and is pushed through the entire process, sometimes in various buildings, from counter to counter, office to office, and comes out the other end deprived of all his rights, robbed of all his money, and bearing only a scrap of paper telling him to leave the country within fourteen days, but he is sent to a concentration camp.[4]

Encouraged to register with the agency, the Jews of Vienna were directed to crowded ghettos where they would find hunger and ever harsher deprivation.

Among the first members of the Rosés' circle to leave Vienna were Alma Mahler-Werfel, her husband Franz, and her daughter Anna (now divorced from her third husband, Paul Zsolnay, Franz Werfel's publisher). Fleeing to Italy, Switzerland, then France, they joined tens of thousands of stateless refugees. At one time Alma Mahler had been convinced that baptism into the Catholic faith would afford protection from Nazi tyranny, but recently she had resorted to another ploy. Both her daughter and Werfel's secretary, Albrecht Josef, were scandalized when after the Anschluss, they saw Alma Mahler-Werfel wearing a swastika beneath her lapel, hidden from view but accessible.[5]

For the Rosés, an important ray of hope came from Carl Flesch, the eminent violinist and teacher, in England.[6] Word arrived that he was soliciting money for a fund to help support the elderly Rosé. Flesch wrote scores of letters to fellow artists around the world appealing for contributions. Among many others, Elizabeth Sprague Coolidge, the former U.S. first lady, sent a contribution.

ALMA AND ARNOLD watched anxiously as Alfred and Maria worked out plans to emigrate. Invitations in hand from Louis and Lotte Meijer in The Hague and Leila Pirani in London meant they could leave Austria on short notice. The United States became a possibility when Maria's mother, Alice (Lisl) Schmutzer—a poet and arts writer whose work appeared frequently in the *Neue Freie Presse*—asked a friend in New York, the aged Abraham Beller, to provide an affidavit for them. This precious document was the key to entry into the United States, proof to the U.S. consulate in Vienna that would-be immigrants had financial backing in the U.S. and would not become a burden on the state. Beller's advanced years were a concern at the consulate, however, and again the Rosés' departure was delayed.

Another stalwart friend, Elly Burger—formerly the children's governess and later Alfred's secretary—came to the rescue. Elly had emigrated to the United States and was living in Cincinnati, Ohio, where she worked as secretary to an opthalmologist, Dr. Sattler, who had his own clinic. With Mrs. Sattler's help, Elly was able to assure U.S. authorities that the couple had a place to live in Cincinnati: the third floor of the clinic could be converted into a small apartment.

Alfred had been warned not to leave the house in Sternwartestrasse lest he be arrested, so Maria stood for whole days in queues to get the necessary documents. For weeks, the couple's suitcases were packed and ready for a telephone call from Meijer in Holland telling them when they should leave to catch their ship, the *Veendam* of the Holland America Line, which was scheduled to depart from Holland on 5 October 1938. The date of departure by rail from Vienna was set for 28 September.

On 27 September, their last night in Vienna, Alfred and Maria went to the apartment at Pyrkergasse for a last visit with Arnold and Alma. It was a farewell without farewells, since Alfred and Maria had decided it would be easier for Arnold to learn of their departure after the fact. Alma, however, guessed their secret. After they left Father Rosé and descended to the street, she came running down the front steps after them. "You are leaving tomorrow?" she said.

Emotionally, Alma embraced them for the last time. She was relieved that they could escape Vienna. All the same, she did not return to the apartment until they were out of sight and she had composed herself sufficiently to face her father.

The next morning Maria's mother, her sister Susanne, and Susanne's fiancé Paul Peschke were at the Westbahnhof to see the couple off. Their trunks were to be shipped separately. Except for jewelry, the layers of clothing Maria wore, and the contents of their suitcases, their worldly assets were reduced to the equivalent of U.S. $5 cash at the German-Dutch frontier.

Here they met another barrier. Inundated by refugees, the Dutch had passed a law prohibiting immigrants in transit from entering the country more than five days in advance of their scheduled exit date. At the border, however,

Alfred and Maria learned that the departure of the *Veendam* had been delayed. Alfred was able to telephone Louis Meijer in Scheveningen and explain their plight. He and Maria sat on their suitcases a few meters from safety in Holland until 3 a.m., when Louis was able to obtain ministerial clearance for them to enter the country for a stay exceeding the stipulated limit.

The *Veendam* did not sail until 15 October. The Rosés spent the intervening time with the Meijers in Scheveningen, blissfully out of harm's way. On a visit to Amsterdam, they had the pleasure of attending a Rachmaninoff concert with the Concertgebouw Orchestra. Afterwards they found the pianist backstage in a long fur coat raging over the treatment Mengelberg, the autocratic conductor, had given the concerto in which he was soloist.[7]

The *Veendam* docked briefly at Southampton. Leila Pirani drove from London to greet the young couple and to give them £30 she had collected. Five pounds had come from Dorothy Beswick Hetherington, the Rosés' beloved Dory (then living in Hertfordshire), and another five from "Miss Jessie" Thompson, two former governesses who remembered the family fondly.

In her autobiographical *Letter to My Grandchildren,* Leila described her brief reunion with Alfred:

> Alfred was very troubled about Alma, and he begged me to do something about her. "You can't imagine what a dreadful life she is leading. . . . Now she can't go inside a theatre, a cinema, a park or any other public place."[8]

Vati wrote to Alfred and Maria six days after they left Vienna:

> The way you said goodbye, I was convinced you were leaving. It was good of you to spare me the upset. Tell Louis and his wife how grateful I am for the help they have given you. It shows that people still have a heart.
>
> Alma has devoted herself to me completely. She takes care of all the business, knits and cooks, shops, and looks after me so well that I have no needs.
>
> She corresponds all over hoping she can get an extra week's work. Twice since you left, we have been at Lisl's [Alice Schmutzer's]. Almschi is concerned that I am not left alone too much. Because the tram is the only way into town, I never go there. I am sending this letter without a word from Alma because she is with Heini, who came only for the day.

On 7 October 1938, Alma wrote to Alfred and Maria in Holland:

> If only we were away! Can you please ask Louis to send us an updated invitation so that we can be ready for a surprise. In all cases it is prudent

> to have an invitation in hand so that one will have someplace to go at a moment's notice. At the same time write to the friend in London C. F. [Carl Flesch] to seek the same thing. Hurry it please, as soon as possible, so that we can have the invitations in an emergency and escape at the first opportunity.
>
> At the moment I am so happy—but for how long! Manina [the Czech cook Marie Jelinek-Klose] returned yesterday. So pleased.[9]

This letter was written during a five-day terror that swept the Döbling district of Vienna. From 5 to 10 October, Jewish households were raided. All passports were marked with a "J," and Jews without passports were forced across the Czech border and given a mere 40 marks—the equivalent of U.S. $10—to make their way. It would have been dangerous for Alma to mention these events explicitly in her letter.

TWENTY-EIGHT September 1938—the very day Alfred and Maria left Vienna for Holland—was recorded in history as "Black Wednesday." Hitler had issued an ultimatum for the "return" to the Reich of the Sudeten region of Czechoslovakia, home of three million Germans, although in fact the mountainous northern section of the country had belonged to Austria but never to Germany. Repeatedly, Hitler had assured Neville Chamberlain, the British prime minister, and other heads of government that once the "Czech problem" was solved, he would make no further territorial demands in Europe. Prague, however, had rejected Hitler's call for the immediate evacuation of the Sudetenland, which would force hundreds of thousands of Czechs to leave their homes, abandoning even the cattle in their fields. "Black Wednesday" was the deadline Hitler had set for capitulation of the Czechs or armed invasion. His troops were massed at the borders, and war seemed inevitable. Czechoslovakia and France were mobilizing troops, and the British were digging trenches and evacuating schoolchildren from London.

At the last moment, Mussolini sent word that he and Fascist Italy stood behind the Führer on the Sudeten question but begged him to delay military action. Hitler, pleased by the Duce's loyalty, agreed, and a conference was hastily called in Munich for the next two days, 29–30 September 1938, with the sole purpose of settling the "Czech question" while averting war. The nation Hitler sought to dismember was not invited to the conference of the four Big Powers: Great Britain, France, Italy, and Germany. Toward the end of the sessions, two Czech representatives were invited to sit in an adjacent room, where at the conclusion of the talks they were handed a map showing the large territories to be evacuated immediately. The fate of the Czech republic was sealed.

The German army marched across the borders on the first of October and occupied the Sudetenland by the tenth. Among the leaders of the West, only

Winston Churchill seemed to understand what was happening. In a speech addressed to the House of Commons on 5 October 1938, he declared:

> We are in the midst of a disaster of the first magnitude. . . . All the countries of Mittel Europa and the Danube valley, one after another, will be drawn in the vast system of Nazi politics . . . radiating from Berlin. . . . And do not suppose that this is the end. It is only the beginning.[10]

The Munich Conference sacrificed the Czech nation, weakened the French position, and strengthened Germany militarily, thereby postponing war by eleven months. Without firing a shot Hitler had made another major conquest, and he was now in an excellent position to press on with his drive for more German "living space" in the East.

From Vienna, the Nazis launched a radio campaign designed to inflame the nationalist passions of Slovaks in Czechoslovakia. The German government actively fomented "disturbances" and "clashes." By 21 October 1938, the Führer had issued a top-secret memorandum to his military chiefs calling for "liquidation of the remainder of Czechoslovakia" as quickly as possible. The weak, newly pro-German government of Czechoslovakia was soon convinced to dismiss all editors and officials who opposed the Nazi regime and to outlaw the Jews of Czechoslovakia as the Jews of Germany and Austria had been outlawed.

Whatever safety Alma might have found in Czechoslovakia had evaporated at Munich. Anny Kux Poláková, whom Alma and Michal Karin had helped to flee with her parents from Vienna and find refuge in Bratislava, lived with her husband Eduard Polak less than an hour away, and Alma knew she would always be welcome in their home. But she feared, realistically, that all Czechoslovakia would soon be in Nazi hands.[11] Alma's options included possible offers from the Grand Hotel Central in The Hague and from Athens, but she worried that Holland and Greece were also among Hitler's targets. In any case, she could not bring herself to leave her father or to separate from Heini.

On 11 October 1938, Arnold wrote to Alfred, "Alma's only worry is that Heini should be able to leave with us." A day later, on 12 October, Alma herself wrote:

> Of course I won't act precipitously, but there have been such wild happenings here that I wrote that letter [of 7 October, asking Alfred to help with invitations from Louis Meijer and Carl Flesch] with Vati's agreement. However, meanwhile everything has been reversed.
>
> One would have had to leave within twenty-four hours otherwise. Until Monday I had visitors [a veiled reference to Nazi callers]. Sometimes I would love to simply pitch everything away and leave, never to return.

> Amazingly, I have no desire to play. I just wish I were rooted somewhere, but that does not seem to be my destiny. Tell Louis [Meijer] that if it is in his power, he should help us.

Alma's next note, dated 13 October 1938, was surprisingly buoyant:

> We are enjoying the autumn sun. This is my favorite time of year. That is the only diversion in the small circle in which we are cramped. Next week I'll send Father to the doctor, but there seems to be nothing serious. I give him all my attention. I beat my head to breaking as I strive to find out how and where we can go with Heini.

Alice and Susanne Schmutzer, who met with the Rosés as often as twice a week, also exchanged letters with Alfred and Maria. Frau Schmutzer's reports from her theatrical and literary circles, and Arnold's with news about musical Vienna, contained veiled allusions that amounted to almost daily accounts of the terror in Vienna.

From her letters it is clear that Maria's mother disapproved of Alma. On 22 October 1938, Frau Schmutzer wrote: "Father is well and astute. Alma is a difficult case, and she is not ideal for this environment—[father and daughter are] not good for each other. I preach to her as well as I can. She always has visitors and in the evening is invited out."

This judgment seems harsh. The same day, Alma sent a warm note to Mrs. Nina Maxwell, a well-known supporter of musical projects and a close friend of Bruno Walter's: "My father today received your dear invitation and beautiful flowers. He thanks you very much—your warmhearted words touched him. He will be glad to see you Monday. Would you allow me to accompany him? Would you be so kind as to telephone us with your reply (at B10-5-38)? We are unable to get your telephone number."[12] The letter reflected Alma's desire to be with her father at all times, for she feared he would encounter difficulties if he ventured outside Pyrkergasse 23. Invitations from Mrs. Maxwell and others worked wonders, and Vati's spirits lifted.

Good friends of twenty years' standing, Dr. Hans and Stella Fuchs (who met the Rosés when Stella and Justine worked together for the Red Cross during World War I), had recently moved close to the Rosé apartment in Vienna. Their proximity was a tonic, and Arnold saw them frequently.

Late in October Frau Schmutzer wrote again, disturbed because the Rosés were suddenly incommunicado:

> I must say that Alma has curious ways. When I didn't hear from her for some days, I called and found out that *sans adieu* she had gone away the day after she was here about a week ago.
>
> She has gone to see Mrs. Doubleday [Leila Doubleday Pirani] in

London, and she hopes to get an invitation to Holland from Louis couldn't even write me a note, which she could have done in a hear.

The important thing is that all is well with Father. He has become outspoken and sociable. He is invited out very often. He makes plans like a youth but is very, very reasonable.

Alma had maintained silence about her coming trip because she did not want to risk alerting the Gestapo to her travels. She had indeed left Vienna on 29 October on a multinational "scouting trip" suggested by Arnold, hoping to find a way to secure the future for her father, herself, and Heini.

WHILE ALMA was away, Vienna suffered the worst anti-Semitic violence in its history. It was an "earthquake," Frau Schmutzer wrote, referring obliquely to explosions that destroyed the synagogue in Leopoldgasse and to the notorious Kristallnacht—the "Night of Shattered Glass"—that swept German Europe on 9–10 November 1938.

In Paris, a seventeen-year-old German Jew, Herschel Grynszpan, had shot a young German diplomat, Ernst vom Rath, on 7 November. Vom Rath died of his wounds two days later. Grynszpan's Polish Jewish parents, residents of Hanover for more than twenty years, had been rounded up and deported in boxcars to the Polish border, where they were detained in a camp under deplorable conditions. By his rash action, Grynszpan expressed his rage at his parents' plight and at the brutal persecution of Jews throughout Nazi Germany.

In retaliation for the shooting, the Third Reich orchestrated the worst pogrom yet, a night of "spontaneous" demonstrations that resulted in the burning of over two hundred synagogues and many Jewish houses and shops, the arrest of some thirty thousand Jews, and an untold number of sadistic attacks against individual Jews. Close to ten thousand Jewish shops were looted, and the damage in Germany in broken glass alone amounted to five million marks (about U.S. $1,250,000). To compensate for damages, the German government ordered the Jewish community to pay a billion marks.

In Vienna, a few blocks from Pyrkergasse, the synagogue in Döbling was among twenty temples destroyed or vandalized. Fifteen thousand Viennese Jews were rounded up, and many were severely beaten during questioning. Some were sent to Dachau, others held on a barge in the Danube. Days later some five thousand Jews were still in custody.

Fritz Molden reported a joke circulating at the time in Vienna. God had endowed man with three attributes: intelligence, decency, and National Socialism. But things being what they were, a German could have only two of them at a time. "Generally speaking," Molden went on to say, "virtually everyone in the Third Reich was classifiable under these three heads. For . . . an intelligent and decent National Socialist had become an impossibility."[13]

In his next letters Arnold mentioned resumed contacts with Paul Fischer, the quartet's former violist, and Julius Stwertka, a violinist with the Philharmonic. Guido Adler was a caller of special note.

When Alfred expressed concern about Alma's bold actions, Arnold wrote on 12 November:

> I will tell you everything about Alma. Her stops will be Hamburg, Amsterdam, Leila, and perhaps on the return, Paris. Her progress is wonderful. Heini shares her dreams—she is lucky.
>
> I play every day. At the end of the year my pension is to be cumulated! [Payments due over a period of years would be paid in a lump sum, which would leave Arnold shortchanged.]

An event of 15 November brought a change of tone. Writing in careful shorthand Arnold said: "I've had a 'visitor' who wanted to know about you." Fortunately Alfred had escaped Vienna before the Nazis came to arrest him.

In Amsterdam Alma stayed briefly with Bruno and Elsa Walter, who were en route to France. At the Grand Hotel Central in The Hague, where the Wiener Walzermädeln had performed in 1935, she renewed old acquaintances. Both Walter and Mengelberg—two titans in European music—gave her recommendations. On 21 November 1938, Mengelberg wrote to the Concertgebouw management. After summarizing Alma's background, he concluded: "She is a first-class artist and soloist. I can recommend Alma Rosé most sincerely to all concert organizations."[14]

A day later, Leila Doubleday Pirani met Alma in London. She described the scene in her unpublished memoir:

> Alma was dressed entirely in black when she got out of the train (because of her mother having died) and was frightfully pale. Her appearance was therefore disappointing. She was also highly nervous and tense, so that after ten minutes I knew that difficulties lay ahead.
>
> I had photographs of her father and mother in my room which I had not removed, as I thought they would please her; but on sight of them she had a nerve storm, and it was difficult to calm her down and get her to eat some supper before she went to bed.
>
> It was painful for me to see Alma in this state, but I realized that the failure of her marriage to Příhoda, the difficult conditions she had been living under, and moreover something of which I had not yet heard, had all contributed to her mental upheaval. She was idolized by her parents, spoiled by society and the public, so that she was not able to tackle the changed conditions.
>
> After she had settled down a little, we went to see Professor Flesch, who had not spared himself in collecting as much as possible so that

the fund for Rosé would be sufficient to satisfy the British government to allow Rosé an entry visa.

Flesch, sixty-five, had the utmost respect for her father, was exceedingly nice to her, and said it would be the greatest satisfaction to get Arnold out of the clutches of the Nazis. The next day, we went to Broadcasting House to meet Sir Adrian Boult. Sir Adrian was polite and kindly. He invited Alma to a performance of Mahler's *Das Lied von der Erde,* which was attended by Gucki [Anna Mahler] as well.

Pianist Wilhelm Backhaus was performing a Beethoven piano concerto. Alma told me that the German Backhaus was a great friend of all the family and always visited them when he concertized in Vienna. She was looking forward to meeting him in the artists' room after the concert.

Boult greeted us nicely, and Alma was about to turn to Backhaus but stopped, because on seeing her he turned his back and walked through a passage. Alma's face twitched, and of course I realized what a shock this was to her: a stab in the back from this cowardly man, who for fear of his Nazi masters could not behave decently, even in England.[15]

Still in London on 1 December 1938, Alma wrote to Alfred about her trip:

I was not going to write you, but your birthday is coming, and I am thinking of you so much that I am unable to wait until I get back to Vienna. From here I want to wish you every good fortune and blessing for the next year of your life! Unfortunately I cannot at present send you anything, as I have no money—

I have been away from home for four weeks. It had become impossible; my nerves were simply on strike. After a week in Amsterdam I came here to the Piranis. They are angels!

Flesch has stood by Vati fabulously. Naturally I do not touch the money—on the contrary, I try through all people possible to add still more. Bruno [Walter] has given me something. I also stayed with them in Amsterdam. Mengelberg has written a wonderful recommendation for me, as has Bruno. I hope as a result still to receive something [referring to work prospects]. In any case I have engagements in Holland for a few weeks, very well paid.

On the day you left, the SA called on us. Thank God Vati was already asleep. They took my car. We have by the way lived through a number of such nice little intermezzi. We absolutely want to be someplace else. I won't hurry anything, don't worry. But I am on a scouting trip.

Buxbaum only yesterday received his permit for permanent residence and permission to teach. Beautiful, isn't it?

Tomorrow I shall be with Sir Adrian Boult.[16] It takes so long to set up appointments! I want very much to be back with Vati—I can hardly

> wait. But if I were to hurry back before I have spoken with all the people here, the whole trip would have been in vain.
>
> My dear one—please try to understand and do not condemn me for leaving Vati alone. Had I not gone, I would have had to leave him alone even more. It was his idea because he had seen that things could not continue as they were.

When Alma met with Boult, she presented a plan to reform the Rosé Quartet in London with Buxbaum as cellist and herself as second violinist. Sir Adrian was enthusiastic. He himself would underwrite Arnold's work permit.

Friedrich Buxbaum and his family were already in England, but as late as 7 November 1938 Arnold wrote to Alfred: "Bux plans to return to Vienna because he is too old to get a place in London." Emigration to the United Kingdom had become exceedingly difficult for anyone over fifty, and both Buxbaum and Rosé were well past the magic age. Buxbaum, ousted from the Vienna Philharmonic the same day as Arnold, had been trying for months to become established in London but could not find work. With Alma's plan to resurrect the quartet, a place for Buxbaum suddenly opened in London, and Bux was rescued along with Arnold.

Arnold's letters to Alfred while Alma was away complained that he was vegetating, confined to "these four walls, reading and playing violin." He was grateful when Susanne Schmutzer made a wooden cross to mark Justine's grave until a permanent headstone designed by Carl Moll could be erected. He was looking forward to a chamber music session at Pyrkergasse with three loyal colleagues from the Philharmonic. His sense of alarm was growing. His nephew Wolfgang had sent an SOS from Berlin. "Wolfi" was seeking an affidavit for emigration to the United States, and Arnold asked Alfred to solicit help among his new acquaintances in Cincinnati. (Alfred was later able to get support for Wolfgang's emigration.) In London, Arnold reported, Alma had lunched with "Rudi Bing," at the time artistic director of John Christie's Glyndebourne Opera. Bing pledged to help the Rosés as he could and asked to be warmly remembered to Arnold.

Alfred wrote from Ohio that he was desperate for employment. He had taken an advertisement in the *Musical Courier* with his picture, stating that he had "returned to America" with the objective of presenting the music of his uncle Gustav Mahler and was available immediately for engagements.

Still in England, Alma moved quickly through the paperwork of clearing Arnold's emigration with the English Home Office. Thanks to a special request for expediency Bruno Walter had sent to the daughter-in-law of the viceroy of India, Alma was able to make a direct and immediate application on behalf of her father. On 15 December 1938, she wrote again to Alfred:

> News has just arrived that Vati has received his residence and work permits. It was rushed through the Home Office in three weeks! Since I

> arrived here I have collected another £100 [for the Rosé Fund]. I wrote to all possible people. You can imagine how I have reacted. . . . I have several offers to play in Holland, Athens, and elsewhere.
>
> First, I will go back and get everything in order for Father's emigration. Then I shall settle him in London in Leila's neighborhood. And then I want to earn some money. All the gathered monies, together with the fund, now amount to about £300, so that for the first time we need not feel nervous. Don't you, either! Father's only wish is *away!* Fuchse [Dr. Hans Fuchs] will probably also come [to London] soon.
>
> After three months, Bux obtained the same [work] permits as Vati. I have heard, without seeing your letter, that after Christmas you have the prospect of a job. I need not tell you how happy I would be to be with you. These last days have been terrible—I am so alone in this terribly large city. My nerves have again completely given way. But now I have new courage to live . . . .
>
> My dear one, do you realize that now Vati can visit you anytime as soon as we earn the money? Is that not marvelous? The future still holds what I hope will be only a brief irritating time in Vienna—but then!!!
>
> For Christmas and New Year's I send you warmest wishes—the same that I send to Vati; 1939 will certainly be a happier year. May God bring it to pass that we may soon hold you close and find a real home. You and Maria, praise be to Heaven, have this blessing already in that you are together.

In November, while Alma was in London, a boundary settlement between Hungary and Czechoslovakia, enforced by Italy and Germany, sliced away another piece of Czechoslovakia. Alma, still relying on her Czech passport for safe passage, was reminded that she was on borrowed time.

As Christmas 1938 drew near, a pall hung over the Rosé apartment at Pyrkergasse. Arnold's letters from Vienna were still edged in mourning black, and the day did not pass when he did not think of Justine. Alfred and Maria were far away, struggling to build a new life in America. Both Arnold and Alma still wrestled miserably with their banishment from Viennese musical society. This New Year's there would be no performance by the Wiener Walzermädeln in the Ronacher theater, and Arnold would hear only secondhand accounts of the traditional Philharmonic concert.

Alma's personal life, too, hung by a thread. In London, she unburdened her soul to Leila, who gave this account:

> Alma finally confessed to me that she had a lover in Vienna to whom she was devoted, but he was a good deal younger than she, and his rich father would have cast him off without a schilling if he attempted to marry a woman of the Jewish race.

> Alma also told me that when her mother became ill, she felt the need of the help and consolation of a formal religion, and shortly before Justine died, [she] had been received into the Roman Catholic Church.
>
> She said she hoped that Heini and she would be free to marry in England. There was no English law, such as the Nazis instituted, that would prevent her marrying a Gentile and Roman Catholic such as Heini.[17]

Arnold was elated by Alma's news from London, yet he worried constantly about her delayed return. Friends sought to distract him: on 23 December he dined at the Schmutzers' (where he extolled Alma's successes in England), and he spent Christmas Eve with Hans and Stella Fuchs.

For her part, Alma was striving feverishly to return to Vienna before Christmas. On her last day in England, she almost panicked. Her precious ticket for mobility—her Czech passport—was mislaid at the Home Office. She had to return to the office to retrieve it and missed the train she meant to catch.

She took the next train out, but the trip to Vienna was an ordeal, forty-three hours in third class in uncomfortable, unlit coaches. Arriving in Vienna at 3 a.m., twelve hours late, she called the apartment at Pyrkergasse and asked Manina to meet her at the station. She slipped into bed without waking her father so that he would be fresh for Christmas Day.

On Christmas morning, Arnold awakened to find the exhausted but triumphant Alma in her bed. With her "impulsive nature," as he proudly wrote to Alfred, she had achieved in weeks what others would require months to accomplish. As Arnold liked to say about his daughter, she had the energy of a Mahler.

9

Another Blow

Scorn poverty: no one is as poor as he was at birth. Scorn pain: either it will go away or you will. . . . Scorn fortune: I have given her no weapon with which to strike your soul.
—Seneca, *On Providence*

With the new year 1939, the Nazis were flush with victory. The city that had rejected Hitler as a young artist thronged to welcome the triumphant Führer along the route of his motorcade to the Hotel Imperial, whence he paid visits to the theater and other sights of the imperial city.

Alma spent long hours in lines with the hundreds of other Viennese waiting to launch appeals to the Nazi bureaucracy and to comply with the new laws governing Jewish households. A mistake could bring disaster, and she had to thrust her impatience aside and take each small step required to get the necessary exit permissions and to pay the "refugee taxes" levied on Jewish emigrants. The Pyrkergasse apartment was to be "Aryanized" the first week in March 1939, and she and her father would be forced to move. It is a tribute to the future occupants of the apartment that they told the Rosés they could wait to take possession until father and daughter had wound up their affairs.

For weeks Alma passed up lunch, too busy to take a break. Fortunately Arnold had overpaid his taxes, which allowed him to pay the many special levies. Arnold asked Alfred to request yet another "invitation" from Louis Meijer in Holland, in case he and Alma had to leave in haste despite Alma's preparations for an orderly departure.

Heini and a friend of his from childhood pitched in to help as they could, but the burden fell on Alma, with Manina working faithfully at her side. In negotiations with the bureaucracy, Alma enlisted the aid of a few friends still in the administration. If all were done correctly, she and her father might be able to leave Vienna with most of their possessions.

The news from Alfred and Maria was encouraging. Alfred had a music teaching job, and his Second Quartet had been performed in Cincinnati. Maria, a musician in her own right and also a trained couturière, was earning money sewing. The couple were also baking Viennese confections that Alfred delivered before dawn. Later they would supplement their income by giving lessons in Viennese baking.

The miracles Alma performed in the first weeks of 1939 impressed even Frau Schmutzer. Eventually two truckloads of treasured possessions were sorted, packed, and hauled away from the apartment. Most of the Rosés' belongings were destined for England, although a substantial number of crates were left with Martha Setzer, Alfred's loyal colleague at the Volkskonservatorium, who also pledged to tend Justine's grave. Alma wrote to Alfred that perpetual care of their mother's resting place was her "personal commitment."

Arnold and Alma were pleased but envious each time they learned that a friend or relative had found asylum beyond Vienna. Some of Arnold's colleagues left for Lima, Santo Domingo, Trinidad, and Australia; others simply disappeared.

It was Vienna's coldest winter in years. Despite repeated warnings from her father, Alma refused to slow down. By mid-February 1939 the hectic pace had taken a toll, and she was burning with fever. Arnold finally called the doctor. To save Vati from worry, Alma did not tell him that she scheduled a tonsillectomy for 24 February. A week later, she was still in pain and having difficulty talking. She had lost momentum in preparations for departure, and once again her nerves collapsed.

As Alma put the finishing touches on plans for escape, calls to the Rosé home were fruitless. Manina was cryptic about Alma's whereabouts, even with Frau Schmutzer, and Arnold would not come to the telephone. Arnold also began to veil references to himself in his letters, calling himself Uncle Josef (his middle name). Father and daughter, Alice Schmutzer wrote, had dug underground like badgers.

Arnold remarked in one letter that both sons of his brother Eduard, who would be eighty at the end of February, had risked a trip to Weimar to visit their father. His next letter reported that both Ernest and Wolfgang intended to flee Germany, taking the arduous route through southern France and Spain.[1]

As March approached, the news from Czechoslovakia was ominous. On 15 March, Alfred and Maria heard that Hitler had accepted the surrender of Czechoslovakia. They knew that Alma's Czech passport was henceforth useless.

A reassuring letter from Alma arrived from London. On 19 March 1939, she wrote:

> My Dearest Alferle,
>
> You can now be free of worry. Tuesday [14 March] I was still at the last office for Vati's passport, standing for eight and a half hours without a rest, and they told me he would receive it in a few days. I'm sorry

I couldn't wait any longer, but had to leave Wednesday evening [15 March] to escape here. It was like the movies. Terribly exciting. Heini came with me!

I'm almost sure I was the last one let in with a passport. Two others were sent back from the airport. We were examined in Croydon for many hours, singly, and interrogated. Terrible!

I had reserved a place on an airplane from Hamburg to London. I left by train Wednesday evening and was supposed to transfer in Leipzig to another train, but the train was late and I missed the connection. Now I had to fly to reach the other plane. Under the most complicated arrangements I got a seat, changed planes in Berlin, and flew on to Hamburg. Heini was waiting. We pretended not to recognize each other.

The departure went smoothly. We were the only passengers in a beautiful little English plane. Only when it left the ground did we speak to each other. In three and a half hours we were in London.

In London, Leila had received a telegram from Alma giving the time of their arrival. "Both arriving," it said ambiguously. Here Leila Pirani takes up the story:

Why from Hamburg? I thought.

I waited and waited. Finally, I was convinced there was some mistake, as no passengers seemed to be coming in. Suddenly a small messenger boy appeared and asked me if I were Mrs. Pirani. He requested me to go to the Interrogation Office and said, "your friends are in trouble, I am afraid."

Poor old Professor was my first thought. However, there was no tall professor waiting for me, but a tall, fair young man was with Alma. I guessed immediately that this was Heini, the lover of whom she had told me. Alma, swathed in furs, rushed towards me, putting both her arms around my neck, and whispered "you are responsible for Heini and Dory [Dorothy Beswick Hetherington] for me."

Released from the embrace, I went straight to Heini and said I was so glad to see him, with a few platitudes about having had a good flight, etc., after which the examiner wished to question me.

The whole atmosphere was so fantastically unreal that it was made easy for me. . . . The examiner looked troubled and said he thought the persons in question, Alma and Heini, had arranged their flight together, and he wished to know whether there was any intention of marriage between them. To this I answered neither "yes" nor "no" but said, "I think you will find that there is a great discrepancy in their ages."[2]

Alma and Heini—every nerve taut—moved in with the Piranis. Repeatedly, they went over the plan for Arnold's escape to England, worrying that something would go wrong.

In a long letter of 19 March, Alma told Alfred about their last days in Vienna:

> At this time, we are living in Leila's attic but looking urgently for a furnished flat for Vati. He is in good hands, staying with the Fuchses [in Vienna]. I wrote down everything for him, and a friend of Heini's is very attentive and will see that everything is taken care of. . . . You can imagine how quickly we had to do everything.
>
> Both violins [the Mysa and the Guadagnini] and all the jewelry are out, also the watch from Franz Josef [a gold watch on a chain presented to Arnold by the emperor]. Sorry I could not get permission to take out the silver. . . .
>
> The delay in Vati's passport was the result of a tax to flee the country. Everyone who earned more than 30,000 schillings was required to pay a year's tax. . . . I told Vati to pay the balance owing in cash.
>
> It is too sad that I could not be the last one to leave the apartment, like the captain of a sinking ship, rather than leave Father to come afterwards. But it would have been worse if Father could not get out any more, and everything would have had to be repeated for me.
>
> I could not say goodbye to anyone in Vienna. In two hours I was gone. Maybe the tremendous hurry made it easier. Still, it was painful.
>
> Sunday [12 March] we were at Mutti's [Justine's grave in Grinzing]. Forget-me-nots will be planted over her grave, and from May to November, pink begonias. You will receive a photo after the headstone [by Moll] is erected.
>
> I embrace you. Much love to Elly!

Alma and Heini soon wore out their welcome as houseguests. The Piranis, professional musicians with demanding schedules and two small children, Felix and Gina, had one maid, Anny, who was hard-pressed to keep up with household work. Alma and Heini paid little heed to the Piranis' routines and rarely offered to help. Often they slept late and sat at the dining room table all morning smoking cigarettes. "Alma did not, or did not know how to, clear the table and set it for the next meal," Leila wrote. Anny was often irritated and complained to Leila that her efforts on behalf of Alma and Heini were excessive. In reply, Leila said, "I told her how good the Rosés had been to me, and nothing I did would be enough to show my gratitude."

Soon, to everyone's relief, Alma and Heini found a small place in Maida Vale and moved out. Alma took a small room close by for Vati. The wait for his arrival stretched to six weeks.

In letters to Alfred during this suspenseful time, Arnold used musical references to carry on a discourse only his son would understand, so that no censor could fault his reports. On 10 April 1939, Easter Monday, he wrote that Alma had arranged an engagement for him to play on 1 May with Buxbaum and Paul Weingarten. He said that the program called for Dvořák's *Dumky* Trio (music with pensive, brooding passages), when it should be the "*grosse B* [great B] of Beethoven," the triumphant "Archduke" Trio. He knew Alfred would get the message that this was the day his father would arrive in England.

Traveling via Berlin and Amsterdam, Arnold reached London on schedule. His first card to Alfred from England, written 8 May 1939, showed an enormous sense of release. Arnold had met with Viennese friends and visited Carl Flesch as well as Dory and the Piranis. At a Toscanini rehearsal in Queen's Hall, the conductor had embraced him repeatedly. The same night Arnold attended a violin concert by Bronisław Huberman,[3] and the next night a concert by Richard Tauber. He had met with Sir Adrian Boult to discuss the rebirth of the quartet.

With a friend, Arnold had visited Justine's grave in Grinzing before leaving Vienna. He reported that the Carl Moll headstone was in place, with room for his name too. He hoped one day to return to his homeland, in life or in death.

During Arnold's first weeks in London, the Piranis held a series of musical soirées in his honor. Often the Piranis and the Rosés took turns performing. Alma made a few tactless remarks about the Piranis' repertory and playing skills, insisting, for instance, that Leila play a violin piece Alma and her father knew well—"the César Franck or a Handel sonata"—to allow them to judge her strength with virtuoso pieces. Leila, who was eager to please her former teacher and could have played either piece "standing on my head if necessary," was stung by the challenge.

Alma's emotional, sometimes thoughtless behavior strained relations with the Piranis, and it was not long before Leila detected disturbing signals between Alma and Heini. It seemed to her that Alma was too overbearing for the mild-mannered Heini. "She never left him out of her sight," Leila wrote; often she was "draped around him like a fur neckpiece."

In late May, Alma wrote to Alfred about their progress:

> You have written so lovingly that it greatly touched my heart. There is so terribly much to be done all day long that I can hardly get to my practicing. We cook at home—especially Heini, who has proven himself an unspeakably talented cook—and we must also clean up everything. Vati has a pretty room a few houses from here and comes to all meals except breakfast.
>
> Heini finally received his military leave until August. Meanwhile we MUST find a job for him. We are looking constantly.
>
> At long last we have found a very pretty flat—a two-story maisonette—and we hope to move in next week. When Father will again be with his familiar furniture everything will be much better. As soon as possible, I will send you a drawing and photo. You will have a very nice

> room with us when you come to Europe someday. This seven-room dwelling is cheaper than the two rooms we have now. . . .
>
> If we finally begin to earn something, we will feel quite at home here.

Early in June, Alma wrote that Heini's efforts to find work in England were fruitless. It was impossible for a German to find work. Meanwhile she and Arnold spent hours on end playing their violins. Much of Arnold's old repertoire was new for Alma, and she bent herself to the task of mastering it. Soon Arnold boasted that his daughter was the best second violin he had ever had. The musical work, all-consuming for Arnold and Alma, left Heini on the sideline.

Evenings spent with fellow Viennese, who could communicate with Arnold in German, were especially enjoyable. One summer night, Alma, Heini, Arnold, and Lotte and Franz Zuber—also immigrants to England—composed a joint postcard for the Rosés in Cincinnati. Alma wrote happily: "This has been one of those rare evenings when one feels complete. Franz Zuber is always the wonderful optimist, and through Lotte our whole youth is relived."

TOWARD THE end of June 1939, Leila came home at noon from a break in rehearsals for a production of Handel's *Rodelinda.* Anny told her that a man with a German accent had telephoned several times and said he would call again at 2 p.m. At first Leila thought it was one of the many Austrian refugees she befriended, but Anny said she did not recognize the voice. When the telephone rang at the appointed time, the caller communicated devastating news for Alma:

> "You do not know me, Mrs. Pirani, but I am a friend of Heini's father, and I have to tell you that Heini, after repeated appeals from his parents, has agreed to go home and has left Madame Rosé this morning. She will no doubt be upset when she finds Heini's note to her, and she will naturally go to her father. Heini requests that you go to them immediately."
>
> I said I certainly would, but as he was responsible for the message, I asked him to give me his name, telephone number, and address, which he did.
>
> Off I went to the Professor's little hotel, and went up to his room to find Alma lying prostrate against her father, and tears pouring down his face. . . . How broken he was now, without any control at all! Alma kept weeping, too, and saying she couldn't go back to the flat and the stark reality that Heini had left.
>
> "You needn't do that, Alma. You can come home with me."
>
> Professor said: "*Ja, nimm sie doch zu Dir.*" ["Yes, take her with you."]
>
> I then suggested I should go next day and pay off the flat and col-

lect Alma's things. The Professor came with us and I told them of the gentleman who had telephoned. Alma got through to him, and asked him to come to 32 West End Lane [the Piranis' home] and tell her what he knew of Heini's going. I remember he DID come, and all sat around the table; it must have been tea-time; and there was suddenly an awful moment when he said that Heini might still be in England, as the plane didn't leave until about 5.

Alma jumped up from the table, asked Max [Pirani] to drive her to the airport at once. Max explained that he couldn't, for he had to drive me to the theater by 7 p.m. for the performance of *Rodelinda* and couldn't get back in time if he went to the airport.

At that moment Kings [Kingsley Doubleday, Leila's brother, who spent the summer of 1910 at Bad Aussee with the Rosés and remained one of Alfred's closest friends] appeared in his little car. Alma practically threw herself on him, begging him to get her to the airport.

Poor old Professor looked completely bewildered, as he knew only a few words of English. He didn't know what Alma wanted to do. Kings in his usual gentle way said he would, and Alma told her father to hurry. The three went off.

The plane had already left when they arrived at the airport.

Alma spent the night at Leila's, sleeping in the master bedroom. The next morning, Leila wrote, when she delivered a breakfast tray to the room, she found Alma "in a fearful state." As she got out of bed, Alma "fell faint on the floor." Leila couldn't get her up and called for help.

Later, when Leila was in the West Country of England on tour with the *Rodelinda* company, she received a letter from Heini. "He tried to explain and justify himself and begged me to let him have news from time to time of the 'two beings I love best in the world.'" Thinking Heini's words might console Alma, Leila reported them in a letter. As she recounted:

> Alma was out when the letter arrived, and, coming home at night, she decided in her impulsive way to telephone me. The call woke everyone in the house, much to my consternation and embarrassment. She wanted me to read the letter over the telephone and I had to go up again and get it.
>
> She informed me then that she had taken [another] maisonette in Maida Vale for herself and her father, and there would be plenty of room for Heini as well.

Arnold wrote to Alfred and Maria about the disaster in Alma's personal life. Out of nowhere, he reported, two Viennese—a friend of Heini's and a friend of his father's—had arrived in London and convinced Heini to return to the Continent with them. Almost in the same post, Maria's mother wrote to ask what had happened. Heini and his brother Thomas had been seen together in Vienna, and rumors were flying. In March, Heini had disappeared with Alma with no explanation to his family; three months later, just as suddenly, he was back again.

Upon his return, Heini seemed to be tormented. He made frequent visits to Alma's friends and relatives asking for news about the Rosés in London and seeking consolation for his own remorse and guilt. Viennese friends quoted Heini as saying that in London he could not find a job, he was too often on his own while Alma and Arnold concentrated on their music, and he was left with too many domestic chores. Perhaps more tellingly, word circulated in Vienna that his father wanted to retire from the family business and threatened to bring an outsider into the firm in Heini's place unless he came home immediately. Both Alma and Arnold believed that through the mysterious visitors from Vienna, Heini had received an ultimatum from his father concerning his future with the company.

Years later, Thomas Salzer emphatically denied this report:

> There never existed a plan to divide our firm between Heini and myself. Never was such a proposal made, not to me and not to Heini. We were, together with my father, co-owners of all our firms until Heini's death.[4] . . .
>
> There was no pressure on Heini because of Alma's Jewish ancestry on the part of our family. But of course my mother especially wanted him to come back because of the threat of war [between Germany and England], and my brother and I were surely to be forced into the German army.[5]

In an interview at the Viennese headquarters of the Salzer firm almost half a century after Heini's return to Vienna, Thomas Salzer—himself retired, his two sons the seventh generation of Salzers managing the firm—affirmed that as early as 1939 he knew that his father wanted to retire, yet he knew of no threat to bring an outsider into the firm in Heini's place. Thomas added:

> I know Heini was very much in love with Alma. But Heini liked the good life, and he knew this would be difficult in England, which he at first was willing to risk. With war coming, however, he certainly knew he would be interned. . . .
>
> As far as I know, Heini never met Alma again after London, but they had contact through friends and letters.

To put the best complexion on Heini's desertion, it must be realized that Heini could not prove himself a refugee and was not able to work legitimately anywhere in England. Further, in the summer of 1939, the threat of war between Britain and Germany grew daily. Had Heini remained in London when war broke out, he would have been classed as an "enemy alien" of the most dangerous category. To escape internment, it would have been necessary to go into hiding and Heini would have become a fugitive, the role Alma would have assumed had she remained in Austria. If Heini had been apprehended, he could have been sent to the Isle of Man in the Irish Sea, Canada, or Australia, where the British established internment camps. Thus the decision to remain in London could well have meant internment for the duration of the war, and Heini and Alma would have been separated in any case, possibly forever.[6]

There is no evidence that Alma and Heini ever had a face-to-face discussion of his predicament in England before his departure. Perhaps he realized that worries about his future career and fears about having to go underground would carry little weight with Alma, whose nature was so excitable and unyielding. She had given Heini her heart, and for her, separation under any circumstances was unthinkable. She would have fought his decision tooth and nail.

Arnold, writing sadly to Alfred, said in summary: "Alma has bad luck with men."

10

The Need to Sacrifice

One doesn't know what to believe, one doesn't know what to wish for.—Arnold Rosé

Alone again at thirty-two, Alma felt the weight of responsibility for her seventy-seven-year-old father. She was enraged with herself when she began to chafe under responsibilities for her beloved father's last years. Arnold wrote to Alfred that his art was his refuge, yet: "Imagine, I go into the city to look for work." Alma could only watch and pity.

Housekeeping was a physical burden to which Alma was not accustomed. She tried to learn to cook, using the book her mother had written out for her and soliciting recipes for her father's favorite dishes from friends. In addition she tackled a full schedule of studying and practicing the violin repertoire.

"Alma becomes thinner, and her sadness is a worry," Arnold wrote to Alfred in July. Alma reported that Heini wrote daily, insisting that despite his return to Vienna, he wanted nothing to change in their relationship. To Alfred the statement rang as hollow as Váša Příhoda's protestations while his marriage to Alma disintegrated. Arnold too was skeptical, predicting to Alfred that Alma's love affair with Heini would become a "vaporous memory." Soon Heini's letters became less frequent.

EARLY IN the Rosés' stay in England, Karl Doktor, the violist of the Adolf Busch Quartet, who lived with his family in St. John's Wood, offered to help Arnold and Alma reform the Rosé Quartet in England. Doktor's commitment was to Busch, so he was not available for Rosé. His son Paul (who went on to a brilliant career of his own) was suggested as violist for the quartet, but the senior Doktor felt the difference in ages would be a problem. Rosé and Buxbaum both tried to convince Leila, a violinist, to take up the viola, but she declined, although she was tempted to change instruments in mid-career for the sake of her Professor.

On 9 July 1939 Karl Doktor sat in for a performance featuring the two Rosés and Buxbaum—the first in a series of Haydn Memorial concerts in Duke's Hall at the Royal Academy of Music. On the program were the "Emperor" Quartet, opus 76, no. 3, and "The Bird," opus 33, no. 3. Paul Weingarten on piano and baritone Mark Raphael also performed.

The Doktors opened their home to Arnold and Alma to audition violists for the quartet. After many hours, the Rosés chose Ernest Tomlinson, formerly with the Royal Academy. Tomlinson, who was in his sixties, had the necessary experience and proved to be a wise choice; he remained with Arnold through the war years. Late in July 1939, the reconstituted quartet had its first engagement. Both Alma and Arnold were overjoyed with the fee of 40 guineas, a little over U.S. $200.

In July Rudolf Bing and Fritz Busch invited Alma and Arnold to Glyndebourne, where Bing was general manager and Busch artistic director of the summer opera season. Bing sent train and bus fares along with tickets for a performance of Verdi's *Macbeth,* and Busch treated the group to dinner.

For the most part, the Rosés' social life centered on an older generation of Viennese. Käthe Buxbaum, Bux's wife, became Alma's confidante, and Lotte and Franz Zuber arranged frequent get-togethers. Leila Pirani had moved to the country with her children, so Alma and Arnold saw her less frequently as the summer progressed. Dory Hetherington, although she lived fifty miles away in Radlett, Hertfordshire (which Arnold pronounced "another world"), remained in close touch. Arnold's inadequate attempts to learn English added to Alma's sense of isolation; she saw few people her own age and had little opportunity to seek out new friends. As the weeks passed, the chances of a reunion with Heini seemed increasingly remote.

Alma was grateful for opportunities to perform as second violin with the quartet, yet she longed for her own musical life. She hoped to play again as a soloist and even to organize a women's orchestra in the style of the Walzermädeln, but her British work permit allowed her to play only in the quartet. She and Arnold appealed for revised work permits, again with the aid of Sir Adrian Boult. Alma hoped to expand the scope of her activities, and Arnold sought official status as a teacher comparable to his former position in Vienna. But London was crowded with unemployed émigré musicians as well as native musicians seeking work and careers, and the permits were denied. Alma had to abandon her plans to establish a women's orchestra in Great Britain.

She was acutely aware that the fund founded by Carl Flesch would soon run out. Bruno Walter, seeking to reassure both Arnold and Alma, wrote from New York on 13 July 1939 to remind them they still had the Mysa Stradivarius, which Arnold could sell if necessary. To Alma the letter was more alarming than cheering. To her mind, selling the Stradivarius would be the crowning catastrophe for her father, and saving Arnold's Mysa became her personal crusade.

Elsa Walter added a note to Arnold recommending patience, the very quality Alma found in perennial short supply. She added: "Alma will certainly put out her antennae to Amsterdam. [Finding work] seems to be easy in Amsterdam, and there seem to be possibilities she will probably find useful. That she has been so brave during these difficult times is very fortunate for you."

In mid-August, Alma wrote to Alfred. Hitler was menacing Poland, which had vowed to resist aggression and marshaled the support of Britain and France. World war was imminent. Twice in her letter Alma pleaded for Alfred's advice. "Politics at present is my only interest," she declared.

Taking Elsa Walter's suggestion to heart, Alma began to explore possibilities for work in Holland, which was expected to remain neutral even if war broke out, as it had remained neutral during World War I. Friends in England surmised that she was also hatching a plan for reunion with Heini in the event of war between England and Germany. It is true that with Alma on neutral ground, the couple could have met at least occasionally, since Heini would be free to travel to Holland.

In August Alma received a letter from The Hague offering an engagement at the luxurious Grand Hotel Central. In a letter to Alfred she weighed the risks and benefits of such a move. In its favor, she cited the example of Carl Flesch, who had accepted a position with Holland's Royal Conservatory of Music, also in The Hague.

ON 25 AUGUST Arnold began a letter to Alfred that lay unfinished for three days. He had received a midnight phone call, he explained; now "I cannot write another word." The British newspapers had a report that Bruno Walter's daughter Gretel had been killed in Zurich by her estranged husband, who then committed suicide, and a reporter had called Arnold for background information. Still in shock, he managed a brief note of sympathy to the Walters in Lugano on 1 September 1939:

> Deeply shattered by the news of the tragedy that has befallen you and your family, I am hardly able to find the proper words to convey to you my warm and heartfelt sympathy. We feel your loss as though it were ours. Bound to you and to yours through a friendship that has stood the test of time, I press your hand from afar, fully participating in your sorrow, and I wish with all my heart that time, which has inflicted such deep wounds, will also serve to let them heal again.

Bruno Walter replied on 26 September:

> My Dear Arnold,
>
> We thank you for your words of sympathy. The terrible tragedy that has struck us has destroyed our lives. Our very dearest child has

been taken from us by the hands of a murderer. I shall never be able to understand this unfathomable event.

My Gretchen, my sunshine, the reason for my life, has been taken from me in this bestial manner. Even time will not be able to eradicate the wound. I only hope for the peace of my singularly beloved Gretchen. Without her and with this desperate hope in my heart, I shall only be a source of worry and embarrassment for my dear ones. Forgive me that only these few words should tell you how things are with us. Maybe later I shall be able to write further to you with more equanimity.

ON 1 SEPTEMBER 1939, German troops invaded Poland and Luftwaffe planes streamed over the border to bomb military and civilian targets alike. Hitler's armies introduced the world to *Blitzkrieg* to prove they were the strongest in the world. After initial confusion, Britain and France honored commitments to their ally, and as the Polish army fought valiantly with horsemen and swords against tanks and vastly superior German firepower, World War II began.

On 3 September, England and France declared war against Germany. Within a week, the Polish army was defeated. Cracow fell on 6 September. The garrison in Warsaw held out until 27 September, when the nation's capital also fell. Poland, like Austria and Czechoslovakia before it, disappeared from the map. By the end of the month, Hitler and Stalin, in a secret pact, had divided up Eastern Europe.

ALMA, WHO was desperate for income, had her one and only adventure as an office worker in late summer 1939. One afternoon she and Arnold visited a café with Lotte and Franz Zuber. Hearing Alma and Arnold speaking French and German and Alma also conversing in English, a man at a nearby table approached and said he was looking for a secretary and chauffeur. If she could type and drive, he said, she was hired to start work the following Monday. The pay was £2 10s. per week.

Alma leaped at the opportunity. She was able to engage a Viennese friend, Lisl Kraith, to look after Vati. Lisl was a fine cook and would be attentive in personal ways as well. With Lisl's help, Alma hoped not only to earn wages, but also to devote time to her "more serious calling," as her father put it—her violin.

Arnold described the adventure in a letter to Alfred and Maria. Alma's employer, an energetic sixty-five-year-old, chased her constantly. Her third day on the job, he proposed that he move in with father and daughter. The next day he invited himself to dinner, brought the ingredients and prepared the meal, and again appealed to move in. Fortunately the Rosés were expecting Hans and Stella Fuchs, who were soon to arrive in London, traveling from Vienna via Sweden, and they could honestly say they had no room.

The first Saturday, Alma's employer invited her for dinner and dancing at an elegant hotel. He arrived in tie and tails, a flower in his lapel. When they left the apartment, he took Alma on a bus to a corner near the hotel then summoned a taxi so they could arrive in style. A handsome middle-aged woman joined them for dinner. Alma was home by midnight, dismayed.

At the office the second week, Alma's boss continued his amorous pursuits. One morning he brought his hunting dog into the office. Announcing that his lumbago made it impossible for him to bend over to wipe the dog's eyes, he ordered her to do it for him. Alma drew the line and resigned. Undeterred, the eager chap called the following Sunday, asking Alma to drive to Folkestone with him. After this brief encounter with the business world, Alma was more than ever determined to make her way in music.

Arnold's pleasure in the reviving quartet was tempered by concern over finances. Despite their straitened circumstances, Arnold continued to pay Lisl in order to relieve Alma emotionally and socially. Only when Lisl managed the household was Alma free to rebuild a life of her own.

A letter came from Heini toward the end of September; "he was very worried about us," Alma wrote to Alfred. She had not heard from him since the end of August, shortly before the invasion of Poland. Perhaps this letter, as well as the minuscule household budget, encouraged her to look to Holland for work.

Alma broke the news to Alfred casually. "I now have an offer of about £14 a week from The Hague," she wrote. "But as yet I cannot here get guaranteed assurance that I can return, and I fear that Hitler will march into Holland. It's too bad about the engagement. I was to lead six men."

On 6 November 1939, Alma wrote again, sounding alarm. "Something has to be done," she said; "everything is too makeshift." Without further delay she signed a contract for a two-month engagement at the Grand Hotel Central, which would bring in 1000 fl. (about £14) per fifty-two-hour workweek beginning the first of December. Lisl agreed to live with Arnold in the apartment and keep house for him for £1 a week. Using her Czech passport, which she jokingly referred to as "Jan Masaryk helping in the nicest way," Alma obtained British permission to leave the country for five months, until May 1940.[1]

A day after Alma reported her decision to Alfred, on 7 November 1939, feelers Arnold had put out in London brought results. Acclaimed British pianist Myra Hess wrote that she was honored he had offered the Rosé Quartet for an appearance in concert at the National Gallery in London. Unfortunately Alma could not perform with her father at the concert, since her plans had gone too far to be canceled.[2]

Among Alma's last performances with Arnold was a memorial ceremony held by the Austrian Club in honor of Sigmund Freud in November 1939. The Rosé Quartet played the second movement of Beethoven's Quartet opus 59, no. 2; Stefan Zweig delivered a eulogy. The quartet, with Alma as second violin, played two other unpaid engagements for the club in the same month.

Justine and Gustav in Budapest in 1889, the year their parents and older sister died. Gustav became the Mahler family patriarch, and twenty-year-old Justine managed the household.

The Rosé Quartet in 1905, composed of Arnold Rosé (at left), Paul Fischer, Anton Ruzitska, and Friedrich Buxbaum.

Cartoon mocking the "new music" of the Mahler years in Vienna. As Mahler lights a bomb and twirls a noisemaker, Rosé plays feverishly at left, Schoenberg performs on a sewing machine at right, and Richard Strauss (at top left) prepares to drop a heavy weight on the public. Cartoon by Theo Zasche from *Illustrirtes Wiener Extrablatt* 88 (31 March 1907).

Meinem lieben Freunde und
„Wahlverwandten" Arnold Rosé!
Wien Juni 98
Gust. Mahler

Gustav Mahler, signed photograph inscribed to Arnold Rosé in 1898. Photog. R. Werner.

Gustav and Justine, 1899. Three years later Justine married Arnold Rosé.

Arnold Rosé, concertmaster of the Vienna Philharmonic and Court Opera Orchestras, 1907. Photog. Martens, Mai & Co., Vienna.

Silhouette of the esteemed concertmaster by Hans Schliessmann; from *Wiener Schattenbilder* (Vienna: R. Mohr, 1892).

Little Alma and her brother Alfred—"Almschi" and "Alfi"—with Arnold in 1907. Photog. Rudolf Jobst & Co., Vienna.

Aussee, 1910. Alma became "Tommy" and dressed in lederhosen for the summer, holding her own with the rough-and-tumble Rosé boys. Photographs courtesy of the family of Leila Doubleday Pirani.

Almschi (above, at right) with her cousin Anna Mahler and Dory Beswick (later Dorothy Hetherington), the Rosés' governess, in Vienna.

Summer holiday at Wolkenstein, 1914—snapshots (top left and above) from the Rosé album.

Almschi with her violin, ca. 1914.

Justine and Arnold in 1915. Photog. d'Ora, Vienna.

Alfi, Alma, and Justine in 1915. Photog. d'Ora, Vienna.

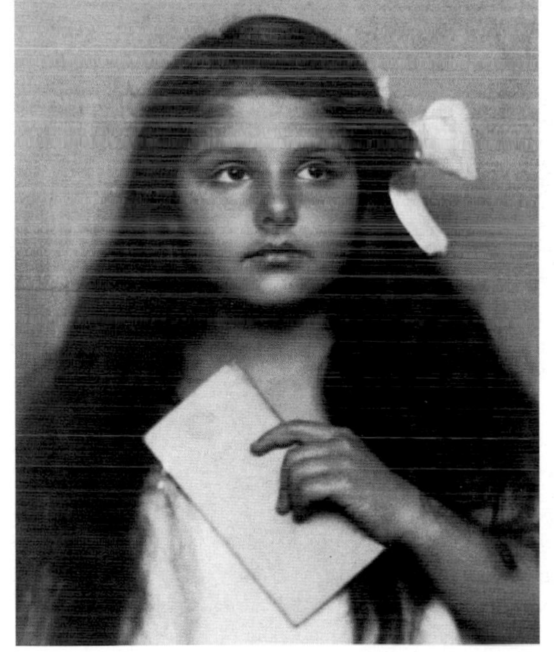

Alma holding a letter, 1915. Photog. d'Ora, Vienna.

A family celebration in the Rosé dining room in the early 1920s; in the background is a bust of Beethoven.

Rudolf Bing visiting the music room at Pyrkergasse, winter of 1926–27. Rumor had it that Alma was the chief attraction.

Alma Mahler-Werfel, Alma Rosé's aunt and godmother, with Franz Werfel. Photograph courtesy of the Alma Mahler-Werfel Papers, Special Collections, University of Pennsylvania Library.

Alma in the cockpit of a Czech-built airplane, traveling with her violin from Vienna to Prague in June 1925.

The Rosé Quartet with Alfred as pianist and tour manager aboard the *SS New York* en route to the United States in April 1928 (standing, left to right—Anton Walter, Anton Ruzitska, Paul Fischer; sitting, left to right Arnold Rosé, Alfred Rosé).

Arnold in Salzburg in 1925 with (left to right) Richard Strauss, Rosé Quartet member Paul Fischer, and a fellow Philharmoniker.

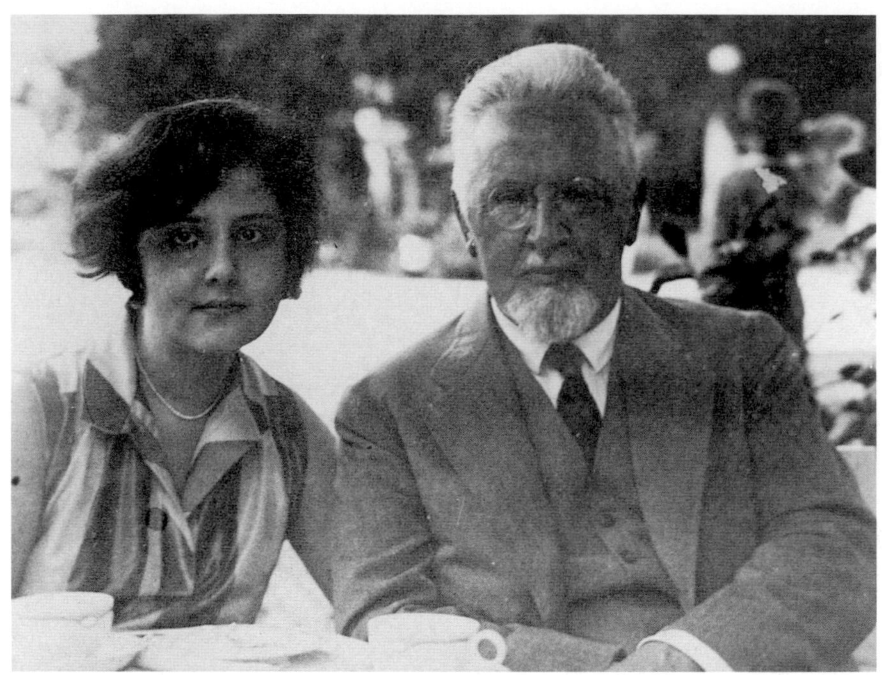

Alma and Arnold at the luxurious Hotel Römerbad in the Black Forest in 1927. Father and daughter had secret surgeries that summer.

The same summer, the Rosés met Váša Příhoda, the young Czech violinist whose technique was compared to Paganini's. Váša visited the family at Pyrkergasse in the fall.

Alma and Váša married in 1930. Alma was an aspiring violin virtuoso and Váša a star of the concert stage.

Příhoda's big white Mercedes was his trademark.

È
VIETATO
AMARE
ROMANZO DI
MARIO MORTARA

Sheet music for the song "È vietato amare" (Forbidden to Love) by Mario Mortara showed Váša as he appeared in the film *The White Wife of the Maharajah.* Rumor linked him romantically with his glamorous costar, Isa Miranda.

Alma as a newlywed at Váša's villa in Zariby, on the Elbe near Prague.

The portly Příhoda of later years, as depicted in *80 Jahre Musikverein in der Karikatur* (Vienna: Verlag der Gesellschaft der Musikfreunde, 1950).

Arturo Toscanini congratulating Rosé on his seventieth birthday, 24 October 1933, Vienna.

Alma Mahler-Werfel and Franz Werfel with Justine at Semmering in 1932.

Alma Příhoda-Rosé performing in 1931.

Alma with the Rosé pets, Arno (at top) and Pepsi. Photog. Willinger, Vienna

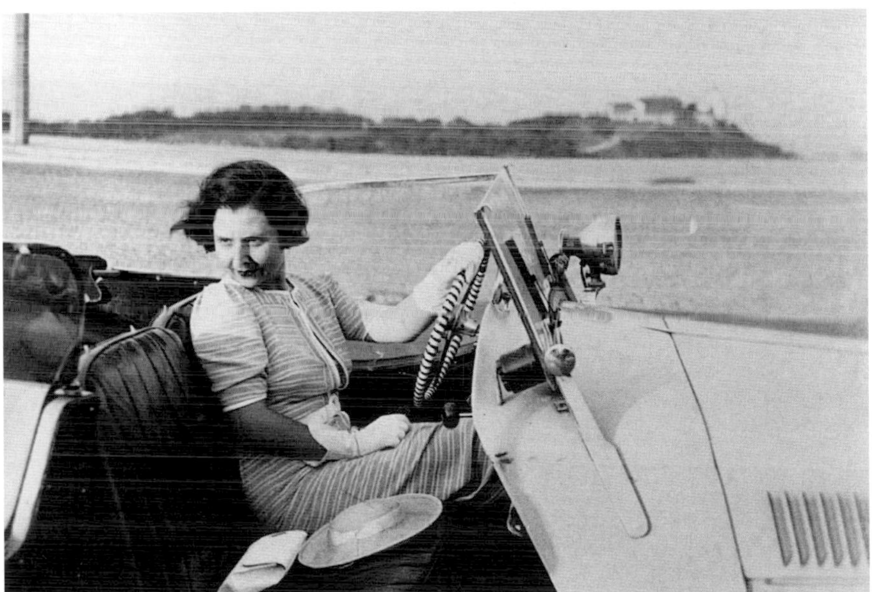

Alma in her white Aero convertible, a gift from Váša in the early 1930s. Arno, the Rosés' black German shepherd, was a familiar sight in Vienna's Ringstrasse, riding behind Alma in the sporty car.

Alma in a 1930s publicity photo.

Alma's girlhood friends Margarete Slezak (left)—in a photo dated 1927 and signed with the familiar "Greterl!"—and Erica Morini (above left), whose spirited playing style was captured in *80 Jahre Musikverein in der Karikatur* (Vienna: Verlag der Gesellschaft der Musikfreunde, 1950).

Alma and her orchestra the Wiener Walzermädeln (Vienna Waltzing Girls) in the 1930s.

Alma Rosé og hendes Valse-Piger.

Forrygende Aften i Tivolis Koncertsal.

Alma Rosé omgivet af sine nydelige Partnersker ved Koncertens Afslutning i Aftes i Tivoli.

Newspaper clipping from a Scandinavian tour (Anny Kux, Alma's concertmistress and close friend, is second from left in the front row), and an advertisement for an engagement in France.

The custom-designed motif of orchestra stationery and programs, and calligraphed initials "AR" from the cover of the orchestra's brochure.

The Waltzing Girls on tour in the 1930s.

Heini Salzer, Alma's Austrian lover after Příhoda divorced her in 1935.

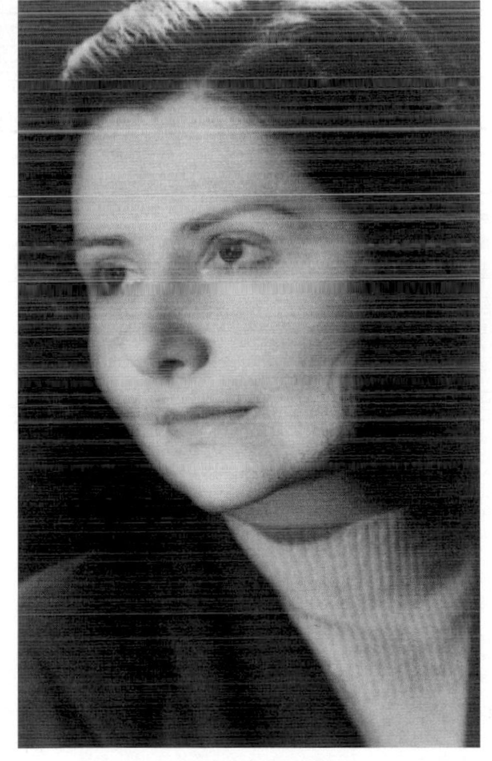

Alma soon before her flight from Vienna to England in 1939.

Clipping from a May 1939 Croydon newspaper announcing the Rosés' arrival in England.

The last photograph of Arnold, in England with his Viennese friend Moriz Tischler.

The publicity postcard Alma used in Holland in the early 1940s.

Alma at the home of Marye and Paul Staercke in Utrecht. She is holding her tiny datebook.

Marye and her daughter Hermeline, a photograph Marye sent to Alfred Rosé in 1946. Hermeline was born in June 1942 while Alma lived with the Staerckes.

The last photograph of Alma, taken on the Staerckes' balcony shortly before she tried to escape from occupied Holland in December 1942.

BOTH SEA and air travel were dangerous in wartime, but Alma risked a flight on Sunday, 26 November 1939. She bade farewell to Vati during a violent storm. Her plane had to avoid both British and German patrols, but the real trial was turbulence over the North Sea, with a fierce tailwind that cut almost half an hour from anticipated flight time. Alma wrote to Alfred that she was so airsick, it took her three days to recover.

Arnold found an English violinist, Walter Price, to replace her for the quartet's first National Gallery concert, which reached an audience of a thousand. The program included Beethoven's Quartet in C-sharp minor, opus 131, and Schubert's Quartet in A minor. Price and Tomlinson would continue as loyal members of the reformed quartet, respecting Arnold's leadership so absolutely that his sense of musical authority was soon restored.

Although Alma regretted leaving the quartet at the moment its fortunes turned, she was delighted to see the lighted streets of Amsterdam after the prolonged blackout in England. She had friends in Holland, and the move reawakened her hope of reunion with Heini. On 18 December 1939, she wrote to Alfred:

> Thank God I earn wages. I rejoice that I have already sent Vati £10.
>
> This is the best solution as long as Lisl can look after Vati. For extra money, I am playing in cafés and restaurants, performing solo pieces I used in concerts previously.
>
> The Meijers are indescribably friendly. I lunch with them often, because I am never free in the evenings for dinner. I live like a miser in an unheated room.
>
> On [December] 24th I'm scheduled to take part in a charity matinée with Otto Wallburg, Willi Rosen, and Fritz Steiner.
>
> The responsibility I have felt for Vati has given me numerous white hairs. On the other hand I am infinitely happier to be able to do something for him. I hope even more will evolve from that. . . .
>
> From Heini I receive more news. Just think, he went to Grinzing [to Justine's grave] by himself and will regularly look after things. Have you heard from Ernest [Rosé, who had found refuge in the United States]? Max Ehrlich was here with a revue [from Berlin] and asked about you with great interest.
>
> Vati now has very nice social connections in London and is not so lonesome.
>
> Just imagine, Mr. [Neil] Phillips, who together with you studied with Professor [Walter] Robert,[3] plays in the hotel.

At first Alma's experience at the Grand Hotel Central was disappointing. She was expected to lead an ensemble of such varying capability that she persuaded the hotel manager to let her play solo violin with piano accompaniment. After her presence was advertised, faces from the past appeared as if magically to lend support. Among the first were Mady Meth, formerly a singer with the Wiener Walzermädeln, and her brother Eugene. With their mother, the Meths too had fled Vienna, stopping in Holland where Mady could resume her singing career and Eugene found work as an engineer in the Dutch aircraft industry. Alma and Mady were delighted to be reunited, and Alma took a room with the Meth family.

Another who reappeared in Alma's life was Theo Bakker, her favorite dancing partner at Badenweiler in those long-ago summers when their families vacationed together in the Black Forest. Now a young Dutch lawyer, Theo revived memories of those sunlit holidays, and he and Alma met frequently in the months to come.

Alma and her father wrote to each other every two or three days. The early letters reveal a sense of freedom and happiness on Alma's part and a certain tension on Arnold's: Alma would justify her absence, and Arnold would urge her to return to London, as the quartet was receiving new engagements. Neither dwelled on the ominous signs on the war scene, although various telegrams and letters from friends in England cautioned Alma to return to London as soon as possible. After the successful invasion of Poland and Hitler's pacts with the Soviet Union, the Germans were confident of economic and military stability on the Eastern front. Now, during the "phony war" when the mighty craft of the Luftwaffe dropped propaganda sheets instead of bombs, fear was growing that the ambitions of the Third Reich left none of its neighbors safe.

Alma could not be dissuaded from her course. Her worried cousin Wolfgang had written to Alfred from Berlin a few weeks earlier, in reference to his own affidavit for emigration to the United States. Wolfgang, who knew Alma well, added the following:

> Some time ago I had a very lovely letter from Alma. She is still a bit upset about Heini's return home, but I am hoping she will surmount it. She is a lovely but, sorry to say, very complicated human being who, in her own way, almost artfully obstructs her own happiness. I only hope for the well-being of your father and herself, and that her plans will succeed.

IN JANUARY 1940, Arnold reported to Alfred that Alma was healthy and happy. She exchanged letters with friends in Vienna, confiding especially in Marie Gutheil-Schoder and Ernestine Löhr. Through Alma, Arnold learned that his brother Eduard was still living in Weimar, and that Wolfgang had given a Christmas concert in Germany. Arnold had registered with British authorities and now described himself as a "friendly alien" with permission to travel about the country at will. Happily, he had also received permission to teach.

At Christmas Rudolf Bing sent a gift of Russian caviar with the message: "Take refuge through the violin." More than an allusion to the comforting power of music, it was a reminder to Arnold that if pressed, he could survive by selling his gem-caliber instrument. Arnold wrote to Alfred that the Mysa was appraised at £4,000 but was certainly worth more. After rummaging through the music shops of Europe in a half-century of touring, the old master knew the value of a Stradivarius.

Arnold's letters to Alma were warm and appreciative. On 4 January 1940 he wrote, "I am very proud of you and admire you. You have been possessed by Mahler's spirit, for in my family, there never were such dynamic people." On 24 January, replying to his daughter's pleased announcement that a letter had arrived from Heini, he wrote: "That you have received news from Heini naturally makes me very happy. Greet him for me, if you think you should. The Meths must be a great comfort to you . . . such neighborly love."

As Alma's successes in Holland multiplied, she repeatedly postponed her return to England. Arnold expected her in London at the beginning of February 1940 to prepare for an April concert series in which the quartet would perform the late Beethoven quartets. He reminded Alma that the repertoire required intensive study and encouraged her to come back immediately, but her sights were firmly set on Holland. Her hopes for a career as a soloist were revived by an audition with Willem Mengelberg, for whom she played the Wieniawski Violin Concerto. The conductor suggested that she might be engaged to play the piece with the Concertgebouw Orchestra in Amsterdam. A lunch with Carl Flesch further bolstered her faith in the future.

On Valentine's Day, Arnold wrote to Alfred that Alma hoped to return to London at the beginning of March. Meanwhile she was directing a small ensemble in a month-long tour of Holland. Her Dutch notices were favorable, and she was pleased by her renewed success. "Heini is loyal," Arnold added cryptically.

In Arnhem in mid-February, Alma encountered the musicologist and critic Louis Couturier, who gave her a copy of his book on violin technique inscribed with a quotation from Beethoven's 1814 diary recommending courage in the face of mankind's sad fate. Today the well-worn book is in a rarely touched file in Amsterdam's War History Documentation Center, among other items Alma left in storage in the hope of one day retrieving them. During her visit to Arnhem, she sent Alfred a publicity postcard of herself with her violin, inscribed in English with the message "Don't forget me—with love and kisses, allways yours, Alma."

Late in February Alma performed a solo program over Radio Hilversum, the voice of Holland. Arnold heard the program and was thrilled. He reported to Alfred that Alma was soon to give a house concert in The Hague in the home of a wealthy patron, Meta Lissauer.

Although Alma sent money to Arnold in London whenever she could, his resources were almost exhausted. In March, swallowing his pride, he wrote to the Toscaninis in New York asking for help. Carla Toscanini replied immediately:

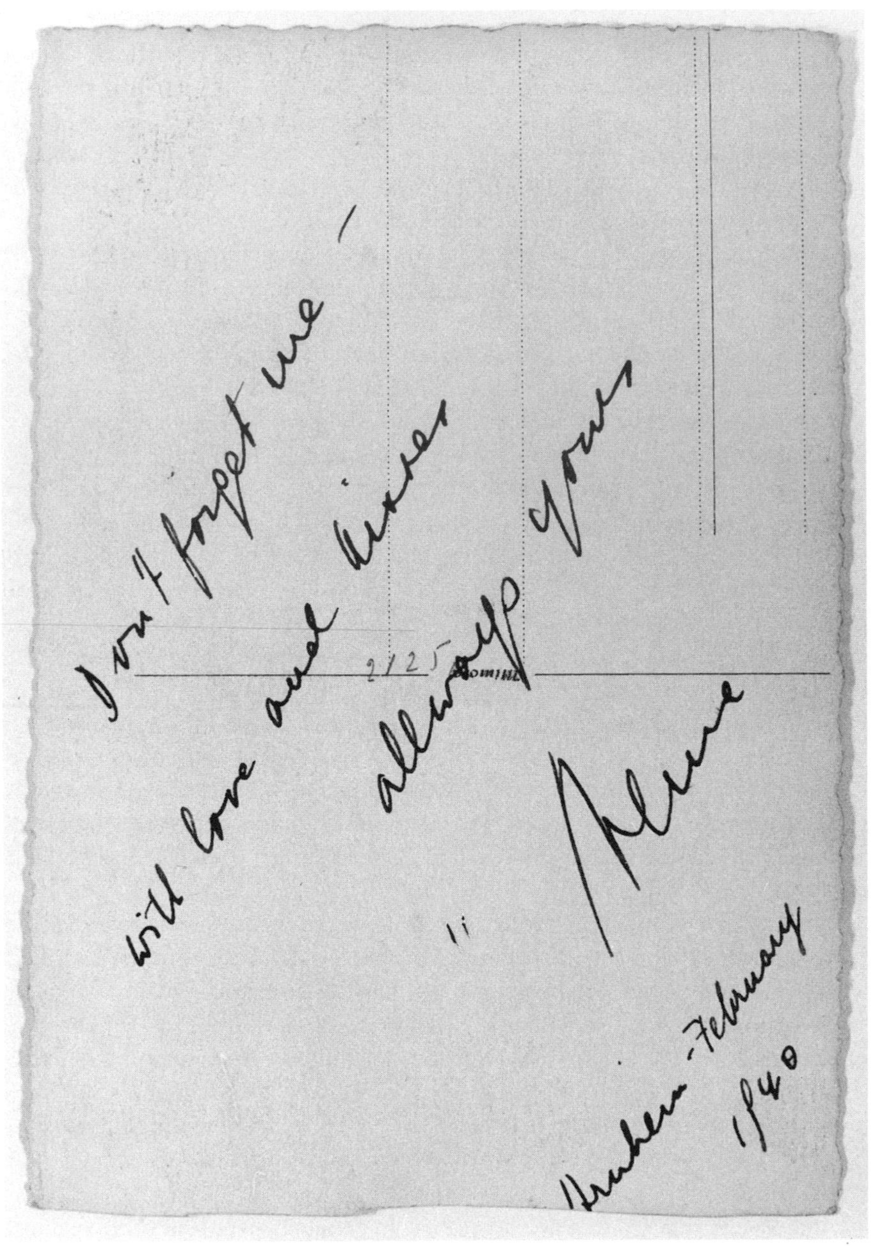

Don't forget me!
with love and kisses
allways yours
Alma
Arnhem-February
1940

Note to Alfred in Alma's hand, sent from the Netherlands in February 1940.

We were very distressed to learn that you, too, were suffering the consequences of these present conditions. We cabled one hundred dollars the day after your cable came and today have cabled two hundred more—Several of your devoted friends are here, and we plan to do whatever is possible to assist you during these trying moments. We have tremendous admiration for the splendid spirit and courage shown by the English people. . . .

Affectionate remembrances, dear friend—

From California Bruno Walter sent another hundred dollars, helping to stave off crisis.

A LETTER from Heini written 12 March 1940 became a talisman Alma carried in her purse.

My Dearest,

Your two letters and two pictures with inscriptions arrived. I was very happy. And yet I didn't write you for such a long time, my dearest. First, I didn't get to it, and then, when I had time, I wasn't in the right mood. Don't misunderstand, my dearest. . . . I always think of you so much, and my thoughts are always with you.

When a letter comes from you, especially with dear pictures, I am so happy and so sad at the same time, because we are not together. I have to pull myself together and bury myself in work. Otherwise I would be overwhelmingly unhappy.

Sometimes I don't write a letter because I am afraid to do it. On the other hand, my thoughts are always with you, and I long for you and dream of you. Just last night I had a long, long dream about you!

But I want to write you more, my dearest, because I know you are sad when you don't hear from me for such a long time. My dearest. Sometimes I feel glad that I am at least able to write to you, although I can't be with you. My heart is very heavy already, and I don't want to add to your sadness.

You have certainly got a heavy heart—I can feel it. When I say that, I know you will be pleased and even a little happy. But it makes me unhappy. Sadly, I think of you and our happiness, when I can put my hand in your hand. When one knows and feels that, nothing else really matters!!

The other day, Dr. Kraith [Lisl's father, whom Heini sometimes called "Uncle Kraith"] was here and told me about you. He was very nice, and it made me so happy to be able to speak to someone about you. I am pleased that you have successes and are able to earn money, and I look forward to the day when you write to me again. That Vati is as well as he can be pleases me, for I think of him very often.

The Sunday before last I went out of Vienna alone and took a long, lonesome walk through the snow-covered vineyards, over Sievering to Grinzing. Throughout the walk I thought of you and felt you were next to me. In Grinzing [at Justine's grave] I thought especially of you and felt you were completely inside me, at the same time and place. It was so peaceful and quiet, so much snow that the gravestone was hardly visible. I will go there again very soon, with your person again inside me, the way I always feel you are with me.

Darling—This letter is quite different from the one I wrote you from the office. If you only knew how important and true it all is, I think you would sense that we always belong together, and totally.

In a few days it will be a year since we left here. Do you remember? It is terrible how time goes by.

After all, I don't have to write you again how I love you, how I have always loved you. I know you must feel it most deeply. But I will tell you PASSIONATELY when I am again complete, completely happy with you in my arms, and kiss you long, long on your mouth and all over. You—you my dearest. Happiest am I when I think about it. I belong to you completely.

Write me immediately. I think only of when we will completely, completely come together.

ALWAYS COMPLETELY YOURS—

Heini's ardor shines through these lines. The letter, among the documents on file in the Amsterdam War History Documentation Center, shows the wear of being folded and unfolded again and again.

11

Rebirth

We shall fight on the beaches, we shall fight on the landing grounds, we shall fight in the fields and in the streets, we shall fight in the hills; we shall never surrender.—Winston Churchill

Hitler's "phony war" ended with the approach of spring 1940. Now the Führer was ready to mount an offensive in the West. Seeking to circumvent a British blockade across the North Sea, the Germans' first move was a surprise attack on Norway and Denmark, which could provide the Reich with naval and air bases as well as access to the open sea.

On 9 April 1940, an hour before dawn in Copenhagen and Oslo, envoys from the Third Reich roused the foreign ministers of the respective states from sleep and presented them with the Reich's demands: they must accept, without resistance, the "protection of the Reich" or be invaded by troops already poised for attack. As bombers roared over the Danish capital, the king of Denmark and his government capitulated the same day.

The Norwegians resisted, knowing they had little chance of success. Allied forces came to their aid: the war's first land engagement between British and German troops took place at Lillehammer, Norway, on 21 April 1940. But like Austria, Czechoslovakia, Poland, and Denmark before it, Norway quickly succumbed to superior force. On 7 June the Norwegian king and his government fled to exile in London, and the Reich was again victorious. In the battle for Norway, even the support of Anglo-French forces failed to halt the Nazi advance.

Publicly Hitler had proclaimed that war in the West would settle none of the problems in the East, which Germany and Russia would solve between them. To his generals, however, as early as September 1939 he expressed his resolve to attack the West. He had no intention of respecting the neutrality of the Low Countries—Belgium, Holland, and Luxembourg. Due to the harsh fall and winter of 1939–40, he postponed the attack date fourteen times. Yet he was eager to push westward, with the aim of destroying the armies of France and Britain and gaining positions on the English Channel and the North Sea that would allow Luftwaffe bombers to raid Great Britain.

As the war edged closer in April, the last month covered by her British travel permission, Alma again postponed her return to England. "With all my strength I wage a battle that we may not have to sell the Mysa," she wrote to Alfred on 8 April 1940, the eve of Hitler's attack on Norway and Denmark.

> At the moment I am playing in the *Count of Luxembourg* [an operetta by Franz Lehár]—on stage [Sarasate's] "Zigeunerweisen," and all evening in the orchestra otherwise. Since February, I have played it eighty-six times, including over Radio Hilversum last Saturday. The next day I had a private afternoon concert which earned me 200 fl., and in the evening the operetta performance.
>
> We are now on tour all over Holland by bus with the operetta. It is terribly demanding. The show is over at 11:45 p.m., meaning that we drive back to The Hague, sometimes not arriving there until 4 a.m., then sleep until noon and start off again to the next engagement.
>
> Besides I have over-played my right arm. To save it I have written as little as possible, except to Vati.
>
> With Heini, I remain in close contact. . . . In a way I am lonely, but I have so much to do that I don't have time to dwell on it.
>
> I see the Meijers at most once a month. I can't manage to get to Scheveningen to see them. One thing I must do, and that is sleep—otherwise I shall not survive. I eat a warm meal every fourth or fifth day, otherwise bread and cheese.
>
> I am embarrassingly often with Gutheil [Wilhelm Ernst Gutheil, the journalist son of Marie Gutheil-Schoder]. It is awkward for he is embarrassingly friendly. He lives in Amsterdam. I see Flesch very seldom even though he lives in The Hague. . . . I am sending a few newspaper clippings about me; perhaps you will find them funny.
>
> Up to now, I have sent £50 to Vati in London. Not bad, is it? . . .
>
> Alferle, even when I don't write, my thoughts always revolve around you. For people like us, genuine closeness does not have to be spelled out in letters. . . .
>
> With much, much love!
> Your Alma

Alma was still in Holland on 11 April 1940 when Arnold launched a series of four Tea-Time Concerts in Queen Mary Hall, London, sponsored by the Christian Council for Refugees from Germany and Central Europe. He was disappointed that his daughter was not at his side for this important appearance. With Walter Price in her place, and with Tomlinson and Buxbaum, the Rosé Quartet played the four last Beethoven quartets—one in each program—

along with selections from Mozart and Haydn. Proceeds from the concerts went to the musicians' benevolent fund.

Alma's letters to Arnold reported only successes; often they included enthusiastic critiques clipped from Dutch newspapers. She wrote that she hoped to return to England at the beginning of May.

In one letter to her, Arnold jokingly complained that Lisl Kraith denied him delicacies at the table. Whatever was most delicious and acquired with most difficulty, he said, Lisl kept for the return of the prodigal daughter.

On 2 May 1940, Alma's permission to return to Britain expired. She continued to bank on the freedoms her Czech passport had provided. On 5 May she was in Scheveningen with Louis and Lotte Meijer, who warned her to return to London as soon as possible. The political situation was unstable, they said; the Low Countries lay in Hitler's path to the West, and they did not believe the Germans would allow Holland to remain neutral during the war.

The Meijers' warnings went unheeded. Cheered by her reborn career, able at last to send money to her father in London, and still able to communicate with Heini, Alma replied simply: "*Es ist gemütlich hier.*" She was comfortable in Holland.

In a letter to Alfred of 7 May 1940, Arnold complained that he had received no news from Alma, as she had left The Hague on a short trip. Three days later, on 10 May 1940, the Germans struck without warning before dawn, launching a meticulously prepared attack across a front of 175 miles through the Netherlands, Belgium, Luxembourg, and northern France. Ministers of the Reich summoned ministers of Belgium and the Netherlands to inform them that the Germans were invading to "safeguard their neutrality" against possible Anglo-French attack.

Hitler's daring took Britain and France by surprise. In London, a three-day crisis within the government was resolved the evening of 10 May, the very day the Germans launched their campaign. Replacing Neville Chamberlain, Winston Churchill became prime minister and leader of the Western Allies, now facing a massive assault by the most powerful army in the world.

It was a five-day war for the Dutch, who were completely unprepared to defend themselves against the first large-scale airborne attack in history. Rotterdam was leveled by one wave of bombers after another. The Dutch royal family fled to Britain. On 14 May the commander of the Dutch armed forces ordered his troops to lay down arms; the next day Holland officially capitulated. The Nazis' first concern was to take the cream of Holland's rich food supply back to their homeland. Thus began five years of German terror in this peaceful land.

Tiny Luxembourg could only bow to the military invaders. Grand Duchess Charlotte and her cabinet fled to London, where they established a government-in-exile. King Leopold III of Belgium surrendered on the morning of 28 May. The Belgian army had held out for eighteen days.

Alma was trapped in Holland as surely as if a cage had dropped around her. In the confusion, it was impossible for her to communicate with Arnold. At last she was able to contact Anny Kux Poláková in Bratislava, who cabled Alfred in Cincinnati that Alma was safe.

By 26 May 1940 the Germans had swept through France to the English Channel, and the miraculous evacuation of Allied troops at Dunkirk was about to begin. Trapped by the Germans in a narrow triangle, the soldiers seemed doomed. But a massive rescue effort between 27 and 31 May carried a third of a million men away from the besieged port and open beaches in a motley armada of over eight hundred vessels, from cruisers to small sailboats piloted by civilians.

The French continued to resist, but they had lost their best units and most of their armor in Belgium and northern France in the early days of Hitler's offensive. On 10 June 1940, France collapsed before the invading force. The French government left Paris, and by 14 June the swastika flew over the Eiffel Tower. On 16 June, Marshal Philippe Pétain replaced Paul Reynaud as the French premier; the next day the cooperative Pétain asked for an armistice. At Compiègne, where the Germans had surrendered in November 1918 at the end of World War I, Hitler forced humiliating terms of defeat upon the French.

An armistice was signed on 22 June 1940. Although it left the French government in nominal control of an unoccupied zone in the south of the former French state (the area that would be known as Vichy France, whose government was disavowed by the postwar French republic), Hitler's triumph was complete. Most of the European Continent—a hundred million subject people—lay under the Nazi yoke.

Alma realized the enormity of her miscalculation in leaving England for Holland then letting her travel permission run out. On 29 May 1940 she made an urgent call to Louis Meijer, but by then it was too late. As a Jewish journalist who had written widely on the political upheavals of the 1920s and 1930s, Louis knew he would be on the German list for "special treatment" once the occupation was established, and he and Lotte had a baby son to protect at all costs. When Alma asked what she should do and if he could help her, he could only reply gently that he could no longer help—he didn't know how he could save his own family.[1]

By a decree of 18 May 1940, Arthur Seyss-Inquart, Hitler's chancellor of Austria in the crucial four days following the Anschluss and later deputy governor of conquered Poland, became Reichskommissar of Holland. From her experience in Vienna, Alma knew to expect no mercy from Seyss-Inquart, a balding former lawyer who wore thick glasses and walked with a limp. Now any illusion of safety was gone.[2]

During the first months of the German occupation, the Dutch administration sustained the attitude that Holland had no "Jewish problem" and Dutch Jews faced no major difficulties. The Nazis' first overt anti-Semitic action was to pronounce the Jewish population ineligible for air-raid duty and to expel German and foreign Jews from coastal areas. A behind-the-scenes struggle led to a November 1940 decree banning Jews from civil service, including academic positions, and the usual restrictions on Jewish businesses and residences soon followed. In the end the Nazis forced the application of the German race laws in the Netherlands as elsewhere in occupied territory, obliging Dutch authorities at every level of government to implement Nazi policies. The registration of Jews in Holland, Belgium, and France proceeded systematically, following the patterns tried and proved in Austria, Czechoslovakia, and Poland.

Still able to contact Alfred in the neutral United States, Alma wrote on 31 May 1940:

> I'm very sad that I cannot see Vati. Have done everything possible, yet the difficulties are invincible. You will have received the cable from Anny Kux, asking that you advise Vati. I have always provided for him as well as I could, but as I will not see him for a long time, he will no doubt have money problems.
>
> Please write to him that he can turn to the Flesch fund. Hopefully, he will no longer pay Lisl the large honorarium.[3]
>
> I must now see how I can survive myself. Prospects for engagements are poor. I believe I shall have to become a chambermaid.
>
> Please, Alferle, write IMMEDIATELY. I languish for news from you, and hopefully you will be able to tell me how Vati is getting along!
>
> I had intended to go to him in the next few days (after my last letter) but was waiting for the completion of a contract in which I was to play in a revue for between four and five months, beginning in August.
>
> [On 12 May 1940, Mother's Day,] I was so contented that Mutti did not have to suffer anymore—Just think of that!

Alfred worried incessantly about Alma's welfare, and Arnold sank into depression. In a cable to Alfred of 1 June 1940, he speculated that Alma's Czech papers might still afford protection.

Without Alma's assistance, Arnold's financial future was precarious, and he again considered selling the Mysa. He worried that he would have to let the precious instrument go for too little and asked Alfred's advice. Where was the Mysa's pedigree? He would need the papers if he decided to sell.

Alma had foreseen that her father, in his growing frailty, would consider selling his precious violin, and to forestall a hasty decision she had taken the papers with her to Holland. Now that Alma was trapped there, she realized that the papers essential to any sale would be safer in Alfred's possession, and she promptly sent them to him.

Alma remained in The Hague, playing violin in the café at the Grand Hotel Central. Her friendly treatment of hotel patrons, including Germans in the audience, led to difficulties with the Meths, who saw her attitude as accommodation and could not accept it.

Eugenia Meth, at the time Eugene Meth's fiancée, remembered evenings in the café when Alma would join the couple between performances. Alma was strikingly beautiful, Eugenia said, with expressive eyes and dark, dramatically styled shoulder-length hair. Yet she had a hunted look and sometimes squinted furtively around the room, as if to reassure herself that she was seeing clearly. This squinting was disconcerting, Eugenia commented: Alma seemed to be looking through the people she was talking with.

Alma's strong will and flair for drama were intact, and she minced no words on subjects she felt strongly about. At one point, Eugenia recalled, Příhoda came up in conversation, and someone dismissed his artistic mastery. Alma flew to his defense, insisting with her old fire that he was the greatest of violinists.[4]

Alma was able to get word to Arnold through his old friend Edward Breisach in Budapest in still-neutral Hungary. A welcome telegram carried the message "ALMA WITH KIND FRIENDS ALL RIGHT HAGUE LONGING FOR NEWS WRITE."

Heini wrote to Alma on 13 June 1940:

> My Dearest Almschi,
>
> I am so happy to have news from you again after such a long time. I was very much disturbed, fearing what might have happened to you and where you might be. I'm now very happy that I know you are well and everything is all right so far. I was very much worried about you. I was reassured when Uncle Kraith told me he had had a card from you, and now, finally, your dear letter has arrived.
>
> Please do not be upset that this letter is not handwritten. One should type, like this, now [to cooperate with the censors], and maybe you will get this letter more quickly. Otherwise, the fact that this has been typed has no meaning, and it should not be considered less sincere because it is typed.
>
> As you can see, I am still here, and I'm also quite well. Everything is fine. We do not suffer deprivation and are grateful. The idea of going to your brother's is a good one, and probably now the best solution. I hope you can arrange this.
>
> You don't need to worry about Vati. He can be taken care of as well as it is possible in these times. [Between us] everything is as it used to be, for certain, and nothing has been destroyed. I am always thinking of you, and the time—so long since I heard from you—has been terrible.

Please do not misunderstand when I close this letter so soon and write only briefly. Everything remains as it used to be.

I send you all—total—love. Please write again soon.

Dein Heini

ON 18 JUNE 1940, still in The Hague, Alma wrote pleadingly to Alfred:

I beg you, give me some news!! Otherwise I perish!

If only I could cable you. I would give my last cent to know what the situation is with Vati! Are you in constant contact? Is Lisl still with him? I suffocate with worry.

An indescribably good lady [unnamed for her own protection] has taken me in with her.[5] She arranged the private concert I gave in March for which I earned 200 fl. If it were not for this lady, I don't know what I would have done. Now there is another possibility that I might play again. Even then, I quake thinking of another appearance. My nerves are not up to the demands of performing.

Alferle dear, can you see a possibility to bring me across? I would in no way become a burden to you, and as always I would unquestionably earn my way. After all, I have been successful here.

Perhaps as a matter of form Uncle Bruno could do something for me? In any case, do at long last get in touch with me—I am quite frightfully alone. Heini continues to write, but one cannot live on that.

I wish you every good fortune and embrace you and Maria (praise God you have her!) with all my heart.

Do write, I beg you!!!

Germany had launched a series of air attacks on Britain, and Alma began to worry about Vati as desperately as he worried about her. Through the Red Cross, she was able to send a direct message on 29 June 1940:

Cared for by the concert woman—again engaged. Can you move in with the Fuchses? Can the Flesch money be stretched? Only thought is to see you again still healthy. Kisses and love.—Alma Příhoda-Rosé

By July Arnold's depression had deepened to despair. He practiced his violin two hours daily, saw occasional students, and "waited from one day to the next—what for?" he wrote to Alfred. He hoped to restore his spirits by adhering to a plan he called his "renaissance": he would play through his entire repertoire, writing down all the works alphabetically, beginning with Bach.

Alma replied to a letter from Alfred on 12 July, saying that she was in touch with friends and relatives in Vienna and in Weimar, where their Uncle Eduard still lived. She expressed her worries about Vati in view of the recent bombings and said she was thrilled to hear that Alfred had sent his composition *Triptychon* to Koussevitzky in Boston, so that it might yet be performed. Only then did she write about herself.

> You don't ask me how I live!
>
> For the past fourteen days I have again been playing in a cabaret: Paganini, Viennese music, "Zigeunerweisen," and so on. The lady who arranged my private concert in March and I share the work at her place since she took me in. This is a great piece of good fortune, for my immediate worries are over. All the same, the chances for further engagements do not look rosy. This lady, who has a married daughter living near Vati in London, lives all alone in a flat. Apparently she is also happy to have a houseguest.
>
> Wilhelm Ernst [Gutheil] has disappeared for a month, and I am anxious about him.
>
> It would be wonderful if Vati could see my letters and if I could see his handwriting again. My heart aches so much!
>
> Kisses for Maria. . . . I embrace you with all my heart.

IN LATE summer, Alfred undertook a campaign to bring his father to the States. Asking for letters in support of Arnold's immigration, he and Maria wrote to Arturo Toscanini, Bruno Walter, Thomas Mann, Elizabeth Sprague Coolidge, Serge Koussevitzky, Eugene Ormandy, and Albert Einstein. (Einstein was Maria's target, as she recalled the famous scientist visiting her father's studio in Vienna to pose for a Schmutzer etching.) The response was heartening. An elite group endorsed Arnold's admission to the U.S., some even soliciting others to write letters on Arnold's behalf.

Despite the outpouring of support, Arnold was at a disadvantage because of his age. Had he been younger and still actively teaching, he could have qualified for entry under U.S. immigration policy, but he had been retired in Vienna. As a native of Romania, he fell under the very limited Romanian quota, another barrier to immigration.

Simultaneously Alfred continued to pursue the precious affidavit that would allow Alma to come to the States. Cincinnati friends Robert Fries and his wife Frances put their bank account in his name, so that Alfred could show U.S. authorities he had the resources necessary to support his sister if she entered the country but could not find work. Still, without a contract to join or perform with an orchestra, Alma had little chance of meeting the stringent U.S. entry requirements.

In August, responding to an anguished letter from Alma, Heini wrote by hand:

> My Dear *Wiebraut*! [a pet name, suggesting "as a bride"]
>
> I finally received your letter of 27 July. I'm always happy to hear

from you and cannot understand why you write to me and to Dr. Kraith that you have no news from me. I received your lovely books and wrote you right away, and I answered your last letter. When I wrote on the typewriter, it was for a reason, and you shouldn't take it amiss. At the time there was a new official order, and I thought it was necessary to type all letters.

In any case, the letter wasn't meant to be cold and detached, my dearest. Of that you can be sure. I worry a lot about you, my dearest. I hope you are able to live halfway decently. I gather from Lisl's father that you have the possibility of some work. I hope you will earn a little bit for yourself.

There is not much news here. . . . I don't want to make you sad, but it will please you endlessly that I am more unhappy each day, and have more longing for you and feel more and more that I can belong only to you, and I love only you!

I sometimes feel better when I am at work in the day. When things go well and I see that I accomplish something, I almost imagine that this is the right situation, that [work] alone can be sufficient. Yet when I sit alone in the evening in my room—as I am doing now—and I am lonesome, I realize this is not true. One needs somebody not only beside oneself, but inside too, with whom one is only US. And that can only be you.

Do you understand now why I fear writing to you? When I am by myself, I think of you and feel your presence so completely that I have to admit to everything I am feeling. Dearest, when I look at your lovely pictures, which I am so happy to have, and when I think how happy we could be, then I feel complete and true, although it can no longer be. . . .

Please, dearest, stay with me. . . . I am sure you still love me—understand the way it is with me!—and I know that you belong to me, and this is certain. . . .

I have the same amount of work all the time . . . so many things to do that nothing gets done and I am always busy.

A few weeks ago I was in Grinzing [visiting Justine's grave]. . . . So peaceful. My dearest, I always feel so near you when I am there that I am very sad and lonesome. It is now more than a year since I last saw you—terribly long, yet you are so real to me that it seems only a short while ago. I don't understand why I get so little mail from you. I write you every time I receive a letter from you.

Now I take you in my arms, my dearest, and kiss you long and fervently.

Totally, totally yours,
Heini

Despite Heini's soothing words, Alma was on the verge of hysteria. Outside the U.S. embassy she waited for days for an opportunity to register for emigration, in sun and rain joining the crowds of the hopeful. Every hour, an official with his surprising American accent would emerge from the building and say, "Sorry, folks, we're trying to get you out, but the Germans won't give you permission!"

Camilla Youssef, a British teenager, was in the crowd. During the weeks of waiting for the all-important "quota number," she and Alma struck up a friendship. "We were terribly frightened, but Alma maintained a quiet dignity that made her special. She told me she had already had encounters with the Nazis, seen them in action, and she was terrified of them, but I could see she would never kowtow to them."[6]

For weeks Alma heard nothing from Alfred. On 24 August 1940, she wrote anxiously:

> Now I'll try writing for the last time. If I don't receive an answer, I shall telegraph even though I am saving furiously. I have almost collapsed with worry about Father. . . . What does he live on?
>
> I am playing on the stage of a moviehouse at present and hope it will continue. IT'S A STRUGGLE FOR LIFE! Even if you do not hear from me, you MUST write to me from time to time, Alferle. Just consider how lonely I am.
>
> Yesterday I again had a very nice letter from HEINI. These recent days you must also have thought of me [on the anniversary of their mother's death]. Yes, Alfi? I am truly thankful that SHE is at rest. But that I can do nothing for Vati makes me ill!
>
> Alferle, do tell him how very, very much and how constantly I think of him. Just now, he would be very satisfied with my playing—that is the only thing I can do for him at the moment. That Malchen [a Rosé cousin who replaced Lisl in Arnold's service] is looking out for him is greatly reassuring.
>
> That YOU have no immediate money cares means much, and I am very happy about it. Have you heard from Koussevitsky regarding your *Triptychon*?
>
> Kiss Maria for me, and know yourself embraced with all my heart, from your nearly despairing
>
> Alma
>
> P.S. Do make it possible somehow to get news to me from Vati.

The next letter from Alma was written on 18 September 1940 in Hilversum:

> After the most maddening difficulties, I was able to get fourteen days' work playing in a moviehouse [the Passage theater] in The Hague—excellent critiques, one of which is enclosed. ASTONISHED?

After that, there was a lot of action for me—I received excellent offers and began to feel less shattered—then along came SOMETHING. ALL [Jews] must move to the middle of the country within forty-eight hours. At first, I was at a loss and quite dizzy, being so entirely alone. The lady with whom I have been living could not take me with her where she was going. All prospects again amounted to nothing.

That's when the BAKKERS [the family of Theo's aunt in Hilversum] called. Would I come to them? Thank God that was permitted, and once again I was out of danger. I have now been here since 8 August and am trying to get work. Amsterdam also is off limits. Remember those days in BADENWEILER?

Inform Vati immediately!

Now, tell me at last, WHAT does Vati live on? I feel so desperate that I cannot care for him!!

When I inquired some time back at the [U.S.] consulate, I was told that if I applied, it would take fifteen years until my turn came up! Therefore I have not registered at all. But the consul indicated that if I could obtain a contract or an engagement, emigration would be possible.

I would rather not remain there [in the United States], but be with Vati. That is really the goal in my life—to be with Vati again and to be able to care for him. Ironically, this was the reason I left him. I have, of course, earned considerable amounts. And who could foresee this forced separation?

Wilhelm Ernst [Gutheil] has been transferred to Zurich. I have heard nothing from him. The reasons you can imagine.[7] I spend my life waiting.

I was married ten years ago last Monday. Currently playing in The Hague are the movies *G'schichten aus'm Wienerwald* (Tales from the Vienna Woods) with Vati [a movie in which he appeared with Leo Slezak, Arnold portraying a conductor of the Vienna Philharmonic] and at another theater, *Die Weisse Frau des Majaradja* (The White Wife of the Maharajah) with Váša. I wanted to see it but was forced to leave—who knows what good fortune that was! But Vati I would not have had the heart to miss.

Sometimes I feel I cannot bear it. Please tell him that—how I long for him. I am sure he will be pleased. And I beg you with all my heart: he should write me, just one line in his hand, Alferle. Were the roles reversed I would surely achieve that for you.

Alferle, do write to me even when you have no news from me—I cannot help it when the mail is slow. Remember that I am alone. Tell me how your work goes at the moment—everything interests me.

On 17 October 1940, Alma registered with authorities at the American consulate in Rotterdam and received a quota number. Despite the upheaval around her, she again felt hopeful.

She was aware that on 27 September 1940, an onerous decree regarding the status of Jews was passed in occupied France. On 3 October, even Vichy France in the unoccupied south enacted the first of more than 160 laws excluding Jews from public life. In Warsaw, on 10 November, Jews were herded into the city and sealed into a ghetto. Inexorably, the Nazis tightened their grip on the Jews of Holland.

Alma wrote to Alfred on 8 October 1940 that she scarcely knew where to turn. She had seen enough for twenty lifetimes, she said. Letters from her brother were her lifeline: "There is nothing else for me. Keep them coming, or I shall not get through." To add to her misery, she felt she was being maligned within the family, and her judgment and motives in leaving Britain for Holland questioned in the cruelest way. She complained to Alfred:

> Now it comes out that Malchen has spread a stupendously stupid piece of meanness into the world that I did not get back to Vati for private reasons [her feelings for Heini] and was clumsy and inept!
>
> Only when you all hear of the tragic happenings [on the Continent] will she be ashamed. I have wept for hours about this and still do. As long as Vati does not believe anything like that! Please, do tell him all this!!!

Even Vati was party to this vexing speculation. On Christmas Eve, he wrote to Alfred that Alma might have lingered in Holland in the hope of a rendezvous with Heini.

Whatever her own circumstances, Alma never failed to show love and concern for Alfred and Maria. They were still struggling to support themselves in Cincinnati—Alfred lecturing and teaching irregularly, and Maria taking orders for knitting and doing alterations in a dress shop (on one occasion, for actress Mae West) for $29 a week.

"We must keep our heads high, Alferle," Alma wrote. "You too, because of your students my dear. At the last moment something will surely come."

Alma had one card left to play. In Amsterdam she had met Hugo Kolberg, the former concertmaster of the Berlin Philharmonic, whom Wilhelm Furtwängler had protected in that position as long as possible. At the time Kolberg and his wife were on their way to America; Furtwängler had helped to arrange their flight. Alma knew that Kolberg went to Pittsburgh and wrote to him about the possibility of joining the orchestra there. Alfred, too, promised to contact him. At Kolberg's request, Alma sent copies of her recommendations from Bruno Walter and Willem Mengelberg. After several months Kolberg replied that no orchestra job was available, but if Alfred could get her a teaching position, she might obtain a non-quota visa for entry to the United States. Her hopes were dashed, and visions of emigration grew dim.

WITHOUT SPECIAL permits, Alma was now barred from Amsterdam and The Hague and the relative wealth of musical prospects these cities offered. She wrote to Alfred: "I have placed myself on the waiting list but am forbidden to go to Rotterdam to the U.S. consulate." In Holland, as in other occupied countries, the Nazis had banned not only public performances by Jewish artists, but even the performance of Jewish composers' music. This year Willem Mengelberg and the Concertgebouw would not hold the customary Mahler Festival in early May, coinciding with the anniversary of Mahler's death.

Alma wrote sadly of the Meijers' disappearance from her life. "They probably feared I would suddenly appear abandoned on the street. But that is not like me. I originally tried to find a place as a chambermaid, but managed to obtain something as a violinist." The truth, which Alma would not know for weeks, was that her friends had gone underground, fearing for their lives.

The woman with whom Alma had lived in The Hague was now in Utrecht. She gave Alma her daughter's bicycle, and Alma, cycling from the Bakkers' home in Hilversum, visited her weekly. The continuing friendship was a bright spot in a life harsher than anything Alma had known.

Through diligence and clever maneuvering, Alma suddenly received permission to play again in The Hague. She had a two-week engagement at the Passage moviehouse and another two weeks at the Grand Hotel Central, she reported to Alfred on 10 November 1940, and she was "delighted to be working again."

Italy, under Hitler's ally the Duce, had invaded Greece on 28 October. Alma wrote that she feared for Maria's brother, Johannes Schmutzer, his wife, and her parents.[8] She and Vati had been right, she now knew, to reject offers of work in Athens, which could no longer look after its own.

Alma had found ways to communicate with Vati through relatives and friends in Brazil, Switzerland, and Portugal. With sudden optimism she wrote to Alfred on 21 November 1940:

> Someday all our worries will be over—perhaps sooner than we think. I'm very happy that at last Vati has my letters. I have written so often. Above all [if both she and Vati are admitted to the United States], at long last we will be able to live together again. . . . I think with gratitude of Maria, who means so very much to you. That amounts to 80 percent, to have for this life a companion through thick and thin.

In the same letter Alma reported that the Meijers had been in contact: they were safe, and all was well with them. "Fortune plays a role in everyone's life," she observed, and she went on to describe the solace she found in her violin.

> The three-week theater engagement was just in time. I get together with Flesch once in a while. He is very nice, but I never ask him for any-

thing. That is my way, as long as I can earn something. As you can imagine, I pull every string, and I was among the first of the refugees and émigrés to play again. . . .

I am very happy that you are better off professionally. You really should never despair, for when one is completely down, then comes a turn for the better. I was terribly lonely and miserable. I played, and played well—and that lifted my spirits.

In four weeks the days will again be longer, and once Christmas is over, we shall be closer to the day when we will all be united. On the eleventh [of December, Alfred's birthday] and the fifteenth [Justine's birthday], we will be more aware of the distance between us than usual. . . .

If only I could earn for Vati again. Oh, how much else I would like to ask!

Alma knew that a bomb had fallen close to Arnold's rooms in London and blown out his windows. Not only did she worry about his safety, but she tormented herself with the knowledge that the rent at the Maida Vail maisonette was too high for him. In fact, with the help of Dr. Paul and Nora Nathan, Arnold had moved in early November to Welwyn Gardens City in Hertfordshire, where he had a pleasant, quiet accommodation. The Nathans had arranged for him to receive welfare assistance to pay for his rooms.

In an emotional state, Alma wrote again on 5 December 1940:

Since 28 October [when she received a letter from Arnold], I have been a different person. And now you tell me Vati is in the country and, so to speak, looked after. If only you could take him to your home!! Despite the greatest of efforts, I am again without work, although I had some in the past three weeks.

It is tremendously capable of you to have acquired all the papers for Arnold's immigration. This is hard to imagine. What worries I have had. [In the following sentences she refers to herself in the third person, disguising her identity for the censors.] All the documents on Váša's wife are in the writing desk. Shall she request duplicates to be sent to her or rather have them forwarded later? Do advise, for she shall surely require them.

Because of the cold, I cannot sleep, have chilblains on hands and feet, and my arms ache so much. Very unpleasant. . . .

I will not celebrate Christmas at all because of loneliness and a shortage of money. Your letters are the brightest spot in my life. Still, there are pleasant and understanding people who are good to me—mostly older women, and it does me good! I could easily enter a cloister. I don't even know a man who could interest me—crazy, isn't it?

All my energies are concentrated on a reunion with Vati and with you and Maria, and obtaining a fixed position to offer Vati a secure living. That is all I desire. . . .

Alferle, just another extra kiss for you from your ever lonesome (notwithstanding my old ladies),

Alma

LITTLE BY little Arnold was disposing of possessions, selling or storing items brought from Vienna. Dory, whose home in Radlett was closer to his new lodgings, helped in the process, which would pave the way for emigration to the States.

On 10 December 1940, Alma was officially labeled a Jewess: Alma Sara (Maria) Příhoda-Rosé.[9] An enormous red "J" was stamped on the new passport no. 5326-40 she received in Amsterdam that day.

All mention of Heini had disappeared from Alma's letters. Was she prepared for this letter, written on 20 December 1940, when it arrived at Christmas-time?

My Dear Alma,

I haven't written you for such a long time despite your nice letters. But everything has changed so much. Also I forgot your birthday. At the time, I was on business in Stuttgart. Uncle Kraith visits me from time to time. He will have written to you already. In the meantime, I got married.

I cannot write everything that transpired, because it would be read by so many people, and it would be meant for you only. It is not the greatest good fortune, but that can never be. . . . I am happy and content this way, and peaceful. I know this is best for me. I might not have found the right answers, but for me this was the best, smoothest and best, compromise.

I know how hard it must be for you to hear this. When I left you, I already had the feeling that it must come to something like this eventually. Maybe it was too right, too beautiful and too harmonious, to stay forever as we were!

Why should I write you lots of words now? You must certainly know all I leave unsaid, and how I feel about you.

I will go to Grinzing at Christmas-time, and will feel your presence as always, and think of you. That is the best Christmas greeting I can offer you.

Dein Heini[10]

This was not the happy letter of a bridegroom. "Not the greatest good fortune" was indeed a clue to the truth of Heini's marriage. He did not know, when he married a well-known Viennese sportswoman, that she could not have children. A widow, she had had a hysterectomy, a fact she did not reveal to

Heini before the wedding. Thomas Salzer said that it was a lonely marriage for Heini. His wife was a furiously competitive tennis player and horsewoman and led a life quite separate from his. Her aggressive character was a complete contrast to Heini's extreme gentleness.

ALMA'S NEXT letters to Alfred came from Utrecht, where she had suddenly fled from Hilversum. She reported harrowing experiences beginning the night of 23 December, when a son of the Bakker family, her friend Theo's cousin, "suddenly lost control . . . armchairs were thrown . . . and I ran through the pitch-black night to the home of an acquaintance." Alma did not link the outburst to a specific incident.

Alma's stubborn sense of her own birthright could have led to the rupture with the Bakkers, although Theo Bakker's wife in later years, Antonia Bakker-Boelen, remembered hearing of only one dispute during Alma's stay with the family in Hilversum. Kathleen Doyle Bakker, Theo's aunt, considered Alma's dark, shoulder-length hair too noticeable and urged her to have it cut short, in the fashion of most other women. In Antonia's words: "Aunt Kathleen kept saying to her: 'Really, Alma, you should cut your long hair; it draws too much attention.' Alma kept saying: 'No, I would not be Alma Rosé anymore if I did.'"[11]

Alma was shattered by the young Bakker's December outburst and left the family home soon afterward. In a letter of 14 January 1941, she wrote: "Now a nice young married couple [Ed and Millie Spanjaard] have taken me into their home and treat me colossally well."

> They have arranged a house concert for me on 26 January in their home [in Utrecht], and so many tickets are sold already that the concert will have to be repeated. I must now rely entirely on house concerts, Herr Bürgermeister! Now that I have a warm room I again practice regularly, and it does me good psychologically. Since I got a handwritten letter from Vati yesterday, I feel much better. . . .
>
> I have high expectations from the house concerts. Through this couple I have come into a magnificently musical circle and am playing almost daily—and becoming very well known.
>
> For both Christmas and New Year's I was with the young couple at Hilversum, before coming here. They had a tree, and at midnight I happened to be all alone in front of the lighted tree, and I played the violin. It was a magical moment! The others had gone to take an elderly lady home before twelve, since no one is allowed on the streets between midnight and 4 a.m. They arrived back here breathless ten minutes past the deadline, but I was alone when the clock struck twelve.
>
> I firmly believe we shall be celebrating together next year—
>
> Your still embattled
> Alma

Please write to Vati that things are going well for me. I tell you how it really is, just as you should do with me. Alice [Schmutzer] wrote me most lovingly at Christmas!

In Nazi-occupied Holland, many Dutch musicians, Jewish and non-Jewish, refused to join the Reich Kulturkammer in protest to its anti-Semitic doctrine. Musicians identified as Jews were limited to appearances with Jewish ensembles playing "Jewish music" or to performances in the homes of affluent Dutch citizens who thus flouted the Nazi rules. The "house concert" became a fixture in many occupied countries, and a welcome outlet for the beleaguered Jewish artists.[12]

During her months in Utrecht with the Spanjaards, Alma became a regular on the house-concert circuit. Ed Spanjaard, a lawyer and a conductor who frequently led the Netherlands Radio Chamber Orchestra, was well known in Dutch music circles and helped Alma to establish useful contacts.[13] Most of her programs are on file in the War History Documentation Center in Amsterdam, with Alma's orderly notation of her earnings from each event.

For her first performance, at the Spanjaards' home, she earned 87 fl. The eminent Dutch composer, organist, and pianist Johan Wagenaar was her accompanist.[14] Alma, in her element as soloist, played the César Franck Sonata in A and the Handel Sonata in D as well as two virtuoso Příhoda arrangements of Paganini and Richard Strauss.

Although Alma was virtually a prisoner within the Spanjaard home, she felt a new sense of belonging. Her hosts were genial and cultivated, and the ambiance in their home evoked her old life in Vienna.

Ed Spanjaard's younger brother, Dr. Jaab Spanjaard, a psychiatrist and accomplished pianist, was a frequent visitor. He enjoyed exploring the four-hand literature with Alma; the two often played piano transcriptions of the Mahler symphonies. Their friendship never veered into romance, although Jaab recalled with a twinkle in his eye that when Alma emerged from her bath, she had a most alluring glow.[15]

Millie Spanjaard—later Mrs. Millie E. Prins-Marczak living in Bilthoven, the Netherlands—remarked that she and her former husband organized Alma's first concerts in their home.[16] Alma kept the proceeds and remained in the household as a boarder for seven months. She became so popular that impresarios eventually took charge of arranging her house concerts.

Alma persisted in her efforts to get travel permits, which came under the official jurisdiction of the newly formed Dutch Zentralstelle. For a time she avoided regular bureaucratic channels and miraculously made her way by working through unofficial sources. According to Millie, "the reality was that Alma got her permission several times in Bilthoven. She deliberately avoided the big-town administration in Utrecht and expected she would have better chances in a small village."

The mystery of Alma's success, which eluded so many others, was illuminated one night when Alma and Millie were alone in the kitchen cleaning up after the evening meal. Alma's young hostess found it hard to hold her own in the face of Alma's dominating personality, and they did not often share confidences. Tonight, however, Alma held nothing back.

Millie recalled:

> She had been to Bilthoven that day, where a more cooperative German—possibly one of the many Austrians serving in Holland—was able to make special concessions involving permission to travel. She was helping me wash the dishes. I could see a special glow about her. I asked her what had happened in Bilthoven.
>
> "Can you see it so easily?" Alma asked.
>
> I came from behind her and then she said there was a man—that she liked him and he liked her. Then she told me that behind the villa of the *Ortskommandant* [the German town major] was a garden with a swimming pool.
>
> The door to the villa was slightly open when she arrived, and there was absolutely no one to be seen in the house. In the hallway, Alma waited and waited. She pushed on a bell, and finally out of the garden came "a tall blond god" wearing a very small bathing suit, the sun behind him and droplets of water gleaming on his skin. If you make an acquaintance in this fashion, and you are charming and alone—well, you can understand.

People of the district still speak of the sympathetic hearings they received from the same official, "who was certainly no Nazi." He was known to have advised the Dutch to warn Jews when raiding parties were planned. One former Dutch official in the town of Bilthoven reported that the officer in question was later given a court martial and executed by the Germans.

Was Alma seen as a collaborationist because of this adventure? In the opinion of the former Mrs. Spanjaard,

> Alma was not avoided because of her relations with an enemy officer, whom she visited several times. No one ever judged her for it. I would not be surprised if he were an Austrian. Talking with someone in a familiar accent and with a similar mentality must have been very attractive to Alma. Dutch men certainly don't have the charm and light way of conversation that Austrians often have. . . .
>
> Alma must have needed and appreciated the recognition of her femininity—especially at that time—and that had nothing to do with collaboration.

Millie Spanjaard found her houseguest demanding and sometimes difficult, but she confessed that Alma was very beguiling.

> Shall we say she had sex appeal? High-born Vienna, she carried herself with elegance. She was always well groomed. She knew how to make something out of nothing—she always had a neatly folded handkerchief in the breast pocket of her blouse or dress.
>
> She favored black, with a touch of red or white, and wore little jewelry. Through all her troubles she remained distinguished and charming. She did not give in to her moods, nor did she let her worries cloud her days. We were all worried, but none of us showed our fear, and nor did Alma. She had an extreme will to carry on.

In February 1940 a sickly young man came to board at the Spanjaards', and Alma had to give up her private room and move into the dining room of the house. The new pensioner was Dr. J. J. (Jaab) Henkemans, a tuberculosis patient thoroughly demoralized after three years of treatment. A near-invalid when he arrived, he needed a warm room and lots of rest. Previously a musician and composer, he was now a psychotherapist. Upon his release from the sanatorium, his doctors, believing he was as well as he would ever be, had ordered him to restrict his piano playing to fifteen minutes a day.

Dr. Henkemans, who has since had a notable musical and professional career, said gratefully, "I was resurrected by Alma."

> Alma made me overthrow those rigid rules, and in no time at all we were playing together quite regularly. Of course, I was a convalescent, and after playing a sonata with her I was wet with honest sweat. But it was sheer delight to play with her, and I did not care about my health anymore, much to my advantage.
>
> Of course Alma could not "appear" in Holland. But we played to our hearts' delight and gave a few modest "at homes" for a select public. I found it amazing how quickly I could regain my technique, but almost surely it was working with Alma that helped me. I remember that after one month, I was able to play the very difficult piano part for the César Franck violin sonata to perfection. Alma was very demanding, very critical of herself as well as of me, and we went over the sonata again and again until it was perfect.
>
> She was an excellent musician. To be able to play at all was medicine, but to make music with a skillful violinist was a godsend. If she had survived, she would have had a great career.[17]

Alma put considerable stock in Henkemans' opinions and enjoyed his company. Their friendly banter could add to an evening's entertainment. For instance, her new musical partner was not as enthusiastic about the late Romantics as Alma was. One night after they played a Brahms sonata before a group of friends, she asked him how he liked it.

"Long," said Henkemans.

"Is that all you can say?" Alma demanded.

"Slow," said Henkemans. The discussion ended amidst laughter from all.

When he recovered from his illness, Henkemans went back to work as a medical doctor and psychotherapist and lost track of Alma, whom he warmly recalled as his personal musical therapist.[18]

LIFE WITH Alma was never smooth. She could display temperament and insisted on the prerogatives of life as an artist. This sometimes clouded her stay with the Spanjaards, as it had marred her visit with the Piranis in London. After Henkemans' arrival, she slept in the warmest room of the house—the dining room—and she liked to sleep late in the mornings even when she had not performed the night before. She paid no attention to the inconvenience this might cause the family, who thought nine o'clock late enough to rise from bed. Millie Spanjaard also resented Alma's liberal use of talcum powder after her baths, which left billows of fragrant dust for her hostess to clean up.

Upon the success of the Utrecht concerts, Alma was engaged for a house concert in Amsterdam on 2 February 1941. Her accompanist was Olga Moskowsky, who was later killed by the Nazis. Another concert was scheduled for 29 March.

Early in her stay at the Spanjaards' Alma caused a sensation. One evening as she was descending the stairs to the living room for a performance, she tripped on the top step. She fell face forward, smashing against the wall where the steps took a right-angled turn to the ground floor. Dr. Henkemans said that she broke her nose. Onlookers were amazed at Alma's discipline. Instead of raising her hands to break the fall and protect her face, she held them and her violin behind her back as she fell.

On 15 February 1941, she wrote to Alfred about the incident:

> A week ago today I fell down the stairway—square on my face to save my hands. It was terrible—my eyes were no more than slits, and blood hemorrhaged into my eyes. Today it is greatly reduced or I could not write about it. My arm, too, is all right again.
>
> I sleep on a bench in the dining room here and pay only for meals. Am not so alone—and last but not least, it is warm! While I was unwell, I continually received flowers and candies—it did me a world of good psychologically. Dental care I received for nothing! I play chamber music with the dentist, and he treated me for root infections. Now I have a nose specialist free of charge too.
>
> If you could see what your letters do for me, you would write more often.
>
> Your faithful sister,
> Alma

Giving up hope of returning to England, Camilla Youssef had married a Dutch farmer who promised her shelter, a wartime arrangement like many others. Learning at Christmas-time of Alma's difficulties, Camilla wrote and offered her a place on the farm with her husband and herself.

Alma responded in English on 21 February 1941, keeping up her brave front:

> I think I wrote you I had a house concert on 26 January. It is much better for me to stay in Utrecht. On 16 March I have another house concert at the home of Dr. [J. L.] Noest and one on the 29th in Amsterdam.
>
> I had two letters from my father !!!! telling me that he is living in the country at Welwyn Gardens City (Herts.) and that Toscanini is helping him financially. Well—you can imagine how pleased I feel! Here I got two answers from the Red Cross—so I suppose you will have heard from your parents too by now?? . . .
>
> I've been rather ill. Imagine, I fell down the stairs on my face! I was afraid to hurt my hands—I look marvelous!
>
> There is no chance to get to The Hague at the moment, but it is awfully kind of you to want to help me. I'm sure we would have a wonderful time together, but I don't believe I could get permission.
>
> I am terribly glad to read and FEEL that you are happy! How many dogs have you got at the moment? I can imagine how lovely it must be with spring coming!
>
> Well, dear, do write again—A big kiss and heaps of love from
>
> Your Alma
>
> Try to keep smiling!
> I am so homesick for Father.

12

Musical Fortress

I cannot escape my loneliness. Only when I play do I rise above it.
—Alma Rosé

Carl Flesch, although he shared Alma's plight in Holland, enjoyed some protection as a native Hungarian. Moreover the Nazis had dubbed him a "blue knight" (a special category of Jews, possibly designated for ransom purposes, that afforded protection from arrest and exemption from wearing the yellow star). Early in February 1941, he wrote to Alma that he hoped to leave Holland by the end of the year. He was awaiting final contracts from the Curtis Institute in Philadelphia and planned to travel to the States via Berlin and Barcelona.[1]

Flesch understood Alma's role in getting her father safely out of Vienna, and he knew of her dangerous wartime flight to Holland in search of support for both Vati and herself. "You are a most courageous person," he wrote, adding emphatically: "You possess the chief qualities fitted for these times: adaptability and enterprise. I have no fear for your future."[2]

An anecdote still told in Holland bears out Flesch's faith in Alma's nature. The house concert Alma was to give at the home of Dr. J. L. Noest in Utrecht on 16 March 1941 was important for her career. Not only would she perform with Dutch music critic Rutger Schoute, a fine pianist, but she would play the Beethoven A major "Kreutzer" Sonata, opus 47.

At their first meeting, Schoute produced the edition of the score edited by her father. Alma was pleased and surprised by his gesture. Schoute never suspected that the work was not already in her repertoire.

During their first rehearsal, Alma had difficulty with the fingering prescribed for the long solo passage in the opening movement. Undaunted, she told Schoute they could go on to other passages. She would study the solo part on her own, and she would find out exactly what her father had intended.

Schoute was skeptical. In occupied Holland, how could she get an answer from London in time? Alma wrote to a friend in either Lisbon or Rio, who relayed the letter to Arnold in England. He responded immediately, via the same circuitous route, taking pains to elucidate his earlier suggestions. "*Der Fingersatz ist schön aber schwer*" ("the fingering is beautiful but difficult"), he wrote; then he proceeded to tell her finger by finger of an alternative: "*Folgender ist auch gut,*" he said—"the following is also good."[3] Alma complained that in Arnold's haste to answer her musical question, he neglected to send personal news.

Although she did her best to hide her tensions, Alma's nerves were at the breaking point. Schoute and his wife recalled that during the first practice, their three-year-old son Zweder brought his small chair into the room to watch and listen. The child was absolutely still, but Alma became so agitated that the parents finally asked if he were bothering her. She admitted that the boy upset her, so they took him away. Schoute and his wife were amazed that such a veteran performer could be undone by the presence of a child.

The Sunday afternoon concert, at which Alma earned 150 fl. (enough to support her for three months, she wrote proudly to Alfred), was a splendid success. In addition to Alma's debut in the "Kreutzer" Sonata, the program included the Brahms Piano and Violin Sonata in G major and Debussy's hauntingly beautiful Sonata in G.

Schoute recalled: "It was a major event. Admission was by invitation only. People were shown to their seats by liveried ushers wearing red and white striped vests." Schoute agreed enthusiastically to a later concert in Hilversum, for which he would go so far as to truck in his treasured Gaveau grand piano.[4]

On 29 March 1941, Alma gave a concert in Amsterdam that brought in 60 fl. She was now in demand outside Amsterdam and Utrecht; concerts were scheduled in Drachten in mid-April and in Wageningen in May. On 20 April and 11 May, she and Schoute repeated the program they had performed at Dr. Noest's, and Alma earned another 134 fl. In a 16 June performance in Hilversum, the same pair performed the Handel Sonata in D, the "Kreutzer" Sonata, and the César Franck Sonata in A, and Alma earned 146 fl.

After the Hilversum concert, Mrs. Schoute, a physician, saw Alma to the train station. Decades later she recalled the risks of travel at the time, even for the Dutch, but particularly for Alma. Informers and secret police could be anywhere. A German-speaker was suspect if not in uniform; a Dutch-speaker had to fear being questioned. It was particularly dangerous to travel with a child. "You never knew who was listening," Mrs. Schoute remembered. "You were afraid to draw attention on a station platform or in the train."

The house concert required considerable daring; yet Alma became so confident that on one occasion she performed at noon in the coffee shop of the most prestigious bank in Amsterdam. An attendant at the War History Documentation Center recalled four decades later that her performance at the bank created a sensation. Neither Alma nor her audience realized the magnitude of the risk she ran.

As Alma's concert career blossomed, the Germans instituted increasingly stringent measures against Jews throughout the occupied territories. Neil Phillips, a friend of Alfred's who had met Alma in The Hague in 1939 shortly before he left Holland for the States, sent Alfred a stern letter of warning on 10 March 1941. Although Phillips was American-born, it had taken him almost three months to get out of Holland. He wrote that it was absolutely necessary for Alma to apply to the Germans for her exit permit immediately—as soon as all her documents were together. Because she was registered as a "non-Aryan" and because permission would have to cover all the countries she would pass through en route to the U.S., it would take at least three months to get the necessary clearances. He urged Alfred to send the required affidavits of financial support directly to the U.S. consul in Rotterdam in order to expedite the process. Alfred set the wheels in motion at once.

Alma allowed her anxieties to surface in letters to her brother. On 3 April 1941 she wrote:

> I have written Mrs. Meta Lissauer, who is staying at the Waldorf-Astoria. I have asked her if she can do something for me. When she was at The Hague, she arranged my first house concert and was indescribably good to me. Besides, her two sisters are still here and treat me as though I were their daughter. I had lived with one of them [perhaps Frau Ashkenazy] for three months in The Hague. . . .
>
> I beg you with all my heart to do everything possible to get my visa. Once over there, I shall get along without difficulty. I have many recommendations—many well-to-do relatives of my motherly friend want to help me. I would begin with house concerts, having had excellent experience with them here.
>
> I think of you so often and so much—I am sometimes lonely beyond belief. If I did not have my violin, it would be awful. I am now studying *Tzigane* by Ravel, a very effective and difficult piece. . . .
>
> Tell Vati everything I write.

After the joy of receiving a letter from Alfred on Easter Monday, Alma replied on 15 April 1941:

> Every night I have had the most terrible dreams about Vati, then during the day I am exhausted. I am so glad that he plays. . . .
>
> So often my head is full of your song *Nach dem Regen* [After the Rain]—I am so fond of it. And your poem *Mauerkatzen, Grüne Ranken* ["Alleycats and Green Vines"].[5] Do you remember, Alferle? I live almost exclusively in the past—wrong no doubt, but I cannot escape my loneliness. Only when I play do I rise above it, and then I enjoy being alone. You understand, don't you? . . . I sometimes have a longing for Vati that is almost impossible to bear.

On 1 May 1941 Alma sounded alarm:

> Now, concerning Almschi. You mention at the beginning of your letter that the quota sequence has been abolished, but then you still ask twice when mine comes due. Only then would you set everything in motion. I cannot comprehend it. Can this lady [Mrs. Fries] not send me the affidavit as quickly as possible?
>
> Of course, that alone is not enough to allow me to leave immediately. It is necessary that you, as my brother, send me a security bond. The fact that you might not be employed at the school next year does not concern the consul here. He only needs to see that I want to get to my BROTHER. Then my turn will come up regardless of the quota.
>
> You may take for granted that I will not become a burden to you. I have now received the promise of my first house concert in New York. Very rich people have also invited me to live with them. Even here, under much more difficult conditions, I am able to take care of my needs myself, thank God.
>
> From all this, you can see that your guarantee for me is an unqualified necessity, but for you a mere formality. At present, it is most important to send these two guarantees.
>
> As for travel costs, I shall one of these days speak to my motherly friend, who a few days ago received her emigration permit and plans to leave shortly. I hope to ask her wealthy brothers and sisters to lend me the money, since she knows me well and is convinced that once I am over there, I shall be able to repay everything in a short time. She is nearly always at my concerts and wants to help me build a career that she is certain is possible once I am there.
>
> I know you scratch your head over all this, and worry as well about Johannes [Schmutzer]. But it's all or nothing. Once I am again able to unleash my full energy, there will be no worry for any of us. I would so much like to provide a quiet life for Father as well.

A letter from Bruno and Elsa Walter in May offered Alma scant encouragement with respect to job prospects in the United States. Even the eminent conductor found his American career developing slowly. Competition among émigré artists was intense, he wrote, and American musicians erected hurdles in order to protect jobs for fellow countrymen.

On 17 May, Alma wrote to Alfred again to say that "everything else is secondary" to the affidavits and the bond from Mrs. Fries. Several friends had offered her the money for passage to the United States. "Numerous promises have been made to me," she reported, "and they have given me a much more optimistic outlook."

> With all the energy I have regained, I absolutely want to bring about a normal life for us all—for Vati above all. Tell that lady [Frances Fries]

what I am like and that—terrible as it might be—I would again play even in a coffee house. . . . Know yourself embraced with all my heart—for you an extra kiss from

Your Sister

On 17 June, Alma described more "wonderful" house concerts in which she was accompanied by Paul Frankel, a pianist who had toured for six years with violinist Bronisław Huberman. Suddenly her tone became pleading:

> But I beg you over and over again, do get me that affidavit. . . . All my acquaintances are leaving one after the other. . . . Believe me, Alferle, it is serious. It is surely the first and the last time in my life that I shall be asking you to help me. You know, it is not like me. I have to do more than EVERYONE here. Nevertheless, my life depends on my getting over there.

To his great relief, on 11 June 1941 Alfred had received official notification that the two affidavits Alma so desperately required had gone by diplomatic mail directly to the U.S. consulate at Rotterdam the same day.

The precious documents arrived too late. On 15 June 1941, President Franklin D. Roosevelt ordered the closure of all German government agency offices in the U.S., which were suspected covers for intelligence operations. In retaliation, on 19 July, Berlin and Rome ordered all U.S. consulates and American Express offices closed and personnel evacuated. Alma's fate was sealed.

Her next letter was dated 22 June 1941, the day the Germans launched a massive attack on their former ally the Soviet Union:

> Just received your letter of 23 May. I thank you with all my heart. Events are upside down. In another two weeks, the two American consulates will depart. Therefore everything reaches me too late.
>
> But the fact that you—my brother—have stood up for me has done so much good for me. The longer road that is still necessary and all that will be required to get a visa I know only too well, for everyone I know is so busy trying to leave that they can do nothing else.
>
> Frau Ashkenazy, with whom I lived last summer, is in Havana. . . .
>
> Next Saturday I have a concert with Johannes Röntgen, whose father played with Vati many times. It is the last one of the season. But I can again live a few months without worries.
>
> I find it splendid that you are having such a big student evening—I only wish I could be there. I often reminisce about the one in Sternwartestrasse [at the Schmutzer villa in Vienna] and how pleasant it was.
>
> Of course I shall thank Mrs. Fries. It is certainly Fate's decree that I received [the affidavit] only now. Don't you see it that way too?

AMONG THE JOYS of Alma's constricted life were weekly meetings with a threesome of amateur musicians Alma led in quartet sessions. One young cellist came to mean more to her than her other musical partners. He was Leonard Barend Willem Jongkees, a doctor who would distinguish himself in the field of otolaryngology as a researcher, clinician, surgeon, and writer-editor. Six years her junior, Jongkees was not yet thirty when they met. Tall, handsome, and meticulously groomed, he was well known—even notorious—in Utrecht for his amorous conquests. A colleague recalled that in his youth Jongkees loved to act the "enfant terrible" and "certainly had something of the frolicsome exuberance of a 'puppy.'"[6] Leonard's energy was a match for Alma's, and she was delighted when he became a regular at her quartet evenings.

In interviews and correspondence in the 1980s, Leonard Jongkees recounted his "dear but sad" memories of Alma. His first words were: "Yes, I was—and sometimes think I still am—in love with Alma."[7]

"Considering how difficult the times were, we had many laughs," Jongkees said in impeccable English. "Alma was always the first to get a joke." Her intensity, the contradictions in her character, attracted the young doctor. "She was a romantic," he said; "her playing was romantic." He loved Alma's high color and willful spirit."I could never have fallen in love with a 'sweet' girl," he commented. Alma was a woman of extremes living in an extreme time, "a time for deeper depressions and higher elations":

> Considering the threat all were under—Alma in particular—the birds sang clearer to us and the flowers were more beautiful than ever. Everything we did had significance. On our walks, those things we now take for granted became more meaningful than ever, and they remain so in memory.

Alma was never foolhardy, Jongkees said; yet "she often told me she wished she could get in a car and drive three hundred miles an hour to get away." She was fascinated by "the sins of Alma Mahler," although she resented the way her godmother had treated her mother.

The amateur quartet, which included Leonard's father, Willem Jongkees, on the viola, and physicist J. J. (Jaab) Groen on the violin, played in the afternoons because a strict curfew prevented Alma's participation in the evenings. It is almost impossible to comprehend how Alma was able to carry on the weekly sessions given her full schedule of practice and formal performance, complicated by travel restrictions that all but forbade her appearance on the street.

Recalling the quartet sessions, Leonard described Alma as a strong musical leader. Occasionally she was troubled and distracted, but she rarely missed an entry. If her concentration failed her, one of the other players would say "Come now, Alma," and she would proceed without embarrassment. It seemed to Leonard that she was fanatically attached to her instrument.

"Alma talked about Váša Příhoda with respect, some love, and perhaps a bit of resentment," Leonard remembered. She never mentioned Heini Salzer, although in her purse she was carrying Heini's heartbreaking last Christmas greeting.

Looking back, Leonard said, "I never thought about marriage to Alma as deeply as I do now." At the time he was not ready to settle down—he was still somewhat "wild," as he put it, and keenly focused on his scientific career.[8] Nonetheless he and Alma became deeply attached, and marriage was never out of the question. His family in Zwolle offered to shelter Alma if she decided to go into hiding, but she demurred.

IN THE SUMMER of 1941, Alma again contacted Margarete Slezak (whom she still affectionately called "Gretl"), asking for help. She knew that Gretl's brother Walter, now in New York, would be a valuable contact if she got to the United States. Gretl's breezy reply to Alma—on file at the War History Documentation Center in Amsterdam—is dated 24 June 1941 and came from the Slezak enclave at Rottach-Egern am Tegernsee:

> I am beside myself. I was in Holland in April, singing daily a whole week in Hilversum, was naturally in Amsterdam and The Hague, and once in Utrecht. [She was no doubt entertaining German troops as part of what her father called her "war work"—a requirement for women under forty-five.]
>
> Too bad. I will certainly come again next season, and we will see you there then. I'm happy that so far it is well with you and your father, as we can say for ourselves. I always have a lot to do and next week I go to Rome for a few days. I travel a lot, sing a great deal, and always go farther and farther away. Hopefully the war will soon be over. . . .
>
> Have you heard nothing further from Heini, poor Alma? . . .
>
> The parents are staying during the war at Tegernsee, have closed the Berlin house and given up the Vienna residence. My daughter Helga has passed her exams and is currently engaged to a Viennese. That is all the news for today. Many kisses and loving greetings to your father.

It was obvious that no help would come from this quarter. Gretl did not mention that in September she would be in Paris, co-starring with Elisabeth Schwarzkopf under Herbert von Karajan in a full-scale Berlin Opera production of Johann Strauss's *Die Fledermaus,* a 200,000-Reichsmarks propaganda extravaganza to be mounted in the Nazi-occupied city.

Surrender did not come easily to Alma. On 30 July 1941, she wrote graciously and optimistically to Frances Fries, who had supplied the bond for the affidavit that arrived too late: "Someday I hope to come to the United States and thank you personally for what you did for me. I'm trying hard to keep my head up and wait patiently. My violin helps me to get through these difficult times."

In a letter that crossed Alma's, Mrs. Fries—unaware of the dire developments in Holland—wrote that when Alma arrived in Ohio in a mere few weeks, she would find it resplendent with autumn color.

ALMA WAS under intense pressure during the months she lived with the Spanjaards in Utrecht. Their home was a few blocks from Gestapo headquarters in Maliebaan, and the streets teemed with German officers. In addition, just across a park was the headquarters of the leading Dutch Nazi party, the NSB (Nationale Socialistische Beweging). When anti-German resisters in Hilversum took ten physicians hostage, the Dutch Nazis rounded up more than three hundred Jewish youths and sent them to Germany in reprisal, and marauding gangs burned synagogues in Amsterdam and vandalized Jewish homes and businesses.

Through the summer of 1941 Alma remained surprisingly mobile, although caution guided her every move. A postcard she received from a Bella H., sent on 17 June from Leeuwarden, has every appearance of normality. Unfortunately, Bella advised Alma, a Leeuwarden concert would have to be canceled, but a performance in Drachten was still on. The change in plans also forced the cancellation of a program at Groningen. Because Bella would be working and could not meet Alma at the station, her host, Mrs. H. E. Dikboom of Drachten, would meet her instead. Alma did indeed play in the Dikboom home, accompanied by H. E. Dikboom-Beckhuis and earning 80 fl. The concert was one of a series in which Alma played the Beethoven "Kreutzer" Sonata, by that time a keystone of her repertoire.

The summer was long and hot, and the Spanjaards too were under pressure. One evening at the dinner table, tempers flared. As Millie Spanjaard recalled, Alma had been included in an invitation to dine with family friends but refused to go. Ed Spanjaard thought she was being rude. He acknowledged that she might not enjoy the evening with his friends, but he added, "So long as you live here, you go through everything with us, and you should go through this in order not to hurt these other people. You are young, and if you are not going to fit in with what we do, then you might as well live elsewhere."

To this Alma replied hotly: "That is unequivocal. I will leave." Both she and Spanjaard later regretted their words, but the confrontation had been too bitter for Alma to stay. She began casting about for a new place to live.

Alma spent the last days of the summer alone, while the Spanjaards were on vacation. Preparing to move and refining her repertoire for the next season of house concerts, she stayed busy and tried to maintain a cheerful countenance. On 18 July 1941 she wrote to Alfred,

> I'm happy to tell you that I move on 1 August [1941], again as a paying guest—with a very nice young Dutch couple. I will have my own room

> again, and a bed that is long enough. I will have a chance to practice all day since Paul Staercke is a medical doctor at the hospital and comes home in the late afternoon.
>
> I now cook by myself. For me that is not without adventure. . . . I'm not as gifted as you are.

Alma reported that their cousin Wolfgang was among the lucky would-be emigrants: he had received his visa in Germany one hour before the U.S. consulate closed, and he would meet his brother Ernest in the U.S. on 5 August. She was overjoyed, she wrote, that Alfred was composing again. Although she had not heard from Vati since 20 May, she was pleased to know that he had given a successful concert in London.

On 9 August, Alma briefly dropped her facade and confided that her only hope of escape was a visa to Cuba. Her health was beginning to suffer from the strains of life in Holland, and she was being treated for migraines and arthritis. Doctors prescribed a drug called Almedin—with such a name, she quipped, she could hardly refuse it.

> Just think, I am best friends with Kurt and Liselotte Röders from Vienna. [The Röders had fled Austria with their baby and were living in Amsterdam.] She is the sister of Annemarie Selinko and a cousin of Lotte Zuber. . . .
>
> After a very successful concert, I heard from Louis and Lotte [Meijer], but I don't see them. However, I am in good standing with his sister in Amsterdam and often eat there. [Louis van Creveld and his wife, Louis Meijer's sister, lived on Krammerstraat in Amsterdam.]
>
> How splendid that you hear operas—I can hardly imagine anymore that concerts and movies still exist! Dear Alferle, do write again quickly. My most precious moments are when I receive mail from Vati or from you.

After the first of August 1941, Alma lived comfortably in a third-floor room in the home of Dr. Paul Staercke and his wife Marye (formerly Marye Lobry de Bruyn), a hospitable young couple who would shelter her through harrowing times. "I am received here as if I were at home," she wrote to Alfred, "and that is just what I miss so intensely." She would spend the next year and a half as the Staerckes' boarder.

The family circle was small and intimate. Sam Engers and his wife lived on the ground floor of the building in which the Staerckes had the second and third floors, and Alma's friends the Röders were close friends of the Engers'. Very soon Alma was as much at home on the ground floor as above, and she shared many meals with the Engers as well as the Staerckes.

Tragedy had already struck the Engers family. After the Nazi invasion of Holland, the Engers' son had let his beard grow, paraded through the streets in

Orthodox Jewish garb, then committed suicide. Engers himself, a former teacher, had lost one leg and had to contend with a wooden prosthesis of his own making. Still Engers held to faith in the future and predicted an early end to the war. In contrast, Paul Staercke was a brutal realist whose outlook grew bleaker with each new German victory. Yugoslavia and Greece were Hitler's latest conquests.

Over the next nineteen months, Alma and twenty-year-old Marye Staercke became fast friends, holding philosophical discussions long into the night and preserving a warm rapport through many a heated spat. Similar in spirit to Alma, the volatile Marye treasured the company of her sophisticated friend and admired her vivid postures. The two women often laughed and joked. Life was never dull with Alma around, Marye remembered. Her caustic wit and "sometimes not very charitable comments about people we both loathed met with my hearty approval. . . . You had to love her, for she was fun to be with—even when you wanted to kick her!"[9]

Marye laughed as she revealed that despite Alma's pride in her progress as a cook, she was hopelessly inept in the kitchen, as indeed with housework of any sort. At the time, Marye remarked, it was necessary to boil the milk, which was delivered to the door. One day Alma angrily announced that the milkman was cheating—adding water to the milk. She had "discovered" there was less liquid after she boiled the milk than when she first put it on the stove.

Sometimes Alma's sense of herself as a patrician deserving of special privileges triumphed over her more generous instincts. Marye remembered an especially galling incident when gas for water heating was rationed, and the Staerckes proposed that each of the three in the household take only two baths a week. Alma objected, saying that she was accustomed to her hot bath each day. When the Staerckes said they too liked daily hot baths, Alma insisted that they, not she, should make the sacrifice. "You are accustomed to doing without, I am not," she said haughtily.

In a disagreement over almost anything, Marye recalled, Alma would say, "But I am older, and you are not as I am." On the other hand, at the height of an argument, "she could give it all a little twist with a witty remark, and we'd both burst out laughing—agreeing it had been a silly thing not worth arguing about." The fact remained that Alma was not easy to live with.

Alma could be a giddy romantic, and she could also be coldly practical. Said Marye, "Her mind was so perfectly organized that first things always came first. Above everything else, she saw herself as a great artist."

One story the Staerckes cherished from Alma's months with them involved a relative of theirs named Pyke Koch, a painter known for his "magic realism." Koch fascinated women. He also held Nazi sympathies, which made him an outcast within the Staercke family. Marye and Paul occasionally invited him to their apartment to spare him the pain of complete ostracism and also to keep him abreast of anti-Nazi views. In Marye's words:

> Aware of the delicacy of the situation with Alma in the house, we told Alma well in advance that he was going to visit us one evening. She stewed all day, whether she should come down and meet him. Her curiosity was aroused by his artistic status and his reputation as a lover.
>
> We were all suffering from chilblains, and Alma had them in two fingers. When her itching curiosity enticed her down to join us, we introduced her. Aware of Koch's great charm, Alma stole the show when offering her hand, saying: "I have only three hands—sorry, three feet—sorry, three fingers to offer you."
>
> All of us knew exactly what she was saying, for we and Koch had been brought up on Freudian word games, as Alma obviously had been. Her "Freudian slip" got her message across. She was telling him: "I welcome you (three hands), I could kick you (three feet), but I offer you my hand."

Marye saw her friend as resourceful and resilient. "Some people going through sad experiences would merely push them away, but Alma would do something about her suffering. She would take the things that upset her most and make them grow into something positive, even if it were only making music."

Alma continued averaging at least three house concerts a week, earning between 25 and 150 fl. at each one. It remains a mystery how she was able to continue to get travel permission. On 15 September 1941, the Sonderreferat Juden, or Jewish Council (the administration charged with Jewish affairs), was established to enforce the severe travel restrictions. The council could issue temporary travel permits valid for four days in the case of "urgent business and family needs." Marye said that she never questioned Alma's ability to circulate as she did to concerts and rehearsals. "But Alma had a personality that could get things done. And she was able to get to know the right people and thus make all things possible."

Confronted many years after the war with Millie Spanjaard's tale of Alma's relations with the enemy officer in Bilthoven, Marye shrugged her shoulders and said only, "It was like the things we might have had to do to save our families during the occupation."

MUSICALLY, ALMA'S season began early—and on a high note—with house concerts in Apeldoorn on 3 August 1941 and again on 24 August. At these significant concerts, her pianist was James H. Simon, who had studied with the composer Max Bruch and taught for fifteen years at the prestigious Klindworth-Scharwenka Conservatory in Berlin, until the advent of the Nazis. Simon, who was also a composer, had worked in many genres and written an opera. Fleeing Berlin, he established himself in Zurich, where he remained safely out of the Nazis' reach for several years. Then, like Carl Flesch and Alma herself, he decided to pursue opportunities in "neutral" Holland, where he took up residence on Courbetstraat in Amsterdam and was ultimately trapped.[10]

Two hundred and fifty attended the second house concert presented by this distinguished pair, and they received a rousing ovation. In a letter of 29 August Alma reported to Alfred: "People again stamped their feet—something that does not happen in house concerts!"

She had made the acquaintance of an "elderly lady" who "took a fancy" to her, she wrote. Upon discovering that Alma suffered from arthritis, her new friend gave her two pairs of long woolen underwear, which she would wear without a thought to fashion. All in all, her letter was optimistic.

> It's been raining all August. Your heat wave would be trying. Come to think of it, I prefer rain.
>
> I'll be eating at her place [a reference to her elderly friend] while my landlords are away in the country for the next two weeks.
>
> I have so many concerts for the next month, and will have to practice so much, that my friends worry I will again neglect to eat. I don't feel so much alone.
>
> The Staerckes are really very good to me. Nor am I so hungry any longer, and I have gained some weight, but it doesn't matter—a little reserve for the winter.
>
> Just think, I now cook sometimes, and everyone likes the taste very much. I don't have as large a repertoire in that department as I have on the violin.
>
> The Röders had an enlargement made of Vati from the best picture in the Vienna Philharmonic book, so I finally have a picture of him.

Alma did not identify the elderly lady who had entered her life, but it was certainly Marie Anne Tellegen, a law graduate from an eminent Dutch family. In the summer of 1941 Miss Tellegen headed the Utrecht Department of Social Affairs and Statistics. A few months later, when Dutch Nazis took over the city administration, she resigned.

Miss Tellegen, considered "untouchable" because of her family connections, became an important leader of the Dutch resistance. She lived at Maliebaan 72b, separated by a single house from the Gestapo headquarters at Maliebaan 74. There, she explained, she could keep an eye on the enemy. A powerful personality possessed of great courage, she became a legend.[11]

Marie Anne Tellegen described her first meeting with Alma in the summer of 1941. Alma had become friendly with a lawyer named Meijer and his wife Frieda, who were also friends of Miss Tellegen's. One day, she recounts,

> I dropped in [at the Meijers' home] for a moment of talk and to hear the news on the BBC as I often did. With them I found a young woman with black hair, unusually big dark eyes, and an engaging laugh who was presented to me as Madame Rosé. I remember her well as she was that evening, charming in a black frock with a small white collar, with her dark hair and beautiful dark eyes. I loved her at once.[12]

From Miss Tellegen, Alma learned the full story of Louis and Lotte Meijer's underground life. Indeed it was Miss Tellegen who had come forward to help when Louis was confronted with inevitable arrest after the German conquest of Holland. As Louis and Lotte prepared to go into hiding, they faced a heart-rending choice. Their son was only a few months old, and their greatest fear was that if they were found and arrested, the child would share their fate. Miss Tellegen herself offered to take the baby. Fearing that her prominence and her activities in the underground entailed too great a risk, Louis and Lotte decided instead to place the baby with a large Gentile family, who provided him with a safe and happy home throughout the war years.[13]

ALMA'S JUNE 1941 house concert with Johannes Röntgen in Baarn gave rise to a significant musical partnership. Links between the Röntgens and the Rosés stretched far into the past. Johannes' brother Joachim, born the same year as Alma, was the former concertmaster of the Winterthur Orchestra in Switzerland and a contributor to the Rosé Fund in England. Their father, Julius Röntgen, a composer, conductor, and pianist, had played with the Rosé Quartet in formal concerts as far back as 1897 and also in the Röntgen home in The Hague in 1922 during one of the quartet's tours of the Netherlands.[14]

Johannes' wife, the former Julia Fentener van Vlissingen, was a mezzo-soprano who enjoyed singing Mahler songs with Alma at the piano, and the threesome struck up a friendship rooted in music. The Röntgens had two daughters, who remembered Alma warmly.

Johannes—who was named after his father's friend Brahms—bore one of the most honored names in Dutch music. The Nazi administration invited him to join the Reich Kulturkammer, but he refused. In retaliation he was barred from public performance or a teaching position of any kind. Banishment from his profession was only the beginning of the pressure the Nazis put on this cheerful, passionately principled musician, according to his daughter Annemarie de Boer-Röntgen.

> There was harassment. There was a threat that my father would be taken away and sent to Germany to work in a factory or, worse, a labor camp. We had to be careful opening the door. Sometimes the house would be searched from top to bottom in the middle of the night as the Germans or the Dutch police under them looked for incriminating papers.

> For many nights, sometimes for long periods, my father stayed across the street, where friendly neighbors hid people—Jews as well as my father—on the top floor. They even had a fine piano up there that my father could use. [At one point a neighbor commented that the piano player across the street played better than the famous Röntgen.] Not until after the war could we tell her that the pianist across the street and my father were one and the same.[15]

The situation was to get worse for the Röntgen family. At times the house was cold and food was scarce, so Johannes would play for coal or flour. But when Alma, Johannes, and Julia were together, they felt secure inside a musical fortress manned by Mozart, Bach, Beethoven, and Brahms.

Only once did Alma mention Röntgen in a letter, but between June 1941 and May 1942, the two played twenty-three concerts together. As a rule the programs included a major sonata from Alma's growing repertoire; a section of Dutch compositions by Johannes, his father, or other Dutch composers; and a French selection. Most of the concerts took place in the afternoon because of curfew restrictions.

Rehearsals required Alma's presence in Amsterdam. When curfew made it impossible for her to travel home, she spent the night with the Röntgens, becoming almost a member of the family. Annemarie, a teenager, would sit on the stairs long after she was supposed to be in bed and watch the three adults through the banister, marveling at the joy they found in music. She remembered Alma's "long black frocks and red handkerchiefs." She had "fine dark hair with a wave," Annemarie said, "and a strong profile matched by a strong personality. When she talked her voice had a special quality; she had a very musical voice." The Röntgens found Alma's performances of Brahms unforgettable: "Alma played Brahms as he should be played," said Annemarie.

Alma brought a glow into the Röntgens' family life, Annemarie recalled, "despite the fact that by the beginning of October there was little to laugh about concerning the war." German forces had pressed far into Russia, and Hitler was launching the battle for Moscow. The Führer was confident that the Soviet Union would soon fall, and Britain, with its deplorable "martial spirit," would be the only enemy yet to crush.

Alma's intimate association with the Röntgens was illuminated forty years later when a young Utrecht artist, Charlotte Obermeyer-Groen, went through the music cabinet of her late father, Dr. J. J. (Jaab) Groen (who with Leonard and his father played in Alma's quartet in Utrecht). In the cabinet, Charlotte found a manuscript copy of a Johannes Röntgen composition, "Nocturne nach A," dedicated to Alma Rosé. Attached to the manuscript was a card dated 3 November 1941 (Alma's thirty-fifth birthday), which bore this inscription in Dutch:

Yearning for Alma

Sometimes I awaken in the night,
and my yearning grows for you and our music:
the absolute, when two souls become one,
the highest, most beautiful experience of mankind.

My yearning calls to you in the night—Alma, Alma.
It urges me toward you, and we know it is good.

I put my yearning into this piece of music,
and afterwards I was calm in the knowledge
that when you play, you reflect my soul,
as when I play, I reflect yours.

The dedication—testimony to a musical friendship of exquisite depth—had become separated from the nocturne until Charlotte found it in Dr. Groen's music cabinet.

Alma described her birthday and Röntgen's gift in a letter to Alfred of 6 November 1941. Foreseeing that communication with her brother would be severed if America entered the war, she affirmed her devotion to Alfred and Vati in every letter as if it might be the last.

First Alma expressed pleasure at an upturn in Alfred and Maria's fortunes in Cincinnati, adding that she fervently hoped Eugene Goossens in Cincinnati would agree to a performance of Alfred's composition *Triptychon.* In Ohio he had completed the orchestrations himself—"a laborious task," his sister commented sympathetically.[16]

The winter in Holland was bitter and cold, she wrote. She continued wistfully:

> Would it be possible to send me your *Regenlied,* Alfred? Mrs. Röntgen would love to learn it—I have sung it for her. . . . I am now playing the Vitali *Chaconne,* which Váša had in his repertoire.
>
> My birthday this year was as beautiful as it could be under the circumstances, seeing that I am really quite alone. I received exquisite flowers and from the Röntgens splendid fur mittens and a Nocturne which he composed for me. From Marye (where I live), a splendid black leather bag which she had, of course, owned previously, for something like that is no longer available. A tiny packet with genuine tea for about three or four cups. Wonderful, isn't it? Writing paper with a monogram. A piece of lavender soap. It is wonderful how everyone tried to give me joy, and I was happy to see that in spite of much turmoil, I have made friends here. . . .
>
> By the way, the daughter of Hendrik Andriessen, the well-known Dutch organist, is teaching me gratis. It is very good for me because I am quite bent with arthritis. . . .

I am really beginning to cook. Marye now lets me do it entirely on my own. . . . I would so love to master Vati's favorite dishes.

Your lonely
Alma

Heini sent birthday wishes in a letter from Vienna dated 15 October 1941. Evidently Alma had written to Heini earlier. Now, it was clear, he was ready to end the relationship:

Only now am I able to thank you for the nice letter. We were on vacation for a few days, and I found your letter only on my return.

For a long time I had contemplated writing you once again, but for one thing, I never found the right time and the peace, and besides I did not know your present address. I previously heard about you through Dr. Kraith, who visited me sometimes, but this is no longer the case. That you are materially fairly well off is very good news. I have often been very worried about you and wondered what would happen to you, and now I'm very pleased that you send me such favorable news.

About myself, there is nothing new to say. I am very satisfied and happy in my marriage, and have found the peace and contentment that I wanted. I'm pleased with the results of my work. I have found it satisfies me so much that perhaps the most important thing (although marriage is not everything) has been put into the background and sometimes almost disappears completely.

I think I have changed quite a bit. You might not be able to imagine it, but it is so. Everything is not quite 100 percent. In my daily life I seldom encounter extraordinary change or excitement, so I cannot write much about that.

Above all there is a lot of work. Otherwise I am mostly at home—we go out rarely, and I mainly read and rummage in my books. Up to now I have bought for my little library almost two thousand books, and they give me great pleasure.

In addition, I have found a place among practicing musicians. I tell you this only so you can laugh about it a little. With perseverance, I play the most beautiful songs on the accordion.

You might be interested that . . . Tom [Heini's brother] and his wife, who were married a few weeks after I was, are expecting an heir within the next few days with great excitement. I myself will postpone this for a time, because we have an apartment that is too small. We are urgently looking for a house to buy, but hardly anything is to be found.

I have now written you quite a lot, but probably not what you wanted to hear. And I would like to write you more about that, but it is impossible. In any case, I think of you very often.

> I wish you a happy birthday, which is now quite close. All the best, with all love and good will,
>
> Dein Heini

The letter, preserved in Alma's file in the War History Documentation Center in Amsterdam, does not mention that the same month, Heini's father turned over management of the publishing side of the Carl Ueberreuter enterprise to Thomas and the Vienna-based paper-making operation to Heini. Thus the brothers became the sixth generation of Salzers to head the conglomerate.

Despite his frequent expressions of concern about Alma's and Vati's finances, it should be noted that Heini—like Váša Příhoda—never offered material help.

IN THE FALL of 1941 Marye became pregnant. Alma was almost as pleased and excited as she was. The details of the pregnancy became a major topic in her letters to friends and relatives in Vienna.

Grasping at every hint of safety and continuity, Alma devoured letters from every source and was eager for any scrap of news. She sometimes asked Alfred for word of Alma Mahler-Werfel and Bruno Walter in the States. Arnold, in London, renewed contact with Anna Mahler, who sculpted a bust of her Uncle Arnold during this period,[17] delighting in his rambling tales about his early years.

Alma had not heard from Vati directly since the previous spring, when she received a brief message through the Red Cross during a brutal Luftwaffe blitz. Determined to destroy the British Royal Air Force and demoralize the British people, the Germans had continued their air offensive and stepped up fearsome night bombings. Alma worried endlessly about Vati. She was reminded of him, she wrote to Alfred, when she heard a radio broadcast featuring a Schubert quartet that was one of the last pieces they played together.

Alma begins her last letter to Alfred, written 20 November 1941, with a birthday wish for "my dear, dear Alferle" and ends with an apology for "writing when I am so 'down'—but is it any wonder?"

> Last night I dreamed I was in New York—and I was so happy.
>
> Aren't you glad that Vati is no longer at home [in Vienna]? . . . If I did not have my music, I would not know how to deal with life—but that is my good fortune (as compared with others). For the first time on Monday I shall play the *Chaconne* by Vitali, which Váša always played. It is a splendid piece of music.
>
> We all have stomach disorders—am curious how long that will go on. When will there be a *Wiedersehen* for us? This lack of living one can never retrieve.

If only I knew how Vati was getting along—it's been such a long time since I have heard from him. . . .

I often play four-hand piano now, so I fondly remember how we used to do this together. . . .

Your Alma

Correspondence between Alma and Alfred ended abruptly after 7 December 1941, when Japanese bombers attacked the U.S. Pacific Fleet at Pearl Harbor, taking the Americans as well as the Germans by surprise. It was a sneak attack worthy of the Führer himself, and Hitler applauded the Japanese aggression. In a matter of days, Germany and the United States were at war, and direct communications between Nazi-controlled Europe and the U.S. ceased.

13

Council of War

Experience and reflection pitilessly presented me with the blackest, most hopeless view of the world; longing, intuition, and the revelations music brought me were the only things that calmed and consoled me.—Bruno Walter

One cold December morning in 1941, the composer Géza Frid and his wife were surprised by a telephone call from a woman whose name—Rosé—they recognized, although they did not immediately recall meeting her previously. She reminded Frid that they had met the year before at a house concert, when they had talked about the terrors of bombing, a raid on Italy in particular. She asked if she could visit him at home in Amsterdam and possibly play some music with him; she said she would bring her violin.

Frid extended an invitation, and on the appointed day Alma appeared at the door, her cheeks bright from the winter wind. Frid and his wife recalled greeting a tall, strikingly attractive woman who was "perhaps a little overweight."[1]

Frid was thirty-seven at the time and known internationally as a composer of works drawing on Hungarian folk music and as a pianist and interpreter of Bartók, who with Kodály had been his teacher in Budapest. Frid had settled in Holland in 1929 and built an outstanding career; he had known Ravel and Debussy and played with orchestras conducted by Pierre Monteux, Serge Koussevitzky, and Willem Mengelberg. With some reverence, he recalled hearing the Rosé Quartet playing in Hungary when he was a youth.[2]

After polite preliminaries and a warm drink, Alma and Frid began to play together. Four decades later, Frid remembered the pleasures of the encounter. In his lifetime, he said, he had played with a hundred and twenty of the world's foremost violinists, and Alma remained prominent in that company. "She was such a special somebody . . . such a pleasant person to play with. She didn't put herself ahead of another artist. She was not a show-off. It went so wonderfully well that we immediately played sonatas. We played the three Brahms, the Beethoven 'Kreutzer,' and Mozart sonatas. We decided to arrange house concerts." Frid added, "Words cannot describe her 'Kreutzer' Sonata."

There was no question of romance, but Frid, like Johannes Röntgen, became an intimate and adoring musical partner. He and Alma continued their practice sessions at the Frid home, and on 28 December 1941 they presented an afternoon sonata concert in Utrecht at the home of Frieda Meijer. Alma noted on the printed program that she earned 70 fl. Their practice sessions broke off in January and February 1942, which were so cold that both Alma and Marie Anne Tellegen moved in for a time with the Meijers, whose home had central heating.

By the time Alma and Frid met, the Germans were exerting severe pressure on the Jews in Holland. Frid said: "We had to be very careful. Sometimes we met only at the house where the concert was being held." He and Alma usually traveled to their engagements separately, because when they were together they might be tempted to communicate in German, a language they had in common. If the Dutch heard them, they would be frowned upon; if the Germans heard them, they would very likely be questioned. For engagements in Leeuwarden and Groningen, which required overnight stays due to curfew regulations, he and Alma never stayed in the same house. To protect them both, Frid at no time asked where Alma lived. Nor did he ever ask her age, because "you don't ask a violinist of her stature how old she is." In fact, she was only two years younger than he.

Frid never knew anything about her travel permit, "for that was her business, whether she used false papers or not." He did know that Alma's status had changed by March 1942.

Their last two concerts, in Hattem then in Hilversum on 6 April 1942, were acts of special courage. In Frid's words:

> We knew it was the last time we would be able to travel and play together. We played unbelievably beautifully. We played through until four in the morning, and the people gave us a lot of money—hundreds of guilders. They gave it with open arms. . . .
>
> She played everything outstandingly. Why, oh why, had she been so stupid as to return to Holland after she was safe in England in 1939?

By the time Hitler invaded Russia, in June 1941, he had given orders for the annihilation of European Jewry. At the Wannsee Conference in Germany on 20 January 1942, Reinhard Heydrich, the chief of the SD (the Nazi Security Service), addressing high officials of the SS as well as the SD, said frankly: "In the course of the Final Solution of the European Jewish problem, approximately eleven million Jews are involved." The clear message was that all were to be exterminated. Heydrich proceeded to lay out the Nazis' plan. Jews who were not already in the conquered lands of the East were to be taken there, separated by sex, and used as labor. Those who were able to survive—the strongest among them—would be "treated accordingly, since these people, representing a natural selection, are to be regarded as the germ cell of a new Jewish development." In other words, survivors would be put to death.[3]

By April 1942 the Germans were showing their design beyond conquest, and the Jews of Holland were completely terrorized—they were either in hiding or preparing for the worst. All Jews had been ordered to register a year earlier. After May 1942, they were forbidden to use trains. Westerbork, a camp the Dutch had built to house refugees from Germany, became a holding camp for Jews destined for forced labor and concentration camps.

Alma risked lunch with Mady Meth in January 1942. Mady's brother Eugene had fled with his fiancée through France to safety in Spain, and Mady and her mother had moved to Utrecht, where Mady and Alma renewed their friendship.

On 4 February 1942, Alma made an ominous entry in the small notebook where she jotted down reminders: "Hollandse Schouwburg—van Raaltje." Had Albert van Raaltje, conductor of the Jewish Symphony Orchestra—the Jewish musicians permitted to play only Jewish music in Jewish venues—been summoned to a former Dutch theater now known as the Jewish Theater? Jews were ordered there and kept until their transfer to Westerbork or to Vught, another holding camp. In fact, Van Raaltje was deported a few months later.[4]

As Nazi pressures mounted, Alma's safety became a critical concern for her Dutch friends. People liked her so much, explained Miss Tellegen. "She was so much more spontaneous in her reactions, so much warmer in her friendships than we are accustomed to."

Alma knew that if she could marry a non-Jew, she might be safe. She was in love with Leonard Jongkees, and he professed to love her. But they had decided against marriage, at least for the time being. If Leonard and Alma married, it would be for love, not for the safety a marriage document could afford. To complicate the situation, Leonard was soon to leave Utrecht for Zwolle to complete his residency, and he and Alma would be separated.

Alma's first thought was Theo Bakker. She was fond of him, and they had continued to see each other regularly even after her stormy departure from his aunt's home. They did not meet as lovers—indeed they rarely spoke of their personal lives; but Theo, as a young lawyer dealing with the problems of the occupation, understood Alma's dilemma and in many an open-hearted conversation had shown his eagerness to help her.

It is a measure of Alma's desperation that she swallowed her pride and proposed that Theo marry her to give her the protection of his name. As gently as possible, Theo said that he could not help her in this way. He was in love with Antonia Boelen and committed to marrying her. Moreover, his career presented obstacles. He had acquired the right to represent fellow Dutch accused of offenses by the Germans, even to carry their cases to courts in Germany. Professionally he was walking a tightrope, and marriage to Alma would have compromised his ability to represent his Dutch clients. It might also have hastened Alma's arrest.

In early February 1942, Ed Spanjaard and Marie Anne Tellegen, both lawyers, met privately with the Staerckes at their home to discuss Alma's plight. Alma herself was not present. Gathered around the dining table, her friends held a council of war. They too had concluded that Alma should marry a non-Jew, and quickly. The Germans, aware of the growing number of "mixed" marriages intended to protect the Jewish partner, had announced that after March 1942, such marriages would no longer be recognized.

All agreed that marriage was the best course, but marriage to whom? It was clear that the prospective husband should be "whitewashed Aryan," as Marye recalled. Under the circumstances, and out of respect for Alma, they decided that the candidate need not be interested in women, nor have any expectation of consummating the marriage.

Ed Spanjaard, embarrassed by his own suggestion, came up with the most likely candidate: a thirty-four-year-old Dutch cousin of Paul Staercke's born in Singapore when his parents had lived in Indonesia. A sickly child, the young man had grown up in Holland depending on his mother for support. Now he was a childlike dreamer who wandered Utrecht aimlessly, sometimes calling himself a medical student but in truth, in Marye's words, "just loafing and wasting his mother's money." His name was Constant August van Leeuwen Boomkamp, and he was "Aryan" through and through. At least Connie and Alma shared a love of music: "If you heard someone in the streets whistling any classical tune, almost note perfectly, day or night, it would be Connie," said Marye. During the marriage, he and Alma would continue to live separately, and annulment would be easily accomplished once peace returned.

For Connie, as he was known to his relatives and acquaintances, the matter was simple. When his family tracked him down and made the proposal, he replied warmly, "That is something I can do."[5]

The situation was awkward. Marye continued: "We didn't know how to break it to Alma, but we banked on her good sense and her desire for self-preservation. We asked Ed Spanjaard to tell her, complete with the warning that it was the only way out."

Alma offered no resistance. A penciled entry in her notebook dated 8 February 1942 shows that her sense of irony persisted: "VERLOBUNGSTAG—engagement day." Her immediate response was to send a message through the Red Cross to her father. She did not mention the coming marriage but assured him that she was safe.

Alma and her friends moved quickly. Public notice of the coming marriage, akin to banns, was issued on 16 February 1942. It was a delicate moment.

The Germans, aware that marriage could serve many purposes, were known to have arrested other couples who published such notices, but Alma and Connie were not challenged.

The marriage was not simple to arrange. Connie had to have an affidavit confirming his birth in Singapore, which was now controlled by the Japanese, and Alma had to provide an affidavit confirming her divorce from Příhoda. The date for the civil ceremony was set for 4 March 1942.

Marye described the wedding day as traumatic, not because there was any question of not going through with the ceremony, but because it was so difficult to keep track of Connie, who was likely to wander off at any moment. Alma and Marye had lunch together then joined Connie and Paul at the public building where the wedding would take place. The couple took their place in a long line.

It was terrible, Marye said, to see so many waiting to be married with so little fanfare. The motley crowd included those obviously in love, those whose bulging dresses revealed their own kinds of necessity, and those—like Alma—for whom matrimony could mean life or death. The Van Leeuwen Boomkamps came away with marriage certificate in hand. Alma would continue to live with the Staerckes, and Connie would resume his wandering. The contrast could not have been more total between this hollow ceremony and the joyful event in 1930 when Alma married Váša Příhoda.

Alma was quick to notify her correspondents in Vienna of the change in her status. By the end of the month, she was receiving mail addressed to Alma van Leeuwen Boomkamp–Rosé.

DUTCH CELLIST Carel van Leeuwen Boomkamp had grown up with Connie, his cousin, and knew of his marriage to Alma. He also knew there was no chance that Connie and Alma would live as man and wife.[6]

Carel van Leeuwen Boomkamp recalled with some bitterness a day not long after the marriage when as a young teacher, he was giving a lesson at the conservatory in The Hague. Director Henk Badings opened the door and berated him for hiding his secret marriage.[7] The musician, who was not married, denied the accusation. Badings then produced a copy of a letter the Nazis had sent to him for approval or rejection. Signed "Mrs. C. van Leeuwen Boomkamp," the letter was an application for permission to tour France.

Obviously Alma was hoping to be mistaken for the well-known cellist's wife. Had her "tour" been approved, she could have passed some checkpoints with semi-official status and might have escaped from Holland to Allied territory. She had neglected to forewarn Carel van Leeuwen Boomkamp of her plan, and he saw her use of the family name as opportunism. The cellist never forgot those tense moments during the occupation when he was challenged by all-powerful officialdom. Permission for Alma's tour was of course denied.

IN LONDON, the Rosé Quartet continued to make frequent appearances, including a performance at Wigmore Hall celebrating the centenary of the Vienna Philharmonic. Arnold played with his customary exuberance; audiences could not suspect the weariness in his heart.

In May 1942, Oskar Kokoschka presented Arnold with a watercolor still life inscribed with the dedication "To the god of the violin, in your winter of exile." The painter's expression of friendship and sympathy touched and pleased him.

AFTER MAY 1942 the Jews of Holland, Belgium, and France were required to wear a six-pointed star outlined in black on bright yellow cloth the size of a palm, bearing the inscription "*Jood*" or "*Juif*" (Jew). This was to be affixed to the left breast of outer garments and worn at all times. Typically of Alma, she did not wear the star—at least Leonard and her other friends do not remember her wearing it.

Protesting the humiliating yellow star order, many non-Jewish Dutch wore yellow flowers in their left lapels. Others in Holland as well as France and Belgium boldly wore the star themselves, taking it as a badge of honor. The Germans were quick to stamp out such protests, jailing "friends of Jews" and even sending them to concentration camps.

Some Germans, too, were shamed by the yellow stars that marked Jews as separate from the rest of humanity. Writer Ernst Jünger, who served in the German army of occupation in Paris that summer, recorded his reaction in a diary entry of 7 June 1942:

> In the Rue Royale, I encountered the yellow star for the first time, worn by three young women who came by arm in arm. This insignia was given out yesterday, the recipients forced to hand over one point of their clothing ration. In the afternoon I saw the star more frequently. On such an occasion there is no looking back. At such an instant, I was embarrassed that I was in uniform.[0]

At the end of May 1942, Amsterdam's Jewish Council was forbidden to issue further travel permits, and Alma's mobility came to an end. The president of the council, believing the Allies would soon invade Western Europe, said that he went along with the Germans because "in two or three months at the most, the war will be over."

This belief was widespread. The Germans had suffered their first severe setback of the war in Russia during the harsh winter of 1941–42, and Hitler's armies no longer seemed invincible. By the third spring of the war, in 1942, Axis forces—including German, Romanian, Hungarian, Italian, Slovak, and Spanish divisions—were engaged in the Soviet Union, in the West, in North Africa, and on the open sea, attempting to carry out multiple offensives simultaneously. Some doubted that they possessed the military strength to prevail across such scattered fronts. With Roosevelt, Churchill, and Stalin now united in opposition to Hitler, waves of optimism swept through Holland, nourished by BBC and Radio Orange broadcasts predicting an early liberation. The Germans themselves reinforced rumors that the Allies would soon arrive in the West by undertaking extensive work on seaside defense installations and moving seasoned troops from the Russian front to the coast.

In May 1942 one German officer reported to Colonel Lang, the Wehrmacht field commander based in Utrecht, that the "English radio had been heard to promise the Dutch would be liberated by the end of the month." With reviving hopes of liberation, the Dutch engaged in every form of foot-dragging.[9] In official reports to the military hierarchy, Colonel Lang noted that "sickness" had become the most popular Dutch sport, as the people of Holland avoided any activity that would help the Germans.[10] Doctors went so far as to drug patients to prevent their deportation from Westerbork or Vught.

For the Jews of Holland, these were nightmarish days. People one had come to love suddenly dropped out of view, never to be heard from again. It was impossible to know if they had gone into hiding, escaped, been picked up for work in Germany, or been arrested and "sent East."

One day the Engers were gone, the downstairs flat suddenly abandoned. A notice had been posted on their door ordering the inhabitants to report to Westerbork. The resourceful Engers were prepared: they had obtained a medical certificate permitting them to enter a hospital. This was a detour en route to a hiding place, where they spent the remainder of the war. Marye and Alma, finding the apartment deserted, spent a day retrieving valuables the Engers were unable to take with them and putting them into storage. When the Germans came to the house, little remained to be confiscated.

Kurt and Liselotte Röder were less fortunate than the Engers, although they had many offers of help if they chose to go into hiding. They made every effort to send their baby to Denmark to the home of Liselotte's sister, Annemarie Selinko, who had married a Danish diplomat. When that proved impossible, they opted to report to Westerbork and requested to be taken as a family to Theresienstadt, where they had heard that families had a chance of survival.

In her letters Alma mentioned the Röders for the last time on 13 June 1942; it is unlikely that she ever knew their fate. Liselotte and the baby were gassed in Auschwitz. The grieving Kurt reportedly escaped briefly from the camp, was captured in Budapest, and perished in an earthen bunker cell designed for torture and slow death.[11]

IN MID-JUNE 1942, Johannes Röntgen presented Alma with a hand-copied version of his violin sonata, which she had played with him fourteen times since their first shared engagement almost a year before. They would have only one more opportunity to make music together, during a rehearsal in September, when Röntgen came to visit Alma in the Staerckes' home.

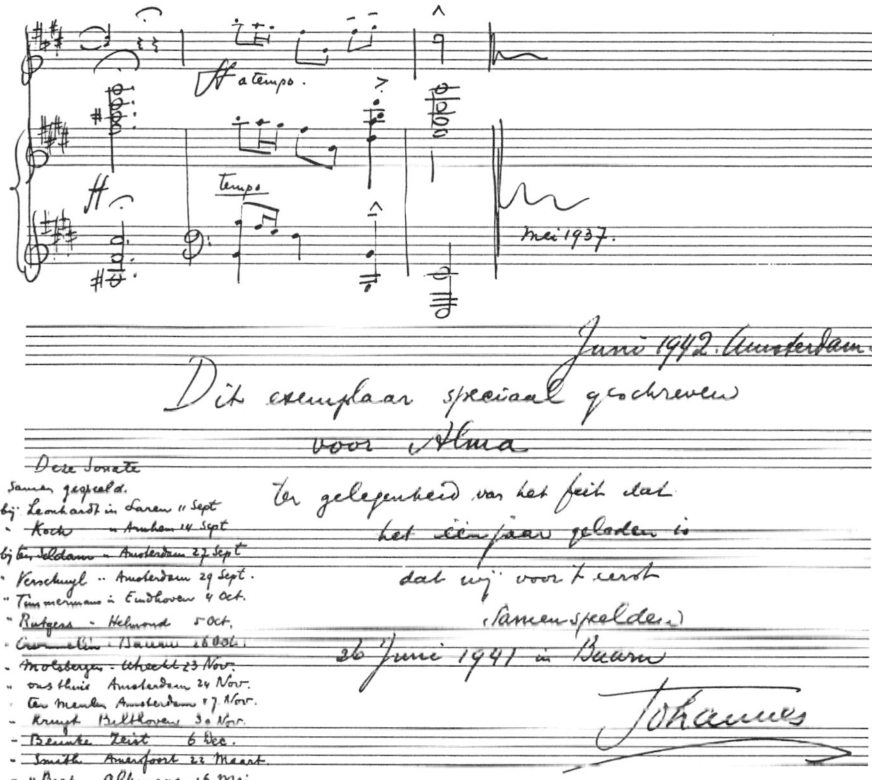

Johannes Röntgen's farewell gift to Alma: a copy of his violin sonata, inscribed to her and listing (at left) each occasion on which they had performed the sonata together.

On 22 June 1942 in Berlin, Adolf Eichmann, head of the "Jewish office" of the Gestapo, announced his plans for Holland. Forty thousand Jews were to be sent east for what was euphemistically called "labor service." Deportations via the transit camps Westerbork and Vught began in July. "Times of warning" were finished, wrote Wehrmacht Colonel Lang.

In June 1942, the Staerckes had a baby girl. Marye and Paul decided to call her Jessamin. When they went to the appropriate bureau to register their daughter's birth, they were told the name could not be used: it was not on the list approved by the Germans. The baby was rechristened Hermeline, a name acceptable to the officials. Alma shared her hosts' joy at the birth and their outrage at the compulsory name change. Marye, touched by the depth of her feeling, said years later: "I remember Alma's admiration of the baby, and my feelings of sympathy. She had the kind of life in which a child had no place, and she suffered constantly from the fact that she didn't have a child of her own. I remember thinking that. She didn't put it into words, but I felt it."

DURING THE summer of 1942, Alma spent a good deal of time with Marie Anne Tellegen in the country and only occasionally made music with her friends. On 7 July she wrote to Anny Kux Poláková in Bratislava that she and Mady Meth had celebrated Mady's birthday in May. Her mother had died, and Mady too now lived alone. Alma concluded, "Loneliness is really the worst thing in life."

The BBC carried a report that Váša Příhoda had killed himself in Prague in response to persecution by the Gestapo. The next morning, German police burst into his room and photographed him still in his pyjamas, holding a calendar and pointing to the date to prove he was still alive. For the Germans, it was a chance to discredit the much-trusted BBC. The radio report of Příhoda's demise prompted Dory Hetherington to write to Alfred: "Alma will be sad."

On 9 July 1942 Alfred received a note from Alma through the Red Cross telling nothing of her present predicament. The day the note arrived, the Jewish Symphony Orchestra, which included many musicians Alma knew well, gave its twenty-fifth and final concert; a week later it was deported. Systematically, the Nazis began to deport foreign-born Jews then proceeded to deport Dutch Jews.

The Germans treated France, Belgium, and Holland as one in handling the "Jewish question." On 14 July 1942, all Jews born between 1902 and 1925 were declared eligible for the labor force. The next day Jews were denied telephone service. In France, Adolf Eichmann demanded that the three deportations of Jews from Paris each week be increased so as to rid the country of Jews as quickly as possible. In a mass raid in Paris, twenty-eight thousand Jews were rounded up and jammed into the Vélodrome d'Hiver, a sports stadium designed to hold fifteen thousand.

In this time of stepped-up depredations against the Jews, Fryke Oostenbrug, a Hollander, cycled the back roads of Friesland to carry provisions to those in hiding, "sometimes getting help for a sick child." Engraved in her memory to this day are the terrified "brown-eyed ones in a country of blue eyes."[12] The comfortable Jews of Holland had become hunted people.

Alma appears to have had a plan for escape as early as 21 July. Without revealing any details, she wrote to Anny: "I am happy that I will finally be with Vati, and then I can take care of him. . . . I know a lot of people here who are very nice to me, but I do not belong with them. I do belong with my violin. I think these difficult times have improved my playing."[13]

On 2 August 1942, Alma again wrote "Hollandse Schouwburg" in her small notebook. She made no further entries until 8 September.

On this day in August, the Germans began a roundup of Jews who had been baptized Catholic, although for a time they would spare Protestant-baptized Jews. The Catholic church had left to its clergy whether or not to read a letter of protest, originating with the Protestant Synod, against the deportation of baptized Jews; many clergy chose to read and affirm the letter. In contrast, the Protestant hierarchy had accepted the German offer of a bargain: if its clergy agreed to suppress the letter of protest, the Germans would not seize and deport Protestant Jews.[14]

On 2 August Alma was home alone; the Staerckes were away on vacation. Uniformed police burst into her room, arrested her, and took her to Hollandse Schouwburg in Amsterdam.

Alma was unprepared for the scene that greeted her in the former theater. Some prisoners and their families had been held at the Schouwburg for weeks, appealing for their freedom or awaiting the moment when they would be herded into trains for transportation to "work camps" in the East. Auschwitz was the usual destination.

During the day, chairs were arranged in the main hall in facing rows, with a center aisle leading to the stage. In the evening, the chairs were stowed away and straw mattresses thrown on the floor. Those held at the Schouwburg had been incarcerated without any preparation, and hygiene and sleep were next to impossible. Children screamed night and day, and the terrified crowd milled about, taunted by Nazi guards. So many prisoners were driven to suicide that on 5 August, an order at the Amsterdam police headquarters called for the regular posting of lists of Jewish suicides.[15]

Plunged into this chaos, Alma insisted that she was a partner in a mixed marriage, but her protestations fell on deaf ears. After several frantic hours, she managed to get messages through to the Staerckes and to Marie Anne Tellegen, who rallied to her aid. The influential Miss Tellegen went to the top of the German command to make the case for Alma's release. At the same time, the Staerckes located Connie van Leeuwen Boomkamp and alerted him to be ready with papers showing the Van Leeuwen Boomkamp family tree and the certificate affirming his marriage to Alma. The concerted efforts bore fruit, and Alma was released before nightfall.

Leonard Jongkees, though often away at Zwolle, was in Utrecht when Alma returned from Hollandse Schouwburg. Alarmed at news of her arrest, he rushed to the Staerckes' home, where he found Alma alone and desolate in her third-floor room. Her nerves had been shattered by her experience. He stroked her hair and tried to comfort her, as she cried and laughed at the same time. Leonard recalled: "Alma was hysterical. She had seen her own death for the first time. I stayed with her for hours. She had never cried as she did that day. Like a drowning person, she saw her whole life flashing before her. She talked for hours."

To Leonard, her ravings sounded like a "first-person obituary." Finally

Alma said, "I'm so tired, I had better go to sleep now." She asked if she could name him in her will.

KNOWN IN Dutch history as Black Thursday, 6 August 1942 was a raiding day when two thousand Jews were arrested in a brutal display of force because too few Jews were reporting for transport to work camps, and the trains to the East had to be filled. The next day, the Dutch underground paper *De Waarheid* carried a daring exhortation to the Dutch police: "Think of your human and personal duty—arrest no Jews and only make a show of carrying out orders directed against them. Let them escape and go into hiding. Remember that every man, woman, and child you arrest will be killed, and you are their murderer."[16]

The same day Alma, in despair, wrote a letter of farewell to Carl Flesch, who was still in Holland, protected since March by his status as a "blue knight":

> There is no other way to take leave of you. With that you will know everything! I'm leaving—trying to get to freedom. Otherwise I shall perish.
>
> At this time I would like to tell you once again: I know that only you made it possible that my father now lives in a free country. No human being in this world can do more for me than you have done. And my feelings for you I do now commit to paper. I want you to know them.
>
> Shall I see you again in this life? God protect you. I embrace you in spirit.

Following the crisis of Alma's arrest, Leonard and Alma wrote to each other almost daily. Leonard urged her to hold on to her strength and courage, signing his letters "*T à T*" for "*tout à toi*" (entirely yours).

On 18 August 1942, Alma appealed directly to the office of Reichskommissar Arthur Seyss-Inquart in The Hague to be allowed to remain in Holland for the remainder of the war so that she could see her father again when peace was restored. She hoped the name Rosé might strike a sympathetic note with the music-loving Nazi from Bohemia. The response, from culture department director Dr. Bergfeld, was a form asking for information about her two marriages and their status and inquiring whether either marriage had produced children.

Still another letter in which Alma sought to save herself was probably prepared in the office of Marie Anne Tellegen, who was immersed in a campaign to protect her. Writing in stilted legal language, Alma sought to exempt herself from further roundups of Catholic Jews:

> On the 24th day of September, the secretary of the City of Utrecht (second administrative division) has, on my behalf, forwarded a "statement

> of arrangement of a mixed marriage." On instruction of the administrator, this statement names my religion as R.C. (Roman Catholic), since this was the religion given on my first registration form.
>
> However, I was a member of the Roman Catholic Church for only a short period, and left the church some years ago. At birth I was baptized in the Evangelical faith, as you will see from the attached copy of the certificate of baptism.
>
> I request that in consideration of this, the submission forwarded to your office be changed from R.C. to Evangelical-Lutheran, and that the secretary of the second administrative division of the City of Utrecht be empowered to change the first registration form accordingly.[17]

In September 1942, Jewish partners in childless mixed marriages were marked for deportation. The Jewish marriage partners could escape the new rule only through sterilization, which would render them "racially harmless." The decree led to an illegal traffic in sterilization certificates, but Alma did not resort to this maneuver.

In his reports to the Wehrmacht, Lang noted mounting resentment among the Dutch against the German treatment of the Jews, the holding and shooting of hostages, and the seizure of fifty thousand bicycles. Among his lengthy reports was an account of an incident at Bergen op Zoom when a crowd of non-Jewish Dutch, in sympathy with Jewish neighbors forced to report to Westerbork, accompanied the Jews to the railway station with tears and open mourning. Another report complained that Dutch children were encouraged to play with Jewish children as a way of showing "overt sympathy" for the Jews.

The anti-German mood reached a peak in August 1942 just as hopes of liberation plummeted with the failure of an Allied raid at Dieppe, France, on the English Channel. The disastrous Allied attempt to gain a foothold on the Continent hit the Dutch "like a cold shower," Colonel Lang reported. The Hollanders' spirits were further dampened by low food stocks and the prospect of a cold winter short of fuel.

In mid-September Alma sent a twenty-four word message to Alfred via the Red Cross (the maximum length was twenty-five words). Again she asked whether his *Triptychon* had been performed, and she urged him to write to her every month.

On 14 October 1942 Alma received an order, complete with permission to travel, to appear two days later at the Zentralstelle for Jewish Emigration in Amsterdam. She was to bring all her documents as well as her husband's. A terse entry in her notebook—the two words "Marie Anne"—suggests that Miss Tellegen again saved her from arrest, for the travel permit was never used and remained among Alma's papers.

By this time the Jews of Holland had to remain at home from 8 p.m. to 6 a.m. and were forbidden to shop until after 3:15 p.m., after everyone else had

REPLY — RÉPONSE — ANTWORT

Message to be sent to inquirer—Message à renvoyer au demandeur
Mitteilung an den Anfragesteller zurückzusenden

(not more than 25 words, family news of strictly personal character.) (*25 mots au maximum, nouvelles de caractère strictement personnel et familial.*) (*nicht über 25 Worte nur persönliche familiennachrichten.*)

HAPPY RECEIVED YOUR NEWS.
SEVERAL INQUIRIES WITHOUT ANWSER
DONT PLAY SINCE MAY. WAS YOUR
COMPOSITION PERFORMED?
DO WRITE EVERY MONTH
OTHERWISE UNBEARABLE
LOVE KISSES

Date — *Date* — *Datum* September 13th 1942

Signature — *Unterschrift* Alma Rosé

Please write very legibly **Prière d'écrire très lisiblement** **Bitte sehr deutlich schreiben**

The Red Cross telegram Alma sent to Alfred in September 1942.

picked over the scarce goods in the stores. (Two years later, starving Dutch in every "racial" category would resort to eating flower bulbs.)

Roundups became more frequent. Thirteen-year-old Anne Frank, already in hiding in Amsterdam, noted in her diary in mid-October 1942 that the Gestapo were taking away her family's Jewish friends and acquaintances in droves, treating them roughly and sending them in cattle cars to Westerbork then on to "faraway and uncivilized" places. "We assume that most of them are being murdered. The English radio says they're being gassed." In mid-November, the young Anne made this chilling entry: "In the evenings when it's dark, I often see long lines of good, innocent people, accompanied by crying children, walking on and on, ordered about by a handful of men who bully and beat them until they nearly drop. No one is spared. The sick, the elderly, children, babies and pregnant women—all are marched to their death."[18]

Alma's notebook contains only a few entries after her terrifying experience in the Schouwburg in August. She jotted reminders of her final rehearsal with Röntgen in September and two sessions with the quartet; another entry says merely "Brahms." In November she noted an overnight visit to the Jongkees family in Zwolle, carefully copying Marie Anne's telephone number on the same page in case she should need help while traveling.

Anny sent Alma best wishes for her thirty-sixth birthday, adding that she was trying to arrange an invitation for Alma to perform in Czechoslovakia.[19] Such an invitation would prove useless, Alma replied in a letter dated 7 November 1942, because she would never get permission to leave. She continued:

> I am so happy that you thought of my birthday. Dearest, don't be sad if you don't hear from me. Things are not going well. Alfi's sister [disguising her own identity] was away in August. She had a terrible shock from which she could not recover for a long time.
>
> From Vati, I had a Red Cross letter. Thank God everything is all right there.
>
> I can't take this being alone anymore. Anny, I was never alone before and could always have the nice atmosphere of a home. And now—already three years alone! Will it never end? Please write me every fourteen days, and I shall write you. Quite often now I play chamber music, and I would like to do so again in Vati's quartet if it continues.
>
> I have again fallen hopelessly in love—on schedule, every three years after a terrible separation. He is a doctor thirty years old and moves this month to another city. Is that not bad luck? But maybe it is better so. Living here for the duration is impossible—at least that's what I keep telling myself. But the loneliness is unbearable.
>
> If you read this letter to anybody, please leave out the last sentence. A fervent kiss for you and your mother.

Alma drew up her will on 24 November 1942. She was brief and to the point: "I direct that my husband will not inherit any of my possessions. I name Miss Marie Anne Tellegen in Utrecht (upon her death or default, Doctor Leonard Barend Willem Jongkees) to arrange my funeral and dispose of my possessions."

14

Flight

We perish by that through which we thought we'd live.
—Baudelaire

With the wisdom of hindsight, many considered Alma's decision to leave Britain for Holland in November 1939 foolish and headstrong. Now a chorus of Netherlanders, pleading with Alma to go into hiding, encountered the same firmness of mind. Despite knowledgeable advice to the contrary and many offers of shelter from Dutch friends, Alma decided to attempt escape.

Marie Anne Tellegen described Alma's deliberations:

> I never understood why she did not try to leave Holland between the 10th and 14th of May 1940, as many people from Scheveningen did. When I asked her, she said friends had dissuaded her. . . .
>
> It was autumn [1942] when her plan to get away ripened. At first we tried very much to convince her to drop the idea and advised her to go into hiding, as so many others did, if they did not feel safe any longer. Thousands of people had to "take a dive" [*onderduiken* or *untertauchen* —literally, go below the surface]. But she always refused.
>
> She said she would be unable to bear the strain of living concealed, with the continuous dread of being discovered. Perhaps she was right. Many, many people who tried it were discovered and taken to Germany afterwards.
>
> It was a very hard time. We talked and talked, and at last she made her decision.[1]

Alma's reasoning proceeded from the depths of her psyche. She did not want her Dutch friends to run risks on her account. As she told the Staerckes and others who offered help, she could not live with the possibility that her actions might endanger them. If the Nazis came again for her at the Staerckes, even the baby Hermeline, whom she adored, could be taken away. Moreover, her identity was closely bound to her music. Without it, shut away in a hiding place, she felt she would cease to exist.

Marye Staercke, by that time "chained together" with Alma, who had lived in her home for nineteen months, wrote to Alfred four years later: "She was also terribly anxious that her temperament would not permit her to go underground, that she could not get along with unpredictable strangers with whom she might be placed. At the same time, she feared being held in a room by herself." These anxieties outweighed the fear of capture on the road. Marye, who understood Alma better than anyone else, had to agree that for her friend, who could not be content with anonymity, flight was the best course.

Alma also yearned to see her father. He would be eighty the following October, and she intended to celebrate this birthday at his side. She wanted to show Vari how hardship had honed her talent, and to care for him in his final years. In hiding she knew she could find no peace from her nagging concerns.

On 15 October 1942, Alma received an order to report to Westerbork. The Nazis in Utrecht, both German and Dutch, knew who she was and where she lived. The artificial nature of her marriage to one of the city's most visible eccentrics was public knowledge. It was essential that she set her plans in motion without delay.

Through Marie Anne Tellegen, with her contacts with officialdom, Alma knew the risks she ran. Miss Tellegen was certainly aware that only a small number of those transported from Westerbork and Vught to the East for "resettlement" were ever given the promised work. From the camps in the East there had been far too many reports of deaths due to "cardiac arrest" and "pneumonia."

Alma, Miss Tellegen, and Alma's other Dutch friends weighed her alternatives. There were two escape routes from the Netherlands—one leading through France to Spain, the other to Switzerland; but the "Spanish Road" was said to have been breached, and only the "Swiss Road" remained secure. Because Alma had numerous musical contacts in Switzerland, the northern route was preferable in any case.

The political situation, too, favored the Swiss Road. British and American troops under the command of General Dwight D. Eisenhower landed on the beaches of Morocco and Algeria on 8 November 1942, securing the Mediterranean for the Allies in one of the turning points of the war. Although Pétain, the leader of Vichy France, promptly broke off diplomatic relations with the U.S., Hitler doubted the Pétain government's desire to fight on behalf of the Axis. Violating the terms of the armistice, Hitler gave orders to seize unoccupied France, and on 11 November 1942 the Germans crossed the line that had divided the country since 1940. Under the circumstances, Miss Tellegen and Alma's other friends reasoned that the Germans would be so busy in southern France—especially in the month before Christmas—that they might be less vigilant along the route to Switzerland.

Outwardly Alma remained calm; only Marye and Marie Anne knew the extent of her feverish preparations. She took the time to tidy her affairs, writing to a Henk Viskers in Eindhoven to tell him he could keep a book she had lent him and sending out Christmas letters bidding her friends and relatives "*Auf Wiedersehen,*" which could be read as a standard Christmas greeting or a hopeful farewell. She sent goodbyes to the Bakker family and to Mady Meth. To Vati, she sent a Red Cross message saying merely, "All is well."

On one of their last nights together, Paul Staercke, with Alma and Marye, reviewed Alma's dilemma. If she insisted on trying to flee, he said, she should be prepared for any eventuality. False identity papers could put her in jeopardy. The dangers of betrayal, capture, even torture, were real. With this prelude he produced a surprise gift—a capsule of deadly prussic acid poison, which he had ordered made up at the hospital—and Marye proceeded to embed it in a tube of lipstick. Staercke assured Alma that the capsule's contents would bring certain death within fifteen seconds.

Alma accepted the capsule without batting an eye. Marye said forty years later: "She was so determined, there was never any doubt that Alma intended to use the bead of poison if circumstances demanded it."

MONDAY, 14 December 1942, was Alma's D-Day. On the eve of her departure, she sent a last message to Vati through the Red Cross with a veiled but reassuring message: "Justine's daughter is married."

She bade an emotional goodbye to Leonard, who had begged her to go into hiding. For the last time, she held the violin that had been her comfort and her provider; she could entrust it only to someone she loved and trusted. She handed her Guadagnini to Leonard with a postcard photograph of herself holding the violin; on the back was the handwritten message, "Not to be lost."

On a dark December morning, Alma slipped away to rendezvous with a man she had never met. The Staerckes were never to see her again. That morning they found a note on a table in her third-floor room, written in her firm, resolute hand: "I thank you, my dears. What we have endured together—that I have not forgotten, nor ever will. Alma—1941–1942, August–December."

Except for a picture of Alma that Marye kept for years, this note was the only evidence of Alma's presence in their home. To avoid incriminating the Staerckes, she never discussed the details of her escape plan with them, and she left her remaining possessions with Miss Tellegen, including her passport, programs of her house concerts, and her small notebook. Together they constitute a tangible memory of Alma in the files of the War History Documentation Center in Amsterdam. The concluding entry in her notebook signifies both release and resignation: "*Die längste Zeit ist vorbei.*" (The longest time is past.)

On the final page, Alma wrote her married name and that of her husband, Constant August van Leeuwen Boomkamp. Those were among the few personal references in the small diary. Even the Staerckes could not remember the exact day she left.

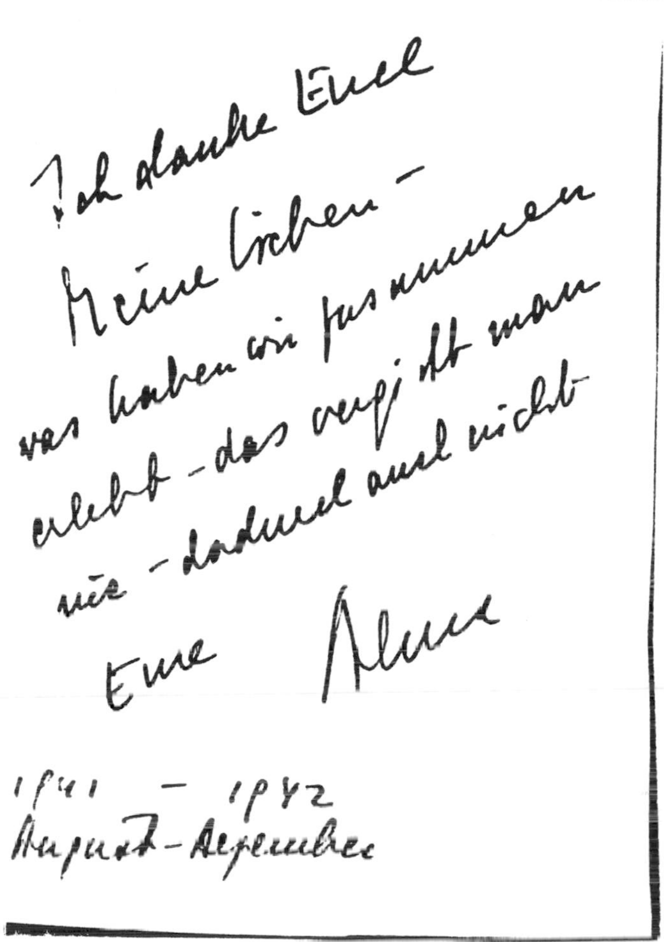

Ich danke Euch
meine Lieben –
was haben wir zusammen
erlebt – das vergißt man
nie – dadurch auch nicht
Eure Alma

1941 – 1942
August – Dezember

The note Alma left for the Staerckes when she fled Holland on 14 December 1942.

THE DETAILS of Alma's flight may never be verified. At least four versions have come to light, including the guarded recollections of the young man who accompanied her on the journey, reports that reached Alma's friends in Holland through Miss Tellegen, and closely related reports that reached her relatives after the war.

A young Dutch Jew was Alma's companion that December morning. He will be called "Martin" because, having spent many decades trying to forget the trauma of his flight with Alma, he has refused to allow his name to be used in this biography. He remembers only fragments of this critical episode in his life.

Both Alma and Martin had been near-fugitives for months, relying on their wits to evade the German and Dutch Nazis. Miss Tellegen had arranged both their passages, and the urgency of their situation was among their few common bonds.

Since 1941 Martin had carried false papers to avoid being sent to a German work camp. He worked in a safe house in Amsterdam (the former home of Antonia Boelen, Theo Bakker's sweetheart), a house in which many downed Allied airmen found shelter and avoided capture.[2] When he learned that a tradesman was going to inform on him, he attempted to escape. In his words:

> My first attempt to flee was, of course, without Mrs. vLB. In fact, I was alone, except for the people who helped me cross the borders. That "chain of escape" was infiltrated, of which I was warned in Lille in northern France. I managed to get back to Holland.
>
> My second attempt, together with Mrs. vLB., was one or two months later.[3]

Martin was doubly cautious the second time around, but with arrangements made by Miss Tellegen, he had new confidence.

Early that December morning, Martin and Alma met as strangers at Breda. The reluctant Martin did not say how they recognized each other. Neither wore the yellow star, and the papers that provided them with new identities did not bear the letter "J." Both carried a large sum of money, an amount prescribed by Miss Tellegen. Said Martin, "I was twenty-three. I was not interested in my traveling partner. I was trying to escape because I was—and am—a Jew. I was of an age when people were being sent to Germany."

It was prudent not to become too friendly and to remain as inconspicuous as possible. The less the two knew of each other, the better. If they were caught, they were on their own and would not be able to betray each other even under torture. There was no small talk. Martin did not know that Alma was a musician, nor that she came from Vienna. "I think Madame van Leeuwen Boomkamp spoke a little bit of Dutch," Martin recalled. "I certainly didn't speak German with her. I certainly did not speak French with her." (He added that he did not learn French until it became necessary when he was interned in France for the remainder of the war.)

There were a number of "lines" of escape to Switzerland. At each contact point, Alma and Martin received new instructions directing them to the next rendezvous. While they knew their destination was Switzerland, they at no time knew their full itinerary. This was another vital precaution: if they were captured and interrogated, they could reveal only a fraction of the resistance network.

From Breda, Martin and Alma took a bus to a point near the Belgian-Dutch border, then they walked to the home of a professional smuggler who was to help them across the frontier. Such smugglers, familiar with the routines of border guards and patrols, were available for hire: fugitives paid in cash. Martin remembers the first night, at the Belgium frontier, when he and Alma had their first contretemps. The smuggler told them in Flemish that it was too dangerous to cross the border that night and advised them to stay in his cottage with him and his wife. There was only one bed, which the smuggler and his wife offered to Alma and Martin. Martin said that Alma refused to share the bed with him, "although nothing could have been further from my mind at that moment than a tryst. I do not remember how the problem was solved, but I suppose I slept with the smuggler and Alma slept with his wife."

The next day, on foot, they crossed the frontier, guided by the smuggler. Martin does not recall the route they took from that point. Various people helped them on the way. "I assume each one gave us instructions on how to get to the next point and how to find the next contact." No doubt Alma, who was conversant in French and twelve years Martin's senior, helped in negotiations along the route. It took two or three days to reach Dijon. According to Martin, he and Alma were together every moment.

In Dijon, Martin says, "we certainly were betrayed, probably by the man who supplied us with false papers," for which they paid a handsome sum. The papers were to permit them to cross by train the two "red" zones forbidden areas between Dijon and the Swiss frontier. Martin's fragmentary version of events runs like this:

> We arrived in Dijon, somehow got in contact with the man who was to sell us the papers, who made an appointment with us in the restaurant where he gave us the false papers. I seem to remember that we had to wait for him a long time, and we got more and more nervous.
>
> We were already on the train which was going to take us to the Swiss border, standing in a very crowded compartment, when a couple of Germans in civilian clothes came in to check the papers. They were obviously interested only in us and said immediately that our papers were false.

Martin remains convinced that the Frenchman who sold them the papers in the "very big sort of restaurant in Dijon," or this man's "boss," betrayed them to the Germans. In another interview, he recalled that one Dijon contact appeared to signal to a woman in the background. His memories are as bitter as they are vague: "The whole trip cost a lot of money, which we paid to various people who helped us get to Dijon and to prison." Without warning, he and Alma were arrested on the train before it left Dijon for the Swiss frontier. The date was 19 December 1942.

"After our arrest," Martin said, "we were separated immediately." Taken to Gestapo headquarters at 9 Rue Docteur-Chaussier, he was told to drop his trousers so that his interrogators could see whether he was circumcised. During the interrogation Martin turned his false identification papers over to the Germans and told them his real name. He was not subjected to torture.

Back in Holland, confusion reigned. Leonard heard that Alma was safe in Switzerland. Some days later, he was stunned by news of her arrest. The version of events that eventually filtered back to Alma's friends was relayed through Miss Tellegen. She reported that Alma and Martin arrived at a safe house in Dijon and were arrested on the spot by the Gestapo, who had infiltrated the resistance network. This account of the arrest was believed for more than four decades.

As a main railway junction and communications center, Dijon teemed with Germans. According to Maquis Commandant Alberic Bernard Guillemin (known during the war as "Commandant Bernard"), a leader in the French underground, entering this city was like walking into the "lion's jaws." He and fellow Maquis veteran Raymond Pallot described wartime Dijon as a hotbed of covert operations. Both Britain and the U.S. had agents working in the city, and German surveillance was keen. "There were eyes everywhere to look over all Dijonnais, and especially to view new arrivals with suspicion," remembered Guillemin.[4]

Still another version of Alma's flight and capture, replete with detail, has surfaced in recent years. This is the account of Jean-Paul Gay, a native of Dijon who was a young courier for the French underground in December 1942. Gay's memory of Alma and Martin was triggered by Dijon author and journalist Jean-François Bazin, who in 1985 published requests for information concerning Alma's arrest in *Le Bien public* and *Les Dépêches,* two Dijon newspapers

The aristocratic M. Gay came from a noble line related to the Dukes of Burgundy and traceable, Gay says, to the family of Joan of Arc. During the war he lived with his parents, Léon and Mélanie Gay, in an imposing stone house the size of a small hotel at 57 Rue de la Préfecture, in the midst of German offices and billets and next door to the local préfecture. After Hitler came to power in 1933, the Gay home became a stopping point for those in flight, where many meals were served to hungry refugees. Every Monday funds would arrive from Paris—donations to be distributed among refugees in need. In Gay's memory, Alma and Martin were among these refugees.[5]

In a quiet voice devoid of pretense, Gay—interviewed in 1989—described the Dijon scene in mid-December 1942. According to his account, Alma arrived at the Gays' home before Martin did (although Martin said they were separated only after their arrest). Gay remembers that at the time, his parents were sheltering a Jewish family from Strasbourg, a well-known banker named Hem, Heym, or Hayem, with his wife and son.[6]

Although Alma was traveling under the name of Mme van Leeuwen Boomkamp, Hem introduced her by her full name to young Gay, who realized that it was dangerous to know the names of people on the run lest one were questioned by the Germans. Said Gay, "I think I knew her name was Alma Rosé, but I must confess to you that we preferred not to know family names—and immediately forgot them."

Gay found her charming and very distinguished, with "a sober elegance, very reserved, wearing a light-colored dress." He believed that she had lightened her hair to help in her escape, and he noticed that she favored one hip and leaned against the back of a chair for support when standing (a detail consistent with Alma's complaints about arthritis during the cold months in Holland).

It was warm for December, a "St. Martin's summer." Gay recalls the unusual weather because about the same time, he was infuriated when he saw a German in a neighboring building lean out the window in shirtsleeves and scrape the contents of a mustard pot into the Gay courtyard.

In a purse-sized datebook later found in Alma's room in Auschwitz-Birkenau, Alma had written the name "Suzanne Tikhonoff," with the address "Avenue Ville Neuve 39, Choisy-le-Roi"—a village south of Paris.[7] When Gay learned this, he began to fill in the blanks in the record of Alma's and Martin's itinerary. Emphatically, Gay said: "I know that after Choisy-le-Roi, Alma was being followed by the Germans. She explained the situation, but I don't know too many details. A contact in Choisy told Alma and Martin they had to leave. The Germans were watching them." He remembers that after her arrival in Dijon, Alma made several vain attempts to telephone Choisy. He also remembers that she received news from Choisy and came back from the telephone in tears. "Somehow, she seemed to feel responsible for something that had happened in Choisy."

Gay recalls that one of the escape routes from the north went through Choisy-le-Roi, despite the fact that the area was considered extremely dangerous, and he believes the Gestapo had taken over a safe house there. "I think the place was very close to the German offices," he said. "The Germans had 'marked' the house and the floor on which Mme Tikhonoff lived." At the time, he heard a report of a "great coup by the Gestapo in Choisy." Word had it that "someone was killed." Mme Tikhonoff was executed for her role in the French underground, Gay concludes, adding that "anyone with a Russian name was under Nazi suspicion anyway." Had Alma and Martin embarked on their flight from the Nazis on a route already breached by the Gestapo? Had they arrived at the supposed "safe house" in Choisy only to find it under Gestapo surveillance? Gay suspects that undercover police followed the fugitives from Choisy to Dijon in the hope of exposing other links in the underground chain.

A search of the archives in Choisy-le-Roi reveals that a Suzanne Tikhonoff (also spelled "Tichonow" in village records) lived at no. 9 Avenue Villeneuve rather than no. 39 as Alma had noted. Had she and Martin inquired at no. 39

by mistake, thus drawing hostile attention? According to Choisy archives, Suzanne Tikhonoff was arrested on 4 October 1942—more than two months before Alma and Martin left Holland—and released to an unknown fate on 24 April 1943. The reason cited for her arrest is "*question raciale juive*" or "Jewish racial question," a catch-all covering any number of charges that could be a pretext for arrest. The term "released" could also mean anything. A knowledgeable Choisy-le-Roi official surmised that Mme Tikhonoff died (possibly under torture), was executed, or was sent to Germany for forced labor or east to one of the death camps. City archives and local cemeteries yield no record of her presence in Choisy after April 1943.[8]

The Choisy-le-Roi archives further reveal that a "Boris Tichono"or "Tchikonoff" lived at the Villeneuve address until 1946. No "Tikhonoff" by any spelling still lives in Choisy-le-Roi, and none is buried in the local cemetery. Nazi hunter Serge Klarsfeld's records of deportations from Drancy, the transit camp near Paris, do not list a transport to any of the concentration camps in April or May 1943 after Mme Tikhonoff's "release" by the police, which supports Gay's contention that she was killed.

Gay continued with a bizarre story:

> I learned one day that Martin and Alma were walking down the Rue la Liberté from the Ducal Palace toward the Place Darcy and the eighteenth-century gate. Halfway down the street was the largest brasserie in Dijon at the time, the Brasserie du Miroir, much frequented by Dijonnais before the war, but during the war hardly ever patronized by anyone except Germans and a few French who went to listen to German concerts played in the loggia by five or six soldiers or officers. The orchestra played on a balcony overlooking the tables and bar. A staircase led to a high mezzanine.
>
> [In the brasserie, which Gay also entered] the Dijon natives mostly sulked and Martin lost patience, didn't stay very long, and wanted to take Alma along with him. But she lingered to listen to the music. . . . Her happiness could be read on her face, and when it came out that she was a musician, it was proposed that she go to the loggia to play with the orchestra. She went after some persuasion.
>
> I don't know whether it was her idea or someone else's that she should play with the orchestra. People next to me urged her to play with the orchestra. . . . After that, it was proposed that she should return to the restaurant and play regularly with the orchestra.

Had Alma behaved impulsively during Martin's brief absence from the Brasserie du Miroir? Or was the pressure from patrons at a neighboring table attracting so much attention that she had no choice but to play? As far as Gay is concerned, "It was Alma's love of music that caused her downfall." Gay's description of the Brasserie du Miroir meshes almost perfectly with Martin's recollection of the "very big sort of restaurant in Dijon," which he too described as having a "kind of loggia."[9]

Gay continued:

> On the main floor was a long bar down the left side of the room, ending where a woman cashier sat. Next to her was a room where an employee washed dishes. Three tables in front of the cashier, a young civilian perpetually watched the room, concerning himself with people he saw alone. He appeared to single out individuals, encouraging them to talk about themselves.
>
> This individual was a member of the *milice* [the "militia," French collaborators], possibly related to the cashier, and the server from the scullery was also from the *milice.* The cashier as well as the *milice* members were informers.
>
> An unknown courier then took Alma and Martin to obtain identity cards in the Café de l'Union in Place des Cordeliers,[10] which at that time was operated by a Monsieur Lacharnay, himself a member of the resistance. He was in touch with a resistance leader named Georges Picard, who obtained identity cards from the préfecture when needed. The cards were free; yet M. Lacharnay told M. Picard that in his presence, they had been sold to Alma and Martin.
>
> I found out too late—after their arrest—that Alma and Martin had paid for their cards.

Gay explains his detailed knowledge of Alma's and Martin's arrest by the fact that the banker Hem sent his son to follow the courier and the fleeing couple. Hem felt that if the courier were reliable, he might choose to follow the same course as Alma and Martin. According to Gay: "The son followed them and saw they had been arrested. We were all desolate. . . . M. Picard, of the liberation committee, later told me that justice was done [to those who had betrayed Alma and Martin]."

Alma and Martin were taken to Gestapo headquarters on Rue Docteur-Chaussier. Gay, his parents, and the Hem family feared that under torture they might reveal their route and contacts, but the Gestapo did not come for them. If Alma was tortured (Martin has said he was not), she did not betray her benefactors in Dijon.

Jean-Paul Gay wrote the above story and verified it in person to Professor William Bush of the University of Western Ontario in 1986. Seeking to confirm that Gay was not confusing Alma in Dijon with another escapee, Professor Bush showed him a picture of Alma. Gay exclaimed three times: "Truly, truly—that is she!"[11]

The register of the Dijon prison has vanished, but Alma became identified in German documents by various versions of her married name, Van Leeuwen Boomkamp.

Klaus Barbie, the Gestapo lieutenant later known as the "Butcher of Lyons," may have been in Dijon at the time of Alma's and Martin's arrest and instrumental in their capture.[12] Barbie had operatives in the city and kept rooms in Dijon's Hotel Terminus after October 1942. The brutal Barbie, the nemesis of Dutch Jews prior to his posting to France, was especially relentless in the Nazis' war on the underground network.[13] According to Barbie biographer Tom Bower, by the time Alma and Martin arrived in Dijon, the Gestapo had cracked the resistance in the city, and the escape route to Switzerland was closed.

Gay's memories contradict this statement, as does the testimony of John Weidner, a hero of the Swiss Road who saved the lives of nearly eight hundred Jews. In a letter of July 1986, Weidner insists that "the Swiss Road was never infiltrated, though arrests were made" through means other than penetration of the network.[14] Indeed Commandant Bernard and his Maquis were still making lightning attacks on the Germans from their forest camps when the Allies liberated Dijon in 1944.

In this debate it seems fitting that "Martin" should have the last word. In a letter of 15 October 1986, Martin wrote from bitter experience: "Mr. Weidner's statement that the Dutch road to Switzerland was never infiltrated is untrue. There was more than one road, and both roads I used [during two escape attempts] were infiltrated."

15

Enter Alois Brunner

Woe is wondrously clinging: the clouds ride by.—Anonymous

For almost a month after Alma's arrest, the record bears no trace of her existence. There is no evidence that she was tortured in the Dijon prison, but the practice was common. Word eventually reached Holland that she had suffered excruciatingly in Dijon and never fully recovered.

She and Martin were transported separately to an internment camp at Drancy, a satellite city still under construction on the Saint-Denis Road in the northeast suburbs of Paris. During the war years, seventy-six thousand Jews would be deported from Drancy, which the French memorialized as "the antechamber of the death camps." Most were sent to Auschwitz.

Drancy entry records of 12 January 1943 list Martin's and Alma's names. The latter is misspelled yet unmistakable: "Van Leeven Boomkamp, Alma (Rosé) Hol. 3.11.06 Vienne—Utrecht (Hollande)."[1] Alma's birthdate, 3 November 1906, was given correctly, as were her birthplace (Vienna) and last residence (Utrecht). For the first time in her life, Alma Rosé became an anonymous cipher: at Drancy, she was 18,547.

It was a busy day at the camp. There were fifty admissions and three departures. A fifty-seven-year-old woman died, and two prisoners were freed.

The Drancy complex consisted of five tall concrete buildings surrounded by wire fencing. Internees were held in four buildings in the center, which French police guarded and administered for the Gestapo. In these stark surroundings, Martin observed his twenty-fourth birthday five days after his arrival.

Political events had diverted the complex from its original purpose of providing low-cost housing. The Third Republic used it to house Communist prisoners, then the Germans used it for French prisoners of war. Finally it became the stopping point for a helpless mass of men, women, and children—Communists, Jews, and "friends of Jews" whose crime was to oppose Nazi policies.

Alma knew better than to try to contact her cousin Eleanor Rosé in Paris. For Eleanor's sake, it would have been unwise to make contact, and the chance that she or her daughter Farouel could help was remote.[2]

SS Colonel Helmut Knochen, who took over the Paris police on 26 January 1943, ordered that all Parisian Jews subject to deportation be dispatched to a holding camp such as Drancy to be ready for the next available transport. Massive roundups followed in Paris and elsewhere—anti-Semitic French officials called them "hygienic operations." Soon the rooms at Drancy were filled beyond capacity and inmates were forced to live in the staircases. There was never enough food to end the gnawing hunger. Disease and despair were rife, and personal cleanliness impossible.

The deportation campaign led to feverish efforts to produce baptismal certificates for those threatened with arrest as well as for the incarcerated. The desperate correspondence of Drancy—letters, notes, and cards gathered by Serge and Beate Klarsfeld—fills hundreds of files deposited in the YIVO Center for Jewish Research. Broken families appealed to the camp administration for help in finding children, husbands, mothers, cousins, grandfathers and grandmothers. There were offers to take and provide for inmates' children, and pleas to the clergy to intervene on behalf of baptized Jews or to submit "newfound" baptismal certificates for internees. Much money changed hands in the market for baptismal certificates that ultimately proved useless.

The journal of the Union Générale des Israélites Françaises reflected the turbulence of the era for the Jews of France. Beyond the theological discussions on the front pages were notices of the few Parisian restaurants and public baths still open to them. Pages were devoted to lists of the displaced who had sent messages and others whose whereabouts were sought.

In February 1943, news that the Germans had suffered a massive defeat at Stalingrad rekindled hope among the inmates at Drancy but brought no real relief from their miseries. Overcrowding, hunger, and disease persisted, and transports to the East proceeded like clockwork.

After a month-long silence, Marye Staercke and other Dutch friends began to receive letters from Alma, who seemed confident that with their help she would be released. Alma confided that she was better off at Drancy than she had been in the SS's Dijon jail. "Relocation in Poland" was the fate she most feared.[3]

In Holland, Marie Anne Tellegen leapt into action. On the one hand, she could cajole or negotiate with the Germans, and on the other, she could communicate with the underground. Within three weeks of Alma's arrival at Drancy, a made-to-order advocate in Paris was doing everything possible to help her. This was Emma Louise "Loulette" Villeméjame Wanecq, a young pianist with close connections to French musical society. Widowed when her husband, a French aviator, was shot down, she had since remarried. Loulette, who was devoted to Miss Tellegen, attacked Alma's problems with determination.

In mid-February 1943, two German officers were assassinated in Paris. In response the Germans instituted newly severe measures against Jews. Loulette wrote to Miss Tellegen on 22 February:

> Your friend Alma has written [in early January] to ask me to help her. Twice I have been able to send her food parcels, and I intended to continue with friends or through them to send her a package each week. But I have now learned that she is threatened with going farther away unless she receives her husband's identity papers. He would have to send his baptismal certificate, that of his parents, and those of his paternal and maternal grandparents—in other words, seven certificates.
>
> If it is impossible to procure these documents, he should send a certificate of his "non-Jewish status," his marriage certificate, and his and Alma's baptismal certificates. All these papers can be photographed documents.

Alma, traveling with false identity papers, had left her personal documents in safekeeping in Holland. Her marriage certificate was in Utrecht, attached to a copy of the Van Leeuwen Boomkamp family tree and an affidavit produced by Connie van Leeuwen Boomkamp in which his mother swore to his birth as a non-Jew in Singapore. Alma could only hope that her painstakingly assembled documents would arrive at Drancy in time and prove acceptable to the authorities.

The letter from Loulette continues:

> It is VERY URGENT that at least some of these items be sent to Alma, since she has nothing in her possession at the moment and the extension granted her expires on 8 March.
>
> Your friend tells me to tell you to write as often as possible, enclosing a card for her answer. I don't know what she means, because in her correspondence with me it is she, on the contrary, who furnishes me with the attached card on which to answer. Inquire about that.
>
> I don't need to tell you that I am using all my influence to procure protection for her from well-known musical colleagues. Alfred Cortot [the French pianist and conductor] has been informed about her situation, and I hope he will concern himself with her.
>
> As for me, I shall do everything that I possibly can for your friend, you may rest assured. But what frightens me is the short time at our disposal. You will soon see the young secretary in Rue Auber (a very nice girl), who will be in Utrecht on vacation, but I fear she will not be able to tell you more than you already know.
>
> My dear Marie Anne, when will we see each other? I wish it could be soon. You cannot know how sad and dejected I am. Have you heard of all the cruel deaths in my family? I have suffered a lot. . . .
>
> Hugs and kisses, in loyal friendship,
> Loulette

Marie Anne hastily gathered the requisite papers and arranged for the originals as well as a set of photographs to be delivered to Paris in February by couriers. One young woman assigned to the task was Pietronella d'Aquin Boot, who had shown the same spirit of resistance as Alma's friend Johannes Röntgen: as a member of a professional choir in The Hague, she had resigned rather than sign papers that allied her with the Kulturkammer. Mme d'Aquin Boot recalls:

> I was home in The Hague on holiday from France. Miss Tellegen came to see me at my parents' house, bringing the papers I was to take to France. I received her in my room and told her I was very, very frightened.
>
> With resonating authority, she exclaimed: "Oh, no, no. You must never be frightened."
>
> I said: "I am staying here only a few days, and what would happen if the Germans come and find the papers?"
>
> She said: "No. That's no problem at all." With a flourish, she then lifted the corner of the carpet and threw the documents underneath, and they were gone. You see, she was a very strong person.
>
> She was tall and thin. She was not beautiful. She was about forty-five at the time. She had a very characteristic Dutch face, and she was very courageous. . . .
>
> I visited her once later on. She was from a very old Dutch family. When she sat on the sofa, she resembled the portrait [of an ancestor] that hung on the wall behind her. She was very nice and very enterprising.
>
> So the day came when I had to take my train. To hide the clandestine papers, I put them between pieces of bread and packed them with my lunch right down at the bottom of the big bag. The first test came at the Belgian frontier. I was turned over to a German girl. We called them "gray mice"—they were auxiliary; they were not military, nor were they women SS.
>
> She asked me to follow her. Then she took me right under the station, into a cold, dark cellar, and told me to undress. She felt in my hair and everywhere and didn't find anything. And then I dressed. She began to look in my luggage. She didn't find anything, but she came to my bag where the sandwiches were, and one thing after another, she looked and looked.
>
> Then she came to the package with the sandwiches and said, "What's this?" I said it contained my sandwiches to eat on the train. I was scared stiff. I could have cried, but I didn't. Instead, I remember even asking her whether she liked her work. She didn't answer. She was not a nice person. I tried to be diplomatic, I think. She never opened the package of sandwiches with the documents.
>
> When I came to the French frontier, I was afraid the same thing would happen again, but nothing happened. When I arrived in Paris,

Gare du Nord, a friend who had been on leave a fortnight earlier welcomed me. She had carried the photographed copies of Alma's documents, while I carried the originals. When I told her of the terrible trip, she said the same thing had happened to her two weeks earlier.

Colleagues in the office where I was working—Ruys and Company—went to the German authorities in Drancy, where Mrs. Van Leeuwen Boomkamp was a prisoner. They presented the papers and had several meetings, to no avail. . . .

I never knew how the people in our office knew to go to Drancy. Loulette—whom I hadn't encountered until this time—or Miss Tellegen must have had some contact with them. . . . I think that Alma risked exposing Miss Tellegen. If the Germans had forced her to reveal the Tellegen name, it would have endangered many people.[4]

The next letter from Loulette to Miss Tellegen was dated 13 April 1943—six days before the beginning of an armed revolt in the Warsaw ghetto, the first mass rebellion in Nazi-occupied Europe. The letter indicates that Alma had been very ill. It could also contain hidden code, for its language is curiously oblique:

I suppose you have received all the details concerning the ups and downs of your friend, who has miraculously survived and recovered her health, thanks to the diligence of her friends.[5]

I don't need to tell you that we were very anxious when we heard about her return to the first clinic. Even now, I prefer to see her a little farther away in the good fresh air of the convalescent home where she has already spent some weeks. However, that was not planned, and the main thing is not to lose track of her! It is very difficult at this time to send her wholesome things because there isn't much to be had. I want you to know that I am doing all it is possible for me to do, and that you can count on me. I am less successful with my own good friends than I am with our musician.

One of them has gone far away, and the beloved son of another is on the point of suffering the same fate. I have not been able to do anything for either of them. It is truly demoralizing.

I hope you are well and keeping your courage through this dismal time. I embrace you with all my heart, hoping we shall meet in the near future when peace has come again.

Your faithful
Loulette

Some of Alma's Dutch friends firmly believe that she tried to take her own life when she arrived at Drancy or before, in Dijon; but this is only surmise. The facts of her brush with death and her recovery are unknown.

As Miss Tellegen used her influence with the Germans to relay messages to Berlin and Paris on Alma's behalf, a lawyer in Paris, engaged by Martin's brother in Holland, was working hard on Martin's case. At Drancy various methods of delaying action had become common practice. One was to challenge a prisoner's classification as a Jew subject to deportation through the use of family and church records. Another was to secure admission to the crowded Rothschild Hospital, which temporarily took the prisoner off the Drancy rolls. Either or both these methods could have served to delay Alma's deportation. It is also possible that she was sent to Beaune-La-Rolande, a camp built before the collapse of France to house Canadian troops, which now absorbed the overflow from Drancy. If deportation was stalled, prominent internees were often removed to Beaune-La-Rolande.

Alma's Dutch friends heard that Alma was under the "special protection" of Nazi officials in Paris. It was even rumored that friends in Berlin tried to help her. It appears that no one outside the camp knew why she was held at Drancy for months, although speculation was rampant, and it is clear that representations in her favor came from people of influence outside the camp.

The time of reprieve was certainly not charity on the part of the officer in charge of deportations from Drancy, SS Lieutenant Colonel Heinz Roethke, who directed operations from a base in Paris. Early in 1943, Roethke was the architect of a plan to send eight to ten thousand Jews to Auschwitz by the end of April; numbers, not individuals, were his concern.

Neither Arnold nor Alfred knew of Alma's capture and imprisonment. A note Alfred sent via the Red Cross arrived in Utrecht on 24 March 1943, three months after Alma's departure. Its tone was cheerful and confident: "Happy received your news. Father and we perfectly all right. All three very busy. Have many pupils. Maria working in shop. Father playing often."

By March the transports from Drancy had accelerated, yet the movement of the "cargo in boxcars" was still not fast enough for Adolf Eichmann in Berlin. The French, who continued to operate Drancy for the Germans, were told that if enough Jews were not available for transport, non-Jewish French would fill the places on trains to the East. In June 1943, seeking to speed up deportations, Eichmann appointed SS Captain Alois Brunner, a former Viennese, as his personal deputy in charge of Drancy, and the Germans took over the operation.

Miss Tellegen reported that Alma's confidence as well as her own vanished when Brunner assumed command. His first act was to nullify the various arrangements that could save prisoners from deportation. There would be no more legalistic delaying tactics, no more meetings with clergy or influential friends or drawn-out discussions of racial status. As Miss Tellegen said in a letter to Arnold in 1945: "With Paris friends, we tried to get Alma out. A change in command put a stop to our plans."

In June 1943, Drancy housed more than three thousand internees. The German team that took over in July, consisting of three non-commissioned

SS officers in addition to Brunner, ousted the entire French administration. Borrowing the tactic the Nazis used in the East, Brunner now required the prisoners themselves to run the camp. By creating a small elite with life-or-death power over other inmates, plentiful food, and privileged living conditions, they fostered brutality and obtained the savage discipline they sought.

Georges Wellers described the Brunner takeover in *L'Étoile jaune à l'heure de Vichy* (The Yellow Star in the Vichy Era):

> Brunner arrived on 18 June [1943] and went into the camp alone. Installed behind a small table, he began to interrogate all prisoners for four days. Then he suddenly vanished.
>
> When the French guards and civilian observers were sent from camp and Brunner and his team took over, all the lowest instincts fostered by the SS reigned in complete isolation from the outside world. Even Red Cross personnel were turned out of the camp.[6]

It is possible that as he interviewed Drancy inmates, Brunner recognized Alma as a member of the prominent Rosé family who had fled from Vienna four years earlier. The Austrian connection could have been enough to condemn her.

Brunner had carte blanche not only because of his SS rank, but also because of his record in "liquidating the Jewish question" in Austria and Greece. His handiwork in May alone, the month before he arrived at Drancy, resulted in the murder of tens of thousands of Greek Jews at Auschwitz.[7]

Wellers paints a vivid picture of the new chief of Drancy:

> He had an insignificant physique, small, poorly built, puny even, an expressionless look, small, evil-looking eyes. His monotonous voice was seldom raised. He was perfidious, pitiless, and lying.
>
> His actions were based on cold-blooded premeditation. He rarely struck people. One day he slapped a person to be deported, then walked up and down holding his hand up as though soiled by the cheeks of his victim and wiped it carefully against the posts of the barbed wire fence.
>
> Brunner's three associates were capable of terrorizing and hounding the prisoners, and organized violent public displays of demeaning punishments in the courtyard.[8]

Martin too recalled that inmates were forced to watch prisoners beating other prisoners on order, a revolting spectacle.

Brunner's new regime sustained the fraud that the internees were destined for "work camps." The prisoners' professions and occupations were incorporated into Drancy records, partly to sustain illusory hopes and encourage docility, and partly to supply resource lists for officials of the destination camps in the East and the private industries that purchased prison labor.[9]

With the departure of the French guards, at least the physical conditions at Drancy improved. The prisoners still suffered painful hunger, but they were able to keep their living quarters cleaner and less chaotic.

THE ALLIES conquered Tunisia in May 1943, and on 10 July they invaded Sicily. Five days later, the Russians launched a major offensive. Despite German reverses on the battlefield, the roundup and deportation of Jews in Nazi-controlled territories remained a macabre priority through the summer.

Each transport was thoroughly documented. Early in July, Brunner sent teletype messages to Eichmann and to administrators at Auschwitz informing them that a convoy with a thousand Jews would leave the Paris-Bobigny freight station at 0900 hours on Sunday, 18 July 1943. It would be registered as Convoy 57. On 11 July, Brunner asked Eichmann to authorize the transport.

On 16 July, Roethke, still masterminding deportations from his base in Paris, sent a memorandum to the transport command confirming orders for a "Judentransport" the following Sunday. He ordered a train consisting of twenty-three "solid freight cars" (boxcars) and three passenger coaches to be at the Bobigny freight station between 5 and 6 p.m. on Saturday, 17 July, and ready for loading the next morning. One passenger coach was to be placed behind the locomotive, a second in the middle of the train, and a third at the rear. Guards on the strategically located coaches would be able to patrol the train during the necessary stops. This procedure for making up transport trains had become standard after a full-scale investigation into escapes from previous convoys. As a further precaution, all the tiny air vents of the freight cars were to be secured with barbed wire.

Boarding would begin at 0600 hours on 18 July. The train would depart between 0855 and 0900 hours.

FOR ALMA, as for hundreds of others, there was no appeal. The Jews selected for transport were divided into groups of fifty and placed under prisoner-leaders who would be accountable for each car on the morning of departure.

Two women who knew Alma at Drancy later told Loulette how her courageous spirit had comforted her fellow inmates—how she had buoyed them up in that bleak place, and they had come to love her. Yet the night before she was to leave Drancy, Alma too succumbed to the hysteria and despair that swept the camp like a tide. At her thirty-six and a half years, she was still strong, although she had changed outwardly during her ordeal. Now she surrendered her wristwatch to a cellmate, along with a precious strand of pearls her mother had worn. (Both the watch and the pearl necklace would be in a package Pietronella d'Aquin Boot sent to Marie Anne Tellegen and Miss Tellegen returned to Arnold after the war.) Henry Bulawko, another Drancy prisoner assigned to Convoy 57, described the atmosphere of the camp on the eve of the transport, when "flashes of optimism flickered like weak fireflies, only to be extinguished in the blackest dread of the unknown."[10]

In the pre-dawn of 18 July 1943, orphaned and sick children were awakened without being told where they were going or why. Whole familes—some with children under a year old, others with half a dozen children—clung together, carrying their last few precious belongings. Parents searched in vain for reassuring words, wishing they too had abandoned their children to the care of friends or even strangers, a decision they might have criticized only weeks before.

SS Scharführer Koepler, one of Brunner's ruthless team, drove the deportees forward with methods that would scarcely have been tolerated in the Paris stockyards at Porte de la Villette less than two kilometers away. The prisoners were herded to buses and trucks for the short ride to a cattle train waiting on a Bobigny siding. Anyone who lingered or protested was shouted at and clubbed.

Martin had been on an earlier list for deportation, but at the time he was too sick for even a "Judentransport" to the unknown. If he had survived the journey, he would surely have been judged unfit for work upon arrival. Officials had told him he would be placed on a later train, but in the meantime he received papers that successfully challenged his Jewishness. His change of status resulted in internment in a camp off the French coast for the remainder of the war.

Thus Martin was still at Drancy when the deportees of Convoy 57 went to their fate. In the early morning light, he watched the prisoners assembling in their groups of fifty for transport to the Bobigny station. Alma, dressed in black, was among the last in the lineup. It was the first time he had seen her since their arrest in Dijon seven months earlier, and he was struck by how little he knew about the woman he could identify only as "Mrs. Van Leeuwen Boomkamp." He dared not stand and stare, but from the corner of his eye he watched Alma board the bus that would take her to the eastbound train.

Brunner and his team knew that nothing more would be required of most of the internees once they arrived at Auschwitz, so the passenger manifest was prepared in slapdash fashion. Alma was listed as "Vanleeuven, Obna, 8.11.06, violinist, 2133."[11] Both her name and her birthdate were incorrect.

At 0900 hours, Auschwitz received a signal that the train left Paris-Bobigny precisely on schedule.

R. F. SS

Sicherheits-Dienst

Nachrichten-Uebermittlung

Aufgenommen				Befördert				Raum für Eingangsstempel
Tag	Monat	Jahr	Zeit	Tag	Monat	Jahr	Zeit	
11 JUL 1943				11. 7. 43			16 25	
von			durch	an			durch Kg	

Verzögerungsvermerk

Nr. 43991

Telegramm — Funkspruch — Fernschreiben — Fernspruch

IV B - BdS
Br./Ne.

Paris, den 11. Juli 1943

An das

Reichssicherheitshauptamt
IV B 4

z.Hdn. SS-Obersturmbannführer Eichmann

<u>B e r l i n .</u>

<u>Betr.:</u> Anmeldung eines Juden-Evakuierungstransportes nach Auschwitz.

<u>Vorg.:</u> Bekannt.

Ich bitte für 18.7.1943 ab Bahnhof Paris Bobigy einen Transport von 1000 Juden in das K.Z. Auschwitz zu bewilligen.

Begleitmannschaft 1:20 muß von Metz ab Paris gestellt werden, weil derzeit in Paris keine Kräfte, auch nicht zur Begleitung bis zur Reichsgrenze, vorhanden sind.

I.A.:

Brunner
SS-Hauptsturmführer.

[illegible] 13/7

Portions of the SS order and manifest for the "Judentransport" of 18 July 1943 from Drancy to Auschwitz, reprinted courtesy of the Auschwitz-Birkenau State Museum. Alma is incorrectly listed as "Obna Vanleeuven" (see page 210).

Abtransport
18.7.1943.

57

B. d. S. - F r a n k r e i c h

Ref. IV 4 b

Abschubliste: 57

901	Telila	Jacques	19.1.34	Kind	2921
902	Telia	Salomon	2.7.95	ohne	2075
903	Topobek	Albert	14.1.28	Pelzarbeiter	2052
904	Toporek	Herszel	1898	Schneider	2051
905	Torres	Gentil	8.1.05	ohne	2078
906	Tàrres	Michel	15.5.99	Arbeiter	2077
907	Tragarz	Chaskiel	19.5.21	Heizungsmonteur	2058
908	Treg[illegible]r	Odette	9.3.15	Modistin	2095
909	Treuillet	Lydia	8.12.17	ohne	2059
910	Tuchmann	Abraham	4.11.23	Lederarbeiter	2085
911	Uhry	Yvonne	25.2.03	Sekretaerin	2109
912	Unger	Joseph	3.4.98	Schneider	2112
913	Unikowski	Michel	20.12.92	Markthaendl.	2138
914	Uzan	Joseph	1908	Orthopaede	2151
915	Van Gelderen	Ikarus	11.11.19	Student	2361
916	Vanleeuven	Obna	8.11.06	Geigenspieler	2133
917	Van Lee	Adrienne	30.8.76	ohne	2125
918	Vidal	Colette	6.5.27	Kind	2148
919	Vidal	Nedjma	2.6.87	ohne	2146
920	Vidal	Prosper	5.1.87	Postbeamter	2145
921	Vidal	Rachel	18.1.25	Kind	2147
922	Vieyra	Bernard	11.8.20	Juwelier	2135
923	Vieyra	Jacques	2.2.19	Steinfasser	2136
924	Villerd	Liba	25.10.95	ohne	2137
925	Viner	David	15.12.99	Schneider	2152

16

Instant Nightmare

Auschwitz—a wound in the order of being.—Martin Buber

Here we are in the *anus mundi.*—SS Dr. Heinz Thilo

Convoy 57 hurtled toward the East under tight security. A thousand captives were crowded into the train—522 men and boys, 430 women and girls, and 48 of unspecified sex. Of this number, 59 would survive until the war ended in 1945.[1]

The commander of the train was an officer of the Metz Schutzpolizei Kommando, and there were twenty male guards. An entry in the train's manifest detailed the contents of possibly two freight cars: 6,500 kilograms of early potatoes, 3,500 kg. flour, 80 kg. ersatz coffee, 275 kg. dried vegetables, 275 kg. pasta, 500 kg. and 540 dozen cans vegetables, 250 kg. lard, 195 kg. sugar, 350 kg. salt, two barrels red wine, 95 dozen tins preserved tomatoes, 195 dozen milk, 371 dozen tins sardines and canned fish, 1,306 dozen tins canned meat and pâté, and about 12 kg. chocolate. The destination for this mountain of conqueror's spoils was not specified, although the manifest included a notation by Brunner than none of the provisions should go to the concentration camp.[2] By July of 1943, these provisions were luxuries throughout Europe; even highly privileged Germans would have found it hard to acquire such delicacies. There is no record of the train's passengers' receiving any food at all during the journey.

Henry Bulawko, among the prisoners on Convoy 57, described the experience of spending two nights and three days in sealed boxcars:

> We were loaded 60 (the manifest required 50) people where 30 would have had difficulty fitting. There wasn't enough room for all to lie down at the same time. A big pail in the corner of the car took care of our needs. For modesty's sake, we encircled it with blankets.

Only once, at Cologne I think, we were allowed out of the wagon for some minutes. It happened that some prisoners risked all in an attempt to escape at one stop, the "passengers" still sealed in their cars. They set fire to their car, gambling on someone opening the door to attend to the fire.

But they paid for it. When the fire attracted attention, a German policeman put his head up to the small barbed wire–covered opening and ordered the leader of the car of deportees: "Put out the fire or you'll burn everybody in there." He disappeared. He was not pleased. The fire was quickly extinguished by my outwitted companions.

On the evening of the third day (20 July), the train slowed down and stopped.

Speculation was rife.

Has anyone noticed the "canning plant" that the allegedly "well-informed at Drancy" spoke of at the office of the administration?

Prisoners asked each other a thousand and one questions.

Will families be separated? What will happen to the children? And the sick ones? Will each person be allowed to work at his own specialty?

The propositions bounced back and forth:

"I know German well. Perhaps I can get an easy job."

"Me, I will go to the commander. He has been deceived. I am not a Jew."

"Me, I'm a war veteran."

"And me, part Aryan."

The feverish movements of each one—the re-tying of bundles, the re-buttoning of a gabardine, holding a child more tightly—betrayed the inner hopes, questions, and a great anxiety.

The door opened brusquely and the answer came to all our questions. A response unexpected, unimaginable, and inhuman.

An instant nightmare. Strange figures in striped clothes crawled over the train like gnomes, hideous escapees from hell. Behind them, the SS, machine guns pointed at us. And more cries: "*Los. Raus. Alles raus. Schnell.*" (Out. All out. Quick.)

Each bent over to pick up suitcases and bundles. "My goodness," cried someone, "my case is not marked. Where and how shall I recover it?"

But there was no time for questions, not even to think. How to go faster? We trampled on each other, astounded by the unprecedented ferocity. Women cried under the blows, trying to protect their children.

We are down. At once we were separated in two lines: the men at the left and the women at the right.

In front of each group, an officer. He passed us, paused between the lines, cast a rapid glance at us and said dryly, "Left" or "Right."[3]

Trucks with Red Cross insignia were waiting for those the officer directed to the left—440 women and children, and some older and sickly men. They were crowded into the vehicles and taken away. A neighbor of Bulawko's, still new to Auschwitz, murmured approvingly: "They even have chic! They give rides to women and children."

Bulawko heard a man ask, "Do you think I will find my wife and little girl again?" Someone nearby said reassuringly: "Of course. What have they got to gain by separating you?"

As a heavy rain began to fall, those the officer directed to the right waited to walk into the camp. Unwittingly, they had survived their first "selection"—the process by which Nazi camp doctors determined which prisoners would work and which would be put to death. Within the hour they would learn the first awful truths of Auschwitz-Birkenau: the prisoners herded into the trucks their wives, husbands, parents, children and grandchildren—went to a gas chamber for extermination.

There they were told to strip for a shower and to leave their possessions where they could recover them afterwards. To maintain the illusion of legitimacy and to keep the victims calm, seats were sometimes numbered and towels and bits of soap issued; the gas chamber itself was equipped with useless shower heads. By day's end, all were dead. Their last material possessions—their clothing and the precious items they carried with them, any jewelry they were wearing or had sewn into their clothing, even gold teeth and gold or diamond fillings, had been systematically plundered. Their clothing joined the mountain-like piles from other victims on the trains streaming into camp from all over Nazi-occupied Europe. Valuables that were not stolen were sent to Berlin or put in safekeeping for the treasury of the Reich. According to Danuta Czech, of the group from Convoy 57 who were gassed on 20 July 1943, 126 were children under the age of eighteen.

The day Convoy 57 arrived, thirty-three prisoners arrived from nearby Katowice, as well as forty-seven other males and nineteen females. Five boys and two girls were born to Gypsies. Twenty-four male and eight female prisoners came from Cracow. Prisoner Stanislaw Stepinski, who had escaped on 16 July but was recaptured, was put in the punishment bunker in Block 11 and later shot. Transferred to Buchenwald were 152 Czech inmates. The day was not busy by Auschwitz standards.

Also according to Czech, from 15 January to 15 March 1943, twenty thousand inmates, those fortunate enough to have gained admission to the camp, had died violently—shot, beaten, gassed, euthanized, or killed by starvation or disease. The figure included seventeen hundred Gypsies who were gassed when typhus (spotted fever) broke out in their area of the camp.[4]

Through the avalanche of orders, Alma might have heard that the day before her arrival, twelve prisoners on the camp's survey team, suspected of plotting to escape, had been hanged outside the camp kitchen. Also still on the tongue of every inmate were tales of the thirteen-and-a-half-hour selection in February 1943, a roll call on a freezing meadow during which a thousand women were selected for gassing. After the long hours of standing at attention to be counted, those who could not jog back to their barracks were clubbed out of the ranks and sent to Block 25 in the Birkenau women's camp to await death without food or water.

Auschwitz (Oświęcim in Polish), in German-occupied southern Poland in Upper Silesia, was one of six annihilation camps in Poland. Established in June 1940, it was initially a typical concentration camp, where prisoners, chiefly Poles, were required to work as part of a program of humiliation and terror. In addition it served as a quarantine and transit camp for prisoners bound for camps in Germany. Even as the increasingly desperate war effort increased the need for labor, the Nazis' goal of eliminating the Jewish race remained a fundamental priority, and the predominant function of the camp became mass murder. Many lives ended before prisoners were officially admitted to the camp, as SS doctors performed "on the ramp" selections of new arrivals and took the doomed directly from the railway platform to the gas chambers. Those who survived to join the work force were beaten, exhausted by forced labor from three or four in the morning until dark, and slowly starved; malnutrition or its consequences, such as pneumonia or infectious disease, claimed an untold number of lives.

Jews, marked with their yellow badges, were designated for death from the moment of their admission to the camp. Other internees were Gypsies, Poles, Russians, and non-Jewish prisoners arrested because they had opposed the Nazi regime, among them Communists and resistance fighters who had tried to help the beleaguered Jews. Ironically, the elite at the camp wore the triangular insignia denoting "asocial elements," a category that included prostitutes and common criminals along with homosexuals, political prisoners, and Jehovah's Witnesses; these groups were known respectively as the black, green, pink, red, and purple triangles. Those who entered camp "with a file"—the *Karteihäftlinge*—had an immediate advantage since they could not be sent directly to the gas chambers, in case as prisoners convicted of crimes they should be summoned to court.

The Auschwitz complex rapidly grew to a network of almost a dozen camps that stretched into the countryside for miles and supplied labor to such factories as the I. G. Farben plant known as "I. G. Buna" (*buna* was a synthetic rubber needed for the war effort) and the Krupp industries. To balance the two overriding concerns of the camp—the work and the killing—doctors regularly performed large-scale selections. Thus they reduced overcrowding and halted typhus and typhoid epidemics, rid the camp of weak and dispirited inmates, and replaced them with healthier prisoners who would carry on the work of the camp until they too became debilitated and were weeded out by gassing.

Auschwitz I, the main camp or *Stammlager,* was built on a damp, swampy plain in the industrial heartland, a region known for its brutal winters. In August 1942 it was joined by Birkenau (Brzezinka in Polish), also known as Auschwitz II, an adjunct built three kilometers from the main camp in a birch woods, from which it derived its name "Birch Grove." Birkenau would eventually house more than three times the number of prisoners in the parent camp—as many as two hundred thousand at a time, twice the capacity Himmler originally ordered—in a constellation of subcamps known as BI (the women's camp), BII (the men's camp and family camps for Czech Jews and Gypsies), and the partially completed BIII, known as "Mexiko."

Birkenau would become the most efficient death factory ever created. Four of Auschwitz-Birkenau's five crematoria were located here, and the air was constantly fouled by a thick black smoke that issued from the chimneys. The newer gas chambers were built beneath the crematoria and partly obscured. Elevators carried the corpses upstairs. The crematoria were operated around the clock; each could burn over five thousand corpses daily. At its height, it was said that Auschwitz had the killing machinery to process twenty thousand victims each twenty-four hours.

Mass murder with Zyklon B (Cyclon-B) gas, a preparation of prussic acid previously used for killing vermin, began 3 September 1941 with the "trial" killing of 600 Russian prisoners of war and 298 patients chosen from among the sick. By late 1941 or early 1942, large-scale gassings were routine. By paralyzing the lungs, the gas caused death in three to fifteen minutes. Camp commandant Rudolf Höss took pride in the gassing procedure, which was quick, certain, and less disturbing for the executioners than the face-to-face killing formerly used to implement the "Final Solution." Still the supervised slaughter was onerous, and it was a Nazi doctor, Heinz Thilo, after participating in a selection of deportees from Holland, who gave the camp the name forever linked with its memory: *anus mundi*—anus of the world.

In "Children," a poem published in 1978, survivor Wojciech Gniatczyński wrote of Zyklon-B as a cyclone:

The sky was blue
like the Cyclone in the gas chamber. . . .

Outside, a hard
Polish winter.
Withered weeds
on frozen earth.
Only in the gas chamber
is it warm.
Only in Man's heart
is Hell.[5]

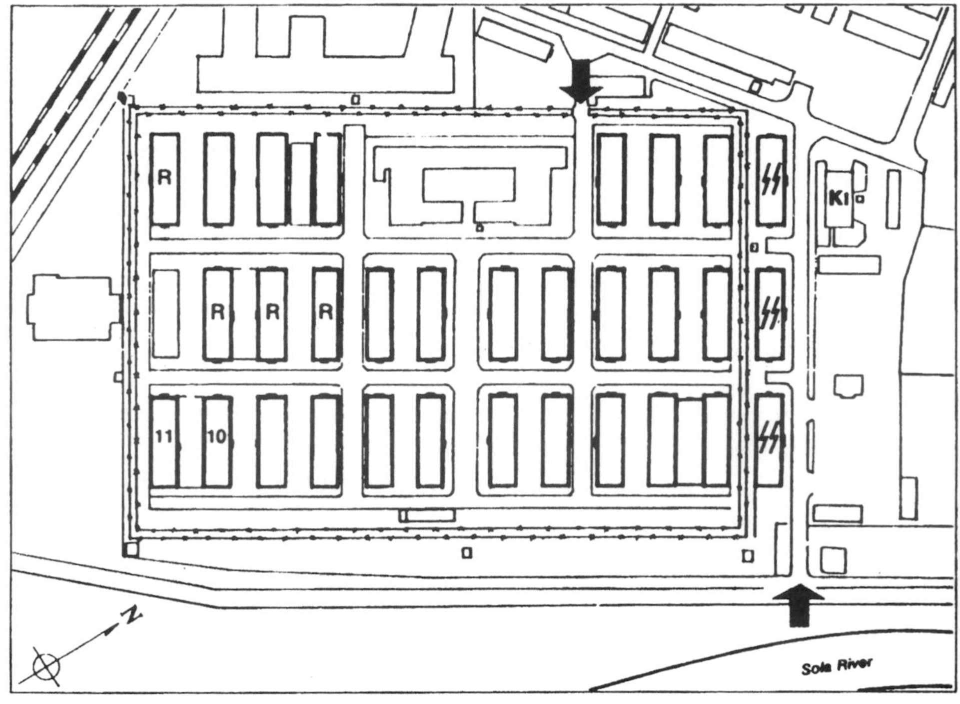

Plan of Auschwitz I, the *Stammlager,* 1944. Blocks within the electrified barbed-wire fences show barracks and other buildings; small squares locate watchtowers. The large building at top center was the camp kitchen. 10: the Experimental Block; 11: the "Death Barrack," a punishment block linked to Block 10 by the infamous "Black Wall." R: hospital barracks. KI: gas chamber and crematorium. The main gate (with the motto "*Arbeit macht frei*") is marked by the black arrow at top. Map reprinted from Pawełczyńska 1979 courtesy of the University of California Press, Berkeley.

AT THE TRAIN STATION, Alma was pointed to the right and funneled into a group of a dozen women. With 369 men and 179 other women, her small group marched for half an hour through the rain under SS guard, some to Birkenau and others to the main camp. Some arrivals reported that the SS guards extorted valuables from them during the march into camp. Alma's group was separated from the others at the gate to Auschwitz I, where they passed under the brightly lit archway with its famous motto, *Arbeit macht frei* (Work Makes You Free).

The great majority of men and women admitted to the camps were separated by gender and processed according to a well-tested pattern. They were ordered to undress, putting shoes in one pile and clothing in another. Some-

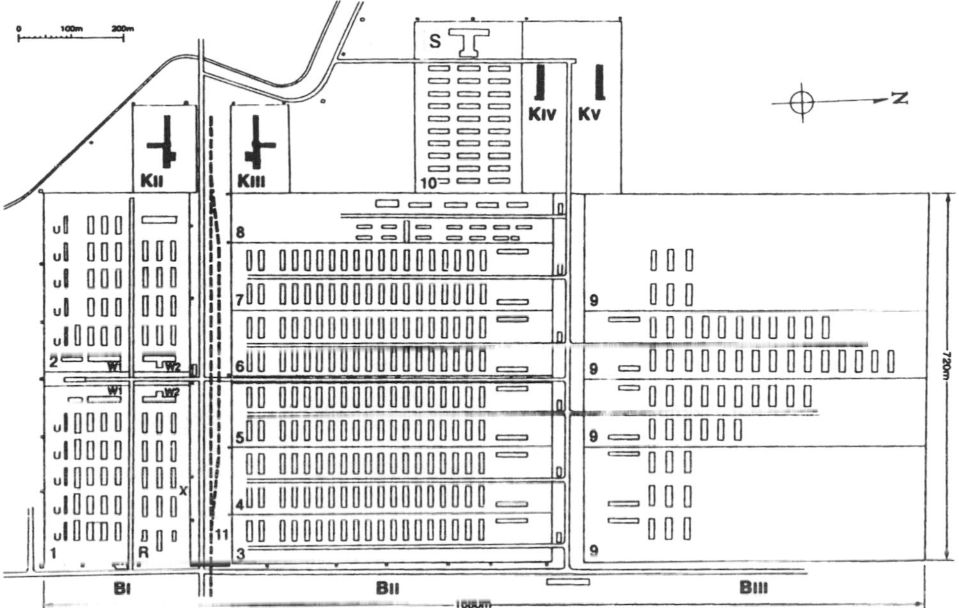

Plan of Auschwitz II Birkenau, 1944. Blocks show barracks and other buildings; continuous lines around sections represent electrified barbed wire fences; tiny black squares indicate watchtowers. The broken line shows the railway built from the Auschwitz train station, through the gates of Birkenau, to crematoria II and III.

BI—1 and 2 (BIa and BIb): women's camp; R: the Revier, women's hospital blocks; X: the Music Block; W1: kitchens; W2: bathhouses; U: latrines and washrooms.

BII—3: Quarantine Blocks; 4: Czech Jewish family camp; 5 and 6: men's camp; 7: Gypsy family camp; 8: men's hospital blocks, 10. "Kanada" storehouses. S: the Sauna, main camp bathhouse. KII, KIII, KIV, and KV: gas chambers and crematoria.

BIII—9: "Mexiko," an unfinished camp extension.

Map reprinted from Pawełczyńska 1979 courtesy of the University of California Press, Berkeley.

times they were given towels and even "wardrobe tickets." As they stood naked and shivering, prisoners in striped camp garb came into the room with soap brushes and dull razors and shaved off the hair on the newcomers' heads, under their arms, and between their thighs. The prisoners were locked in a shower room, doused briefly with cold water, and disinfected as a control for lice and skin diseases. Prisoner-attendants then drove them from the shower and thrust new clothes and shoes at them, the belongings of former prisoners who had died or been murdered in the camp.

From this initiation, an extreme of degradation, the prisoners emerged as slaves. Survivor Primo Levi recalled:

> Nothing belongs to us anymore; they have taken away our clothes, our shoes, even our hair. . . . They will even take away our name: and if we want to keep it, we will have to find in ourselves the strength to do so, to manage somehow so that behind the name something of us, of us as we were, still remains.[6]

As a last step in camp registration, the prisoners lined up in rows and filed past tables where still other prisoner-workers, equipped with needle-tipped instruments, inscribed their left forearms with blue numerals they would carry on their skin as long as they lived. The men from Convoy 57 received prisoner numbers 130466 to 130834 and the women numbers 50204 to 50394, reflecting the sequence of their arrival at the camp. Alma received yet another identifying number, 50381. The tattoo alone would tell old-timers at the camp—those rare survivors with four-digit numbers—the history of her arrival from France, even the number of the convoy that took her to Auschwitz.

An announcement was customarily made to new arrivals. This characteristic message was delivered to the men by SS Lagerführer Karl Fritzsch, at one time commandant of Auschwitz I:

> I tell you it is not a sanatorium you have come to but a German concentration camp from which the only exit is up the chimney. If anybody doesn't like it, he can go throw himself against the high tension wires straightaway. If there are any Jews in the convoy, they are not entitled to live more than two weeks; priests have one month of life and the remainder three months.[7]

At that moment, if not before, the new arrivals realized that the pervasive smell at Auschwitz was charred human flesh.

The 179 other women admitted to the camp with Alma's small group were sent to the Quarantine Blocks in the women's camp in Birkenau, a cluster of squat brick buildings. Here, packed as many as five or six to a bunk on plank shelves built one above the other in stacks of three, a thousand newcomers to the camp were isolated before they were assigned to work details. Disease took a daily toll; camp wisdom held that "you don't come out of here alive."

Alma and her small group were not quarantined. They had been picked for a still more terrifying destination: Block 10, the notorious Experimental Block and the only barrack in the main camp then housing women. The two-story brick building accommodated some 395 Jewish women selected for medical experiments, 65 prisoner-nurses, and about two dozen camp prostitutes.[8] Alma and her group, drenched and hungry, soon encountered another of Auschwitz's horrors: the "rabbit warren," as it was known, where Nazi doctors experimented with human subjects.

In the camp rumors flew about sinister activities within the block, which was cut off from the rest of Auschwitz-Birkenau, its windows tightly closed and shuttered. Little was known of what actually went on there. Inmates of Block 10 who peeked through the cracks in the windows saw the courtyard of the "Death Barrack," Block 11, an execution yard where hundreds of prisoners were shot in front of the infamous bullet-stopping "Black Wall." (After liberation, workers realized the purpose to which the courtyard had been dedicated when they found the sand at the wall soaked with blood to a depth of six feet.)

Pseudo-research conducted in Block 10 on Jewish girls and women has been described as the distillation of Nazi racial policy: the doctrine that "the Jew" was a racial poison, an agent of pollution, sickness, and death for the "Aryan" race. In his 1986 study *The Nazi Doctors,* Robert Jay Lifton points out that even the Nazis' use of the Darwinian term "selection" reflected the concepts of "racial and social biology" that converted anti-Semitism into a creed even educated and cultivated adults could espouse.[9] The Jews, unworthy of life, endangered the survival of the pure and superior race and had to be "courageously" eliminated—hence cruel experiments with forcible sterilization for those unfit for propagation, medical killing of individuals with phenol injections into the bloodstream or direct to the heart, mass murder by means of poisonous gas. Faced with complaints about certain Nazi officers' "sensitivity," Reichsführer Heinrich Himmler recommended increasing the number of dogs, which were immune to the qualms of human pity.

Carl Clauberg was the SS doctor charged by Himmler with finding an effective means of "bloodless" sterilization for women. His experiments began in December 1942 in the squalid Revier, the Birkenau women's camp hospital where most of the sick died; later the experiments were conducted in Block 10 of the *Stammlager*. Operated under the strictest security, the Experimental Block came under the authority of the camp office in Birkenau and reported administratively to SS Obersturmbannführerin (Lieutenant Colonel) Maria Mandel, the female officer who commanded the women's camp after its installation at Birkenau. Medically the block was under the command of SS Dr. Eduard Wirths, the chief medical officer of the complex, until the spring of 1943, when camp commandant Rudolf Höss turned the block over to Clauberg. Elsewhere in the camp, SS Dr. Horst Schumann conducted X-ray experiments with two hundred young male prisoners who were eventually castrated.

In the Experimental Block, internees waited in mute fear until they were summoned for surgery. Procedures were painful and rapid. Clauberg and Władysław Dering, a Polish prisoner-doctor the Nazis later released from Auschwitz for his cooperative efforts, subjected young Jewish women to extreme radiation then removed their ovaries under non-sterile conditions in a crude operation that took no more than ten minutes. The ovaries were sent to laboratories that judged the destructive effects of the X-ray treatment with the object of discovering cheap and efficient methods of mass sterilization. Jewish women and girls from Greece, Belgium, France, and Holland, all of childbearing age and including many teenaged Jewish virgins, were "favored" for these experiments. Women inmates also served as guinea pigs in gynecological experiments involving the surgical removal of the cervix for a study of precancerous conditions, and experiments with inducing typhus and testing its communicability.

Often the inquiries reflected the special interests of the SS doctors, such as Dr. Josef Mengele's curiosity about twins, dwarfs, and the condition known as heterochromia, in which a person has one brown eye and one blue. There were no restraints on the use of Jewish subjects, who were destined to die anyway.

"Anthropological research"—another Nazi euphemism for generating inhuman suffering—was also carried out in Block 10, reaching grotesque proportions when the skulls of some 115 men and women, 109 of them Jews, were collected for racial and anatomical studies. Requests from Berlin stimulated a variety of human experiments, many of them fatal.

Surgical procedures were so ineptly executed in the Experimental Block that the eminent French doctor Adélaïde Hautval, a "friend of the Jews" arrested for wearing the yellow star and sent as a prisoner-doctor to Block 10 in April 1943, refused to enter the operating room. Surprisingly, SS Dr. Mengele is said to have announced that if she, as an "Aryan," did not want to take part in medical experiments, she did not have to. The SS doctor who headed the block acquiesced, so that for four months Dr. Hautval attended only postoperative patients. Her brave stand was widely admired.[10]

Another courageous prisoner-doctor, Ella Lingens-Reiner, entered Block 10 as a patient after a rare act of compassion on the part of an SS doctor. A German non-Jew imprisoned at Birkenau, Lingens-Reiner had studied medicine at Marburg with SS Dr. Werner Rohde, head of the women's hospital at Birkenau. When Lingens-Reiner suffered a severe attack of typhus, Dr. Rohde recommended that she be sent to Block 10 of the main camp, where conditions were somewhat better than in Birkenau's Revier.[11] Dr. Lingens-Reiner survived the camp to give extensive testimony about medical activities at Birkenau and at Dachau, where she was also a prisoner.

In five months of 1943, between March and the end of August, 350 women were admitted to the Experimental Block to maintain its strength, according to records compiled by Danuta Czech. The women who entered Block 10 were not expected to live long after their use as experimental subjects. Those who survived the medical procedures were often too weak to escape the regular selections in the medical blocks that sent unproductive prisoners to the gas chambers.

ALMA ARRIVED at Block 10 in a trousers uniform, the prison wear of a former Russian prisoner of war. Magda Hellinger Blau, the *Blockälteste* (block senior) and prisoner-administrator of the block, wrote that at first Alma seemed stunned.[12] Then, from deep in her being, she summoned a rare strength.

On that first July day, the correctness Alma learned from her mother came to her rescue. She assumed a dignified air and a manner of sympathetic curiosity, inquiring about the surgical procedures and the X-ray machines she saw in two ground-floor rooms. In her ill-fitting prison uniform, hiding the horror she felt, she acted the part of a touring artist arriving at an unfamiliar theater.

One of the prisoner-nurses working in Block 10 for the past six months was a twenty-two-year-old Dutch woman Alma had met under happier circumstances. Her name was Ima van Esso, and she was eager for news from outside: she had heard that her mother and father had been sent to Westerbork but had received no further word. When she learned that Alma came from Holland, Ima sought her out.

At first neither woman recognized the other, although both felt they had met before. Only in conversation, when Alma mentioned that she had been married to Váša Příhoda, was Ima's memory of Alma triggered.

Alma had been to the Van Esso home in Amsterdam several times during 1941 and 1942. Ima's father was a doctor, and her mother a singer and supporter of Zionist causes. Ima, who played the flute, recalled the experience of playing with Alma at the Van Esso home:

> Alma was a fine violinist, and she also played the piano. She accompanied both my mother and me. One time I played a Telemann sonata with her, and I remember that she was a real soloist, not following a fellow musician very well. However, I must say it is possible that at the time I was so young, she felt I was beneath her best effort.
>
> Alma always had to be first. Everybody appeared to worship her immediately, although many were jealous of her. She had to be Number One. You couldn't neglect her.
>
> I was so shocked to see Alma in Block 10, so totally changed from the last time in Holland, yet still looking fresh and charming, that I had to tell everybody, even the Hungarian Jewish *Blockälteste* Magda Hellinger [now Mrs. Blau]. This was such unusual news to Magda that she listened, although at the time I felt she didn't like me. At first she didn't know of whom I was speaking. The name Rosé did not set off a reaction immediately, but when I mentioned Váša Příhoda she paid attention. In Central Europe at that time, Příhoda was held in the same esteem as Yehudi Menuhin today.[13]

Faced with the unimaginable circumstances of the Experimental Block at Auschwitz, Alma resorted to the two tools at her disposal: her personality and her music. She later described her reaction to a friend in the Music Block:

"Believing she was going to her death, Alma asked one of the overseers of Block 10 to grant her the condemned person's customary final request. She asked to play the violin for a last time."[14]

Alma's talents presented Magda with an opportunity. As she later wrote, her wits were constantly tested to find excuses to save as many women as possible from the medical experiments and to ease the oppression of their surroundings. Not permitted to write a note to the main office of the FKZ (the *Frauenkonzentrationslager,* Women's Concentration Camp) at Birkenau, which was administratively responsible for the block, she sent an oral message to the Birkenau *Schreibstube* (the camp office).

If she had been caught sending a message on paper, Magda herself would have been put on punishment detail (*Strafkommando*).The message to the *Schreibstube* was to the point: "We have Alma Rosé here, the wife of Váša Příhoda." Magda asked for a violin.

THE INMATES at Birkenau included hundreds of Slovakian Jewish women and girls, who had been among the first transported from the Nazi puppet state of Slovakia (formerly a part of Czechoslovakia) to Auschwitz. Among these was a young commercial artist from Bratislava, Helen Spitzer (later Helen Spitzer Tichauer), who was known as "Zippy" and bore the low prisoner number 2286. Since her arrival at Auschwitz in March 1942, she had seen the arrival of many "Judentransports" as well as the first transport of Jewish women from Paris. She had also witnessed the hasty construction of Birkenau, which she compared to throwing up a city in the Brazilian jungle.

When the adjunct camp was completed in August 1942, the women prisoners of Auschwitz were shifted from the main camp to windowless barracks that were soon infested with lice and rodents. In the move, the count of women prisoners dropped from eight thousand to four thousand. Zippy, among the survivors, became a worker in the main office at Birkenau, which gave her a small room of her own and unusual mobility.

The young Slovakian cleverly utilized her Hebrew name, Zipporah—a name not registered upon her admission to the camp—in clandestine communications with the camp resistance. She became known among her contacts as "Zippy of the *Schreibstube.*" Thus, if any of her messages were intercepted, she could not be identified by the SS or by the informers planted throughout the camp. At least once, Zippy's name was removed from a list of those selected for the gas because of her superbly organized work in the camp office under Czech Jewish prisoner-administrator Katerina (Katya) Singer. As *Rapportführerin,* Katya answered directly to SS Commandant Maria Mandel.

Zippy, a survivor who lives in New York City today, remembers the surprising message from Magda asking for a violin. In Zippy's words, she "could not have wished for more welcome news."[15] A rumor had swept through the women's camp that a well-known woman violinist had arrived on the Drancy train but had been gassed. The news was especially disturbing because a newly formed women's orchestra at Birkenau, modeled on the Auschwitz men's orchestra, was foundering for lack of direction, and its survival depended on immediate improvement.

Zippy, a mandolinist, saw the music work detail as a prime opportunity to save women and girls from the death sentence of *Aussenarbeit,* the grinding work outside the camp as members of a heavy labor *Aussenkommando.* When she and her colleagues heard that Alma was alive and well in the Experimental Block, they advised Katya Singer that a famous musician had arrived in the camp, and her block administrator had requested a violin.

Socially and politically, even artistically, other prisoners in Auschwitz-Birkenau were more important than Alma Rosé; yet news of her arrival spread quickly. Discovery of Alma served several purposes. For the prisoners who passed on a welcome word, there was that rarest of camp commodities, favorable recognition. For the members of the fledgling orchestra, the arrival of a skilled professional could mean increased security. And for the ambitious Maria Mandel, improved performances by the women's orchestra could enhance her reputation, impress her lover (an influential SS officer), and help to satisfy her own passion for music. Magda's request for a violin was promptly granted.

"Getting a good instrument for Alma was no problem," Zippy reported, since prized musical instruments were confiscated each day when new transports arrived.

MAGDA WAS delighted when as if magically, she could hand Alma a fine violin.[16] Eight months had passed since Alma surrendered her Guadagnini to Leonard Jongkees in Utrecht.

Forty years later, Magda wrote of Alma's performance in Block 10 that first night. Violin in hand, Alma waited eagerly for 6 o'clock, when the two female SS wardens left the barrack, locking the door from outside. Inmates were placed as *Torwache*—door watchers—to spread the alarm if anyone came near the building. When all was quiet, Alma began to play.

Without words, she transported the prisoners of Block 10 to the world outside Auschwitz, far from hate and inhumanity. Her music blossomed into memories of family, home, holidays and happy times, and the locks on the barrack doors melted; the operating rooms, the SS doctors, the muffled sounds from the execution yard disappeared.

"Beauty had been a long-forgotten dream in Block 10 until that night. Nobody there could have dreamed of such beauty as her playing at that moment," remembered Ima. Henceforth Alma would be exempt from experiments because of her capacity to make music.

AFTER HER debut in the Experimental Block, Alma played each night after the barrack doors were locked. Women and girls from many different countries gathered in the ground-floor operating room to sing their national anthems and folk songs as Alma accompanied them on the violin. Camp authorities had banned singing in any language but German. But sealed away in Block 10, the guinea-pig girls had their way. The impromptu song sessions led to a bizarre series of "cabarets."

Magda recalls that when she first met with the chief medical officer of Auschwitz, SS Dr. Wirths, she made a bold demand:

> I firmly but politely told him that if this was to be an experimental hospital, the place should look like one—bed sheets, towels, soap, and nightgowns for the women. It was unbelievable, but he said okay! He said I was surely not Jewish, because I was too blonde. Never mind! We got everything. When the nightgowns arrived in bundles of fifty, we distributed them and ordered the girls not to exchange the gowns each of them received.
>
> In the evening when all the SS doctors and SS *Blockführerin* left, we planned that the women should come down the stairs one by one in a kind of fashion parade in the gowns they had received. Imagine the show—a small woman in a big gown, a large woman in a small one. It was a comedy—a tragic comedy. Laughter on the sad faces.
>
> Then I asked who would sing and dance. Polish Mila Potasinski volunteered, and took charge of the cabaret from then on.

Mila, an actress, and Alma, a seasoned nightclub performer, became the leading performers in the Block 10 floor shows, at first held secretly in the evenings. Among other entertainments, Mila recited poetry as Alma provided musical background, or Alma played Spanish-American tunes as Mila taught the tango to women who were well enough to dance.[17]

For Ima, Alma's arrival in Block 10 marked a "new start." She commented that even Dr. Clauberg's first assistant, young Jewish prisoner-nurse Sylvia Friedmann, joined in the cabarets. The women danced as Alma played, and again the horrors of Auschwitz briefly receded. Ima recounted,

> Alma introduced us to the "Czardas" [a dance that accelerates from slow beginnings], played just for us, and taught us to dance it. The Slovakian blonde Sylvia, throwing aside her gruesome tasks, became the man in the dance—her skin as white as ice and with long legs. . . .
>
> The chance to hold someone close, to dance and end it with a kiss —often meaningful—helped the women realize they were alive in the Auschwitz dominion of death.

For some cabarets, the women fashioned gowns from the blue-tinted bed sheets. One inmate made artificial flowers, which the dancers pinned in hair that was beginning to grow back. According to Magda, the revels grew into a production the block finally staged. "It became so popular that we had to repeat it." It was obvious to Ima that Sylvia told Dr. Clauberg about the events, for word about the show in Block 10 spread through the camp, and SS officers began to attend the cabarets.

The SS quickly deemed Alma's talents too precious to be wasted on the Experimental Block. When Maria Mandel heard her play, she arranged her transfer to her own pet project, the women's orchestra at Birkenau. Sadly, the women of Block 10 lost their stellar performer.

Years later, Magda recalled Alma and the brief series of cabarets: "Alma had been the light at the center of one of those small glimpses of humanity, courage, and decency between the inmates, an individual whose behavior and performance—in spite of the pressure from the Germans—made life a little more bearable."

17

Mandel's Mascots

Those who failed to make a niche for themselves were doomed,
although exceptional energy or toughness might delay the end.
A prisoner who had won a privileged position for herself then had
to defend it with efficiency, vitality and iron will . . . and luck.
—Dr. Ella Lingens-Reiner

The top SS woman officer of the women's camp at Birkenau, SS Obersturmbannführerin Maria Mandel, was a commanding figure. Tall, blonde, and impeccable in her black cape, gray uniform, and silk stockings, she had to be addressed as "Oberaufseherin (Inspector-General) Mandel." A woman with a fanatical admiration of beauty and love of music, she could also display sadistic brutality. In her previous station at the Ravensbrück concentration camp, she was credited with a special way of striking women, the first blow making the victim's nose bleed. She is known to have broken a jaw at Rajsko, part of the Auschwitz complex, according to testimony at the postwar Cracow trial of December 1947 when she was sentenced to be hanged.

Born at Münzkirchen in Upper Austria, a few miles south of Hitler's birthplace Braunau am Inn, Mandel was ambitious and demanding. She had a lover among her fellow SS at Auschwitz (variously identified as SS Bischoff, the chief of construction, and SS Janisch), and she kept a handsome horse to ride for recreation. Her love of children was the subject of gruesome legend among the prisoners, yet she is known to have been cruel toward newborn babies and their mothers.

Fania Fénelon, a French singer with the orchestra in its final months, related the tale of a ringleted Polish toddler who arrived at the camp with his mother, destined for the gas.[1] As Mandel strode through a crowd of women and children awaiting their turn in the "shower," the little boy ran up to her. Instead of kicking him away, she bent to pick him up, covered his face with kisses, and carried him off. For a week she took him wherever she went, giving him chocolates and dressing him in fresh blue outfits daily, the finest from the piles of confiscated children's clothing. Then, suddenly, the child was gone. SS Mandel had personally delivered him to the gas chamber, honoring her Nazi loyalties above any human feeling. The SS were trained in such "incorruptibility," the vaunted Nazi hardness, and learned to exercise extreme cruelty without mercy.

Zippy described two encounters with Maria Mandel that demonstrate the deep split in the Nazi personality. On one of her unpredictable inspections of the barracks, Mandel found Zippy in bed in the afternoon, an unforgivable offense. When she demanded an explanation, Zippy said she had severe menstrual cramps. Zippy recalled with amazement: Mandel then "put her hand on my forehead in a motherly way and ordered me to stay in bed until I felt better again."

On another occasion, a runner came to the *Schreibstube* with an order for Zippy to report to Mandel's office. Not knowing why she had been summoned, Zippy responded to the order nervously. "When I entered, she held a book in her hand. It was *The River Pirates*. She asked me if I would letter, with special calligraphy, a dedication for her gift to SS Hauptsturmführer (Captain) Josef Kramer—later known as the "Beast of Belsen"—on his birthday, 10 November. I ventured to say it was a remarkable coincidence, for that was my birthday too."

In response, Mandel told Zippy to go to Block 5, where packages addressed to prisoners (many of them already dead) were stored, and to get a package for herself as a birthday present. Such a gesture toward a Jewish inmate was as disconcerting as it was rare. In the camps, prisoners were deeply moved by any sign of humanity from their Nazi masters.

With the crushing of the Warsaw uprising on 11 June 1943, Heinrich Himmler ordered the liquidation of all Jewish ghettos in Poland, beginning a new phase of mass executions. Tens of thousands of Polish Jews would be transported to Auschwitz by train and by truck, testing facilities to the limit. Zippy and other early arrivals watched with foreboding as new gas chambers and crematoria were built on the edge of the Birkenau camp. On 28 June 1943, the chief of construction, SS Sturmbannführer (Major) Karl Bischoff, announced that all five crematoria in Auschwitz-Birkenau were ready for operation.[2] He assessed their processing capacities per day as follows:

Auschwitz (*Stammlager*) No. 1	340 bodies
Birkenau No. 2 (new)	1,440 bodies
Birkenau No. 3 (new)	1,440 bodies
Birkenau No. 4 (new)	768 bodies
Birkenau No. 5 (new)	768 bodies

Until this time, corpses had been buried in mass graves. Later, in peak times when the flood of corpses surpassed the capacities of the new crematoria, bodies were burned in open pits.

To hide the true function of Birkenau, an order of 13 July 1943 required all surviving Jewish prisoners from Poland and Greece to write to relatives that they were healthy and to request packages. Many would be dead by the time their letters arrived.

Zippy recalled that German setbacks in North Africa, southern Europe, and the Soviet Union, as well as Allied air raids on German cities and pressures on the German industrial machine, only intensified activities at Auschwitz. The Germans commonly instituted newly severe orders when the attention of the outside world was directed away from the camps.

AUSCHWITZ HAD had music since 1941, when a professional men's orchestra was formed in the *Stammlager* after an entire Polish radio orchestra was arrested while performing and incarcerated. None of the musicians in the original Auschwitz orchestra was Jewish. The next year a men's orchestra was formed among the prisoners in Birkenau, an ensemble that did include Jews. The orchestras, known as *Lagerkapellen* or camp bands, pumped out marches as the work kommandos left camp each morning and returned in the evening. They were the pride of the SS commands of their respective camps.

The Birkenau men's orchestra, created in July 1942, was the inspiration of SS Unterscharführer (Corporal) Michael Wolf.[3] Its first director was non-Jewish Pole Jan Zaborski, who was succeeded in November 1942 by non-Jewish German Franz Kopka. Polish-born composer Szymon Laks, a Jewish member of the orchestra, assumed command late in 1943.

Laks wrote in his 1948 memoir that he was mystified by the popularity of the orchestras among the SS. He could never reconcile the Germans' emotional response to music with the brutality of the camp regime. In his words: "Could people who love music to this extent, people who can cry when they hear it, be at the same time capable of committing so many atrocities on the rest of humanity?"[4]

Addressing the same conundrum, Robert J. Lifton, a Yale psychologist who has explored suffering under oppression, describes a process he calls "doubling," which took place at Auschwitz among prisoners, functionaries, and SS alike.[5] Although doubling can occur in many groups, it is most common among professionals, including doctors, clergy, politicians, writers, and artists —people who have developed a "professional self" that can override an earlier "humane self" and even lend itself to inhumane causes. In essence, Lifton defines doubling as "the psychological means by which one invokes the evil potential of the self."[6] Mengele, a "Nazi mystic" who commanded a curious mixture of fear and respect, was the supreme example of this process. His commitment to Nazi doctrine, especially to racial theory, made it possible for him to inflict pain while feeling nothing for the victims, a characteristic of ideological fanatics.[7] Thus he could cut into a child's flesh then offer candy as a gift.

To the extent that the sensibilities of the "humane self" lingered, Auschwitz victims who bowed before Nazi authority could rationalize with such thoughts as *Through my actions many are lost, but some are saved.* The "Auschwitz self" Lifton describes was completely apart from "ordinary experience," giving it "still another dimension of numbing."[8] In the harrowing atmosphere of the camp, to keep a few others alive and to stay alive oneself could become an individual's sole objective. Within the world of Auschwitz, Lifton considers the posture more adaptive than reflective of lifelong patterns.

At Auschwitz, Lifton concludes, the sensitive and caring sides of personalities were subjugated to the "other planet" of the death camp. Rules totally reversed those of ordinary society. As an artist-inmate identified as Eva C. explained, "According to those rules, 'we were there to die and not to live.' And 'to be able to accept being where we were, we had to switch . . . to a different kind of mentality, to a different kind of attitude.'"[9]

Looking back on his Auschwitz experience after fifty-three years, SS Dr. Hans Münch said simply: "You have to realize that murdering people became as natural as carrying out the routine jobs you have to do every day. You got used to everyday life in Auschwitz."[10]

MANDEL, aware of the prestige the men's orchestras conferred on their SS sponsors, conceived of a women's orchestra chiefly as a means of furthering her own career. In the spring of 1943, she broached the subject with the staff of the camp office. Zippy and her coworkers were ready: a survey of the office card files showed that a number of Polish women in the camp had some knowledge of music and played instruments. In most Central European schools, teachers were required to have musical training, so former teachers, in particular, were good prospects for a women's orchestra.

Camp authorities met in April 1943 and decided to proceed with recruitment. Orders posted in various blocks within the women's camp requested non-Jewish prisoners with musical experience to come forward. Player by player, the new ensemble began to take shape.

Violinist Zofia Cykowiak, who was among the first recruits, described the orchestra's earliest days:

> The first to respond to the notices were Zofia Czajkowska [also spelled Cjakowska, Tschajkovska, and Tchaikowska], a former schoolteacher—and political prisoner [since April 1942]—from Tarnów, and Stefania Baruch, another teacher, who played guitar and mandolin, and three violinists.
>
> Czajkowska soon recruited other players from different barracks and new arrivals in the Quarantine Block, resulting in an ensemble of

> fifteen by the end of May 1943. At the beginning the repertory was modest: a few German marches and some popular military Polish melodies. Czajkowska and the guitarist Stefania played from memory and arranged the pieces for different instruments.[11]
>
> The instruments were obtained from the men's camp [from the orchestra in Auschwitz I], whose director was Adam Kopyciński. To get them, we went under an SS woman guard to the men's camp in Auschwitz. A few sheets of music and instructions were received from the Birkenau men's orchestra. . . . The women's orchestra, however, was not important at first. We were a "work kommando" from morning call to evening call, with a short halt for lunch.
>
> The orchestra began to play in the hospital blocks in June [1943]. That month the orchestra was also ordered to play marches for the morning and evening parades of workers leaving for work and returning to camp for the evening roll call. Mandel was especially encouraged when phonetically Czajkowska sounded like the name of the composer Peter Ilyich Tchaikovsky. . . .
>
> Czajkowska, with some musical knowledge, provided a basis on which to begin. Mandel chose Czajkowska as the conductor. The young musicians were so happy to find a refuge away from the camp's horrors that they did not disclose to Mandel that Czajkowska was neither related to the composer, nor had any musical talent. Let the SS be deceived.[12]

Zippy expanded on this account of the orchestra's beginnings. It was important to her resistance efforts that she maintain contacts within the men's camp. In her words:

> We asked Mandel if she would allow us to visit the highly respected orchestra in the *Stammlager.* She gave us a guard to give us official status. We took Czajkowska and every possible Polish prisoner of significance, chosen for their importance as seen through the eyes of pre-war Polish society or for their associations with music.
>
> The whole Polish hierarchy was in Auschwitz-Birkenau. It was such a strong deputation that the men musicians at Auschwitz promised to support the efforts of the women, who truthfully could hardly be called musicians.

According to Zippy, Czajkowska proved to be an excellent negotiator during the orchestra's formative stages.

> We wanted to see how the men functioned. I had a dual role, working with and reporting to Katya [Singer]—the prisoner in charge of the Birkenau camp office—on the negotiations with the men's orchestra. They

> agreed to supply us with violins and all the necessary instruments in abundance. They had their own, and there were thousands of instruments from all over Europe from deportees who had been encouraged to bring along their most precious movable possessions, unaware that upon arrival everything would be taken away from them. Even the sheet music they brought with them was used by the camp orchestras. Auschwitz by this time was the Fort Knox of Europe, with all the possessions taken from people in the countless transports that arrived at the camps. . . .
>
> After four weeks the orchestra had a barracks. It was Block 12.

Maria Moś-Wdowik, a Polish mandolinist and copyist who bore the early prisoner number 6111, told how widely Czajkowska ranged to find her first orchestra players:

> I was sick and Czajkowska noticed my long hair and asked if I'd been in the camp long. I told her I'd been there for nine or ten months. She asked me if I knew and could write musical notation. I answered that I did, because in school we learned how to read music.
>
> Czajkowska invited me to the block set apart for the future orchestra, gave me paper and pencil, and had me rewrite notes for specific instruments, first the violin and mandolin. The first music was the march from *Rosamunde*. Then came little songs which Czajkowska had written down from memory, and I copied them.[13]

An invitation to join the Music Block was a reprieve for the "orchestra girls" (as the women were known in the camp and as they called themselves), most of whom were teenagers separated from their families for the first time. The campwise young Zippy, who became a mandolinist in the orchestra, found herself in two of the best possible Birkenau worlds, with extra food in each place since both the office staff and the orchestra members received double rations. Officially the orchestra was an *Arbeitskommando,* a work detail; yet unlike the prisoner-musicians of the Birkenau men's camp, the women had no duties besides music-making. Unofficially they were Mandel's mascots, and Mandel was determined they would excel.

It soon became evident that the survival of the orchestra depended on its development as a musical ensemble. In May 1943, Czajkowska began to recruit Jewish women from Germany and Greece.

The first transports of Jews from Salonika had arrived in the spring of 1943. Among them were two sisters, Lily and Yvette Assael, and their brother Michael, whose family had been betrayed by Jews in their own community. The Assaels and other Greek Jews in the huge transports arrived at camp in an enfeebled state after seven days of travel in cattle cars. During the selection at the train ramp, Yvette, who was only fifteen, wanted to go with an aunt, but Lily insisted that they stay together. The aunt was directed to the line that led to the gas chamber. Lily, Yvette, and Michael survived the selection and were admitted to Birkenau.

Debilitated by the long journey and isolated by the lack of a language in common with most Jews of Central and Eastern Europe, the Greek Jews admitted to the camp perished in great numbers. Lily and Yvette found sanctuary in the orchestra, which they joined shortly after it was organized. Of the two, Lily, who played the accordion and who had played the piano in a moviehouse in their Greek community, had the broader musical background. (After special training, Yvette would become a double bass player.) Under Czajkowska, they could scarcely hope to advance musically, yet they played as well as they could and were grateful for the opportunity.

By the end of June 1943, the music kommando had approximately twenty members, most of them non-Jews from Poland like Czajkowska herself. Sylvia Wagenberg Calif, a Jewish recorder player from Germany; her sister Karla Wagenberg Hyman, who played recorder and piccolo; and Hilde Grünbaum Zimche, a Jewish percussionist from Germany, with Zippy and the Assael sisters, were the earliest Jewish members of the orchestra. All six would survive the war, exceptions to the rule for Jewish captives at Auschwitz.

Hélène Scheps, a Jewish violinist from Brussels, was one of the first highly qualified musicians to enter the orchestra. When she was eight years old, her father, a cabinetmaker who moved his family from Poland to Belgium to escape anti-Semitism, gave her her first violin, purchased from an old man in tattered clothing. When she was eleven, her father gave her a first-class instrument even as he chided her for never playing a whole piece, but practicing endlessly to perfect musical phrases. For a time she studied with the wife of the great violinist Eugène Ysaÿe. When the Nazis invaded, she entered a paper marriage at the age of fourteen with an older man who sought to help her. Like Alma, she never lived with her husband. Hiding separately from her parents in the country, Hélène and her brother were denounced, arrested by the Gestapo, and sent to the Belgian holding camp at Malines for transport to the East. She lost contact with her brother, who had an outbreak of boils, and never saw him again after he was deported in a "hospital train."[14] Arriving at Auschwitz in early August 1943, she was spared during the on-ramp selection and marched to Birkenau.

Hélène recalled her arrival at the camp and her first encounter with Czajkowska:

> During the tattooing and the humiliating shaving, I didn't flinch. But there, at the side of the block where we were sitting, I broke into tears. A young girl [Elsa Miller, a fellow prisoner from Belgium] consoled me: "If they ask you what you can do, tell them you are a couturière. I will teach you, if it works." But nobody asked me anything. It was desolation, the end of the world, the end of my life?

> Like a Leitmotiv from an opera, it became an idée fixe that I would never again play my violin, and I cried.
>
> Then a miracle occurred. I saw approaching me a civilized-looking woman who was well dressed. I told myself on seeing her: "This is a German!"
>
> She spoke French: "Is it true that you play the violin?"
>
> How did she know? Some women on the convoy told her that I was a musician.
>
> "Yes, I play the violin."
>
> "For how long?"
>
> "I have studied five years."
>
> "Is it true?"
>
> "Yes, it's true."
>
> "Good! Then you come with me."
>
> "That is not the question. I will not play for the Germans."
>
> "Chut!" she insisted: "Come with me."
>
> My friend the couturière said "Shush!" She knew. An angel had come to take me by the hand. . . .
>
> She [Czajkowska] led me to the music barrack. I was dreaming. She gave me a violin. I played the *Chaconne* of Bach. I cried on that violin, and the others cried with me. I did not realize that my life depended on the audition that day. I still did not know that I had the best place in the concentration camp.
>
> Still in the Camp A Quarantine Block as a new arrival, where I had to return to sleep, I walked to Camp B to the Music Block as soon as the roll calls ended each day. As I walked, I could see the horrors of the camp.[15]

Hélène was able to extend her good fortune to Fanny Korenblum Birkenwald, another Jewish prisoner from Belgium whom Hélène had met at Malines.

> Madame Korenblum [Fanny's mother] . . . was intrigued by my comings and goings. She asked me if it was possible for Fanny to get into the orchestra. Fanny played the mandolin.
>
> I spoke to Frau Czajkowska, our leader at the time, who despite her name [which sounded like Tchaikowska] knew nothing about music.
>
> At the audition, Fanny was accepted. We were now three Belgian girls [Else Felstein, a Jewish violinist from Belgium, was already a member of the orchestra], and we stayed together during our entire captivity.

Czajkowska, who had some knowledge of choral direction, showed courage in introducing Polish folk songs into the orchestra's tiny repertoire. Some of its earliest concerts were held in the Revier, the Birkenau women's hospital. Zofia Cykowiak, among others, remembers the effect the simple Polish melodies had among the sick and dying. "It even happened that women who were sick and couldn't move otherwise would get up from their beds, and touch us and the instruments to be sure that what they were hearing was not a dream."

All the same, as Zippy put it: "We could not be proud of our playing under Czajkowska. It was *Katzenmusik.* We were playing and we tried hard, but we were like monkeys to an organ grinder."

THE SITUATION changed completely in August when Mandel discovered Alma in the Block 10 cabaret and installed her as leader of the struggling orchestra. Yvette, the young Greek musician, recalled the moment of Alma's arrival:

> I shall never forget the day the SS brought Alma to the Music Block. She was placed at the third desk of the violins. She seemed to have difficulty seeing the notes.
>
> That day she was merely introduced by the SS as a new member of the orchestra. The next day, the SS told the girls in the Music Block who Alma was, and that she was going to play something for them. She played, I think, Monti's "Czardas." We immediately realized she was really something. Then they announced that she was the new leader.[16]

Hélène Scheps commented that Alma's arrival, a short time after her own, "was an event. It proved that the SS wanted to make a real orchestra in the women's camp out of our odds-and-ends group."

Sylvia, the German-Jewish recorder player, described the shock of the sudden shift in command: "One day the SS arrived at the Music Block. They told us they had discovered a musician conductor, Alma Rosé. She turned the orchestra upside down on its head. Already with mandolins, violins, guitars, cello, banjos, drum, and singers, we played from morning to night."[17]

In the camp office, Zippy kept an eye on Alma's transfer. Said Zippy, "It was an emotional crisis for Zofia Czajkowska, who was showing signs of so much stress that she was given to violent outbursts of temper. It could have been a tragedy for her. But she and Alma were such fine ladies."

Czajkowska, a camp veteran, knew the orchestra had a better chance of survival under the direction of a professional musician, and all the girls in the ensemble would benefit from an increase in its stature. When Alma took over as kapo, or block chief, Czajkowska cooperated in her reduced role as block senior (*Blockälteste* in German, *blockowa* in Polish), also a position that conveyed privilege.[18]

Zippy continued:

> If Czajkowska had not wanted to have Alma in the orchestra—or at least had been unwilling to step down as leader—it is possible that she could have prevented Alma's taking over so easily. . . .

> Alma at first had difficulty with the Polish players, but Czajkowska in stepping down and taking on the position of block senior was able to help Alma overcome those early problems. Alma did not speak Polish, and very few Poles knew German. Instead of sulking and making Alma's work more difficult, Czajkowska proved to be a great help.

As a Polish speaker in the camp at a time when most of the prisoners were Polish, Czajkowska was able to negotiate with the Poles in the *Stammlager* men's orchestra of over a hundred professionals, who at first showed animosity toward the new Jewish kapo. Long-standing Polish anti-Semitism could surface even in the face of a common enemy, and some Poles in the camp felt that Alma had usurped Czajkowska's position as leader of the Music Block. Although there were other Jewish kapos at Auschwitz-Birkenau, they were rarities, and they often had to contend with the opposition of non-Jews. To strengthen Alma's position in the camp, Mandel reportedly had her classification changed from Dutch Jew to *Mischlinge* (part-Jew) and her registration officially changed to her maiden name Rosé.

Zofia Cykowiak had mixed memories of Czajkowska as the blockowa. Although she could be motherly toward the very young girls, Zofia said, she was capable of hysterical outbursts and sometimes beat the players when they did not play the music as she thought they should. She was "very nervous and frequently shrieking," another orchestra member remembered; but "her position was not an easy one. She had suffered many months of torture, as many Poles in the camp had. Czajkowska's good work was in creating the music kommando in the first place, and accepting and coaching girls who hardly knew how to hold their instruments."[19]

In August 1943, as the new kapo of the Music Block—in command of a barrack and an orchestra after less than a month at the camp—Alma joined a select, often despised company of prisoners. Many of her peers in the camp hierarchy were felons given their posts as block commanders by virtue of their willingness to follow SS orders and to show as much brutality to their underlings as the Nazis themselves. Alma's response to being elevated to this questionable position was to cling to her dignity and turn inward more than ever. Separating herself from those she considered unsavory, asserting her full authority over the orchestra, she focused with all the intensity of her nature on the musical work before her.

Zippy commented: "No conductor in the world ever faced a more formidable task. Alma was charged with making something out of sheer rock." The average age of the ensemble she inherited was nineteen; the youngest musician was fourteen, the oldest about Alma's age, thirty-six. Their youth and inexperience posed enormous difficulties.

Even with double food rations and other privileges, the rigors of the orchestra's schedule made it difficult for the weaker players to keep up. Lota Kröner, a German flutist among the elders in the orchestra, occasionally had to be awakened for her entry during a performance. She and her younger sister Maria, a cellist, had joined the orchestra about a month before Alma's arrival. Maria died in the camp shortly after she came to the Music Block, leaving the ensemble without any instruments in the low range. "Tante" (Aunt) Kröner, as Lota was affectionately called, would also die before war's end.[20]

Sylvia described Alma's efforts to procure good instruments for the orchestra by "organizing," the camp term for the bartering that became the prisoners' economic system. Said Sylvia, "Alma picked the best instruments among those brought to the camp by people arriving in transports. She acquired musical scores the same way, using the piano score, which she orchestrated."

One of the first to benefit from the change of leadership in the orchestra was young French violinist Violette Jacquet (today Violette Silberstein, a survivor who lives in Paris). Rejected by Czajkowska at her first audition, Violette had been sent back to her block. When Alma took over, Hélène Scheps, who arrived at Auschwitz on the same transport as Violette, urged her to present herself a second time. She played the violin badly. Moreover the audition selection, from Emmerich Kálmán's *Countess Maritza,* an Alma specialty, was an unfortunate choice.

Violette recalled:

> Alma rightly was not convinced of my talents and told me: "I'll take you on a one-week trial." It meant that each morning, after roll call in my own block—crowded four and five to a bunk arranged in three tiers, with hunger making me even more desperate—I trudged to the Music Block to practice with the orchestra.
>
> The third day, someone stole my galoshes. I arrived with cold, dirty bare feet from walking in the mud. It had rained all night. Before I was allowed in the block, Czajkowska made me wash my feet in icy cold water. As a result, absolutely frozen, I began to cry.
>
> Coming onto the scene, Alma asked why the tears.
>
> When I explained, Alma said: "All right. I'll take you in the orchestra right now."
>
> That was the first time she saved my life.[21]

MARGOT ANZENBACHER (later Margot Větrovcová), a Czechoslovakian Jewish poet and linguist who had studied the violin, remembered her own journey to the Music Block:

> At first I thought I was being sent to Usovic. That meant I was fortunate to be sent to a place near my home, near Marienbad. When I was on the train, I realized how wrong I was that summer of 1943. . . .

> When we arrived at Oświęcim, we were marched to Birkenau. The railroad into the camp had not yet been built. We walked under guard of SS and their dogs. In the lead were young girls and women. The rear, the older women, were hit by SS rifles to make them move more quickly. One young woman went back to help one of the older women who might have been her mother. Finally she was also clubbed.[22]

A "crazy circus of hell and ruin" greeted the new arrivals.

> Women moved around us wearing an unbelievable assortment of men's and women's clothing. Only here and there were striped uniforms. Occasionally one saw a woman nicely dressed with silk stockings, high-heeled shoes, nice shawl, and even stylish hair. They were the prisoner-functionaries in the camp.
>
> As a newcomer, I was given a summer working uniform left by Soviet POWs who had died, and wooden shoes. The trousers and shoes were held on with string. There was no underwear. . . . Every morning there was a long *Appell* [roll call] for hours as we were counted. Those who couldn't or wouldn't live simply lay on the ground so they would not suffer anymore. [In concentration camp parlance these were the *Muselmänner* or Moslems—perhaps because they often lay prostrate as if in prayer or obedience to fate.]
>
> As *Aussenkommando* [assigned to work details outside the camp], we worked hard with the prodding of the SS and their dogs. . . . One stood all day in water. When my foot was injured, I was ordered by a functionary to get pails and bale out the latrines into carts for that purpose and pull them away. It was hell.
>
> A saving grace was the fact I was allowed to give out the food. Because I gave big portions, the food did not go around. For this, the *stubowa* [barrack worker] hit me on the head. Then I got jaundice. I stopped eating the little I received. Then I was sent to the *Strafkommando* [punishment detail].

At one point, "looking at the same section of sky that someone I loved at home was looking at, not knowing that I am alive and fearing that I would never get out of there," Margot noticed an SS dog eating a piece of bread.

> I said to him: "Do you not know that I am not angry with you? You are doing what you are trained for." I say: "Give me a piece of bread." He didn't give it to me, but watched my every movement. As I sat down in front of him, I reached out my hand talking to him quietly and slowly. Finally I patted him on the head.
>
> The SS was watching me. One of them pulled out his revolver. I thought this was my end. Then the dog was ordered to go. The SS man shot the dog.
>
> He ignored me.

From a distance, in her misery, young Margot noticed Alma, whom she described as a "nice, healthy middle-aged woman." Said Margot, "I didn't even realize the music was not a joke. . . . I would become angry when they played wrong notes and made mistakes. 'And this bothers you?' some of my companions asked."

Although Margot wore a numbered triangle, labeling her a political prisoner not ordinarily subject to gassing, her health had deteriorated so much that friends warned her she could be chosen for extermination at the next selection. Joining the orchestra was her only hope.

> At one stage, Alma was sick, but I was told that when she returned she would be asked to take me into the orchestra. Alma arranged for me to be freed from the work I was doing, and I was to be on trial for eight days. In the Music Block they gave me a violin, but my hands had been so badly damaged that I could not hold the violin, and the notes danced in front of my eyes.
>
> Helpless, hopeless. I said to my friends it wouldn't work. I was told: "You don't go there because of your nice eyes. It is because of the party organization. You must survive it. You will go into the orchestra even if you don't play."

A week later, during a rest period, Margot found herself alone in the music room. She continues:

> I was surrounded by instruments. I took up a guitar. It was out of tune. I tuned it. I started to play quietly. Alma approached me: "Who is playing? This is an intermission."
>
> I didn't answer. Alma then said: "That sounds nice. You know notes, and something of music. You know languages?" She accepted me into the orchestra. I was saved—accepted five minutes before midnight. It was not important that I was accepted as a guitarist rather than a violinist. . . .
>
> When we played Dvořák, it seemed Alma was looking at me and in another world. She must have thought the music had a special significance for me and for her and her former husband Váša—when he practiced and she would accompany him on the piano, or playing with her father.

In the constantly shifting camp population, recruitment was an ongoing effort. Hélène Scheps recalled that Alma "looked for musicians among new arrivals. . . . Among the Polish arrivals, she found Helena, a young violinist from Lwów."

Brick-walled Block 25—among the few buildings still standing at Auschwitz II–Birkenau—was a holding barrack for women who had been selected, their last stop before going to the gas. For Helena Dunicz-Niwińska, it was also the introduction to camp life.

Helena and her fifty-five-year-old mother, Maria Monika, arrived as political prisoners on 23 October 1943. They had been in jails in Lwów (Lemberg) for nine months, falsely accused of hiding members of the Polish resistance. Now they were sent to Block 25 because the Quarantine Blocks were too crowded to accommodate them.

Forty-two years later during a visit to Auschwitz, Helena relived her first night in the infamous barrack. They could hear the screams of women in another part of the building. The exhausted mother and daughter shared a straw mattress on bare earth below a row of three-tiered bunks. They tried to sleep under a rain of dust and vermin—including the typhus-bearing lice—as inmates higher up turned and tossed in fitful sleep.

When the block was roused the next morning, Helena and her mother realized they had been placed in a barrack for the doomed. The piece of bread they had saved from the night before had been eaten by rats, and their only food consisted of scraps remaining after the whole camp was fed. According to Marie-Claude Vaillant-Couturier, very often the women in the block "went days without a drop of water."[23]

Vaillant-Couturier told of the cries in all languages day and night of "Drink. Drink. Water!" Roused to an overwhelming pity, she recounted, her friend Annette Épaux, aged thirty,

> came back to our block to get a little herbal tea, but as she was passing it through the bars of the window she was seen by the *Aufseherin*, who took her by the neck and threw her into Block 25. Two days later I saw her on the truck which was taking internees to the gas chamber. She had her arms around another French woman, Line Porcher, and when the truck started moving, she cried, "Think of my little boy, if you ever get back to France." Then they started singing "La Marseillaise."

Non-Jewish Polish prisoner Eugenia Marchiewicz, a teacher before her internment, was haunted decades later by memories of hands stretching through the bars of Block 25 as women cried for food and water. One day she was working on a gravel walk beside the block when a woman begged for a drink. "It had rained, and there was a puddle of water out of which I scooped some in my cup. As I was passing it to the hand, an SS club smashed down on my arm and knocked the cup and water to the ground."[24]

Helena and her mother were soon transferred—Helena to the Music Block because of her violin training, and her mother to another barrack in the camp —but nightmarish images of Block 25 lingered. The morning routine in the latrines—two long rows of round holes in a slab of concrete over a deep trench

—and the mere seconds allowed for washing in a trickle of water left an indelible mark on Helena. From that moment, she confided, privacy became her clearest objective in life.

At the end of Block 25 was the now overgrown "Meadow." Here in a dusty, muddy, or icy field, hundreds of prisoners from the Quarantine Blocks lined up in ranks of five for roll calls that sometimes lasted all day. "You could see prisoners picking lice off each other, some fainting, some beaten," Helena remembered.[25]

After such roll calls, a prisoner work detail was called to remove the bodies. It was best not to be in the front line or at the end of a line, where "you were an easy target for a truncheon," according to Marchiewicz.

A few weeks after Helena and her mother were separated, Helena was marching with the orchestra through the camp after the morning performance at the gate.

> My mother suddenly appeared from beside the road. She said she was dying of dysentery. She pleaded for some charred bread.[26] My friends in the orchestra block prepared some charred bread which I managed to take to my mother.
>
> A few days later, I heard she was dead. Someone said that the bread sent to her was moldy and had made her condition worse.

Yvette, too, told of sharing bread in an attempt to help a family member.

> One day I got a message from Katya in the camp office that my brother was in the camp. I took a piece of bread that I had stored and ran over to the office. I could not appear to be talking with him, so at the corner of the building I looked along one side and he stood around the corner looking along the other. We exchanged a few words and I left the little piece of bread for him on a kind of board for him to pick up.

Through such gifts and attentions, the orchestra women could sometimes spread their special benefits.

FLORA SCHRIJVER JACOBS recalls the Music Block as her "doorway to life."[27] As a young music student, she had received piano training. Her father, a member of the Amsterdam Philharmonic, foresaw the uncertainty of events in Europe and ordered lessons for her in popular music as well as six months' training on the piano accordion. When the family was ordered to report to the holding camp at Westerbork in Holland for "working resettlement in the East," they bought new work clothes and heavy boots. Flora's younger sister went underground (she was later taken from hiding and gassed). With her parents, eighteen-year-old Flora was sent to Auschwitz.

Flora last saw her mother on the train ramp as she was marched to a waiting truck. The young girl dared to approach SS Dr. Josef Mengele, who was presiding over the selection of new arrivals.

> "I'm coming like a Hollander," I told him, "and I would like to go with my mother."
>
> "No," he said. "You are young and you must work. I'll see you in a couple of hours."

Mengele told her there was a shortage of trucks, and she would have to walk into the camp. Flora continued:

> Later I saw what I thought were five factories. A lady came to me, gave me a number, took my hair, and I was all naked with no clothes. She then said to me, "See the smoke, that's your transport. They are burning."
>
> I hit her. "You are crazy; go to a doctor," I said. Then she told me: "No. Old people are burned." That is how I found out that my mother was dead. My father was sent to Russia, where he was shot.

Sent to the Quarantine Blocks, a dazed Flora had no will to live. For forty days she fought grief, hunger, and illness.

> I had all the sicknesses you can think of—typhus and what not. I think I could have lived only four or five more days. A hundred girls from my transport went to the Quarantine Block. Two weeks later, only three other girls and I survived.
>
> You died there from yourself. Other inmates told me I would die or be the victim of the next selection if I didn't do something.
>
> Someone came into the block and asked if anyone played music.
>
> I said I played piano. He said: "No. No piano."
>
> Then a girl came over to me. "Do you play nothing else? Otherwise you'll go to the gas next week." I told her that I took accordion lessons for six months. She then went to the officer and told him I not only played the piano, but also the accordion.

As it happened, Alma was holding auditions for an accordion player. The places in the Music Block were so highly prized that 150 women said they could play the instrument. From the three women selected for a final audition in August 1943, Alma picked Flora. Announcing her choice, she said she was sorry she was allowed only one accordionist. In her joy, Flora felt sorry for Alma, who had to make the decision that may have been a death warrant for the other contenders.

Alma told Flora she had a special love and respect for the Dutch people; she added, "I'm giving you a chance to survive." Flora confessed to Alma that in truth she was a pianist and had little training on the accordion. "I was awful," she admitted. Alma promised to work with her on the instrument.

Flora showed up at the Music Block with bare feet, dirty and skimpily clad in the gray and blue striped prison-issue dress. As a member of the orchestra, she was given better clothing. More importantly, she received a degree of faith that she might leave the camp alive. As Alma herself told her, she could never have survived the physical strain of a work kommando if she had to contend with the lot of common prisoners.

ANITA LASKER-WALLFISCH, too, recalled her first encounter with Alma as life-giving.[28] It had been two years since the seventeen-year-old from Breslau (now Wroclaw, Poland) played the cello, and nothing was further from her mind when she arrived in Auschwitz-Birkenau in a detachment of political prisoners. Her parents had been deported earlier, never to be seen again. She and her older sister Renate had worked in a war industry with French prisoners of war, through whom they formed a connection with the French underground and became involved in preparing false documents.[29] Arrested as they attempted to escape to France, the sisters were tried in a Gestapo court and sentenced to three and a half years of hard labor.

Separated from her sister, Anita arrived at Birkenau in the middle of the night.

> I was well informed about Auschwitz. I knew about the gas chambers and was fully aware that now the fight for survival was on in earnest. My first impression was dogs, black figures in capes and shouting. The "welcoming ceremony" began at daybreak. Taken to another block, we had to take our clothes off, were shaved and a number tattooed on the left forearm.
>
> All this was done—I only slowly understood—not by Germans but by other prisoners all eager to hear "news" from the outside world.
>
> As I was about to surrender my clothes, one of the prisoners asked where I came from. How was the war going? What did I do to be arrested? Would I give her my shoes (which I did, as I would lose them anyway)? I answered all the questions and told her—although it seemed superfluous under the prevailing circumstances—that I played the cello. The girl grabbed me and said: "Good. You are saved! Stand aside. Wait."
>
> By then I was stark naked, shaved, and clutching a toothbrush, which I did not realize at the time was already a great privilege. There I was, in the by-then totally deserted block. Waiting for I knew not what. The block with showers overhead was what I had expected a gas chamber to look like. This was in fact the Sauna, the bath or delousing place. Totally bewildered, I felt I had prepared myself for just this moment in

long agonizing nights in prison, and had mesmerized myself into a state of complete indifference.

I had [previously] survived a "suicide" when a pill I thought was cyanide turned out to be sugar, a Gestapo interrogation, a trial, imprisonment. Now I found myself in a situation that was to turn out completely differently from the expected, just as it had with the "cyanide" capsule.

Alone, I waited for the gas to be turned on, when in walked a tall and handsome lady, dressed in a camel-hair coat and wearing a head scarf. She could have been on the streets of St. Louis.

Was this a guard or a prisoner? She was so well dressed, I was baffled. She greeted me, introduced herself as Alma Rosé, expressed her delight that I was a cellist, asked where I had come from and with whom I had studied. The last thing I had imagined talking about in Auschwitz was cello playing. Alma said I would be saved.

I would have to go to the Quarantine Block, but not to worry—someone would come for me soon and I would have an "audition."...

A few days later, an SS officer who shared Mandel's pride in the orchestra came to the block and called for "the cellist." At the Music Block a cello was thrust in my hands. I was surrounded by a weird collection of instruments. There were several fiddles, mandolins, guitars, flutes, harmonica, and accordion. After a few moments to re-acquaint myself with the instrument, I was asked to play Schubert's "Marche Militaire," which, thank God, was still within my capacity. Alma was delighted that at last she had an instrument in the lower range to play underneath all those high instruments.

Thus began my career as the cellist in the orchestra.... Since there were special privileges in the music kommando, as many people as remotely possible were rescued into it.

Anita's admission to the orchestra also made it possible to save Renate. In Anita's words:

About a week after my arrival a girl came running into the Music Block and told me to go to the reception quickly, as my sister had just arrived. You can imagine my feelings. I had last seen my sister when she was sent to "hard labor" after our trial in Breslau, some six months earlier. I had had very little hope of ever seeing her again.

She was being "processed" by the same person who "processed" me, and my sister noticed the girl was wearing shoes that looked familiar to her. Those shoes had been dyed black after I spilled something on them. My mother had been angry with me at the time for spoiling those shoes. They stood out because they had red laces.

When my sister asked where those shoes had come from, she was

> told that earlier somebody had arrived who was now in the orchestra. Renate knew instantly that it could only be I.
>
> I went to the Reception Block immediately.
>
> The enormity of this coincidence can only be appreciated when you realize how immense the camp was. (A constant enrollment of about twenty-six thousand women.) Our joy, of course, was indescribable. My black shoes had saved her. I dare say she would never have survived the Quarantine Block, except for my membership in the orchestra. As I was the only cellist, I was indispensable. You might say a VIP.
>
> Even apart from the big holes in her legs that oozed pus and would not heal, her physical condition was so poor that she contracted typhus. Such was her suffering that I often wished her dead.
>
> She was not allowed to enter our block, and I had to sneak out the odd mug of soup and some bread, while she stood outside like a miserable beggar.
>
> Eventually I plucked up my courage and spoke to Mandel, and with my enviable qualifications of being the cellist and speaking German, I asked if my sister could be employed as a *Läuferin* (a runner, or messenger) who had to stand by the gate and wait to be sent on errands. Mandel gave her the job. Since it, too, was accompanied by privileges, my sister survived.

To further help her sister, Anita organized medication for her with the help of Henry Meyer, an Auschwitz prisoner who also came from Breslau. Meyer, assigned with Michael Assael to a work party that pushed a wagon around the camp on daily rounds, was able to get the precious medicine to Renate via the Music Block despite the fact that he was forbidden to enter the barracks in the women's camp. As he made his deliveries, fellow prisoners stood guard outside.

Meyer recalled that when he met Alma in the Music Block, even in the dehumanized setting of Birkenau, the Rosé name was magic to him. He had heard Arnold Rosé perform in Prague with Bruno Walter and had attended performances by Alma's pianist cousin Wolfgang.[30]

In her search for capable musicians, Alma added a number of Jewish girls to the orchestra in the first few weeks. Greek accordionist Lily Assael heard an SS officer say to Alma reproachfully: "You have a lot of Jewish girls here." Lily was alarmed. She was aware that at its inception the orchestra had been an "Aryan" project, and although she brought experience as a working musician to the block, the position of her younger sister Yvette would be threatened if the value of each Jewish orchestra member was questioned.

Lily went to Alma with a proposal. The orchestra could use a double bass player, she said, adding truthfully that their mother had purchased a double bass for Yvette at home in Salonika. Alma carried the proposal to women's camp commandant SS Obersturmbannführer (Lieutenant-Colonel) Franz Hössler, an ardent fan of the orchestra, saying that if a member of the men's orchestra could be freed to give her lessons, Yvette could learn the instrument.

A request went over to the Birkenau men's camp for someone to teach one of the girls to play the double bass. Heinz Lewin, a member of the men's orchestra, was excused from his primary duties as a watchmaker and for two months made regular visits to the Music Block to teach Yvette. "It was a happy experience," said Yvette, "for my brother would come with him as a helper, and we would manage visits at the same time."

After two months, SS Josef Kramer questioned the usefulness of the lessons and summoned Yvette to play for him. Alma rose to Yvette's support, saying it must be remembered that she had taken lessons only two months, and that her instrument was essential to the overall sound of the orchestra. Yvette then performed and passed the test. As the only double bass player, the fifteen-year-old had a secure place in the orchestra from that time forth. To her amazement, after her performance, SS Kramer commented encouragingly, "When you get out of here, you will have a career."

ALMA'S SPECIAL efforts to keep Jewish girls in the Music Block are demonstrated by the experience of Regina Kupferberg Bacia, now living in Israel and known as Rivka Bacia. Regina arrived at Birkenau on 1 August 1943 from Bedzin, Poland. She had played the mandolin in an elementary school orchestra and attempted the audition required for orchestra membership but failed. As she prepared to leave the block, Alma asked another question: could she write music notation?

As Regina remembered,

> Then she tested me again, writing music. This time she was enthusiastic . . . and decided to take me as a copyist. . . . Later on, she asked me to help her with her room and personal arrangements. Officially I was a copyist and unofficially Alma's personal assistant. Consequently, close and warm personal relations developed between us.[31]

Hilde Grünbaum Zimche, a young Zionist from Germany who played percussion with the orchestra from its early days, also helped Alma to arrange and copy music. In an interview on Kol Israel, Israel Radio, thirty-five years after liberation, Hilde commented that Alma's attitude was unbelievable in this atmosphere of destruction and death. Who but Alma could conceive of building something of beauty at Auschwitz-Birkenau?

In Hilde's words:

> Alma believed that if we perhaps survived this period, we could prove we could build something in the camp, and survival would be proven worthwhile, and perhaps we could continue [to perform] with the same group of people after the war.
>
> In my opinion, she didn't believe we played for the Nazis, but [that we] played for ourselves in order to survive. She also knew the orchestra had to be good or we would be liquidated.

IN VIOLETTE's words: "They were gassing people every day. It was our world. In our minds we were destined to be gassed too—at any time."

At Birkenau it was common knowledge that 1,000 Jews—727 of whom were immediately gassed—arrived from Paris-Bobigny on 2 August 1943. Zippy reported to the camp resistance that 1,113 women had died in the Birkenau women's camp in July. In the Himmler-ordered campaign to rid Silesia of Jews, according to camp resistance reports, only 10 percent of 20,000 deportees from the ghettos in Bedzin and Sosnowiec were admitted to Auschwitz-Birkenau; the remainder were gassed upon arrival.

A selection took place in the women's camp on 21 August 1943. Of the Jewish prisoners chosen for gassing, 441 were Greek women. At Birkenau, said Zippy, "death was just like you cleaned your teeth. Somebody died. The next day it will be me or my closest comrade."

In August 1943, the month Alma assumed command of the orchestra, 1,438 women previously admitted into the camp died in Birkenau according to the camp resistance. Of the dead, 498 were gassed. These figures do not include the numbers of women sent directly to the gas chamber on arrival, since they were never entered into the camp's records. In an in-camp selection on 28 August in the Birkenau men's Quarantine Blocks, 462 male Jewish prisoners were selected for gassing. The next day, another 4,000 male Jews were selected in the Birkenau men's camp for gassing overnight.[32]

BEFORE ALMA's arrival, many prisoners' main recollection of the Birkenau musicians was the determined beating of the drum by Helga Schiessel. Helga, a German Jew arrested when the Gestapo discovered she had been posing as an "Aryan," was a professional percussionist who had played in a Munich brasserie. Although Alma counted her among the orchestra's more competent players, her drumming and cymbal clanging had to be integrated into a musical ensemble.

Alma's first aim as leader of the Music Block was to change the image of the orchestra. She set out to retrain the existing players and to find and coach new ones, to provide the orchestra with more and better music, and to raise practice and performance standards. Coaching, refining, and conducting were second nature to her. She threw herself into the work with a vehemence that obliterated everything beyond the music room walls.

From the beginning, Alma faced the difficult problem of providing music for the orchestra. She had to arrange from the miscellany of scores or scraps of sheet music new arrivals had brought to the camp along with their instruments, or to enlarge on tunes she remembered or melodies others would hum to her. The Nazis forbade any playing of the proscribed "Jewish music," so the work of Jewish composers was banned.

To write out musical parts and copy them for the odd assemblage of orchestra players, Alma needed paper and pencils. But "no one dared to carry paper and pencil in the camp without the risk of a beating," as Zippy recalled. Working together, Alma and Zippy organized to get the supplies the orchestra needed, and Zippy recruited some of the women in the camp office to draw musical staffs on the pages in preparation for the Music Block copyists. By making her needs known, Zippy explains, Alma extended the sanctuary of the Music Block to still more prison inmates, creating orchestra-related jobs that spared internees from the debilitating work of the kommandos outside the camp. "Alma helped many, regardless of nationality, religion, or language. . . . Her influence went beyond the Music Block," Zippy testified.

Alma's greatest challenge was that of molding her terrified young musicians into an orchestra. Many of the orchestra girls had seen members of their families and friends trucked off to the gas chambers. At best, they knew that surviving loved ones hourly faced the rigors of Birkenau or some other camp.

Adding to the trauma of the circumstances was the fact that the young women had grown up in the comparative isolation deemed suitable for European girls in the society of their time. Many of the Jewish girls had been transferred from ghetto to ghetto. These women had scarcely tasted life in the adult world. In Anita's words:

> These were teenagers who had to live by their wits. Many had come from a restricted environment. Their spirits had been assaulted—if not crushed in the separation from their families and communities—by the depravity of the Nazi system. Even the mature in Auschwitz did things they never would have done in ordinary society—to save themselves and those whom they embraced as comrades and friends. . . .
>
> Alma was sophisticated, she had seen the world at its best, and its worst. We girls had not had similar opportunities as our youth wasted away.

Alma went to extraordinary lengths to build the musical strength of the women's ensemble, and the privileges accorded to its members grew in proportion to the reputation of the orchestra leader. When she took over, she removed a number of girls—primarily the early Polish members—from the ranks of musicians, giving them tasks that did not require them to play. Some became copyists; others took on block maintenance duties. When it was absolutely necessary to oust a musician or worker from the Music Block, Alma and Czajkowska used their influence to find a relatively safe place in the camp for the person dismissed. As many as possible were given the shelter of belonging to the orchestra group.

According to many orchestra survivors, Alma was conscious of her power and conscientious about her responsibility. After several weeks in the Music Block, she said to Zippy: "I have here some girls who are working so hard for me, I will never let them go."

18

The Music Block

What is difficult to imagine in retrospect is the ever-present atmosphere of violent death; not even on the battlefield is death such a certainty and life so completely dependent on the miraculous.—Hannah Arendt

Did you know that hunger makes the eyes shine, that thirst dulls them?—Charlotte Delbo

The Birkenau women's orchestra, forty-five to fifty players at its height, occupied a wooden building with narrow windows under the eaves that let in daylight and the glare of searchlights that swept the camp from watchtowers through the night. The walls were poorly joined planks painted gray. Electric lights hung on exposed wires. The barrack consisted of two main rooms, a large music and practice area in the front (Fania Fénelon estimated its dimensions as twenty six by twenty feet), the beds and a small eating space in the back. Though described by Zippy as typical "lousy Birkenau barracks," the accommodations had a measure of luxury compared with the crowded Jewish barracks and even the camp hospital, where it was common to see four and five people—alive and dead—in the same bed.

Alma and Czajkowska each had private rooms that entered onto the music area. Alma's tiny space was described by Regina as about eight by ten feet, painted white and containing a storage cupboard, table, two chairs, and a bed. It was immediately inside the door to the block, and Czajkowska's room was next to it. The block was beside the road leading to gas chambers and crematoria II and III.

The girls in the Music Block had three-tiered wooden bunks with mattress pads, while in other barracks inmates lay on bare planks or straw pallets. Where others had rags for cover, each of the musicians had a sheet and a woolen blanket, and no more than two slept in a bed. When it was necessary to share, the women slept with their feet by their bunkmate's head.

The musicians were spared the indignity of the thirty-second crush into communal latrines twice a day on a preset schedule. In the Music Block, Jews and non-Jews alike had the use of a small latrine formerly reserved for German women prisoners, located between their barrack and an electrified barbed-wire fence four meters high, the inner of several rows of fences at the perimeter of camp BI. Here they brought buckets to fill with water from the taps, which they carried back to the block to wage an endless battle against the greasy soot that hung in the air and the splatters of yellow mud whipped up by wind and rain. (The Nazis were fanatical about clean footwear; even at Auschwitz, their boots always gleamed.)

Officially the orchestra members received a double portion of soup and extra bread, yet they suffered from constant hunger. Flora described the camp food as "imitations of imitations."

Anita confirmed the paucity of a diet that was generous by camp standards: "No one who hasn't experienced it can know the pain of hunger that was the kind of lingering pain in Birkenau." According to Dr. Lingens-Reiner, three times a week the camp administration allotted four pounds of meat per one hundred liters of soup. Other than the watery soup, there was little more than bread and, for the privileged, occasional minuscule slices of sausage or cheese, a tidbit of margarine or jam, and a coffee-like morning drink.

In Holland Alma had been so terrified of cockroaches that she scrawled the word in her small notebook. Now she lived with the constant threat of disease resulting from starvation, filth, insects, and vermin. Signs throughout the camp warned that a single bite from a louse could infect a prisoner with typhus, which periodically raged through the camp.

The orchestra girls had the luxury of socks and underwear. They were offered a weekly change of the latter, but this was a privilege they rejected, preferring to forego the services of a laundry that relied on steam-cleaning. Alma, trying vainly to control the spread of lice, requested special closets for clothing, which were promptly built. Despite her precautions, during her tenure as orchestra leader at least three girls in the orchestra were stricken and died of the diseases spread by vermin.

It was said that in the name of music, Alma could get almost anything from the SS through the admiring and ambitious Maria Mandel. Although she was always obliging and deferential toward Mandel, Alma dared to make demands. Her iron will could be a scourge within the Music Block, yet even her enemies acknowledged that Alma accomplished marvels.

As winter 1943–44 approached and the days darkened, Alma asked for and received an iron stove for the Music Block, a rare privilege at Birkenau. Cannily, Alma had insisted that the instruments required a constant temperature to stay in tune. During the bitterest cold, she managed to get permission to excuse the players of stringed instruments from the outdoor marching assignment—because, she explained in words Helena recalled, the cold and damp made them "snap like store string." Likewise she requested and was granted unique dispensation from the twice-daily muster and roll call, on the basis that the orchestra players needed more practice time to keep up with their performance schedule. Instead of lining up outside the block for hours each day, "Alma's girls," as the orchestra members came to be called, were counted in the morning and evening inside the Music Block.

Anita reflected the surprise among camp inmates when Alma had her way with the SS. "She commanded an absolute and total respect from us, and by all appearances, from the SS as well. I am sure I am right in saying that she occupied a unique position."

As Mandel's pets, the girls in the orchestra wore a special uniform for concerts: dark blue skirts, some pleated; white blouses; black stockings; and jackets of gray-and-blue-striped prison material. Heather-colored kerchiefs covered their heads. Because "Mandel wanted us to look pretty," said Zippy, girls transferred to the Music Block could let their hair grow.

They were allowed daily showers in the camp bathhouse known as the Sauna, as opposed to the usual fortnightly gang showers of a few seconds' duration. Alma showered in the Sauna with the other members of the block. "She was one of us," Flora emphasized, although others characterized Alma as remaining aloof. The girls tried to make friends with even the most hostile of the Sauna attendants, who were known for taking advantage of ordinary prisoners.

Most camp inmates waited at least two weeks before they had an opportunity to wash, as Dr. Lingens-Reiner wrote in *Prisoners of Fear*. Yet the SS carried on a strict campaign for cleanliness and punished inmates who were slovenly. In the face of an uncertain supply of polluted water, the prisoners carefully prevented any of the shower water from reaching their mouths. They were forced to save their tea or any possible source of clean water for washing, and they had to barter for scraps of soap.

Dr. Lingens-Reiner described her first conversation with a prisoner-attendant in the Sauna:

> How often can we come here and have a bath? I asked.
> "Once—when you are released," she answered.
> And when do we wash? I inquired, a little less self-assured.
> She shrugged: "It's a matter of luck."[1]

Eugenia Marchiewicz, whose experience at Birkenau was that of an ordinary non-Jewish inmate, described another daunting encounter at the Sauna. With a precious onion and potato she had saved from a food parcel received from home (only non-Jews had any hope of receiving parcels addressed to them), she bargained with a woman attendant for a shower. "I also had a little piece of soap. I made the mistake of giving the potato and onion to the Sauna woman before she agreed to let me shower. She gave me less than ten seconds of water, and told me to get out or she would report me." The Sauna attendant kept the soap, the onion, and the potato.

Days in the Music Block were long and repetitive. Each morning the women were awakened an hour before dawn. A detail from the barrack carried music stands and stools to a raised platform atop a small mound near the camp gate. After the group returned, all the women lined up in rows of five within the block for the obligatory roll call conducted by Nazi wardens (often the infamous Margot Drexler and her lieutenant, Irma Grese). Afterwards a drink was served. Anita recalled that it was "not easily identified as anything in particular. But it was hot, and one ate whatever one had managed to save from the previous evening."

The orchestra left the barrack before sunrise, marching in rows of five. Each morning they saw starved corpses in their death grips hanging on the electrified fences like clothes on a line, inmates who chose suicide over another day of life in the camp. Alma walked briskly in front of the orchestra as they marched military style along the cinder road to their platform at the gate, some 300 yards from the Music Block. The road led between other barracks, where work parties waited outside in rigid lines. At daybreak, the workers began to file past on their way out of camp, driven by SS guards, kapos, and dogs. After the morning performance and a march back to the Music Block, the small work detail returned to the gate to retrieve the orchestra's music stands and stools.

In their barrack, the women practiced new arrangements and refined old repertory at least ten hours a day. Before lunch each day, they showered together in lukewarm water in the Sauna, a precious privilege. The barrack staff of caretakers then left for the camp kitchens and returned carrying heavy kettles, from which lunch was served. This was thin soup made of water and beets or turnips with an occasional chunk of potato. Anita recalled that "one's greatest concern was that the soup should be stirred properly before it was ladled out so that one had a fair chance of receiving a possible bit of potato."

During the winter of 1943–44, the rigorous schedule and constant tension were too much for some of the musicians, who had fainting spells and collapsed from exhaustion. Alma persuaded the SS to allow her girls to take a short rest after lunch. "We would go to bed and sleep," Zofia recalled. This too was an unheard-of privilege at Birkenau.

After their rest, the orchestra resumed practice. In the evening a detail again delivered music stands and stools to the platform near the gate, and the orchestra marched to its place to "welcome" the returning work parties. Said Zofia, "More marches—which should have been Te Deums [the processional chants that end certain religious services]. Although Alma as conductor had her back to the procession, we players in our uniquely strategic position were witnesses to all manner of things." Frequently the columns of prisoners carried corpses or workers who were so feeble or so badly beaten that their comrades had to support them.

Prisoners caught with treasures they had bartered for outside the camp were made to kneel and eat their booty. Both Anita and Zofia remembered a woman forced to consume an entire package of cigarettes. After the pathetic spectacle of the daily return to camp, the orchestra marched back to the barrack and lined up for evening roll call.

Zofia described the evening meal:

> We were given our rations, which consisted of a piece of bread—some margarine or a slice of blutwurst [blood sausage] or jam. I am sure that thanks to Alma's intervention on our behalf, we received a special supplement of bread and margarine.
>
> We were luckier than those in other blocks. Our bread was cut and distributed inside the block, so it was not possible for those cutting the bread to cheat by making the portions smaller. Bread was the most precious possession in the camp, and it was the camp currency. One could organize practically anything with bread.

Zippy confirmed the high value of bread: "In Auschwitz, diamonds, even by the handful, could not save a person from death on arrival—or death from hunger, exhaustion, or disease if they were spared for entry into the camp. Bread was far more precious."

Bread could buy all the items coveted at Auschwitz. Undergarments, nightgowns, warm clothing, toothbrushes, soap, eating utensils, tinned foods—all were "for sale" in the camp at the vast storage and trading center known as "Kanada" (so named because Canada was seen as mythically rich, a land of plenty). Here the possessions confiscated from new arrivals and from the dead were sorted for shipment to the Reich or redistributed to supply the camp. Trading, or organizing, at Kanada became a camp institution, to the point that campwise inmates knew the exact price of available goods in rations of bread.[2]

In Anita's words, "workers in Kanada were the upper class of the camp with access to anything they wanted at a price—and that price was bread." Anita bartered at Kanada for a precious angora sweater, which she kept to the end of the war. (The sweater, now in shreds, is on exhibit in England at the Imperial War Museum.)

Only when the orchestra girls won the treat of special gifts from Kanada or "parcels" was the fare more sumptuous. The latter were packages sent to the camp for internees and stockpiled for the privileged. Jewish prisoners did not receive parcels except on special occasions, when packages were directed to the orchestra as a favor through SS Mandel.

Hélène Scheps remembered such a distribution on 7 January 1944:

> As a reward for a concert, each one of us received a parcel. It was extraordinary, for I was seventeen that very day. It was almost supernatural, considering the originally intended destination of the parcel, and the occasion on which I received it. There was an apple in the parcel, and I wanted to offer it to my friend the couturière [the Belgian Elsa Miller].
>
> I went to her block, she wasn't there. It was finished; she could no longer resist. She had died of typhus but did not suffer long.

ALMA REQUESTED and obtained a piano, which allowed her to try her arrangements for the orchestra at the keyboard. She also used the piano to coach individual players. Szymon Laks, her counterpart in the Birkenau men's orchestra, confirmed with a touch of envy that at one time the women's orchestra had a grand piano.[3]

Alma was also provided with a podium, from which she led the orchestra's interminable rehearsals. During practices she arranged the players in the round, so that she was encircled by the musicians and could hear each instrument clearly. Her approach was formal and authoritarian; she had a strong sense of the rights and respect due to an orchestra conductor. When she appeared in the doorway of her room, she expected the orchestra to stand and begin practice. With a traditional tap of her baton on the podium, she began each session.

At Birkenau Alma's famous name conveyed little distinction. Here she could secure her position only through making music and respectfully obeying the SS commandants. Nonetheless her lot was far better than most. Like other kapos she received "Diet," which included an extra ration of bread and grains in boiled milk and sugar. She ate privately in her room; Regina, her personal assistant, delivered her meals to her. Witnesses describe her as more neatly and suitably dressed than ordinary prisoners—some have even called her "elegant" —another privilege attached to her role as a prisoner-functionary. She alone in the block had permission to keep a light burning in her room late at night. Very often, she worked while the rest of the camp slept.

FLORA HAD never played in an orchestra and had difficulty reading the musical parts. Alma sometimes called her stupid for not getting a point. Flora remembered that once she missed an entry and Alma hissed: "If we don't play well, we'll be sent to the gas. Play, Flora!"

Sylvia later remarked: "Alma understood how we could play at all. If the orchestra is good, we survive. And if the orchestra is bad—and does not fulfill the task they have in mind—it is useless to the Germans and there is no need for the musicians to go on living."

To maintain discipline and extract the last ounce of effort from her musicians, Alma sometimes used threats, although the reality of the camp outside the Music Block was enough to terrify the orchestra girls into submission. To

Flora, Alma confided that she had a way to alleviate the horrors of their predicament, which she would share if ever it came to that irreversible moment.

"Imagine," said Flora, "how reassuring it was for an eighteen-year-old to hear that Alma would share the poison she had managed to save. She said she kept it to use if she were ever faced with death at the hands of the Nazis. I did not know how it was possible to smuggle it into the camp. She always promised me [I did not need] to be afraid of the gas chamber."

One might well wonder how Alma had managed to carry that bead of prussic acid, given to her by the Staerckes, from Holland through Dijon, Drancy, Block 10, and the registration at Birkenau. Other friends in the camp reported that she made similar offers to them. Perhaps the bead of poison was a myth she used to combat despair. Many suspected that she had long ago used the suicide pill but recovered at Drancy from the attempt to end her own life.

ELIE WIESEL, whose memoir of Auschwitz appeared as *Night* in 1960, spoke of the relentless assault on the person constituted by camp life. "Our senses were blunted," he wrote. "Everything was blurred as in a fog. It was no longer possible to grasp anything. The instincts of self-preservation, of self-defense, of pride, had all deserted us."[4]

Outside the Music Block, the life expectancy of prisoners ranged from a few weeks to a few months. Never were prisoners allowed to look the SS in the eye; heads had to be bowed. Prisoners were to stand at attention and remove their hats when an SS addressed them. The SS guarding work parties outside the camp were required to keep rifle ready and right hand on cartridge belt. After an incident in which a prisoner snatched a revolver and shot a guard, the SS were ordered to keep a three-meter distance from all inmates; this meant that any prisoner coming closer than three meters risked being shot. The prisoners' subhuman status added to the toll of hunger, little sleep, heavy labor, and utter lack of hygiene and sanitation. Prisoners were tired and numb, disgusted by the conditions of their own existence, sick with longing for home and friends and family.

Dr. Lingens-Reiner believed that it took a special kind of person to overcome the initiation to Auschwitz, which told the prisoner who felt so alone on arrival: "Will you be cold, or will I be cold? Will you risk falling ill, or shall I? Will you survive, or shall I?" Persisting in life required a "glaring egotism" unless companions were found to help. "Hardly a day passed when one's survival was not at stake."[5]

Many survived with the knowledge that they lived because someone else died. For the great majority, surviving was all that mattered. Anita, for one, has said that Alma was the "supreme example of this instinct for survival."[6]

Viktor E. Frankl, an Auschwitz survivor who died in 1997, wrote in his memoir *Man's Search for Meaning* that at the camp, "all we possessed, literally, was our naked existence. . . . Reality dimmed, and all efforts and all emotions were centered on one task: preserving one's own life and that of the other fellow."[7]

Fania, too, wrote of the cost of continuing in life: "To survive, I was not simply going to have to walk over my heart, as the Hungarians say, I was going to have to trample on it, annihilate it."[8]

Zippy described the hysteria in the camp office each time the lists of those selected for death became known. "How could one remove a name, when another had to take its place, to maintain the count?"

THE WINTER Alma spent in the Music Block was one of the worst at Auschwitz. At one stage, Dr. Lingens-Reiner remembered, only fifteen physically fit women doctors attended some seven thousand desperately ill patients. Medications were in pitifully short supply; bandages were no more than scraps of paper.

In the Revier, a selection took place at least every four weeks from August 1943 to February 1944. Eugenia Marchiewicz, in the medical block after a bout with typhus, regained consciousness to find a rat chewing on her flesh. It had already eaten a toe from the corpse lying beside her.

Those who survived the onslaught of typhus suffered debilitating weakness and ravenous hunger during the period of recuperation. Lingens-Reiner, after her own battle with the disease, recalled crying from the painful craving for food as she waited for a distribution of bread.

On 3 September 1943, a hundred women were selected in Birkenau and gassed the same day. To curb corruption among the SS, the camp command issued an order that prohibited the SS from accepting (most likely through extortion) or buying goods brought into the camp by Jewish prisoners. Still another transport of 1,000 prisoners from Drancy arrived on 4 September; 338 men and women were admitted to the camp, and the remainder were gassed.

In Dr. Lingens-Reiner's view, "those who failed to make a niche for themselves were doomed, although exceptional energy or toughness might delay the end. A prisoner who had won a privileged position for herself then had to defend it with efficiency, vitality and iron will . . . and luck."[9] Those who possessed specialized skills—doctors, nurses, engineers, mechanics, tailors, barbers, dentists, shoemakers, artists, musicians—had the best chance of being considered useful by the Nazis.

In her 1979 study *Values and Violence in Auschwitz,* Anna Pawełczyńska gave a sociological analysis of the advantages of belonging to a select group of inmates within the camp. Not only did camp organizations with a distinct function provide some safety from the gas chamber, relatively good working conditions, and extra food rations, but prisoners who belonged to a special unit were better able to preserve a sense of human dignity. As Anita commented, after she joined the orchestra, "I may no longer have had a name, but I was identifiable. I could be referred to. I was 'the cellist.'"[10]

As some of her players struggled with typhus, Alma warned the hospital that each one was enormously important to the orchestra, thus stacking the odds of survival in their favor. Margot wrote that Alma "grasped any opportunity" to help a stricken orchestra member. Polish Helena agreed, recalling Alma's efforts on her behalf during a typhus epidemic that peaked in November 1943: "Alma made a special plea for me, and it was through her that I shared the board bed in the Revier with only one other person. . . . Alma took care of the whole orchestra, regardless of nationality or religion."

Esther Loewy Bejarano, a German recorder player, guitarist, and accordionist who was in the orchestra only a short time after Alma arrived, recalled that the same autumn she fell desperately ill with typhus. Only the intervention of SS Oberscharführer (Quartermaster-Sergeant) Otto Moll, an orchestra supporter, saved her from the gas.[11]

Violette recalled that after a round with typhus, when she had been out of the Revier only three days, she was too weak to keep up with the orchestra as it paraded to the gate. As she lagged behind, SS Franz Hössler stopped Violette and called to Alma, demanding to know what kind of *Muselmann* was this girl. Being identified as a Moslem could have meant that Violette was sent to Block 25 and on to the gas chamber. Violette credited Alma with saving her life a second time at that moment:

> Alma answered truthfully. I had had typhus and was still weak. But she also lied for me: "This is one of my best violinists."
>
> Hössler responded: "Very well. I will see that she gets Diet [extra rations] for the next three months for her rehabilitation."
>
> I was by no means even a good violinist.

Violette has never been able to forget the beating she received from Czajkowska at that time. Left with a severe kidney weakness after typhus, she was forced one night to slip out of the Music Block and urinate in the snow. The next morning, when Czajkowska saw the mark in the snow and identified Violette as the culprit, she delivered a beating to the ailing girl.

As Allied bombings of German cities escalated in late summer and fall of 1943, Auschwitz diarist SS Dr. Kremer was on holiday from his "duty" selecting prisoners for the gas chambers and was moved to write: "Everybody takes notice with wordless bitterness and almost with despair of the heavy bombing raids. . . . Those who attack the achievements of culture wage war against all mankind and not only us."

On clandestine radio the camp resistance followed the news of German defeats in Italy since the Allied invasion of Sicily in mid-July, the disastrous daytime Allied bombings of Rome, and in late July, the overthrow of Benito Mussolini by close subordinates in the Fascist Party, including his own son-in-law. By 3 September 1943, the new rulers of Italy had signed an armistice with the Western powers, and Hitler's chief ally had deserted.

Mussolini, the deposed dictator, was rescued from a mountain lodge high on the Gran Sasso in central Italy by the daring flight of Austrian SS glider pilot Otto Skorzeny. Hitler had hoped that Mussolini would set up a new Fascist government in northern Italy and carry on the fight, but the broken Duce showed little stomach for further battle. Within two months German armies would fail in the last great offensive of the war against the Russians, and the Russians would recapture Kiev in a decisive drive westward.

A DAY everyone in Birkenau would remember was 9 September 1943, when 5,007 Jews arrived from the "showcase" family camp at the Theresienstadt (Terezín) ghetto in Czechoslovakia. Contrary to the basic camp rule, the new arrivals were not quarantined on arrival. In unprecedented manner, entire families were allowed to live (the men and women in separate quarters) in what became known as the *Familienlager* (family camp), to establish their own kindergarten and school for the 285 children in the transport, and even to hold their own theatrical and musical events. Their heads were not shaved, they could receive food parcels, and they were not sent out to work.

Among the heroes of the family community, a man widely loved and admired, was twenty-eight-year-old Fredy Hirsch, a German Jew who had fled to Prague in 1938, only to be interned at Theresienstadt. Hirsch was among the new arrivals at Birkenau, where he carried on his work with the children of the camp, maintaining educational and cultural programs despite the dearth of teaching materials. Rumors flew about the mysterious *Familienlager:* it was under the protection of the International Red Cross, or it was a showpiece for visiting officials, designed to cover up the real business of the death camp.

The family camp was of special interest to Alma because she was sure that she would one day recognize prisoners there. The camp, a section of BII, was strictly segregated from the rest of Auschwitz-Birkenau. It was set up near the Music Block, along the road leading to crematoria II and III; after the railway was built, it was across the track from the women's barrack. Alma often watched the camp, scanning faces with interest. According to some reports, she even found the opportunity to visit. She had lived in Czechoslovakia during her five-year marriage to Příhoda and frequently visited Prague as a touring musician. Otakar Ševčík, the Czech violinist, was one of her teachers. Among those she believed to be at Theresienstadt were her Dutch friends the Röders, James H. Simon (her piano accompanist in Holland in 1941), and her uncle Eduard Rosé.[12]

The same day the prisoners from Theresienstadt were transferred to Auschwitz, 695 of 987 Jews arriving from Westerbork in Holland were gassed. A week later, another 578 from a Westerbork transport of 751, including 119 children, 302 men, and 330 women, were killed on arrival. Of 194 women admitted to the camp, 100 were transferred to the Experimental Block 10 in Auschwitz the next day.

An order issued 25 September 1943 by Auschwitz complex commander Höss advised prisoners not to eat food scraps on 28 September, when rat poison would be spread over the camp. As Danuta Czech points out, the order shows all too clearly that the camp command knew prisoners desperate for food hunted for scraps in dog kennels, pig pens, and garbage dumps.

The ghettos of many cities continued to feed the crematoria fires. The Auschwitz SS tried to break the camp resistance between 16 and 29 September 1943, arresting and later executing suspects. The crackdown did not halt the monthly casualty report, which recorded that 1,871 women died in September, of whom 1,181 were gassed. The Experimental Block recorded 397 women prisoners and 67 prisoner-nurses as of 1 October, the next day, 394 prisoners and 64 nurses. Eleven boys born in the past month in the women's camp were registered as new arrivals in the men's camp, their feet tattooed with camp numbers. For the time being, they were to remain in the women's camp.[13]

In late October 1943, a transport of seventeen hundred Jews arrived from Bergen-Belsen. They had been told they were destined for Switzerland but found themselves in Auschwitz. In the area between crematoria II and III in Birkenau, one woman grabbed a revolver from an SS, fatally shot SS Oberscharführer (Quartermaster-Sergeant) Schillinger, and wounded SS Scharführer (Staff Sergeant) Emmerich. Other enraged women attacked the SS with their bare hands. All the arrivals were shot, killed by hand grenades, or herded inside and gassed.

The next day, in retribution, SS guards fired from their watchtowers, raking the camp with machine guns. Thirteen inmates were killed, four seriously wounded, and forty-two injured, according to Auschwitz records. The Music Block was immediately beneath one of the watchtowers with its deadly spray of bullets.

The previous week had seen the arrival of the first transports from Italy, in the German view an enemy nation since the fall of Mussolini. The latest arrivals from Westerbork—490 of the 1,007 in the transport were gassed—brought the news that the Protestant Dutch Jews among whom Alma had sought to be counted more than a year before had been sent to Bergen-Belsen.[14]

A transport from Drancy, the fourth since Alma's Convoy 57, arrived on 30 October 1943. Of the 1,000 aboard, 613 were gassed according to records gathered by Serge Klarsfeld.

In October, Danuta Czech reported that since the beginning of August, 5,578 had died in the women's camp in Birkenau. Of this number, 3,224 were gassed.

The Birkenau toll of women reached a peak in December 1943, when the camp resistance reported a rise from the November total of 1,603 dead, of whom 394 were gassed, to 8,931 dead, of whom 4,247 were gassed. The high figure corresponded to an outbreak of typhus: at its height, on 10 December, 2,000 Jewish women were selected for gassing in one day.

19

Escape into Excellence

Everything can be taken from a man but one thing: the last of the human freedoms—to choose one's attitude in any given set of circumstances, to choose one's own way.—Viktor E. Frankl

During her tenure as leader, Alma revolutionized the women's orchestra. Anita said that it was "like night and day." Even the slight music the orchestra had played before Alma's arrival sounded better under her direction. The ensemble became musical, and its repertoire broadened to include serious classics. Flora, the accordionist, remarked with pride many years later: "I can never forget the 'Emperor Waltz,' where I had a solo twice."

Hélène Scheps, concertmistress of the orchestra (a post she later shared with Helena), testified to Alma's dedication to music:

> Alma, with the big talent in a family of artists, was to me a virtuoso with profound musical sensitivity. . . . It was an emotional experience to see Alma's desire to make a true orchestra out of us. She was a complete musician. It wasn't something you can learn, nor something you could study. It was born and bred in her. . . .
>
> Music for her was the most beautiful and most important thing. She worked with a determination that was almost desperate to turn us into an agreeable-sounding ensemble—with a special sound that I have never found in any orchestra since. When one day we accompanied her in "Zigeunerweisen" by Sarasate, she complimented us because we had played well. It was a reward of great value to us. We were comrades!
>
> My work with Alma was very pleasing to me, because I understood her intentions, and I think that Alma appreciated this receptivity and my work as the first violin principal.

Praise from Alma was as memorable as censure. Fanny remembered: "One day, Alma was playing "Czardas" by Monti on her violin with her back to us.

She turned around at the conclusion and said we had accompanied her better than her Dutch orchestra had!"[1]

Zofia said that the orchestra often fell short of Alma's expectations:

> Alma wanted the orchestra to be very good. She willed the orchestra to play well. During rehearsals, she wasn't very often satisfied. But when a concert was well done, she acknowledged it. Alma's standards were higher than those of the SS. She therefore established herself as *the* authority. We did not respect SS praises, but we did respect Alma's.
>
> She was a very unusual creature. She knew that. She felt that and lived it. She aimed at a higher goal than the SS or Birkenau.

Anita recalled that Alma's highest praise was to say the orchestra had played something well enough for her father to hear it. "She often talked about him and repeatedly said, as though it was a premonition, that should any of us survive, we should find him and tell him about us."

During a BBC interview in 1996, Anita was asked to judge the quality of the orchestra's music. She hesitated, searching for the right words. Then she said: "How good it was is very difficult for me to say in retrospect. It wasn't as bad as it should have been considering that hardly anybody was a trained musician; but Alma Rosé, being Alma Rosé—she was the conductor, yes—she had such enormously high standards."

Asked whether she thought Alma "understood perhaps that this was the salvation of all of you," Anita replied: "I don't think she was motivated by fear—by fear of the SS, if we don't play well they put us in the gas chamber. I don't think so. It was an escape somehow into—excellence. . . . It sounds totally ridiculous in the context."[2]

Manca Švalbová—a Jewish medical student deported from Bratislava who became Alma's beloved "Dr. Mancy"—also believed that Alma used music as a means of escape. Without it, said Dr. Mancy, she was like a bird with bloodied wings beating against the bars of its cage. Music enabled her to take flight and leave Birkenau behind, "covered as if by a night-cloth."[3]

THE ORCHESTRA's achievement was extraordinary under the circumstances. Anita said with pride:

> I think I am right in saying that there were only four potential musicians among us: Hélène, who led the orchestra, Frau Kröner, who played the flute, myself (cello), and Fania Fénelon, who was the only really accomplished musician. Alma had turned the orchestra into a camp institution of considerable standing long before Fania arrived as a singer [in January 1944]. However, Fania made a major contribution as an orchestrator, both from her prodigious memory and from the piano reductions of music provided to Alma by the SS.

Anita never forgot the night the orchestra first played the Beethoven "Pathétique" Piano Sonata, arranged from memory by Fania for three violins and cello.

> How can I describe that evening, after the SS left the area. It was a link with the outside, with beauty, with culture—a complete escape into an imaginary and unattainable world. . . . In the truest sense, led by Alma, we lifted ourselves above the inferno of Birkenau into a sphere where we could not be touched by the degradation of concentration camp existence. On such an occasion, there was great closeness among us all.

At its height, the orchestra had a large and varied repertoire including marches, fox trots, Viennese waltzes, chamber music, opera, operetta, folk music, Gypsy songs, hit songs and tunes, "German jazz," and adaptations of orchestral music. In Auschwitz, mastering such a repertoire was nothing short of miraculous.

Hélène Scheps said forty-two years later:

> Alma saved our lives because she knew how to make an orchestra of us. If Alma hadn't been there, we wouldn't be here. . . . Alma knew music so well and knew so well what each of us was capable of, she could ask this one or that one to play in a certain way to set off a certain passage. It was not difficult for her to hand a trumpet passage to some violins and tell them how to play.

Helena praised Alma's inventiveness and her ability to communicate her ideas: "The Strauss waltzes were marvelously interpreted by Alma. She explained the rhythm of the waltz as like the bouncing of a ball. The singers were fitted into the repertoire, each in their own range, because Alma could not tolerate any faulty or forced sounds."

Polish Ewa Stojowska, a singing actress who joined the orchestra in November 1943, was amazed by Alma's creative treatments of operatic tunes and her ability to coach the female singers in ranges traditionally covered by men. With a strong, deep voice, Ewa took the tenor parts in operatic quartets Alma arranged (as in the popular Quartet from *Rigoletto,* ordinarily sung by two men and two women). Ewa, who was also a copyist and the orchestra's music librarian, said that Alma's industry in creating or recreating music resulted in a collection that eventually boasted two hundred selections.[4]

No complete record of the women's orchestra repertoire has surfaced to date. But various survivors—Helena, Anita, Violette, and Fania in particular—have contributed to at least a partial list. Violette reported about twenty military marches, including Berlioz and Schubert selections as well as marches by Sousa and Suppé.[5] There were Mozart's "Eine kleine Nachtmusik" and the first movement of the A-major Violin Concerto, Brahms' "Hungarian Dances," Bach's *Chaconne,* Beethoven's "Pathétique" Sonata, Schubert's "Serenade" and

"Lilac Time," Schumann's "Reverie" or "Träumerei," Alabieff's "Nightingale," Leoncavallo's "Mattinata," and Johann Strauss's lilting "Tales from the Vienna Woods" and "Blue Danube."

The operatic selections and ensembles derived from *The Barber of Seville, Carmen, Cavalleria rusticana, Madame Butterfly, Rigoletto,* and *Tosca* and included the Bell Song from *Lakmé.* Arias and medleys were drawn from *The Merry Widow, The Land of Smiles, The Gypsy Princess,* and *White Horse Inn,* among half a dozen Viennese operettas. Selections from Dvořák (actually forbidden music) included extracts from the "New World" Symphony.

The group played Rossini and Suppé overtures and Sarasate's "Zigeunerweisen" with Alma as soloist. "Twelve Minutes with Peter Kreuder"—jazzy music that received a mixed reception from the SS—came directly from the Walzermädeln repertoire, as did "Wien, Wien, nur du allein" (Vienna, City of My Dreams) by Sieczyński. Hits of the day included "Under the Red Lanterns of San Paoli," "When Lilacs Bloom," songs by Zarah Leander and Marika Rökk, the "Laughing Polka," and of course "Lili Marlene." "Charge of the Light Brigade" and "Song of the Volga Boatmen" were perennial favorites.[6]

Among the works of Jewish composers performed despite the official ban were "Josef, Josef," a well known fox trot, and the first movement of Mendelssohn's E-minor Violin Concerto. These pieces, like others by outlawed composers, crept into the orchestra's repertoire in disguise, extending a covert message of support to Jewish prisoners. With such selections, Alma tested how far she could go with her captors.

Orchestrating for the odd collection of instruments that made up the women's orchestra was a constant challenge. Fania wrote that in preparing a rendition of the first movement of Beethoven's Fifth Symphony (the signature tune of the BBC and the Free French but a selection the orchestra never performed, according to Anita), she used mandolins for the key phrase, ra-pa-pa-*pum,* with violins coming in to produce a swell on the fourth note.

Certainly Alma recalled her father's pronouncement when more than ten years earlier, she announced her plan to form the Wiener Walzermädeln. There was no disgrace in her project, Arnold had said, as long as she made the music honest by playing it to perfection.

In *Music of Another World,* Szymon Laks said of his fellow orchestra leader:

> The conductor of the orchestra had been the eminent violinist Alma Rosé, who was known especially in Central Europe. She was the daughter of [Arnold] Rosé, founder and first violinist of the world-famous Rosé Quartet. I was told that she had been a good friend and that more than once [she] had stood up to the authorities in defense of the health or lives of her comrades. She had snatched more than one of them from the jaws of death.[7]

Laks commented that the women's orchestra lacked the wind instruments available to the men, especially the brass, resulting in an "effeminate" sound that "did not prevent a serious and loyal musical rivalry from developing in the commands of the two camps. . . . A certain kind of cultural exchange developed against this background: one Sunday we would give a concert in the women's camp; the next Sunday they would perform in ours."[8]

Fania noted that although the men's orchestra was "a real symphony orchestra with excellent players and even soloists, all we had to represent the real musical world was Alma." Elsewhere, Fania referred to the orchestra leader as "our unusual star."[9]

The pride the orchestra women took in their accomplishment was reflected in the survivors' bitter reaction to the portrayal of their music in the 1980 film *Playing for Time.* The orchestra played *poorly,* they objected, and the lead character, based on Fania, sang out of tune![10]

When weather permitted, Alma and the orchestra played twice weekly for the patients in the Revier. For these performances, the orchestra set up their music stands and stools on a grassy island outside the hospital block. The prisoner-doctors referred to the concerts as "sound-wave therapy." Dr. Lingens-Reiner recalled: "With the light Viennese tunes from Lupi Leopoldi stage shows, we tried to imagine we were at a summer spa. Sometimes we managed to laugh and joke."[11] When the weather was severe, the orchestra played inside the Revier.

Maria Moś-Wdowik wrote wistfully of the concerts in the Revier: "They were events in our camp life, and it was difficult not to be deeply moved and also to forget the experience because it was something like a little piece of freedom. What was worse was then the return to the sad reality of the camp." On at least one occasion, at the height of the typhus epidemic in November and December 1943, the orchestra played for the patients in the Revier one afternoon only to discover that most of their audience were gassed the next.

Kitty Felix Hart, a prisoner at the camp who considered the women's orchestra part of the "big lie" at Auschwitz, verifies this report. One day, in a cruelly misnamed punishment called "sport," she was forced to kneel for hours with her hands outstretched before her, holding a stone in each hand. From a distance she saw and heard the orchestra playing for the patients outside the Revier. Kitty said: "The very next day, all these prisoners were sent to the gas chamber."[12]

The orchestra also instituted Sunday concerts on the Birkenau half-day of rest. For many prisoners, these were the only reminder that a gentler world persisted outside the camp. At first the Sunday concerts were held in the square in front of the Music Block, but in late autumn of 1943, the SS halted the practice. Undeterred, Alma persuaded the camp commanders to let the orchestra use the interior of the Sauna as a hall for Sunday performances.

Alma's friend Dr. Mancy described those Sunday concerts. Sometimes they continued for two or three hours, as a hushed overflow crowd stood outside the building straining to hear the music from within. "Thousands more prisoners waited for many hours before it started. Then the Sauna became as quiet as a temple. Those were the most solemn moments in the camp. When Alma played her violin, she took them with her beyond the barbed wire to a faraway world of beauty that had vanished for them."

The Sunday concerts were attended by SS, comfortably seated in the front rows, and privileged prisoners, especially the kapos, blockowas, and other prisoner-functionaries. Ordinary prisoners crowded into the space at the back of the bathhouse and stood during performances. Musical selections began and ended without fanfare. There was no applause.

At large concerts, Alma often played violin solos. Witnesses describe her as tall, dark-haired, now very thin, playing with concentration, her head tilted to one side. With her long, sensitive fingers, Alma played with feeling as never before. One inmate recalled that her huge eyes "mirrored distant scenes."

Occasionally Alma took a group of players to perform at a private celebration—a birthday party within a block or a gathering in the Sauna to commemorate a special event such as a prisoner's discharge from the camp. Such performances were infrequent but added to Alma's reputation among the elite Auschwitz population of prisoner-functionaries, who might be able to command a special performance and thus better their own position in the camp.

In a light vein, Alma sometimes treated fellow prisoners to impromptu serenades. Alicia Rehl, a Birkenau survivor living in New Jersey in 1996, remembers that on her birthday, Alma stopped by the window of her room and played the traditional German birthday song, "Hoch soll sie leben."[13]

Perhaps her most moving solo performances took place within the walls of the Music Block. When Alma wanted to thank the orchestra women for a good performance or merely to help them relax, she played for them. When she played the violin, Fania wrote, Alma became gentle, tender, and warmly sensual; then her eyes were bright with emotion, and she was "incomparably beautiful."[14]

In Cracow years later, Ewa remembered Alma's private concerts: "There were evenings when Alma would play for us—only for us. She was fantastic."[15] In Brussels, remembering the pleasure of those intimate concerts forty-three years later, Hélène Scheps said: "When Itzhak Perlman plays, it reminds me of Alma."

THE MUSIC BLOCK became a meeting ground for prisoners at liberty to move around the camp—the staff of the camp office, the Revier, and Kanada; interpreters and messengers; and kitchen workers. Music-loving SS also developed the habit of dropping in.

Zofia, who earned the nickname "the Philosopher" for her thoughtful ways, said the SS often came to hear the orchestra's music after hours, "and they looked a little more human after hearing us." Whenever an SS appeared in the doorway to the Music Block—sometimes after conducting lengthy selections —Alma and the orchestra members stood at attention. With no warning an officer could enter the room, say "now you have practiced long enough," and order music. Alma attended respectfully to every request, and the orchestra obliged to the point of exhaustion, sometimes performing the same piece again and again.

Margot confirmed that the Music Block became a special refuge for the SS officers, a place to relax and be entertained. "Suddenly an SS woman could ask for Chopin, hear it, and upon leaving, kick an old grandmother. Commandant Höss would ask for an aria from *Butterfly,* then go off on a selection." Sylvia remembered an SS who "drove Fanny crazy with a tango, making her sing it over and over again."

What could Alma, Anita, and the girls in the Music Block allow themselves to feel when the suave SS Dr. Josef Mengele—the "Angel of Death"—asked Anita repeatedly to play Schumann's "Träumerei" for him? This was the man who could stand Napoleon-style, with the thumb of one hand between the buttons of his immaculate jacket, whistling tunes from *La Traviata* as with the other hand he gestured "right" or "left" at the train ramp, deciding life or death for hundreds in an afternoon.[16]

In 1996, a BBC interviewer put the question pointblank to Anita: "How did you feel when you played for such people?"

"I don't think we gave ourselves time to feel anything," Anita replied.

"You knew what they were doing?" the interviewer asked.

"Of course we knew what they were doing," Anita said. "But what was the alternative?"[17]

Fania shared this viewpoint, saying that the orchestra women's great hope was to get out alive. "To survive, what could one do but obey?"[18]

Sylvia remembered Birkenau's notoriously cruel SS overseer Irma Grese and SS Franz Hössler arriving in the Music Block with their dogs. Maria Mandel visited regularly and found the interludes restorative. Said Sylvia: "When Mandel came to listen to music, she was a human being and music lover. But when she returned to the camp, she was by no means a nice gentlewoman." Fania wrote that she became a favorite of Mandel's for her singing of "Un bel di" from *Madame Butterfly.* The same aria won a position in the Music Block for Eva Steiner Adam, a singer from Transylvania (now a part of Romania), who was overheard singing as she begged for bread.[19]

Being Mandel's protégées brought challenges as well as privileges. Fanny recalled her fear when Mandel came to the barrack one day and ordered Alma to perform "Zigeunerweisen" by Sarasate. "She said she came from hearing the piece on the radio and wanted to compare. We played like angels. The German [Mandel was in fact Austrian] responded to an anxious Alma that the orchestra gave a better performance than she had heard on the radio. We gave a sigh of relief."

It was no secret in the camp that the support of their SS admirers was essential to the survival of the orchestra members. One day, when Flora had burned her hand and could not play, an SS remarked bluntly: "It is lucky for you that you are our accordion player; otherwise I would send you to the gas today."

Some camp prisoners referred contemptuously to the musicians as "SS lapdogs" or worse, even spitting at them as they passed, according to some survivors. (Other survivors adamantly deny such accounts. "People did not spit at us," insists Anita.) But the members of the orchestra understood the necessity of bowing to SS demands.

Szymon Laks sympathized with the orchestras' critics, commenting that in his view, "music kept up the 'spirit' (or rather the body) of only . . . the musicians, who did not have to go out to hard labor and could eat a little better."[20]

Adam Kopyciński, the director of the Auschwitz I orchestra, saw the matter differently: "Thanks to its power and suggestiveness, music strengthened in the camp listeners what was most important—their true nature. Perhaps that is why many certainly tried instinctively to make a certain cult of this most beautiful of the arts, which precisely there in camp conditions could be, and certainly was, medicine for the sick soul of the prisoners."[21]

Typical of some prisoners' impressions of the orchestra were the memories of Charlotte Delbo, writing in her often poetic *None of Us Will Return*. For her, in this setting, music was ghastly. In her words:

> The orchestra stood on an embankment near the gate. . . . When the commandant ordered them to play for him, he had an extra loaf of bread passed out to the musicians. And when the new arrivals alighted from the boxcars into the ranks or the gas chamber, he liked it to be to the rhythm of a gay march.
>
> As we passed [at the gate] we had to keep time. Later they played waltzes we had heard in an obliterated past. Hearing them here was unbearable.
>
> Seated on stools they play. Do not look at the fingers of the cellist, nor at her eyes, you will not be able to bear it. Do not look at the gestures of the woman who is conducting. She parodies the woman she was in the large café in Vienna where she once conducted a female orchestra, and it is obvious that she is thinking of what she used to be.
>
> All of them are wearing navy blue pleated skirts, light blouses, lavender handkerchiefs over their heads. They are dressed this way to set the pace for the others who go to the marshes in the dresses they sleep in, otherwise the dresses would never dry.[22]

Laks quotes an especially hateful description of the orchestra as "those dolls . . . in navy blue dresses and white collars—in comfortable chairs. The music is supposed to perk us up, to mobilize us like the sound of a war trumpet that during a battle rouses even croaking horses."[23]

Some SS—among them SS Oberaufseherin Margot Drexler and SS Hauptscharführer Anton Taube—openly opposed the orchestra. They considered its members lazy and wanted to assign them to heavy work in addition to their duties as musicians, following the example of the Birkenau men's orchestra.

Zippy, with her unusual mobility and range of perspective, noted the difference between men and women prisoners—"how the men wanted to keep the SS confused, but the women wanted to keep the SS happy and contented. It actually made the women's camp more easily run." In their collective obedience, if in few other respects, the orchestra women were firmly united. As Alma repeatedly told Hilde, the orchestra "would survive together or die together. There was no halfway road."

Violette observed that Alma was never obsequious in her relations with the SS. "Very much to the contrary. She was correct in her behavior, but with perfect dignity in a painstaking desire for perfection, which dominated her in the service to music as the meaning of her life."

Flora was convinced that Alma hated the Nazis. "She was a goddess to the SS—a goddess who hated them." Zofia remembered an SS who was a composer bringing his violin composition to Alma to sight-read. "Alma played it but made some mistakes because the writing was not clear. She proposed that he make some changes, and he accepted her advice."

Dr. Mancy was struck by Alma's courage in dealing with the Nazis. At one Sunday concert, she remembered, some SS women in the audience began laughing and swearing. Alma stopped the music. "Like a bolt of lightning, Alma took a deep breath and said: 'Like that, I cannot play.'" The interruptions stopped; the orchestra continued.

Rachela remembered the grim humor of one visitor to the Music Block: "One day the [SS] man responsible for the crematoria came to visit us. We asked him what point there was to our playing. He said that when our turn came, he would reward us with a specially strong portion of gas." This sort of humor was not for everyone, but for some it was a welcome reminder of their humanity. Oddly enough, commented Zippy, "you could laugh about death, our constant companion, but you could not joke about food, our greatest need."

Hilde, known in the block for her somber intelligence, could not remember laughing at Birkenau. "Maybe others could because they were so young," she said. "Only after liberation did we try to retrieve the youth that we lost in the camp."

Sylvia pointed out that "we laughed here and there about trivia. But there is a difference between joy of life and laughter."

THROUGH THE cracks in the plank walls of the music barrack, Alma and the orchestra women watched as prison laborers built the much-photographed railway sidings that led to crematoria II and III. New tracks were laid from the Auschwitz train station, through the gates of Birkenau, to the center of camp in preparation for the mass transports of spring 1944, when thousands of Hungarian Jews would be delivered to the camp to perish in the gas chambers. A mere fifty meters away, the musicians could see the processions of the condemned, marching or being trucked to their death in the space between the men's camp and their own, separated from the music barrack by a single barbed wire fence.

In a rare moment in the autumn of 1943, Alma showed her inner feelings as she and Zofia witnessed loaded transports on the way to the gas chamber and the wind carried the screams of the women from Block 25. "It is very, very terrible," Alma said. "Why are the Germans doing such things? I don't want to die this way."

Zofia described the incident: "It was *Blocksperre* [general prisoner confinement during in-camp selections: prisoners remained in their barracks until the selection process ended], and we were hidden on the dark side of the Music Block. I realized that Alma was terrified. Everybody felt that way but practically never said it. It frightened Alma that she would one day see someone she knew selected for gassing and being driven toward the crematoria." In such a case, Alma told Zofia, she would not have trusted her reactions.

The image of trucks crowded with naked women selected for gassing also haunted Dr. Lingens-Reiner. Remembering the hospital concerts, she later commented: "That we went on playing and listening to music, that we never shouted to those in the trucks to jump out—run—resist—is something I cannot understand to this day. How was it possible for us to be so calm?"

THE NEAR-MIRACULOUS difference in sound after Alma took over direction of the orchestra gave rise to many stories about the Jewish kapo, including the rumor that she was abusing the girls. There were reports of harsh punishments for those who played wrong notes, ranging from insults to raps with the baton, slaps, and even beatings.

It is true that stern standards prevailed inside the block. Alma was fanatical about personal cleanliness, although the orchestra women had little means of achieving it. Shoes had to be cleaned and polished daily, and beds made with regulation "hospital corners." Alma's biting comments and authoritarian approach made some girls hate her, even as they depended on her protection and saw their fate as inextricably bound with hers. Even some who fiercely objected to Alma's dominion later asserted that the strict order of life in the Music Block gave the orchestra women an all-important sense of security.[24]

Alma kept her music copyists as busy as she kept the musicians. The copyists sat at a long table on one side of the music room, transcribing orchestral scores in a clutter of papers. For Alma, mistakes in copying were even more unforgivable than wrong notes, and her relations with the copyists were especially difficult. Pin-neat even in these surroundings, Alma hated untidy, messy, careless people and their work. Moreover she did not want to waste the precious music-score paper, with its staves drawn by hand by the girls of the camp office.

There is no doubt that Alma's methods were sometimes harsh. On this sensitive subject, which stimulates heated controversy among the orchestra survivors to this day, Anita cautions that no one who did not live with the orchestra inside the Music Block could understand Alma's behavior. Zippy agrees that the life of the prisoners will remain incomprehensible to outsiders. "Love and hate lived side by side in Auschwitz," she said, "and there was only a fine line between love that meant self-sacrifice, and hate agitated by the need to survive."

Dr. Lingens-Reiner, remembering the struggle necessary to survive in the camp, said all-embracingly: "There was nothing for which I should not have forgiven a Jewish prisoner in Auschwitz."

Remembering Alma, Anita spoke of perfectionism and severity in the same breath:

> Alma had set out to make a real orchestra with standards where only the most perfect rendering was acceptable. These were the standards that she herself had grown up with. . . . Drilling almost every player in the orchestra individually, she threw herself into this task with a fervor that seemed absurd under the circumstances. . . .
>
> Alma gave us severe punishments for playing wrong notes. I remember having to wash the entire block on my knees for playing badly on my return from the Revier after having survived typhus, which leaves one unbelievably weak as well as with impaired sight and hearing. I was by no means the only one punished like that.
>
> I would be dishonest if I said I loved Alma for this at the time. In fact I was furious; but thirty-five years later I view Alma's attitude with nothing less than the greatest admiration. I am still not sure whether Alma was taking a premeditated line or acted by instinct.
>
> What she did achieve, with the iron discipline she imposed on us, was that our attention was focused away from what was happening outside the block—away from the smoking chimney and the smell of burning flesh—to an F which should have been an F-sharp.
>
> Maybe this was her way to remain sane, involving us so thoroughly in this quest that we managed to keep our sanity too.

Hilde had a similar confrontation with Alma when she returned from the Revier after a painful round with typhus. Despite their friendship, Alma would not listen to her. "Alma wanted me to take on the score of some work, and I had a problem convincing her that I could neither hear nor see well enough to do it." All the same, Hilde admired Alma without reservation. "In Auschwitz, she was building. Others were fighting for survival; for Alma, she was actually building. She would argue with me, a committed Zionist, for hours to forget going to Israel after liberation. She said she was building an orchestra that she would take on tour of the world after the war."[25]

As Hélène Scheps put it, the women of the Music Block "were on another planet, although in the camp. Alma sometimes made me forget our imprisonment, our desperate situation."

Sylvia concurred. For her, the mere existence of the orchestra in an extermination camp was too absurd to be dealt with rationally:

> I believe that on a certain level there was complete detachment from reality. If you sit there and make music—not just managing to play—but really tried to improve your playing for eight to twelve hours each day, that was already a detachment from what was happening around you. . . . Either forget everything that happened around you, to live only for the day, or think about it all the time and go mad.

Zofia once said, "I believe we weren't really conscious of what went on. Otherwise, we would have had to commit suicide." Rachela agreed:

> To witness all this, and to bear it, would have been impossible for a logical person. We saw men walk in the snow barefoot. Over their heads they carried their "boards" [wooden-soled shoes that were useless in snow and made it impossible to keep up the pace overseers demanded]. We sat there and cried watching that.

Music Block survivors Rachela, Sylvia, and Hilde in Israel remained stunned by the force of Alma's motivation and the achievements of the orchestra. "It was so beautiful," Rachela said in the Kol Israel broadcast. "We played so beautifully!" Hélène Scheps, too, remembered the sound Alma forged as "beautiful beyond compare."

Alma was no angel, Anita attests, but she was one of the few kapos in the entire chain of camps in Silesia who could declare with authority that she could save a prisoner, and who exercised that power repeatedly. Alma knew full well that other functionaries at the camp, SS enforcers, abused their charges, and she considered herself in a separate category.

"Alma said her job as kapo in the Music Block was better than being a kapo killing girls and stealing their food," Margot remembered. Although camp gossip held that she "lived like a queen," Regina, who tended her room and could sketch its layout years after the war, asserts that it was Spartan. Alma lived plainly, with simple furniture; she did not indulge in the excesses of other prisoners in command of their blocks.

Hélène Scheps, who was devoted to the orchestra leader, will never forget the day she aroused Alma's fury. The orchestra was playing at the camp gate as a group of Belgian women marched past. Hélène said, "One woman recognized me and cried out: 'Is it you, Hélène?'"

> I collapsed in tears. Alma was furious. When we returned to the Music Block, I was still crying. She slapped my face to calm me down and told me never ever to lose control of my nerves. The show must go on! I never lost control again. I never held a grudge against Alma, for I understood the lesson.
>
> How can one analyze my feelings? In self-defense, I gave myself completely to my role in the veritable ghetto that was the orchestra. The crematorium was a hundred meters away. Outside our block, the barbed wire fence gave off sparks in the night. During the night, those selected went to their death in song, in psalmodies or prayers. It was atrocious.

The young Yvette was also particularly sensitive, and she too broke down in tears as the orchestra played at the gate one day. Hélène recalled that "the order came then—reinforced officially by Mandel—that no one was to cry."

Alma has been accused by some—including Fania Fénelon—of beating the girls. Fania further reported that Alma defended herself by saying that the great German conductor Wilhelm Furtwängler, in a "German orchestra tradition," struck his players. According to Fania, Alma, "a real German" with an "empty violin case" for a heart, was fanatical about the commanding position a conductor should occupy.[26]

The distinguished Vienna Philharmonic archivist Professor Otto Strasser admired both Alma and her father. Professor Strasser, who played violin for many years beside Arnold Rosé, wrote that he did not question the sincerity of Fénelon's recollections. All the same, he played under Furtwängler at various times over a period of thirty years in both Vienna and Salzburg. During that time, he said, the conductor "never raised his voice; much less did he ever hit anyone."[27] Strasser strongly doubts that Alma defended a policy of corporal punishment for members of the orchestra in the name of Furtwängler, who was well known and respected in the Rosé home. Nonetheless, Strasser observes, players are often critical of conductors. "It is quite usual," he concludes wryly, "for players NOT to idolize their conductors."

Among the autocratic conductors of Alma's day, one of the most feared and revered was her Uncle Gustav. Her father, too, had strict notions of discipline and was known as an imperious orchestra and quartet leader. (Once, it is said, even the decorous Rosé struck a fellow player on the head with his bow after he missed an entrance.[28])

Kitty Felix Hart recalled that the orchestra members often looked tired and pale, as though they had been beaten. Other witnesses, including Eugenia Marchiewicz, saw no such signs of abuse. Reports of dire appearances were no wonder, say orchestra survivors. They were often exhausted to the point of fainting, often hungry and in pain, their nerves stretched to the breaking point by the knowledge that their lives could hinge on their next performance.

Helena said she is not surprised if the orchestra girls looked worn out, even in their better clothing. Although they were spared the physical burden of the heavy work kommandos, they were under severe strain. The orchestra girls were among the first in the camp to rise each day. Their duties were not complete until well into the night, after an entire day of practice. Helena added:

> I do not remember if Alma ever beat the women. She penalized them in a different way. She would order them to wash the barrack floor. Or she would order them to carry the heavy [50-liter] soup kettles from the kitchen—a job usually taken by the women called *Stubendienst,* the caretakers of the Music Block. Worst of all was banishment from the music room for even a short period—and all that it meant—for it was one step away from being sent out into the camp proper.

Violette remembered Alma's banning a girl from entering the music room for a week.

Sylvia scarcely reacted to Alma's explosions. "I remember Alma falling into a rage over a false note," she said. "I just smiled to myself. It became so absurd to me. After all, I was only playing a little recorder. Only a person condemned to death, as we were, can realize how the life force, the will to live, permitted us to bear it."

In contrast, Violette feared the orchestra leader and went to lengths to avoid her rages. She recalled that one Sunday morning before a concert, she spilled camp coffee on her white blouse. She was singing at the concert and "did not want to be berated and called a pig." To hide the spot from Alma, she covered it with her hands. But Alma was furious at the forbidden gesture and yelled at her, "Are you now the one who does the stage directing?"[29] In such situations, said Violette, Alma's behavior "annulled her humanity."

Tales of Alma's temperamental outbursts have entered the legend of the Birkenau women's orchestra. Alma shouted, slapped her players in the face, rapped their knuckles with her baton, called them "*Blöde Gans!*" (stupid geese) or "*Scheiss Kopf!*" (shithead). In ordinary life, in possession of herself, Alma would never have called another person such names. Yet it is clear that at Birkenau she lost some battles with her own fastidious refinement and sometimes used the brutal language of the ordinary kapo. Helena admitted: "Sometimes during rehearsals, when she was tired, Alma threw her baton at a musician who had made a mistake and shouted '*Du blöde Kuh!*' (you dumb cow)." But Helena saw Alma's lapses in a forgiving light, adding: "The camp atmosphere at its best was always threatening, and even in the shelter of the Music Block there was stress."

Even Fania, Alma's rival and committed detractor, saw her outbursts as lapses born of exasperation. "She was conducting a war of nerves . . . in which she was the loser." Under such circumstances, wrote Fania, "our reactions were understandable: death, life, tears, laughter, everything was multiplied, disproportionate, beyond the limits of the credible. All was madness."[30]

Even when her self-control failed her, Alma was faithful to her role as protector of the orchestra women and did not mete out the ultimate punishment, ejection from the Music Block. Zofia remembered an incident early in Alma's tenure as conductor. During a rehearsal, three girls seated immediately behind the first desk of the violins repeatedly played wrong notes. Alma, becoming more frustrated by the moment, accused the girls of paying no attention and ordered them to scrub the floors. One of them, non-Jewish Pole Jadwiga (Wisia) Zatorska, had been attempting to help Violette, a fellow violinist, and considered herself unjustly accused.

Wisia refused to accept the punishment. Alma, who would accept no challenge to her authority, insisted. Ultimately she decreed that Wisia either accept the verdict or leave the Music Block. Wisia, convinced that she had been wronged, was prepared to face her fate in the outside camp.

Zofia sought to intervene by explaining Wisia's rebellious attitude to Alma. On 24 September, Wisia's brother Władysław had been one of three Polish political prisoners arrested and locked in the punishment bunker of Block 11 in the main camp. On 28 September, after a selection in the bunker, all three were shot by order of the camp commandant.[31] Now Wisia so hated the whole world that she would never under any circumstances scrub the floor. Alma, touched by the story, devised a different punishment for Wisia, who remained in the Music Block and survived.

Anita's respect for the orchestra leader emerged intact after many cloistered months in the Music Block. In Anita's words:

> Driven by her father's expectations, Alma saved the orchestra. It was a prop as real as the prisoners' ultimate need for each other, as real as two sisters holding up one sick sister to prevent her from fainting on roll call. She turned our job into an almost spiritual thing. She might have been as afraid of the Nazis as we were, but she never punished us out of fear. Some girls felt Alma abused them, but they will know better than I.

Recalling Alma's hard work and her battles along the way, Zippy emphasized her pride in the orchestra as it evolved:

> She was achieving something she could never have achieved in normal life. Nothing became something in her hands.
>
> Alma's genius was that she could bring a group of amateurs to a level where they could perform acceptably. For her, it became the tri-

umph of her career. She never would have believed it possible. She also achieved something no other conductor she had known would have tried. She told me she could never go back to her origins. That Viennese society in which she had grown up was totally destroyed. In Birkenau she was creating something of which she could be proud.

A handful of people hated her, but there are many more who loved her then, and still love her. Some could never understand there could be only one leader for the orchestra.

If she did hit anybody, and I don't remember that she did, it would have been nothing in Auschwitz. There you could lose your nerves very easily. You can lose your nerves in normal life. Often a loving mother hits a child. It was not her manner to hit. There would have been all the difference in the world between Alma hitting a girl in the orchestra and an SS or a brutal kapo hitting an inmate in the camp.

I was hit by my best friend in the camp. I was angry, yes, but I could not hold it against her afterwards.

I remember times when Alma would scream in French at a particularly clumsy girl who made constant mistakes. But Alma never turned her out of the block—which would have meant her death, for I know that girl could never have survived anywhere else in Birkenau.

For Violette, too, Alma's comportment was complex but understandable.

I believe very sincerely that Alma failed to realize the situation. Nothing mattered except whether we played well or badly. It did seem excessive and rather revolting. In the name of art she administered two or three slaps or threw her baton at a musician's head.

How can I explain that if certain excesses revolted us, we held the greatest respect for her, and in a certain way we could explain her conduct.

ALMA WAS reluctant to ask the SS for special favors. Violette recalled that Mandel once said to Alma, "If you need bread, ask me. I will have it distributed." Violette continued: "Some days later, we approached Alma reminding her of Mandel's offer of more bread. She replied dryly: 'You played like pigs in the last concert [a performance for the inmates]. To punish you, I will not demand bread.'"

To the orchestra girls this seemed unduly severe. As a kapo Alma received a food supplement, so her own need for food was not as great as theirs. Fania and her French-speaking friends maintained that by refusing to ask for additional favors to ease the suffering of the musicians, Alma showed more care for the Nazi oppressors than for her fellow prisoners.

In the judgment of those closest to Alma, she declined SS favors in an effort to keep her dignity and focus and to inspire the same decorum among the orchestra women. She was determined to improve the scope and quality of the group's music and considered her methods necessary. Without stern discipline, she believed that all the women were doomed. Moreover, she felt that she alone knew how far she could go in dealings with Mandel and the other SS officers.

Flora, among others, had faith in Alma's ability to handle the SS. As Flora stood in front of the Music Block one day practicing a piece of music on her accordion, SS Commandant Kramer stopped her. "That's Jewish music!" he accused. "In self-defense," Flora said, "I replied I did not know who composed it. Otherwise he would have hit me. If he went to Alma about it, I knew she could deal with him."

Although unconnected with the Music Block, Eugenia Marchiewicz heard the insinuating whispers in the camp. She felt that she understood Alma's position, for denunciation was as much a part of Birkenau life as death and dying. According to Eugenia, Alma "didn't want to make too much of the orchestra lest they be denounced." If anyone had a good job, there were others waiting to take it over. Eugenia heard of Alma's demanding ways, her pleading with her players to work harder and rise to ever higher plateaus. It was Alma's appearance of limitless energy that drove the others along, Eugenia believed—not the threat of beatings or reprisals.

Although conflicts among the memories and interpretations of the orchestra survivors will never be resolved, it is certain that the causes Alma embraced with her usual intensity—music of a high standard and the survival of the orchestra women—were in her mind one and the same. She accepted the burdens of her position along with its privileges. Throughout the camp she was acknowledged as the orchestra's strong and solitary leader, to the point that camp rumors tagged almost every piece of gossip about the Music Block with the label "because of Alma." If the musicians were hungry, it was "because of Alma"; if they looked sad, it was "because of Alma"; if they appeared to have been beaten, it was "because of Alma." When the orchestra received privileges other inmates could only dream of, it was also "because of Alma."

At the height of her own career with the English Chamber Orchestra forty years later, Anita offered this evaluation of Alma: "Our orchestra was led in the fullest sense of the word by Alma. She was a most remarkable woman. She showed her very remarkable and strong musical background. She was a very fine violinist herself, but the most unforgettable feature was her powerful personality."

Gabriele Knapp reached a similar conclusion in 1996 on the basis of communications with seven orchestra survivors and research into the existing literature. In her study of the women's orchestra, *Das Frauenorchester in Auschwitz: musikalische Zwangsarbeit und ihre Bewältigung* (The Auschwitz Women's Orchestra: Musical Forced Labor and Means of Coping), Knapp wrote: "In the eyes of her fellow prisoners, [Alma] was a decidedly charismatic individual, an artist through and through."[32]

THROUGH THE autumn of 1943 in London, Arnold kept up a busy performance schedule and did his best to believe that Alma was safe in Holland. He had not heard from her since he received the cryptic note written on the eve of her attempted escape, saying merely "Justine's daughter is married."

On 2 September 1943, Arnold participated in a BBC broadcast to Austria, performing the Beethoven Romance in F for his fellow Viennese. The same month he learned that Carl Flesch, Alma's staunch friend in Holland, had managed to work his way to Switzerland.[33] On 16 September, Arnold wrote to Alfred that he could not rest until he had news of Alma.

Arnold's eightieth birthday, 24 October 1943, was a grand occasion within the Austrian refugee community in London. Many prominent figures in the music world relayed congratulations despite the continuing difficulty of wartime communications across the Atlantic. Official Anglo-Austrian and Free Austria events included a reception at London's Savoy Hotel and a sold-out concert in Wigmore Hall on 27 October, with Arnold at the helm of the reconstituted Rosé Quartet. Dame Myra Hess joined Arnold and Friedrich Buxbaum as guest artist for the Brahms Piano Trio in B major, opus 8, commemorating the occasion in 1890 when Brahms himself was at the piano as the Rosé Quartet played the trio from manuscript in Vienna.

Alma's absence was a cloud over the celebrations. Two days after her father's birthday, Alma had been at Birkenau one hundred days. More than ten thousand women had been admitted to the camp since her arrival in July. Many tens of thousands had been rounded up from every part of Nazi-occupied Europe and delivered to Auschwitz for immediate death.

Shortly after Arnold's birthday, Leila Doubleday Pirani wrote from Vancouver, B.C., that she had heard about Alma's marriage from Karl Doktor, via his son Paul in Switzerland. Arnold was pleased by this report and wrote to Alfred: "I must be relieved by this scant news." He continued to hope that Alma's marriage meant she was being "looked after."

In December Arnold and Alfred exchanged letters, each trying to lift the other's spirits. Alfred, remembering his father's prescription for his own "renaissance," gently advised: "To go to a better world, take the Beethoven piano sonatas and play them through."

20

The Orchestra Girls

There was never a time like it: with the elite of Europe—people we'd never meet otherwise—naked, together in our natural juices.
—Helen "Zippy" Spitzer Tichauer

The bonds which keep the survivors together are closer than any blood ties.—Dr. Ena Weiss Hronsky

Tactics for survival at Birkenau were as diverse as the human spirit. Young Margot Anzenbacher (later Margot Větrovcová) sustained herself by the elaborate fantasy that she was a sports reporter observing a life-and-death game between Hell and Ruin. She had only to remember and report on the contest.

Margot wrote about an incident when SS on horses chased a work gang. She and other girls fled into the water. By submerging herself under a tree branch and keeping her nose above the water, she was able to breathe. "I said to myself: 'Remember you are a sports writer.' Playing reporter helped me in many situations. It gave me strength. For instance, in the very hot sun, thirsty, dirty, sick of being hit by an SS man, I told myself how fortunate I was to be able to work. All the time there were dreams of sleeping in a clean room, or having clean underwear."

Alma also sustained a fantasy: whenever possible, she acted as if she were elsewhere. She entered the music room from her plain cell as if making a stage entrance. Ramrod straight at the podium, baton in hand, she was as dignified and passionate about the musical task at hand as if she commanded a great orchestra. Grete Glas-Larsson, her Viennese friend in the Revier, believed that Alma did not allow herself to realize where she was. She remembered the irony implicit in Alma's explosion one day: "I can't believe it! I cannot stay here!"[1]

The few friends permitted glimpses behind Alma's facade said that she acknowledged her predicament only in the direst situations. Then her aloofness would evaporate, and she would sigh, "If we don't play well, we'll go to the gas."

Friendships—fervent commitments to stand together unto death—also helped to sustain the women of the Music Block. Exclusive alliances grew alongside rivalries and bitter distrust. In Anita's words, life within the small community of the Music Block "generated the vilest hatred and the warmest camaraderie and friendship in equal parts."

When Fanny in the orchestra contracted typhus, her friends felt great anguish. Miraculously, she recovered. Hélène Scheps recalled her return to the Music Block: "Horrible—her face like a triangular mask with holes for her big brown eyes. She was so happy to be among us again." Alma, who had heard that Fanny's mother died of typhus, "asked two of us to break the news to Fanny. We did it with great care. We are one; more than ever sisters."

Friendship groups coalesced along lines of shared language and nationality. Thus special loyalties formed among French-speakers from Belgium and France, Russians, native German-speakers, Czechs, Poles, and the urbane and multilingual. Common cultural backgrounds helped to fuse alliances. According to Zippy, the women separated themselves into islets: "It could be like a glass wall between groups of two or three girls." The divisions gave rise to squabbles Alma could not tolerate. When the weight of pressures on the Music Block led to scenes among the girls, she retreated to her private room.

Many orchestra women—and others throughout the camp—came to believe in Alma so completely that they were convinced the orchestra could not survive without her. Some, including Lily Assael and Fania Fénelon, never forgave her lofty attitudes and her insistence on "Germanic" discipline. They felt she did not give her players the credit they deserved and were always prepared to remind her that, as Lily put it, "she needed us as much as we needed her."[2]

The biggest chasm within the women's orchestra separated Jews from non-Jews. Fania wrote that "Aryan oil and Jewish water weren't mixed," even at the copyists' table. The relations between Polish and Jewish girls were particularly complicated, non-Jewish Pole Helena Dunicz-Niwińska wrote in response to charges made by Fania and others: "It is a very large theme. . . . The attitude of the general lot of prisoners—German, Greek, French, and Polish Jews and Polish 'Aryans'—was appropriate and cultured. Despite the language barriers, close ties were made in that polyglot group."

Helena had a longstanding admiration for the orchestra leader. As a young violin student in 1929, she was a rapt member of the audience when Alma made her first tour of Poland. Fourteen years later, when Helena was sent to Auschwitz-Birkenau in 1943, she considered it a miracle to meet her childhood heroine in the camp, and indeed to play under Alma's direction. Yet Helena remembers speaking to Alma only twice—once upon admission to the orchestra, and a second time when she asked Alma to ease her work in the Music Block so that she could recuperate from illness. Said Helena, "Really there was not much time for conversation in our kommando. Alma was rather alone, and isolated in her separate room. Also, I was not comfortable in front of 'authority.'"

The two main divisions within the Music Block were separated by camp culture as well as by language, religion, and nationality. Under Nazi edict the Jewish prisoners had no future, whereas non-Jews could hope for eventual freedom. This distinction was fundamental at Auschwitz, and Jewish prisoners found themselves at the bottom of the social order. Dr. Lingens-Reiner, among others, has testified that in the Revier, non-Jews criticized doctors for giving precious medication to Jewish patients. "Why do you treat the Jews?" they would say reproachfully. "They are going to die anyway." Jewish women were so badly treated throughout Nazi-occupied territories that most were "dead in spirit before they arrived at the camp gates."

The constant threat hanging over the Jewish women bound them together. When Alma and Czajkowska insisted that the musicians make their beds perfectly each morning and the youngest in the orchestra, Yvette, had difficulty, the older German flutist Frau Kröner made her bed for her. According to Sylvia, the Jewish girls helped one another by sharing their food. When she was recovering from typhus and suffering from all-consuming hunger, she said, "Hilde gave me her portion of food and thus I could survive. Thus one helped the other." The isolation of the orchestra, created in part by Alma's rigorous training schedule, cemented bonds and also accented divisions among the women.

Anita, remembering the few Polish girls who communicated with the Jewish women, said:

> A deep-rooted distrust and even hatred separated the non-Jews from the Jews. The Poles received parcels from home and were because of that in much better physical condition. I don't think that once anybody would have shared anything with any of us. We Jews had to look on when they cooked things on the stove.
>
> The sight and smell of unattainable food did not enhance friendly relations. I remember only two Poles who ever spoke to us. One of them was a highly educated woman, the singer Ewa, who spoke French, and the other was Danka [Danuta Kollakowa[3]].

Representing the Polish side of the rift, Zofia, a non-Jew, reported:

> When it came to cooking "organized" food, Jews had the first privilege on the stove in the block. Czajkowska would say: "You should understand they don't receive packages from home. They only have the camp's food." Of course it is true that the Jewish girls did not have the advantages in Birkenau that non-Jews had. For most of them, no one remained at home to send packages.

The rare food parcel created contention within the Music Block. To share or not to share these precious parcels? Helena spoke frankly: "As for the sharing of packages, some of the Polish girls did not get any from their families, and therefore the packages were shared with compatriots or some relatives or friends —even sometimes with those in other blocks, remembered from previous prisons. However, I am sorry to say that some girls did not share with anybody."

As a result of her camp experience, the simple sound of a fork stirring eggs remained traumatic for Fanny, arousing memories she could barely stand. Many years later, Fanny recalled: "Every time I hear that sound, I am taken back to Birkenau—to a time when I was still recovering from typhus. While we were almost always painfully hungry even in the Music Block, the most uncontrollable hunger took possession of a person after typhus. Anyway, I saw Danka preparing to scramble an egg. I pleaded with her for some, even a mouthful. She refused me."

Yvette speculated that Danka, like many Polish girls, had contacts in other parts of the camp. "She could even have organized the egg through some friend in the kitchen."

Stories of Polish disdain for the plight of the Jews at Birkenau—some claiming that Poles danced and laughed when Jews were abused or sent to the gas—have roused such mild-mannered women as Helena Dunicz-Niwińska and Zofia Cykowiak to fury. The telling of isolated tales out of context does not address the issue of Polish anti-Semitism, they maintain. Where the dire fate of the Jews in their country is concerned, some of those stories have "made the Poles and not the Germans the guilty party," said Helena. Yet "there were people in the camp from many nations who denounced both Poles and Jews. We [Poles] were not fighting Jews."

There is no doubt that widespread anti-Semitism in Poland before and during the war was reflected in the often painful relations between Jews and non-Jewish Poles in the Music Block. For Zofia, however, the elevated cultural level of the women in the orchestra ameliorated any bitterness between factions, for "we were not playing for the SS, but for our own sanity." Sylvia concluded that in the end, the relationships between non-Jewish and Jewish women depended on the persons involved. Fanny emphasized the mutual support the orchestra women gave one another: "I think we all contributed a little to each other's survival."

Alma's loyalty was to the orchestra as a whole. She did not discriminate among Jews and non-Jews so much as between good and bad musicians, and she was always there to protect her orchestra girls.

In defense of the orchestra's Jewish members, Alma had her first major confrontation with an SS official. An overseer accused her of favoring Jewish girls. Dr. Mancy remembered her emotional account of the encounter:

> "Why did you turn away a Polish violinist?" shouted the overseer.
>
> "Because she isn't musical and doesn't play the violin well," replied Alma.

"You lie," said the SS. "It is because she is not a Jewess. Now you take her in the band."

"As you command," answered Alma—correctly, as always.[4]

Alma sobbed as she told of the rebuff. Through tears she did not permit herself to shed in the Music Block, she showed Dr. Mancy "she knew now that elements in the camp challenged her in her music, the one most precious refuge she had left. Discord challenged harmony."

Alma's dilemma deepened after this confrontation. She had to build the quality of the orchestra to please the Nazi officials, and she and Mandel agreed that she should be free to choose Jewish inmates. At the same time, by order, she had to maintain a balance between Jewish and non-Jewish musicians. Although the Jewish women were among her best performers, she dared not highlight them over the Poles, for she knew what awaited the Jewish inmates if the orchestra collapsed. Despite her stature in the camp, she was at the mercy of the SS, who could rule on any piece of music or any musician.

EVEN AMONG the Jewish musicians, united by the extreme precariousness of their position, there were strains due to religious, cultural, and linguistic differences. Lily and Yvette, for instance, did not speak Hebrew or Yiddish; upon arrival they knew Greek, French, and English (they would learn German in the camp). This cut them off from the Ashkenazic Jews of Central and Eastern Europe, who spoke Yiddish or the languages of their native countries. Alma, among the best educated of the prisoners, spoke an excellent, precise French and English and perfect German plus some Dutch and Czech, but she did not communicate in Yiddish or Hebrew.

Hilde described the different groups within the Music Block on yet another level. "There were atheists, Communists, devout persons, and Zionists among us. The Russians wanted to go back to Russia, the Poles wished for an ever-independent Poland. Everyone lived with her own world-view and was convinced she was right." Despite the diversity within the group, it maintained remarkable cohesion.

In the Kol Israel broadcast, Hilde said with regard to Alma: "She did not have a Jewish upbringing but did not deny her Jewishness. She came from a typically assimilated home." Eugenia Marchiewicz remembered that "Jews from the Warsaw ghetto hated Alma because she was an assimilated Jew and because she was like a German Jew, who they said was more German than Jew."

Sylvia did not remember serious differences among the Jewish girls, many of whom sought to carry on religious observances. She, her sister Karla, and Ruth Bassin (a young Jewish musician from Breslau who played piccolo in the orchestra) spent 19 April 1943—the anniversary of Hitler's birth, which coincided with Passover—in a crowded freight car en route to Auschwitz. As the train sped over the tracks, they tried their best to arrange a Seder evening.

Hilde remembered that in the camp, Karla read from the Bible on the Sabbath, "which we tried to keep." For holy days, the Jewish girls fashioned a menorah from one of the boards in a bed, carving out the branches of the traditional Hanukkah candelabrum.

The Jewish holy days sometimes provoked the Nazis to especially cruel measures. In particular the Jewish orchestra players remembered the approach of Yom Kippur in 1943. On 8 October, SS doctors performed selections in both the men's and the women's camps at Birkenau, and several thousand Jewish men and women were sent to the gas chamber.[5]

Asked by a Kol Israel interviewer whether inmates at Auschwitz turned to religion for comfort, Sylvia said: "There are indeed people who were atheists who have returned to religion today. Their argument is that we were saved to prove there is a God. I, however, wonder if there is a God who could look on while five thousand children were burned in a ditch because there wasn't any more gas for them. How could there have been such a thing, or an Auschwitz extermination camp?"

The same doubts would haunt many others. In *Night*, Eli Wiesel wrote:

> Never shall I forget that night, the first night in camp, which has turned my life into one long night, seven times cursed and seven times sealed. Never shall I forget that smoke. Never shall I forget the little faces of the children, whose bodies I saw turned into wreaths of smoke beneath a silent blue sky.
>
> Never shall I forget those flames which consumed my faith forever.
>
> Never shall I forget . . . those moments which murdered my God and my soul and turned my dreams to dust.[6]

Jewish philosopher Martin Buber, himself a refugee from Nazi Germany, echoed the anguish of camp inmates when he spoke of the Holocaust as "the eclipse of God."

Polish Christian Eugenia Marchiewicz said: "Some of us were afraid to pray. I was not strong enough to face the thought that God might have heard me and did not help me."

Dr. Mancy wrote of a December 1943 selection by Dr. Mengele when hundreds of Jewish women were thrust into Block 25. Crazed, naked, without food and water and surrounded by corpses, the women were held until it was discovered that the selection had taken place without prior approval from Berlin. They were then released only to be re-selected for the gas chamber once the official order came. Those who ran to escape the transports were clubbed to death or shot.

In mid-December, an additional 5,008 men, women, and children arrived from Theresienstadt, joining the survivors from the September transport who had established the Birkenau family camp.[7]

The chief of surgery in the main Auschwitz camp announced that between 16 September and 15 December 1943, doctors performed 106 sterilizations, removing the testicles or ovaries of prisoners chosen for experimentation.

The pre-Christmas rush of transports and gassings eased after 20 December. On that bitterly cold day, 504 deportees in a Jewish transport from Drancy were gassed. The same day, men from the Quarantine Blocks in the Birkenau men's camp were subjected to a long roll call in a blizzard. Too weak to stand at attention in the wind and snow, the men in the front row were beaten. One prisoner was shot in the arm, and four men were taken to the hospital with pneumonia.[8]

Christmas 1943 was the only day of the year when there was no roll call, morning or evening. Alma had worked hard to prepare a Christmas concert in the Sauna. The performers included children from the Jewish family camp, which had some dozen musical ensembles of its own, singing a medley of traditional German hymns.

The concert was disrupted by one of Birkenau's most hated and feared women, "Puff-Mutti" Musskeller, a German from Bavaria and block senior of the Sauna. At the time, she was in the punishment detail under sentence for a misdemeanor. A former prostitute known for crude and vicious behavior, she encouraged others to call her the warm and friendly "Mutti," a paradox that earned her the camp name "Puff-Mutti," or "Brothel-Mama." Musskeller, who was a remarkable yodeler, had made many pleas to be taken into the music kommando, which Alma ignored.

Seweryna Szmaglewska described the occasion:

> In the crowd of women, excited by the absence of the SS men, by the music, and by their own eagerness to forget, flash the figures [of the punishment detail] with red circles on their backs. Musskeller is there too; she has not yet been pardoned. . . .
>
> The ensemble of women artists, collected from all Europe, starts to play a sad tune, a tune so melancholy that with its first chords a spell falls upon the crowd standing so densely that their shoulders touch. Musskeller in her gray dress with the red spot comes up from the crowd and stands by the leader.
>
> She [Musskeller] has grown thin and black in the past months and has lost her self-assurance. She raises bloodshot eyes to the leader's face, panting and swaying to the surge of the music. The leader nods, and Musskeller throws her head back with a smile of ecstasy, spreads her arms, and starts to sing.
>
> Her song is the essence of yearning. It seems that the power of loneliness with which the singer invests the unsophisticated words will blow up the walls:
>
> "*Wien, Wien, nur du allein*" [Vienna, City of My Dreams] . . .
>
> The singing is much too piercing. It is not singing. It is the outcry of an individual who defends herself from having her soul deformed.

> The orchestra senses the passion of the song. Their playing becomes a cry of despair, wrenched from the bowels of their instruments and from the depth of their hearts. The jungle of yearning, as a rule so carefully evaded by the prisoner, suddenly opens and begins to sing with many voices.[9]

Musskeller's singing became so hysterical that Alma stopped the music. Consequently the powerful blockowa came to hate Alma and became one of her most implacable enemies in the camp.

THERE ARE numerous reports of the orchestra playing when trains arrived at Auschwitz-Birkenau and during selections at the camp.[10] Survivors of the orchestra are divided with respect to this heinous legend. Many say that at no time under Alma's direction did they play for a selection, on the ramp or elsewhere. In the 1981 Kol Israel broadcast, Sylvia told of playing through a night-long selection by Mengele, but it is unclear whether this took place while Alma led the orchestra. The percussionist Helga Schiessel, in a deposition on file at the Auschwitz Museum, also says she played for the arrival of transports.

Helena remembered one night during a selection when a detachment of drunken SS summoned a group of musicians to play at a guardhouse adjacent to the ramp, at the road separating Birkenau BIa and BIb. A small group of girls from the orchestra did play during that selection. Helena is uncertain whether this occurred during Alma's term as leader.

Although details are contradictory, Margot wrote in 1979 that she would never forget the morning a request came to the Music Block for a few singers to sing on the ramp. In Margot's words: "It happened that Alma had to select a few singers to sing 'Ave Maria.'" None of the other orchestra survivors remembered that song as part of the repertoire. The reference may have been a message in code for someone Margot expected to read her account, or it may have reflected her recurrent nightmares.

Reports of an orchestra playing upon the arrival of a transport could have several origins. A train may have arrived as the orchestra played for the work parties marching into or out of the camp. The train would have remained sealed until the prisoner details were out of view. In addition, arrivals may have heard the orchestra practicing through the plank walls of the Music Block, a mere fifty meters away beside the fence that separated the camp from the ramp.[11]

Liana Millu, an Auschwitz survivor, remembered Mengele selecting for the gas chambers as her returning work party "marched up to the gate in time to the music's sprightly beat." The doctor stood with a group of SS officers. "With notebook and pencil in hand," Millu reported, "he scrutinized the women filing in front of him, picking out any who looked wasted away. [His Slovak secretary] would read out the number tattooed on the woman's arm, and he would write it down. Then the rows moved on, while the woman selected went to stand apart in a group of gradually increasing numbers, a group of the chosen."[12] The musical background when returning workers were culled in this fashion may have contributed to the mistaken memory of the orchestra playing during selections.

In fact, Zippy pointed out, *Blocksperre* was in effect during in-camp selections. All prisoners, including the orchestra women, had to return to their barracks and remain there until the process was concluded. In any case, the railway sidings that ran up to crematoria II and III were not completed until late March or early April 1944, and Alma's tenure as conductor ended abruptly with her death on 5 April.

21

Frau Alma

I too bleed, and hope for beauty.—Manca Švalbová, on the message of Alma's music at Auschwitz

It was rare for the SS to address anyone with the respectful *Frau,* yet Alma was "Frau Alma" among the Nazi officers who supported her and within the orchestra, and so she was known to her admirers in the camp. Both Mandel and Hössler addressed her as "Frau Alma," Helena and others have testified. The powerful Katya Singer of the camp office was known as "Frau Singer," and Else Schmidt, kapo of the *Bekleidungskammer,* the laundry and clothing storeroom, as "Frau Schmidt." But the use of Alma's first name in combination with the respectful title was a unique mark of honor. Although she was labeled a Jewish prisoner, she became as powerful as any of Birkenau's "queens," as the kapos in the women's camp were called.

Many survivors have reported that at Auschwitz-Birkenau, it was dangerous to become conspicuous. In any group it was best to be near the center of the formation, protected from the kicks and blows of the guards. Attracting the attention of the SS could mean a beating or even death.

In such a setting, the attention Alma drew to herself constituted high risk. Ironically, the independence of mind and reservoirs of pride and hope that made it possible for Alma to act when others faltered—the very traits that ensured her protection and the survival of the orchestra—were also the traits that most exposed her.

Any favors granted through respect for Alma were reflected in amenities of life for all the prisoners of the Music Block. Yet there was something scandalous in Alma's apparently easy relations with the SS. As Dr. Mancy wrote, Alma was often maligned in camp gossip. Her fellow prisoners "at first talked about her quietly; later they began to libel her."

Zofia said the camp was stunned when word spread that Alma was seen seated in Mandel's office, having a normal conversation with the SS commandant as if between two free human beings. Witness to this startling scene was none other than the Belgian Jewish prisoner Mala Zimetbaum, a beautiful young woman and talented interpreter who worked as a messenger and had the run of the camp. Mala was a trusted source of information. She visited the Music Block frequently and was among Alma's confidantes.[1]

Mala's report of Alma's tête-à-tête with Mandel was utterly reliable. Helena said:

> I *know* from Mala and others in the *Schreibstube* that there were examples of Alma being called to the *Blockführersstube* outside our camp, and there, Alma was talking with Mandel and allowed to sit down. They were having a talk sitting. There was also no such example in the history of the camp. THIS IS INCREDIBLE! UNBELIEVABLE!

By the time this tale made its way back to Holland, it had taken on qualities of myth. In a report written in November 1945 to Alma's former host and Ima van Esso's future brother-in-law, Ed Spanjaard, in Utrecht, Ima described Alma as an especially privileged and well-dressed *Birkenau Prominente* who played for the patients and the SS and gave a special Christmas concert at the camp, adding: "She was also once or twice invited to the house of the camp leadership." Ima had not kept up with Alma after she left the Experimental Block in the *Stammlager,* and her broadly sketched testimony showed that she knew little about Alma's subsequent experience at Birkenau.

It is true that the SS supporters of the orchestra showed special concern for Alma's welfare. Mandel repeatedly assured her that she was safe, that she would be the last person at Birkenau sent to the gas chamber. Yet these assurances bore little weight, for as Alma told her friends, she could no longer trust any Nazi.

Zippy remembered an episode that only a friend in Israel confirms for her. During the height of one of the numerous epidemics at Birkenau, Alma suffered from the painful skin disease erysipelas, also known as St. Anthony's Fire, characterized by spreading, deep red inflammation. In the days before widespread use of antibiotics, this infectious disease could kill, and at Auschwitz the standard approach to an outbreak was to step up selections for the gas chamber. Instead, said Zippy,

> Someone came from the Revier each day with an ointment, and Alma persisted in taking the stand in front of the orchestra at the gate. For a few days her face was covered like a mummy's. We commented on the similarity of *Rosa*—the German vernacular name for the disease—and Rosé. In all our misery, and afraid of catching the infection, the girls in the camp office could still laugh to ourselves.

Dr. Mancy disputes this account, insisting that in her months at Birkenau Alma never suffered anything more serious than a head cold. In memory Dr. Mancy may exaggerate Alma's robustness. Fania, for one, wrote that Alma had frequent migraines during her last weeks at the camp, and several orchestra members mentioned that at Birkenau she often pressed her hands to her head as if in pain. Regina, with Dr. Mancy, refuted the migraine report.

DR. MANCY (Manca Švalbová), a young Slovak doctor at the camp hospital, became Alma's intimate friend. Elsewhere their lives would never have brought them together, but at Birkenau they had much in common. Both women, Alma at thirty-seven and Dr. Mancy at twenty-six, had seen something of the world before their deportation to Auschwitz. An early arrival at Auschwitz, Dr. Mancy was tattooed with the low number 2675. Although as a Jew she had been barred from finishing her training, her medical knowledge was extensive; Alma, like many others, considered Mancy her personal doctor. Combining cunning with a generous heart, Mancy had become so campwise that she could organize scarce drugs and palliatives—sometimes merely a digestible soup—for suffering prisoners. Like Alma, she was one of those rare personalities able to help fellow prisoners while evading the wrath of the SS. Sometimes, after giving comfort and care to prisoners, she had to look on as the same people were clubbed, downed by an SS dog, summarily shot, or sent to the gas chamber.

To Dr. Mancy, Alma showed the depths of her disillusionment with love. She had been betrayed three times, she said. She had come to believe that Váša Příhoda divorced her in 1935 because of her Jewishness as defined by the Nuremberg Race Laws. Heini had deserted her in 1939 when her struggle as a Jewish refugee and the imminent war threatened his comforts. Leonard had professed to love her but stopped short of the commitment to marriage that could have saved her. Her loneliness was profound, Mancy said. In retrospect, Alma felt that only her family had loved her for herself, and separation from her father and her brother was a continuing sorrow. Her fondest dream was to again play in a quartet with Arnold; chamber music, she had decided, was the most elegant and satisfying of musical forms. To Dr. Mancy, Alma's violin always conveyed the same message: "I too bleed, and hope for beauty."

Sorting through memories with her friend, Alma returned again and again to the Vienna of her childhood. She longed to relive the family holidays beside those blue Austrian lakes. How she had loved life! she would exclaim.

In Bratislava forty-one years later, Dr. Mancy talked about the Alma she had come to love. Suddenly she was silent, and her face warned that a torrent of emotion might burst forth. She reached into her purse and drew out a plastic envelope containing a card. It was a Christmas greeting showing two girls in costume dancing in front of a decorated tree. "*Frohe Weihnacht*" was inscribed on the front. Inside, Alma had written in her firm, distinctive hand:

Liebe Manzi
Wünscht Dir von Herzen
Deine Alma
Weihnacht 1943

A Merry Christmas,
dear Mancy,
I wish for you with all my heart.
Your Alma
Christmas 1943

This treasured icon is Dr. Mancy's only tangible reminder of Birkenau. Janiny Tollik, a Polish prisoner from Tarnów, had painted the card especially for Alma. Janiny too sought harmony through her art, using it to escape what Mancy called "the frightful dissonance of the surrounding reality."[2]

Alma's friend Hilde compared the orchestra leader to a sabra, a cactus-like Israeli plant with a refreshingly sweet fruit: "Alma . . . was hard and strong as a queen on the outside, but so different inside; outside thorns, and inside soft, sweet, and succulent soothing fruit." Hilde explained: "Alma seemed stubborn and pedantic. But I had a chance to get to know her more intimately. She was a very sensitive woman. She loved poetry and romantic books. There was a great deal of difference between her external manner and her real self."

Hilde, chief copyist in the Music Block, had interests similar to Alma's, including a love of books. Within the block Alma looked on her as a sort of manager, and she confided in Hilde more than in anyone besides Regina, her personal assistant. Hilde had somehow managed to keep a copy of Goethe's *Faust* and a book of Rilke poems she brought with her to the camp. These two volumes were holy texts for her and for Alma, and the two women turned to them again and again for spiritual comfort.

Alma often entertained friends with stories of her encounters with the German and Austrian literary élite—Franz Werfel, Jakob Wassermann, Thomas Mann. Grete Glas-Larsson, the Revier nurse, remembered that she and Alma could lose themselves in talks about Viennese writers and the rich artistic life of the city they had shared. Alma also enjoyed speaking English with prisoners who could keep up with her. Rosa Felix, Kitty Felix Hart's mother, who worked with Kitty in Kanada, became friendly with Alma. Rosa had been an English teacher in Poland and gave English lessons to prisoners in her block. As Kitty recalled, "She enjoyed practicing her English with Alma."

As Alma's reputation grew, she was sought after by the extreme elements of Birkenau. On the one hand, for prisoners with educated and professional backgrounds, she represented remnants of beauty in the world. On the other hand, a nefarious camp elite saw her as a prestigious attraction for what were known

Photocopy of the handpainted card Alma presented to Dr. Mancy at Birkenau in December 1943.

as their "courts." Alma had long ago proven how arbitrary she could be in choosing her companions, and the alliances she formed at the camp were no exception. She embraced some fellow kapos but rejected others—an affront not easily forgiven.

Alma was often in the court of Frau Schmidt of the camp laundry, a Sudetenland German political prisoner said to have served on the staff of Eduard Beneš, who with Thomas Masaryk was considered a founder of Czechslovakia.[3] Schmidt supervised a large staff, including Polish cooks reputed to produce the best food in camp. Zippy said that despite rules against such enterprises, Frau Schmidt enjoyed a clandestine cuisine that even the SS savored.

As THE NEW YEAR 1944 rolled around with no relief from the bleakness of the old, Alma's defenses were crumbling. Her hair was rapidly graying. She tried to hide it, knowing that to the authorities it would mark her as becoming less useful. "Gray hair was a rarity in Auschwitz," said Zippy.

Friends such as Dr. Mancy worried about the escalation of Alma's already feverish activities. She began to swing between deep depression and near-hysterical bursts of energy that prevented her from sleeping. Zofia remembered her toiling through whole nights preparing music. Each time Alma reached a goal, she set another target. Each hurdle she overcame brought more sleepless nights, more desire to perfect the ensemble and enhance its importance in the camp. With each new demand she made upon herself came more stress, more loneliness.

Dr. Mancy felt she could literally see the camp devouring Alma's spirit. As Anna Pawełczyńska wrote in *Values and Violence in Auschwitz:* "The inmate who sought to please would eventually be drained by the system that demanded '*schneller, schneller*' [faster, faster], while privation sought to make the inmate weaker in spirit and physical energy."[4] Frau Alma, doing her utmost, began to falter.

ALMA AND MARGOT worked together to transcribe a song of pure yearning. They began with a popular tune based on Chopin's Étude in E, opus 10, no. 3, which Chopin on his deathbed pronounced his favorite among his compositions. The song in its various versions is rarely heard now, but the music is everlastingly enchanting, both as the original piano solo and with various attached lyrics. It has been recorded under the titles "Tristesse" (Grief) and "So Deep in the Night" by Tino Rossi, Richard Tauber, John McCormack, Bidú Sayão, Paul Robeson, and American popular singer Jo Stafford. In the 1930s a German version with a text by Ernst Marischka became a popular song under the title "In mir klingt ein Lied" ("A Song Echoes Within Me," or "Alone in My Song").[5] Alma's version, preserved in Alma's own handwriting by Hilde in Israel, kept the Marischka title but used a different text:

In mir klingt ein Lied,
ein schönes Lied,
und durch die Seele mir erinnern zieht.
Mein Herz war still.
Nun erklingen wieder zarte Töne,
ruft in mir alles auf.

Leben war fern,
Und Wünsche fremd.
Mein Herz! Wie ruhig warst Du, lange Zeit.
Doch nun kam nah
All mein Glück und mein Verlangen,
Tiefstes Sehnen, schlaflos Bangen.

Alles, alles lebt jetzt wieder auf.
Ich will doch nur
Frieden für mein Herz,
Ruhe will ich nur,
nicht denken wieder (mehr)
An ein schönes Lied.

In me echoes a song, a beautiful song,
And brings back memories.
My heart was still until
Now those sweet sounds emerge again,
Reviving in me echoes
Of a life far removed,
Of dreams no longer mine.
My heart! You were dormant
For so long!
But now all my desire—all my happiness
Springs up again:
Deep longing, sleepless anguish,
Everything now comes to life.
Yet I want only
Peace for my heart.
Rest is all I want,
Never again to think
Of the beautiful song.

From her Wiener Walzermädeln days, Alma was probably aware of the original French words by F. Litvinne, published in 1930 and possibly sung by Yvette Guilbert (who shared the stage with Alma's ensemble), as well as the 1934 German version with Marlschka's text. The French lyrics to "Tristesse," published with the following English verse translation by Paksman, are similarly forlorn:

Tout est fini,
Les fleurs des prés
Se sont fanées,
L'été se meurt.
Les oiseaux peureux se taisent,
La nature est en deuil.
Tout est fini.
Le froid nous étreint,
La nature entière subit l'hiver.

Au printemps les chants des oiseaux joyeux et fidèles
Versaient la paix, la paix délicieuse,
Dans mon coeur grisé.
Et maintenant mon coeur lassé
Pleure ces chants, ses rêves finis.
Triste mon âme s'éteint.
Le froid cruel qui me saisit
A fait mourir tout mon bonheur.
Notre rêve heureux s'efface,
Tristement les fleurs se ferment.

Ô bonheur perdu avec le printemps.
Adieu clair soleil,
Tout est fini, tout est fini.[6]

Autumn has come, dreary is the day;
Silent are the birds that sang their tune fullay.
Withered are the flowers from the north wind,
Faded leaves pass'd away.

High in the sky birds so swiftly fly.
How they skim the air to find a climate fair.
Voice of spring I'm wanting only,
Without song I'm sad and lonely.
Oh melody of dreams,
Those wonderful dreams, wonderful dreams!
Gone is the spring! Gone is the spring!
Deep in my breast, sorrow comes to rest.
My life slowly fades from within.
Dark is the night, darker is my soul.
Oh! The stealthy cold
Will soon be creeping in.

Songs of joy from me have perished,
Songs I've loved and ever cherished.
Fare thee well, my dreams,
Sympathetic friend, sympathetic friend!
Life is at an end, life is at an end![7]

In every language and version, the song is a poignant lament. At Auschwitz it was performed in German with the words Alma recalled. The SS complained of its sadness and banned it unless changes were made, but Alma refused. Henceforth it was sung and performed only when no SS or suspected informers were present. For survivors, it remains a haunting reminder of the camp—a song that defied its own extinction, even by the all-powerful SS. Ruth Bassin, for whom the song was synonymous with memories of Alma, found herself singing "In mir klingt ein Lied" almost daily to the end of her life.[8]

IN JANUARY 1944, tensions in the camp eased briefly. The Germans were under pressure from the Allies, whose bombers were hitting industrial targets deep inside Germany. In dire need of Jewish labor to replace the workers and soldiers called to the Eastern and Western fronts, camp officials announced that Jews could earn special premiums of camp currency by doing exceptionally good work. Thus they too could reap the benefits of a "bonus plan" begun in November for non-Jewish workers. Alma and the Jewish musicians put the Nazis' new leniency in the proper perspective when they learned the details of

Commandant Arthur Liebehenschel's order of 7 January 1944: Jewish women were to be assigned to the arduous work outside the camp and non-Jewish women to details inside, where they were more protected from the wintry elements. In any case, the bonus plan was soon canceled.

By mid-month, the pace of transports and gassings was again stepped up. The resistance reported that in the first two weeks of 1944, 2,661 women died in the women's camp, of whom 700 were gassed. Now 27,000 women were imprisoned in Birkenau, an increase of 10,000 over the November total.

Fania Fénelon arrived in Birkenau on 23 January 1944 in a transport from Drancy carrying 1,153 Jews, of whom 1,113 were immediately gassed. Fania and the singer Claire were two of only forty on their train admitted to the camp. It was the second transport to arrive from Drancy in two days. The day before, 749 of 1,000 Jews were gassed.

On 25 January, 391 men, 435 women, and 122 children arrived from Westerbork in Holland. Of the 948 total, 689 were gassed. The same day, SS Untersturmführer (Second Lieutenant) Hartenburger ordered Jewish prisoners to write to relatives and friends in ghettos throughout German territories that rumors of the mistreatment of Jews at Auschwitz were not true.

Each military setback to the Nazis had repercussions in the camp. The Russians broke the siege of Leningrad on 27 January 1944. On 2 February, 2,800 in the women's camp hospital were selected for gassing. The critical straits of Germany's war industry resulted in a 22 February order to curtail the camp roll calls, extend daytime working hours, and institute night work. Birkenau now held 24,377 women inmates, and the total strength of Auschwitz and the surrounding camps was 73,669.

Near the end of February 1944, Adolf Eichmann, chief of SS Jewish Affairs, visited Birkenau to tour the Jewish family camp and to discuss arrangements for the arrival of 500,000 Hungarian Jews scheduled for deportation and extermination in May. The railway was still under construction, but it would be completed in time to serve its purpose. According to Dr. Mancy, events surrounding Eichmann's visit undermined what remained of Alma's balance.

This was Mandel's opportunity to show off the women's orchestra, and an Eichmann visit to the Music Block was scheduled. Alma could not jeopardize the existence of the orchestra by allowing it to play badly in front of the Third Reich's leading executioner. So began a frenzy of activity.

Eichmann appeared fleetingly at the Music Block, staying only a few minutes. Evidently he was not displeased by the orchestra's performance. Zofia said that shortly afterward, "possibly early March" on a beautiful spring day, the musicians were treated to an extra ration of camp coffee and, still more surprising, a walk outside camp under the guard of a single SS man. The unheard-of privilege of a stroll beyond the barbed wire fence—even under armed guard—remained one of the most cherished memories of Music Block survivors.

Helena and Zofia believe the taste of freedom was the result of Alma stressing the sufferings of the young musicians in talks with Mandel.

Like schoolgirls on a lark, scarcely believing their good fortune and ignoring the disbelief on the faces of other prisoners they passed, the orchestra girls walked through the camp gates into open countryside. Here they saw what they had despaired of ever seeing again: grassy meadows, flowing streams, free people in their fields, farm animals and flowers. Briefly, they laughed and knew that winter had ended. By testimony of many of the orchestra women, for all the hardships of captivity at Birkenau, Alma's kommando was the finest in camp.

The purpose of Eichmann's February 1944 visit to the family camp was not immediately clear. Danuta Czech and others have recorded some particulars. During his inspection, Eichmann spoke to prisoners, in one case lying to Miriam Edelstein, the wife of an elder of the Theresienstadt ghetto, Jakob Edelstein, who had led the Jewish community but remained subject to orders from the SS. Her husband was safe in Germany, Eichmann assured Mrs. Edelstein, when in fact Edelstein had been deported to Auschwitz and confined to the punishment bunker in Block 11 of the main camp the previous December, with the second group of arrivals from Theresienstadt.[9]

On 1 March 1944, a report raced through the camp that the nearly four thousand surviving prisoners in the family camp transferred from Theresienstadt in September 1943 would be moved to a new camp, Heydebreck. On 4 March, the day before the Americans began a series of shattering daylight bombings of Berlin, postcards were handed out to those to be "relocated." During the organization of the new camp, the inmates were told, they would not be able to write letters for some time; therefore they should date their postcards 25, 26, and 27 March.

On 6 March, Katya Singer, at the camp office, overheard an SS telephone conversation with Berlin. It was obvious that the inmates of the family camp were scheduled for *Sonderbehandlung*—all would be liquidated, beginning with the September deportees. At last Eichmann's business in the camp was explained.

The news spread quickly. A group of prisoners talked of burning the barracks the Czech families had occupied since September, and the camp resistance held secret meetings in search of a way to help the people of the *Familienlager;* but each suggested plan was abandoned.

The next day, the camp across the track from the Music Block was emptied, its inmates moved en masse to the Quarantine Blocks in the Birkenau men's camp. On 8 March 1944, youth leader Fredy Hirsch committed suicide rather than witness without resistance the slaughter of women and children.

The atmosphere of Birkenau was charged when *Blocksperre* was announced for the whole camp the same evening, 8 March. Camp streets from the men's Quarantine Blocks to the crematoria were lined with armed SS and machine guns. Through the night, the 3,791 Jewish men, women, and children from the

September transport who had survived the rigors of Theresienstadt and the Auschwitz family camp were taken in relays by truck to the gas chambers and killed. Thirty-five were spared—eleven pairs of twins, whom Mengele wanted for medical experiments, and thirteen doctors and nurses who were assigned to work elsewhere in the camp. Mailing of the postcards began as planned on 25 March.

For a time, the December deportees lived on at the family camp, but they too, with deportees from Theresienstadt in nine subsequent transports, were slated to die at Auschwitz. In later transports, only some 10 percent were selected for work and not promptly gassed. With a second mass gassing in July 1944, the family camp ceased to exist. By war's end, almost 90,000 prisoners had been deported from Theresienstadt to Auschwitz, of whom about 3,000 survived.[10] Of the approximately 7,000 children fifteen or younger who passed through the Theresienstadt ghetto, 6,300 were murdered in the East.[11]

In March 1944, the files of the political department marked with euphemisms for extermination—"SB" for "special treatment" or "GU" for "separated accommodation"—were taken to Birkenau and burned to erase the record.

At crematorium IV, a Polish woman confronted the SS before entering the gas chamber. Her farewell was spoken for herself and the hundreds of thousands of others condemned before her: "Today the whole world knows what takes place in Auschwitz, and for every murder here, the Germans must pay dearly. . . . I say farewell to this world with the knowledge that the time is not far off when your crime will be ended." She went to her death singing: "Poland is still not lost. To the barricades!"[12]

22

Death in the Revier

No, they did not put Alma in chains. She remained a free bird in her feelings and her faith like a naive child. She always thought that she would survive the camp.—Manca Švalbová

On Sunday, 2 April 1944, Alma led and played with the orchestra in an afternoon concert. There was praise from all quarters, and Alma told the orchestra women that she was proud of their performance.

Later in the day, Alma was called to the SS office. She returned to the Music Block in high spirits. Both Regina and Fania said that Alma enthusiastically confided she was to be released from the camp to play outside. According to Fania, she said she was going to play for "the soldiers of the Wehrmacht"; according to Regina, she was to play in the Katowice Opera House "and not for German troops."

Fania wrote that she expressed shock and dismay at Alma's eagerness to entertain German soldiers, "the instruments of Nazism, racism."[1] Alma supposedly retorted that at least Frau Schmidt, a true friend, was happy for her good fortune. Many survivors of the orchestra doubted Fania's report, for as Zofia Cykowiak reported, "Fania and Alma were not that close. . . . In fact, despite Fania's gifts as a musician, her driving ambition and schemes were often at odds with Alma. There is no doubt that Alma respected Fania for her professional musicianship, but I cannot imagine her as a confidante."

The women in the *Schreibstube,* a staff of thirty-five according to camp office survivors Zippy, Wanda Marossányi, and Anna Polarczyk-Schiller,[2] remain convinced that such a prisoner release would have been impossible. "The Gestapo would never have allowed it," said Zippy. Numerous attempts to release the highly respected office chief Katya Singer had been rejected. Wanda added that even if Alma had been allowed to play outside the camp, she would have continued to "belong" to the camp administratively.

In the evening Alma left the Music Block for the *Bekleidungskammer* to attend a birthday celebration for Frau Schmidt. There are many versions of subsequent events.

Rachela testified: "I saw Alma coming back from that dinner. As she passed us, she asked Regina to follow her. A few minutes later, Regina returned and asked Flora, the Dutch girl who with Hilde and Regina and Dr. Mancy was among those closest to Alma, to go inside. Flora went, and when she came back, she told us that Alma was very ill." Regina said that Czajkowska then ordered her out of Alma's room.

When memories were still fresh, three years after the events, Flora told Marye Staercke, a fellow Hollander, that Alma returned from her outing that evening complaining of a terrible headache and dizziness and suffering shaking seizures. After a short time she vomited. Flora and others put her to bed. She appeared to be delirious and said again and again, "The Russians are coming, the Russians are coming." Another witness said that she waved her hands as if she were conducting.

Liberation by the Russians was Alma's final hope. In moments of optimism about the orchestra's future, she often predicted that Soviet troops would free the players to tour the world and bear witness to the Nazis' crimes.[3]

Fania wrote that Regina awakened her, saying that Alma was sick and wanted to see her. Fania resented Alma's enthusiasm for the SS offer earlier in the day and was not happy to be roused from bed. She went to Alma's tiny room.

Alma had been vomiting. She was holding her head and had chest pains. Barely able to articulate, she said that she might not—after all—get out of camp.

Mandel was summoned. After a long fifteen minutes, she arrived with an SS doctor. He examined Alma then called stretcher-bearers to move her to the Revier.

Under special orders from Mandel, the orchestra chief was to be given a private room and a bed complete with bedding. The only room that met this description was that of block senior Orli Reichert, who vacated the room on the spot.[4] It was astonishing for a prisoner who had entered camp as a Jew to receive such attention in medical Block 4.

Outside the hospital, rumors circulated wildly. Manca Švalbová heard that Alma had been taken to the Revier. After the nightly roll call, she ran to her friend's bedside. Alma had blue "bruises" on her skin and a fever of 39.4 degrees Celsius (102.92 degrees Fahrenheit).

Dr. Mancy's first questions concerned Frau Schmidt's dinner party. At first Alma said that she had eaten nothing unusual. When pressed, she confessed that she had drunk some vodka, urged on by others at the party, who included a number of SS. Dr. Mancy scolded Alma, who had told her previously that she could not tolerate alcohol. Doctors gave orders to pump Alma's stomach.

In the analysis of Zippy and her husband, Dr. Erwin Tichauer, both Alma and Frau Schmidt, camp veterans by this time, were far too campwise to be unsuspecting victims of bad alcohol, which was often deadly methyl alcohol. Schmidt had survived from the early days of Auschwitz, and Alma had been in the camp almost nine months, living well past the average life expectancy of camp inmates, whether Jews or non-Jews. These careful and disciplined women would not have accepted a drink without knowing its source and exactly what was in it.

By noon the next day—Monday, 3 April 1944—Alma's fever had disappeared, and her temperature had fallen below normal. The women doctors of the Revier, led by the Slovak Jewish doctor Ena Weiss (later Dr. Ena Weiss Hronsky[5]), suspected encephalitis and noted meningeal symptoms. Six or seven prisoner-doctors, including medical assistants, devoted themselves to Alma's care. Dr. Mancy maintained her vigil and reported increasing numbers of blue "bruises."

Camp authorities were concerned that Alma's affliction might signal the outbreak of another epidemic, which would weaken the prisoner work force and pose health threats to the SS themselves. Further, the emergence of yet another infectious disease would require strict procedures to satisfy public health authorities in Cracow and Oświęcim.

On Monday, as inmates marched out of camp in the morning and returned at the close of day, Alma was not at her usual post. This set off a chain of speculation. By Monday night, conflicting reports were racing through the camp.

The mystery deepened when word got out that Frau Schmidt had disappeared from the *Bekleidungskammer*. In fact, the kapo of the laundry block had been admitted to another section of the Revier with symptoms similar to Alma's. Had the birthday dinner poisoned both women? It was rumored that other guests at the party also became ill. Because the *Bekleidungskammer* kitchen served food organized from SS stores, the health issue for the SS loomed larger still.

Alma drifted from the stench of the Revier into a phantom world. Dr. Mancy remained at her side, holding Alma's slender hands in her own. "You must live for your music," she pleaded. Alma was beyond speech, but seemed to take comfort from Mancy's presence.

The departure from ordinary protocol can be measured by the fact that the next day, on 4 April 1944, SS Dr. Josef Mengele came to consult in Alma's case. Mengele appeared in the Revier of the women's camp only rarely, when SS doctors Werner Rohde or Hans Wilhelm Koenig summoned him for assistance.

Now Alma's dark eyes stared straight ahead, unfocused, as though she were paralyzed; she did not blink, and her near-sighted squint had disappeared. She slipped in and out of consciousness. The Revier doctors gave her a heart stimulant called cardiaca, and Mengele ordered a spinal tap. Dr. Mancy, who assisted at the procedure, noted that Alma's spinal fluid was clear, suggesting that she did not have meningitis. Mengele himself signed the order for a laboratory analysis of Alma's spinal fluid, requesting tests for meningitis and pneumonia.[6]

Hyg.-bakt. Unters.-Stelle der Waffen-SS, Südost

APR. 1..

281/32

Auschwitz OS., am 4.IV.1944

17578/VII/43 7.4

Anliegend wird übersandt:

Material: Liquor cerebrospin. entnommen am 4.IV.1944

zu untersuchen auf Meningococcen u. Pneumococcen

Name, Vorname: Alma Rose

Dienstgrad, Einheit: 50381

Klinische Diagnose: Meningitis

Anschrift der einsendenden Dienststelle: H.K.B. Birkenau

Bemerkungen:

Mengele

(Stempel, Unterschrift)

Request to the SS Hygiene Institute for a laboratory analysis of Alma's spinal fluid, signed by Josef Mengele. Reprinted courtesy of the Auschwitz-Birkenau State Museum.

Dr. Tichauer, with his firsthand knowledge of medical politics at Auschwitz, wondered if Mengele's request for laboratory tests might have been an instruction to find one of the conditions named regardless of the facts. It was common knowledge that death certificates from the Nazi camps drew upon a prescribed list of terms to obscure the true reasons for a prisoner's demise. As Dr. Lingens-Reiner testified: "The hospital office had five model reports which stated as causes of death: pneumonia, acute cardiac insufficiency, general physical debility, influenza, or intestinal disease. The formula was always: 'Patient fell ill on the . . . . Despite careful nursing and adequate treatment with medicaments, she expired on the [date].'" The practice was so routine that it was an act of courage for laboratory personnel to report findings different from any proposed "results."

Again the facts remain murky. If Dr. Mengele suspected that Alma had meningitis, the laboratory report negated his suspicions: the spinal fluid analysis revealed nothing unusual. Alma's leucocyte count was high, but there was no evidence of bacteria. Tests for other infections also elicited the comment "*steril.*" Yet Alma did not respond. It was 4/4/44, a date the women of the orchestra would not forget.

The same day, as Alma struggled with death, 184 Jewish Dutch men, women, and children denounced in hiding in The Hague were gassed.[7] Never registered, they had been held in isolation in the men's camp Quarantine Blocks for two weeks after arrival at Birkenau. Had Alma gone into hiding in Holland a year and a half earlier, it is quite possible that she would have been among them.

Dr. Mancy stayed with Alma into the night, holding her hand and trying to rouse her with questions. But Alma's spirit flew far away in her last hours. Dr. Mancy wrote: "No one would know where she went that night." Only fleetingly did her words evoke a reaction. Then a trace of a smile would appear on Alma's face, a hint that her final journey was into the past.

Through the night Alma's seizures increased in frequency. The doctors worked feverishly but to no avail. Her arms were twisted in epileptic-like contractions, her hands pushing against the invisible weight of death.

Before dawn on Wednesday, 5 April 1944, Alma drew her last breath. The dramatically fascinating set of numbers attached to Alma's death in following years—death in Block 4 at 4 a.m. on 4/4/44—proved to be off by one calendar day.[8] Privileged even on her deathbed, Alma expired in a private room, separated from other sick and dying prisoners.

Dr. Mancy fled the Revier in tears. Conditioned as she was to death in the women's hospital, she was distraught to realize that Alma was gone from the earth forever. With each step, her feet broke through a crust of ice that had formed over the yellow mud in the night. A spring rain diluted her tears as she stared into the distance, trying to see past the expanse of plain and marsh to the peaks of the Beskyt Mountains, where she hoped family and friendship were still alive.

Grete Glas-Larsson, Alma's Viennese friend in the Revier, went to Alma's bed, held her lifeless body, and wept. Grete had grown up with awe for the Rosé name. When Alma died, Grete vowed she would not become "just another corpse," naked and waiting like cordwood for the body wagon to take her to the crematorium. "This is Alma Rosé!" she cried. "She must not lie naked like the other prisoners! She must be covered!"

Maria Mandel, who was deeply attached to Alma, mourned openly. The day Alma died, Mandel came to the Music Block and announced that the orchestra women could visit the Revier to bid farewell to their leader. The invitation was unprecedented at Birkenau. Fania said that all the orchestra members went, although in fact Hilde stayed behind.

In Block 4, the orchestra women were surprised to find Alma's body laid out on a white cloth atop a catafalque fashioned of two stools set side by side in an alcove next to the examining room. Different memories of the scene are topped by Fania's description of heaps of floral tributes brought in from the neighboring village of Oświęcim by the SS: "a profusion, an avalanche of flowers, mainly lilies, and giving off an amazingly strong scent."[9] Without a doubt this is gross exaggeration. But one thing is certain and cause for astonishment: most of the girls in the orchestra saw Alma clothed and respectfully laid out in death.

Orchestra survivors to a person have said that the death scene in the film *Playing for Time* blasphemed the realities of Birkenau. The film ludicrously showed Mengele placing Alma's violin on her breast, a distortion of fact not attributable to Fania's account. Numerous SS passed by Alma's bier to pay respects, Zofia said; but the orchestra women felt that they came to satisfy their curiosity rather than to mourn.

In her post in the *Stammlager,* Ima van Esso heard that a wreath and other greenery were placed in tribute beside Alma's body. Zippy says that even this would have been difficult at Auschwitz, since the grounds alternated between dusty desert, sticky mud, and frozen waste. Ewa, the singer and librarian, recalled that some of the girls managed to pluck a few sprigs of early spring greenery from the fringes of barracks where no one walked on them. With such tokens, the orchestra members paid tribute to their leader. She had come to mean different things to different women. For many, she had built a refuge from terror and nourished the hope of survival. Regina wrote revealingly: Alma's death "was a big shock for me after losing *all my family* in Auschwitz."

Alone in the Music Block, Hilde sought solace in Alma's room. There she found a tiny datebook, a treasured relic she preserves in Israel to this day. In its pages, among other jottings, Alma had written the name of Leonard Jongkees and the forbidden lyrics for the Chopin Étude in E, "In mir klingt ein Lied." In tears and as a form of defiance, Hilde sang the plaintive words, Alma's song of endless longing.

AT LEAST initially, Alma's body was treated uniquely in the Revier. Zofia commented that no one could recall an inmate's corpse being treated with such respect: "Alma clothed in a dress, her hands folded across her breast!" Zofia further stated, and others have repeated it, that on orders of Commandant Hössler, Alma's body was to be taken to the crematorium and disposed of separately instead of being loaded with the day's dead on a *Leichenwagen* and subjected to mass cremation.

Zippy gives a different account. According to her, Alma's body did not go directly, or separately, to the crematorium. Because of the public health questions raised by her illness and death, the SS sent her body to the *Stammlager* for an autopsy. The day after her death, samples of brain tissue and intestine were taken; then her body was returned to the Revier, "to which Alma now belonged

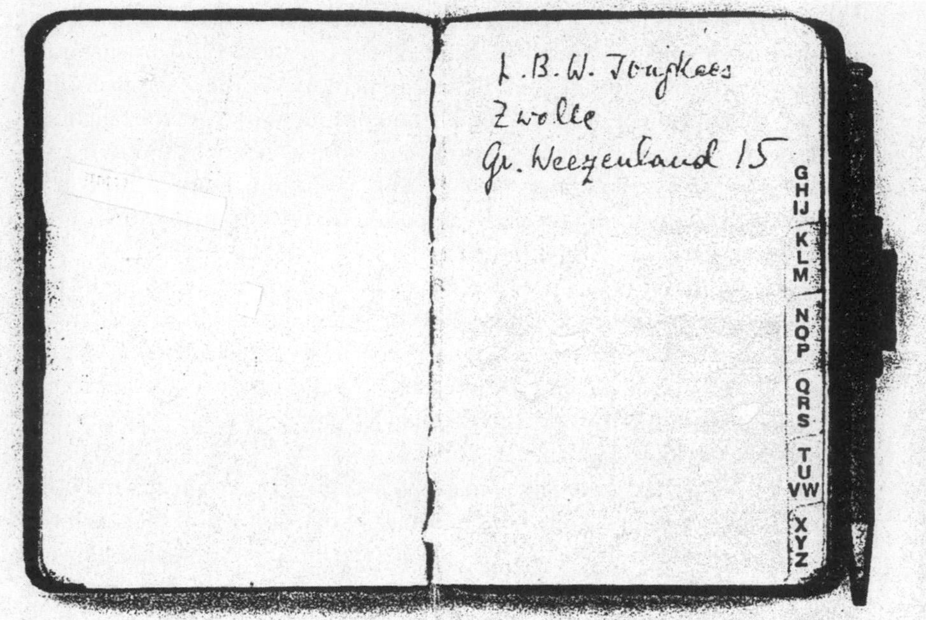

Leonard Jongkees' name and address in Alma's small Auschwitz datebook.

administratively." With her own eyes, Zippy said, she saw Alma's body lying on the body wagon outside the Revier. "She was naked. Her eyes were sunken. Her abdomen was stitched up crudely as a result of the autopsy."

Concerning reports that a post mortem was held after the farewell in the Revier, researchers have found no official record either in Auschwitz or in the archives of Jagiellonski University centers in Cracow.[10] Yet at least three oral reports of an autopsy have survived. One originates from Ima van Esso Spanjaard, who was interviewed in Holland by Ed Spanjaard after the war.[11]

Dr. Tichauer considered Alma's case in light of the formalistic autopsy policy of the SS. If someone outside the "approved research" programs died on the operating table, an autopsy would be ordered. But Alma had not died during surgery. If she had been murdered or poisoned, the authorities would have sought to confirm it; but again, this was not the case.

Dr. Tichauer surmised that the SS wanted to cover themselves in Alma's case. If epidemic meningitis or a tainted food supply were suspected, the death concerned SS and civil authorities as well as prison inmates. The symptoms of meningitis and food poisoning are similar, Dr. Tichauer said, since both affect the central nervous system. After Alma's spinal fluid was found to be clear, the only means of confirming the cause of her death was laboratory testing of the food she had consumed and analysis of her brain tissue.

Dr. Władysław Fejkiel, a doctor active in Block 20 in the *Stammlager* in 1944, did not believe the post-mortem procedures were performed. Attempting to confirm the fact of an autopsy, camp office survivor Wanda Marossányi contacted Dr. Fejkiel in 1985.[12] If Alma's body had been taken to Block 20, he said, he and many others would have known it because the news would have spread like prairie fire. The doctor explained that such a detailed autopsy could only have taken place in the *Stammlager,* since facilities in Birkenau's Revier were too primitive.

The suddenness of Alma's death gave rise to a fantastic array of theories. Typhus was suspected, although officially the camp was free of typhus, so no one could die of it. There was talk of poison and complicated intrigue. One tale portrayed Frau Schmidt as party to an SS plot to get rid of Mandel's favorite. Orchestra player Lily Assael speculated that the first Hungarians who arrived at Auschwitz at the end of the March had brought poisoned wine to the camp, knowing that the SS would commandeer their belongings.

In one interview, two survivors insisted that Alma had become too powerful for the SS and had to be eliminated. Alma had saved many prisoners by declaring them vital to her musical work; at the same time she had slighted enough fellow kapos to become the target of a plot.

Fania advanced a murder theory that some members of the orchestra stick with to this day. Frau Drexler, outraged by Mandel's plan to give Alma her freedom, had bribed Frau Schmidt to accomplish the deed. As Fania wrote: "Frau Schmidt, that 'dear friend,' could only hate the Jewess who was to be freed and who had come to taunt her with her happiness; and she had her revenge."[13]

Dr. Lingens-Reiner mentioned yet another speculation—that "Puff-Mutti" Musskeller, embittered toward Alma, denounced the orchestra leader to the SS, who then ordered her death. Yet Dr. Lingens-Reiner labeled the suggestions of complex plots "preposterous": "If the SS wanted to get rid of Alma, all the SS had to do was tell her—on any pretext—to visit the kapo of the punishment company, who could have killed her with any of the many means of killing available, and she would merely have disappeared."

Dr. Mancy, remembering Alma's despair after the slaughter of the nearly four thousand inmates of the family camp, said that from that moment Alma had no will to live. Afterward she often spoke of the consolation of suicide. If there were no hope of freedom, she would say, suicide was the way to frustrate SS intentions. For many, it was hard to imagine this commanding woman succumbing to a fate she did not design.

In the end, every clue to the cause of Alma's death points to botulism, a theory it took more than forty years to confirm. Botulism produces a neurotoxin that afflicts the brain and nervous system, which would explain the doctors' initial suspicion that Alma was suffering from encephalitis or meningitis, inflammation of the brain and spinal cord membranes.

Dr. Lingens-Reiner, Dr. Tichauer, and other Auschwitz survivors with medical expertise believed that botulism could have resulted from spoiled food from any number of sources, including the blood sausage of the camp's regular rations as well as any tainted food consumed at Frau Schmidt's party. Frau Schmidt had indeed served a tinned delicacy that was Alma's favorite. Some say it was fish; others, such as Dr. Lingens-Reiner, say it was a special sausage, offered as a treat for Alma. Frau Schmidt had only a few bites, but Alma ate a larger portion.

According to some survivors, as soon as "bad alcohol," officially barred from the camp, was mentioned in the gossip following Alma's death, the SS halted their own investigations. An SS doctor who performed autopsies at Auschwitz-Birkenau, Dr. Hans Münch of Munich, commented on Alma's death in a personal letter written four decades later. Considering the alternative diagnoses of "fleck typhus," meningitis, and food poisoning, he wrote: "You can suppose that Madame Rosé lived in better circumstances than a normal prisoner. As a privileged person she had access to better nourishment, especially from 'Kanada'—also the much-desired tinned goods (a potential origin of botulism)."[14]

Dr. Jaab Spanjaard of Holland, whose marriage to Ima van Esso after the liberation of the Nazi camps completed his multiple ties to Alma, held the typhus theory for many years but came to agree that botulism was the most likely cause of Alma's death.[15] The final irony was that Alma had died of a microbe that could have been present in lunches packed for a summer picnic in civilian life, as Marye Staercke remarked in a 1946 letter to Alfred Rosé.

Recovery from botulism is slow, often causing prolonged problems with sight and hearing and requiring months of rehabilitation. In fact, Schmidt and others who attended her birthday party were seriously ill for many weeks after Alma's death. When the film *Playing for Time* was shown on television, Helen ("Zippy") Tichauer was moved to write to *Jewish Week* and *The American Examiner* protesting the film's depicting of Sudetenland German prisoner Schmidt as an SS woman, the orchestra in tatters, and other dramatic falsifications of the facts. As Zippy pointed out: "Frau Schmidt was a political prisoner and NOT an SS woman. She shared the same meal which poisoned Alma Rosé and became as sick as Alma, but responded to emergency treatment."

Frau Schmidt survived Birkenau. Another woman survivor confided that she recognized Schmidt in a Prague restaurant shortly after the war. The survivor invited her former kapo into the vestibule, where she greeted her with a blow. "I told her it was in return for the abuse and beatings she had given me in Birkenau."

Szymon Laks and the Birkenau men's orchestra heard that after Alma's death, the SS hung her baton and a black crepe ribbon of mourning on the wall of the music room, another signal honor for a Birkenau prisoner.[16] Surviving orchestra women do not recall such a tribute, although Fania mentions that a few days after Alma died, Josef Mengele came to the Music Block: "Elegant, distinguished, he took a few steps, then stopped by the wall where we had hung up Alma's arm band and baton. Respectfully, heels together, he stood quietly for a moment, then [said] in a penetrating tone, appropriately funereal: '*In memoriam.*'"[17]

Eugenia Marchiewicz remembered how the news of Alma's death sped in waves through the women's camp. "When Alma died, some said they were sorry she died; some said they were sorry 'it wasn't I who died.'" Even Esther Loewy Bejarano, an orchestra member transferred to Ravensbrück several months earlier, heard of Alma's death and various versions of her demise.

The day after Alma died, Himmler's headquarters in Berlin received an official count of 15,000 men and 21,000 women prisoners in Birkenau. The total number of prisoners in all the camps under the jurisdiction of Auschwitz was reported as 67,000.

Two days later, alarms sounded when prisoners Alfred Wetzler and Rudolf Vrba (interned under the name Walter Rosenberg) were reported as escapees. In fact, Wetzler and Vrba had hidden themselves under a woodpile in Birkenau. After three days, when the hunt in the Auschwitz area cooled down, they were able to leave the camp.[18]

WAS THIS the end of the orchestra Czajkowska and Alma had worked so hard to build? What would become of the musicians? The orchestra women anxiously watched the competition for Alma's job. The Poles had their favorite contender, the Russians theirs. Among the candidates for the position were avowed anti-Semites who might banish the Jewish girls from the sheltering Music Block.

The increasingly powerful Russian element won out. Unceremoniously, SS Kramer visited the block one day to announce that Sonya Winogradowa, a Ukrainian pianist and music copyist, was the new orchestra leader. The Jewish women were upset, for they had heard that Sonya wanted the Jewish girls ejected from the orchestra. Mercifully, they were kept on.

Flora gave an overview of the following weeks: "After Alma died we were not so well off. She saved so many people from the gas room by finding them jobs with us and declaring them indispensable, even though they did not live in the Music Block with us. Alma used to fight for better conditions for us in every way, and she always succeeded."

Sonya, a pretty woman whose musical knowledge was rudimentary, was unable to sustain Alma's musical discipline and quality of playing. The Sunday concerts were canceled, although the orchestra continued to play marches for the departure and return of the work details. Former prisoner Giuliana Tedeschi described the new conductor as "a blond Russian woman who translated the urgency of rhythm and cadence into hysterical gestures."[19] Adding to the players' uneasiness, the SS reduced the conductor's authority and ordered the musicians to take on "useful work," including knitting and mending, in addition to their orchestra duties.

THE ALLIES landed on the beaches of France on 6 June 1944. Deportations to Auschwitz ended in mid-July, after 438,000 Jews had been shipped to the camp in a mere two months. In the summer and autumn of 1944, as the Allies advanced in the West and Soviet forces pressed toward Auschwitz and the Baltic in the East, the Germans began to move surviving Jewish inmates westward toward camps in the German heartland.

In late October 1944, the Jewish girls in the orchestra were evacuated by cattle car to Bergen-Belsen, while the non-Jewish personnel of the Music Block were transferred to the main camp at Auschwitz. In effect the orchestra ceased to exist, although the musicians who remained at the *Stammlager* through autumn and early winter tried unsuccessfully to organize a musical ensemble.

On orders from Berlin, the gas chambers ceased operations in November 1944, and the Germans began to dismantle the tools of the Third Reich's "achievement" at Auschwitz-Birkenau, destroying the crematoria and concealing all evidence of gassings. At the beginning of January 1945, 65,000 prisoners remained in the camp. In mid-month some 58,000 were forced out of the camp on death marches to the west. By 27 January, when four Red Army divisions liberated the camp, the prisoners numbered a mere 7,000, captives abandoned by their captors, many of them dying. According to later Soviet accounts, in six of the thirty-five storerooms of Kanada (the Germans had burned the contents of the other twenty-nine), the liberators found more than a million coats, dresses and suits, massive heaps of shoes, cooking utensils, eyeglasses and other goods, and seven tons of human hair destined for German mattress and carpet factories.

AT BERGEN-BELSEN—little more than a muddy field of tents with wooden slab beds and latrine ditches—the Jewish orchestra women tried to stay together. Their appearance distinguished them from other prisoners. They were still better dressed; their hair had grown back, and they had flesh on their bones. Halina Czajkowska, a seventeen-year-old Polish prisoner at Bergen-Belsen housed in the same barrack as the orchestra women in 1944–45, recalled the beauty of an impromptu performance they gave on New Year's Eve. For their own enjoyment, without their instruments and without words, the orchestra girls sang the parts to a haunting melody, which may have been the melancholy "In mir klingt ein Lied."[20]

At Belsen, starvation and disease overtook the orchestra girls. Flutist Lota Kröner, the oldest member of the orchestra, succumbed to typhus. Fania and others became desperately ill.

In this filthy, makeshift camp, SS Josef Kramer—commandant since December 1944—was earning his reputation as the "Beast of Belsen."[21] One afternoon Flora encountered the former champion of the Birkenau women's orchestra:

> I was in a camp street—no food—no nothing. I knew I was dying. An SS said to me: "What are you doing here?" It was the commandant from Birkenau, Josef Kramer. He recognized me from Birkenau. Listen, in another three days I would be dead. He said then: "I'll make work for you because you have already had the hell of Birkenau. I'll put someone already here out of her job and give you work." . . . He sent for me a few days later. *Achtung!* I stood at attention. *Mein Gott! Himmel!* What have I done? Outside the block stood a woman. She told me that for the next few weeks I would have to look after Kramer's children. Kramer wanted me to form a trio. He gave me an accordion, gave Lily Mathé a violin, and asked Eva [Steiner] Adam to sing.

Thus a trio of women benefitted from the reputation of the orchestra even after Alma's death. Performing for Kramer, his family, and their guests, Lily, Flora, and Eva were able to save themselves, as piles of emaciated corpses around the camp grew ever higher.[22]

Anne Frank, a worldwide symbol of innocent youth confronted by evil, arrived at Birkenau with her family on 6 September 1944, betrayed by an informer in Holland for the price of about one U.S. dollar a head. The Franks were among the Jewish prisoners transported to Bergen-Belsen in October 1944. Anne, the passionate young diarist, succumbed to typhus in Bergen-Belsen, where some fifty thousand men and women died of hunger, exposure, illness, and brutality.

On 15 April 1945, Allied troops liberated Bergen-Belsen. Flora remembers the British soldier who materialized like an angel of mercy and offered her a cup of tea. "Caution," he told her. "You must always put the milk in the cup before the tea."

The outside world could never understand the depths of desolation the orchestra women had experienced, nor the magnitude of their peculiar good fortune. Because of Alma, they were not erased from the living; she had protected them from the extremes of degradation other prisoners had to endure. Most of the women of the Music Block survived and carried on with life as free women, although four and a half million others died at Auschwitz.

Tragically, the orchestra chief was among those who perished. To this day, Flora says, not a day passes when she does not remember Alma and thank her.

23

Reverberations

We who have come back, by the aid of many lucky chances or miracles—whatever one may choose to call them—we know: the best of us did not return.—Viktor E. Frankl

The very day that Alma last led the orchestra at Birkenau, eighty-year-old Arnold performed in London at the Three Wise Monkeys Club—whose motto was "Hear No Evil, See No Evil, Speak No Evil"—in aid of the Red Cross. The club, in the former home of the painter Whistler, had a splendid view of the Thames. On 17 April 1944, twelve days after Alma's death, the Rosé Quartet gave its fourteenth National Gallery noontime concert, attended by two hundred. On 12 June 1944, six days after the Allies landed in Normandy, the venerable Rosé joined soprano Winifred Brown, organist H. Schaechter, and cellist P. A. Wayne in a benefit concert in St. Michael's Church in Blackheath, in a series of recitals for the Church of England Waifs and Strays Society. Schaechter's wife, Arnold noted, was the daughter of one of Gustav Mahler's uncles.

Arnold had not heard from Alma in over a year. His last seven messages sent through the Red Cross had gone unanswered. The house where he now lived as one of the family with Hans and Stella Fuchs had a room for Alma when she came back. He wrote to Alfred: "I would be completely at peace if I received one word from Alma."

Arnold remained in contact with Franz Werfel and Alma Mahler-Werfel in California and with his niece Anna Mahler and her husband Anatole Fistoulari in London. Anna was happy with the birth of their daughter, Marina; another daughter, named Alma, from Anna's marriage to Paul Zsolnay, was with the elder Zsolnays. A movie was soon to be based on Werfel's book *The Song of Bernadette,* and Arnold was enthusiastic. He considered Werfel one of the great writers of the century.

Arnold was still playing violin for two hours every morning and practicing his "three Rs"—rehearsing, reading, and resting. Saturdays he enjoyed sharing the noon meal and making music with Viennese friends Martha Freud and her husband Robert Hollitscher, the daughter and son-in-law of Sigmund Freud. Although his zest for the table had scarcely diminished, gall-bladder problems necessitated a strict diet, and Arnold had lost twenty-five pounds. His doctor said simply that his heart was tired, "having worked so long."

In early July 1944, a V1 "buzz bomb" exploded near the Fuchses' house in Blackheath. Stella was nearly buried in plaster, and Arnold suffered cuts from flying shards of window glass, which Dr. Fuchs promptly dressed. Arnold's typewriter was smashed as it shot across the room. In consequence, later letters to Alfred were handwritten and all but illegible.

By August 1944 Arnold was well enough to visit his friends the Tischlers, Moriz and Anna, in Ashtead, where he spent many a musical evening with Dr. Tischler and fellow Austrian musician refugees. The Tischlers' son, Peter, a commando, recalled Arnold's courtly presence during his extended visits:

> In the summers before the war our family used to stay in Salzburg. One morning I saw Bruno Walter having breakfast with Rosé at the Café Bazar. I had never met him personally, and it really was a great thrill to come home on leave one day and find him staying at my parents' house. Most of the famous people I met were a disappointment when I found out they were merely humans talking about mundane matters like how little they were being paid and telling smutty stories. Rosé was quite different; he commanded respect, even in an intimate environment like the house in Ashtead, Surrey.
>
> It cannot have been easy for him to live on the charity of others, but he made no concessions and did not really behave like a guest in our house.
>
> There was some kind of antique barrel inside our front door, into which one deposited walking sticks and umbrellas. When I came home in commando uniform and put my tommy gun there, Rosé saw it. He said to me: "Put this away—I don't like to see these things!"[1]

Arnold did not speak of charity in his letters to Alfred, writing merely: "Do not worry about me. The Tischlers are my true friends." On 6 September 1944, as the Allied offensive gained momentum along the western coast of Europe, Arnold wrote hopefully: "I hope for a reunion with Alma and wait patiently for news."

Playing with fingers that were growing stiff, Arnold appeared with Friedrich Buxbaum and Franz Osborn at a trio concert in Queen Mary Hall on 26 November, in aid of the Austrian Day Nursery; three hundred and fifty attended. The previous night, he wrote to Alfred, he had encountered a "marvelous modulation" in a composition.

Music and Alma's return remained his preoccupations as the Germans lost their last big gamble in the Battle of the Bulge in the Ardennes forest in December 1944. In January 1945, the Russians were the first to expose the Nazi atrocities when they liberated Auschwitz-Birkenau and found the remnants of what the Red Cross called the Germans' "best-kept secret" in Upper Silesia.

In February 1945 Arnold mourned the death of Elsa Walter, Bruno's wife of many years. In March he learned with horror that his beloved Vienna Opera had burned after four accidental hits by American bombs. The SS, fleeing before the Russian advance, had shelled St. Stephen's Cathedral in Kärntnerstrasse; it too was severely damaged before the Russians captured Vienna on 13 April 1945.

Holland was liberated in May 1945, and on 1 June a joyful Arnold wrote to the Staerckes in Utrecht for news of Alma. Almost simultaneously, Alfred cabled the Staerckes from Cincinnati.

Marye responded with a cable to Alfred on 22 June 1945. Alma had died in Upper Silesia, she said. A letter would follow.

The same day, Marye sent a letter telling what she knew and what she surmised about Alma's death, mixing truths with the half-truths rampant in the postwar confusion. She wrote: "The last message we got from Alma was in the spring of 1944: a postcard saying she was all right and asking after her husband." Asking Alfred to spare Father Rosé the "gruesome details," Marye shattered Alfred with the news that Alma was at first used as a guinea pig for medical experiments at Auschwitz. Marye reported that a doctor, through his wife, a nurse, managed to get Alma a violin so that she "could escape this other fate." Marye continued:

> She was able to get a small orchestra of her own inside the camp and played a lot. After a while, the Germans thought up something rather beastly and ordered her to play at the occasion when other prisoners were hanged. According to this doctor she died at this time, so suddenly that an autopsy was held, which he had to conduct. He could not find a direct cause of her death. He suggested some kind of poison, however.

Marye then told of the small quantity of poison the Staerckes had given Alma when she left Holland, describing in detail its ability to produce "almost instant death—at the utmost thirty seconds between taking it and death, as it is hardly painful and only felt as suffocation. We, my husband and I, guess that is what she used."

She reported that a letter from the German authorities came for Alma three months after she left Holland, ordering her to appear at Westerbork. Marye wrote:

> We know for sure that if she had not gone three months earlier, she would have had to leave at that moment or dive under. The irony, of course, is that although the command [by the Germans] was not obeyed, nor answered, the SD never came for her at our house, and she would never have been interfered with. If we had been able to know everything beforehand, she might just as well have stayed on quietly at our house, and she would never have been picked up. But that chance we would never have dared to take.

Marye ended her letter with the promise that she would join the millions trying to find out how friends and relatives had died. Her hunt for details would continue for three years.

Alfred broke the news to his father as gently as possible. Arnold, replying on 26 June 1945, was so grief-stricken that he could say no more than, "My only consolation is that she had achieved martyrdom."

Bruno Walter sent a letter of consolation dated 17 July 1945:

> I've thought of [Alma] very often and was worried about her welfare. I tried to hope that it helped her, like so many other people, with the help of some good, well-meaning people to go underground and to hide herself from arrest by the beasts until the end of the war. [Now we have learned] the terrible truth, and I cannot tell you how deeply it has shaken us. We knew Alma from the moment she opened her eyes on the world, experienced her growing up, lived with you through all your troubles, and now we hear that she fell victim to those murderers—not really through their violence, but because of it. . . . I have lost a daughter, and Lotte [the Walters' surviving daughter] a sister, through such a gruesome death. . . . Be assured how deeply we feel your pain.

Alma Mahler, writing two days later, expressed shock and grief: "Alma was really like my own child, and I loved her very, very much."

Rudolf Bing spoke for many former Viennese close to the Rosé family when he wrote to Alfred:

> Alma's tragedy . . . shook me to the ground—you know how fond of her I was, and I saw quite a lot of her in London before she left for the Continent. Of all the tragic things . . . this is one of the worst. I was most frightfully upset at the loss of a very dear friend. . . .
>
> It would be nice if we could meet once again and talk about the happy times of a thousand years ago in Pyrkergasse.[2]

ALFRED AND MARIA had long before contemplated the prospect that Alma would not return, if only because of her marriage. Early in March 1944, Alfred secretly wrote to Stella Fuchs, asking a friend to mail his letter from another city so that Arnold would not recognize his handwriting on the envelope. He wanted to discuss bringing his father to America, he wrote, if the move would not be too upsetting.

Stella replied that the old musician was in good health and spirits most of the time but would certainly not consider leaving England until he knew Alma's fate. She feared that if he were again displaced and forced to give up his friends and his music, it would destroy him.

There the matter rested until July 1945, when Dr. Fuchs wrote to Alfred about Arnold's future. Fuchs, a seventy-year-old dental surgeon, was ready to relinquish responsibility for his friend, whose health was failing. In his words:

> Now that the sad fate of poor Alma has been established, we who survived the cataclysm have to make up our minds about the future of your father. . . . As you know he is as helpless as a child in all matters of daily life, and on top of that comes his perfect inability to speak a single word of English and his increasing age. . . . It should not be a sudden decision for tomorrow, but rather a settlement of the matter in principle.

As peace returned to Europe, many refugees went back to their homelands. Maria's brother Johannes, for one—an officer and translator in the British Army during the war—decided to return to the Viennese printing plant he had operated before the war to "help rebuild Austria." His mother and sister, Alice and Susanne Schmutzer, had survived the Nazi occupation of Vienna,[3] and he was eager to be reunited with them.

To this point, Arnold had declared himself undecided about returning to his beloved Vienna. He had received an offer for the Stradivarius. If he sold his violin, his finances would be assured, yet he hated to part with it.

The day Alfred learned of Alma's death, he began proceedings to bring his father to America. He wrote to the Fuchses: "We all hoped and prayed for the moment when Alma would be able to return and establish herself anew with Father. . . . I am absolutely against any idea of his returning to Vienna, a city that is 70 percent destroyed and for him would only be filled with painful memories. His place now is with his son!"

IN AUGUST 1945, Arnold received a letter from Marie Anne Tellegen in Utrecht. Miss Tellegen wrote that Alma's violin and other personal belongings, including her diamond solitaire from Příhoda and a watch and strand of pearls she had entrusted to a friend at Drancy, would soon follow. The letter confirmed that in 1943, Miss Tellegen had fully expected Alma to be released from Drancy. Her own grief at Alma's fate was profound. Arnold took solace in the knowledge that Alma had found such close and true friends in Holland.

The mystery of Alma's death was compounded by various published reports. In October 1945, *Musical America* quoted a report in the *Austro-Ameri-*

can Tribune that she had committed suicide in the concentration camp. It erroneously reported that she had been arrested in Holland by the Gestapo and that she had "organized" the Auschwitz women's orchestra.

Alfred perpetuated the story of Alma's suicide when he sent the following for the 10 October 1945 *Zeitspiegel* account of Alma's death: "After torturous months of suffering, she succeeded in forming a small orchestra consisting of prison inmates. But when the commandant of the camp wanted to force her to play at the executions of fellow prisoners, she took her own life." Alma was reported to have taken poison rather than play for executions, as ordered by the commandant at Birkenau. She died as a "righteous artist" in protest against Nazi barbarity, her brother concluded.

Coincidentally, on 28 September 1945, the New York–based German-language Jewish newspaper *Aufbau* carried a report of Alma's death by suicide, followed on 12 October 1945 by a poetic account of her tragedy by Guenther Anders. Anders' poem, titled "Nachruf" (Obituary), described Alma smashing her violin and hanging herself in her room after the orchestra was ordered to play for executions. Alfred, in particular, did not believe the depiction of Alma's suicide and protested directly to the poet.

A loose prose translation of "Nachruf" follows:

> We are writing it down: if we didn't, even tomorrow no one would believe it.
>
> The girl—pampered, from a well-known family—ran back and forth between the camp's barracks. She assembled a small orchestra from those who were to die the day after tomorrow.
>
> *Midsummer Night's Dream* and *Eine kleine Nachtmusik* helped those who, in despair, lived on borrowed time; their tears gave them relief. In their race with death they were comforted that all was not in vain.
>
> Where will she go? We must not ask. What she has done is what matters.
>
> There was nothing to which the wicked one would not stoop: turning kindness into wickedness.
>
> So the commandant summons the girl. "Your task is the greatest one ever asked of an artist," he says. "Perhaps," she answers. "You are to provide music," he says. "It is what I am doing," she replies. "From now on you will make music at a different time." "As you wish."
>
> Even the wicked one finds it hard to tell her: "At the same time," he repeats. Now she understands.
>
> She understands, although it is beyond the human heart to comprehend such things.
>
> She understands, and she stands still. She whispers, yet clearly: "So you mean, executions with music."

"How easily you say that," he replies.
It is said that she left, walking erectly, and reported every word
to her friends, whispering, yet clearly, urging them to remember
every word.
Those who survive swear it is true—that walking firmly, calmly,
she did what needed to be done.
She smashed her violin against an iron hook in the barrack.
The next morning she hanged herself.
Honor her name: Alma Rosé.[4]

An avalanche of queries descended on Anders after the poem was published. He apologized to Alfred four months later for causing additional distress to the Rosé family, saying that he had written with poetic license: "I don't think of these poems as literal presentations, [but only as] a reminder and a warning." Miss Tellegen, by then secretary of Queen Juliana's cabinet in The Hague, wrote the editor of *Aufbau* that the many people interested in Alma's fate had a right to know Anders' sources of information. There is no indication that she received a response.[5]

The stories about Alma's death became wilder. After the war ended, "Voice of America" announcers were allowed to use their names on the air. When Ernest Rosé, who had used his stage skills in German "Voice of America" broadcasts for many years, finally identified himself publicly, he received a letter from a man in Germany that he chose not to show to the Rosé family. "Alfred, Arnold, and Maria were already suffering too much over Alma," he explained. The man, who remained anonymous, wrote that during a nightmare, his wife said she had poisoned Alma Rosé.

Illness forced Arnold to cancel two performances. He reported that he played his violin for the last time on 2 October 1945. At last he sold the Mysa; he had little heart left for music-making, and proceeds from the sale would finance a move to Vienna or to the States.[6] In preparation for a move, he began to dispose of family papers, including letters to Alma from Váša Příhoda and Heini Salzer and many of Alma's Wiener Walzermädeln pictures. When Alma's diamond ring—the big gift from Příhoda—arrived from Holland, Arnold gave it to Stella Fuchs to sell immediately. He wanted no part of Alma's "bad luck ring."

On Christmas Day 1945, Arnold wrote despondently that his Vienna Philharmonic colleague Julius Stwertka had died in Theresienstadt. When he heard that Anton Webern, another friend, had been shot and killed in error, he wrote in despair: "I have nothing to do anymore. My life is closed."

Honoring Alma's plea to the Birkenau orchestra women, Anita Lasker-Wallfisch (even before she fully recovered her own health) visited the old musician in London to tell of his daughter's unique achievement. After Alma's death, she testified, the orchestra deteriorated: "Alma was irreplaceable."[7]

Anita, like many Auschwitz survivors, disliked speaking of the orchestra girls' ordeal. As she said to one interviewer,

> The KZ [concentration camp] is a very difficult subject. If people want to know, I always say to them, ask me questions. I can answer those, but just to talk, in general, is impossible. Either it will take hours to explain the detail, or you get the impression that people you are talking to think you are lying or exaggerating. It is so foreign to other people's experience, even imagination. The KZ is essentially incommunicable.[8]

Yet Anita firmly agreed with Elie Wiesel (writing in *A Jew Today*) that "not to remember was equivalent to becoming the enemy's accomplice."[9] In *Inherit the Truth*, published in 1996, Anita eloquently conveys how her life was affected "by having lived in Germany at the time of the Third Reich, as a Jew." Her testimony about orchestra life and personalities is the most complete and detailed survivor's account yet to emerge and is necessary reading for anyone interested in the truth of the Birkenau women's orchestra.

Ed Spanjaard also called on Arnold in Blackheath. Spanjaard marveled at Arnold's "mental courage and strength" in view of his great loss

Alice Schmutzer wrote to Alfred and Maria that news of Alma's death created an uproar in war-torn Vienna. On 31 December 1945, *Der Montag* leveled a blast at Alma's former husband, who had weathered the war in Prague. Entitled "Protest Against Váša Příhoda," the article accused him of bowing to the racial policy of the "brown regime" and abandoning Alma to the Nazis to secure his own career: "Alma Rosé died in Auschwitz, and Váša Příhoda counted on man's forgetfulness. He reckons falsely—that Vienna has so little desire, or is so characterless, as to accept this knowledge [without protest]. It is here clearly printed: We want neither to hear nor see Herrn Váša Příhoda."

Příhoda's biographers rightly say that attacks on Váša by the foreign press were so crude as to beg repudiation. Příhoda was at the peak of his musical powers in 1935 at the time of the divorce and did not need to fear for his career. One biographer stresses that Příhoda sued for divorce six months before the Nuremberg Race Laws were established in Germany. Váša's supporters blamed Alma for her fate, saying that her "restless blood" (words that echo Nazi propaganda) inspired her fateful return to Holland in 1939 after she had been safe in England.

Příhoda hotly protested the accusation that he had caused Alma's death, responding that he had "rid himself" of her long before that. Between 1937 and 1942, Příhoda had led a chamber group that included cellist Paul Grümmer and pianist Friedrich Wührer. He gave his last wartime concert in Prague five days before Alma died in Birkenau. By 1946 he was married for the third time. Shortly after the war ended, the Czech Association of Artists certified him as politically dependable, but he later faced difficulties with the Czech regime as the result of a wartime propaganda tour of Germany and Holland he had made with fellow artists and journalists.

On 1 April 1946 Příhoda launched his first postwar tour, beginning in the former Nazi puppet state of Slovakia, where the Jews had been brutally treated. When he arrived in Košice, his first stop, he encountered angry demonstrations. Before the war, Alma's Wiener Walzermädeln had performed frequently in the area, and Příhoda was confronted by a crowd who remembered her well.

As soon as Příhoda and Michal Karin, his accompanist, appeared, a woman in the audience leaped to the stage and led a protest of whistling and shouting Alma's name. Příhoda withered in the face of such hostility. He and Karin retreated backstage until order was restored and the woman leading the protest ejected. Karin recalled that the incident forced Příhoda to leave town the same day in a big Cadillac from his collection.

When they arrived in Bratislava for an engagement, Příhoda's expensive car was immediately recognized. Later he received an ovation for one of his most dazzling performances. Příhoda had sent advance word that he hoped to see and talk with Anny Kux Poláková. Loyal Anny replied that she did not want to see him, although as a violinist in the Slovak Philharmonic she would attend his concert. Disregarding this response, Váša sought her out to talk about Alma and to say how sorry he was that Alma had died at Auschwitz.

In her family's luxury hotel, the Römerbad in Badenweiler, where Váša and Alma first met, Elisabeth Joner Fellmann remembered Příhoda's first postwar appearance in the hotel's celebrity concert series. She asked him about Alma. "Suddenly the great violinist broke into tears. Sobbing, he said her fate was so terrible, and such terrible things had happened in the camps."

Příhoda made his first tour to France in May 1946. When he returned to Czechoslovakia he was denounced, and proceedings were scheduled to begin against him in October. After that he was not allowed to concertize in Czechoslovakia and was able to get only temporary permits to travel beyond its borders.

Embittered because he had been denied a Czech passport and evicted from his Prague apartment (which had reportedly belonged to the family of anti-Nazi political prisoners), Příhoda moved to Rapallo, Italy, where his family joined him in 1947. Shortly afterward he made a fifty-concert tour of the Middle East, using a passport issued by the Turkish government. Exhausted by the tour, he developed chest pains for the first time.

In 1949 the impresario Sol Hurok began negotiations to bring Příhoda to North America. Correspondence about the tour was between Martin Feinstein in the Hurok office and Albert Morini, a New York concert manager who happened to be the brother of Alma's friend Erica Morini.[9] Feinstein wrote on 3 February that Příhoda had been investigated by the court of honor of the Czech Association of Musicians, who ruled that "no objection could be found against this artist as far as loyalty to the Czech state was concerned." Ten days later, Morini replied curtly:

> I had a luncheon engagement last September with a member of the Czech consulate, who told me that Váša Příhoda is on the blacklist and he was not allowed to return to Czechoslovakia.
>
> I am glad that no objection can be found against Mr. Příhoda upon investigation of this artist, as per your statement. However, be informed that I have no time to talk to Mr. Příhoda and am definitely not interested in him.

The Morinis, too, remembered Alma.

Feinstein persevered, and in February and March 1949, Příhoda undertook an American tour under the Hurok banner. After a number of successful concerts, according to his Czech biographer, Příhoda was so upset by the publication of a story recalling the Košice protests in Alma's name that he canceled the tour.

Both Příhoda and Erica Morini performed in New York in March 1949. On 10 March Příhoda appeared in New York's Town Hall. The music critic of the *New York Times* praised the pyrotechnics of his playing; but critical notices were less enthusiastic than those that had greeted his 1920 North American debut at Carnegie Hall, when persistent calls for encores prompted the management to turn out the lights, and he played his last encore in the dark. The next day, 11 March 1949, Erica Morini took the stage at Carnegie Hall as soloist in the Beethoven Violin Concerto, with Bruno Walter conducting the New York Philharmonic in a Beethoven cycle. Her performance received accolades in the *New York Times.* Although in Central Europe Příhoda maintained his reputation, Morini was the violin virtuoso among Alma's intimates who attained lasting international fame. Critic Harold C. Schonberg later wrote that Morini was "a perfect instrumentalist who made the romantic style sound classic, so controlled and elegant was it. With all of the technical finesse, there never was the slightest hint of vulgarity. With Morini the music came first, the ego second."

Příhoda, with his colossal ego and outspoken ways, made newspaper copy wherever he went. He arrived in New York at the height of controversy surrounding appearances by the German pianist Walter Gieseking. In the diner on a train as he left New York for his western tour, Váša became aware of mutterings among passengers who had noticed his cased violin beside him. When he heard the name Gieseking, Příhoda rose and shouted through the car: "Gieseking plays the piano. Příhoda plays the violin. Gieseking is German. Příhoda is Czech. This is not Gieseking. This is Příhoda!"[10]

Postwar students at the Vienna State Academy were surprised at how often their professors mentioned Alma and Váša. New Zealand–born violist Ralph Aldrich, now living in Canada, remembered one impassioned professor pounding on the piano as he recalled pleading with Příhoda in 1938 to try to help Alma.[11]

Five years after Alma's death, in April 1949, a periodical devoted to the violin wrote about Příhoda: "His home at this time being at Rapallo, famous winter resort of the Italian Riviera, sixteen miles east of Genoa, where he and his wife, a daughter of the famous Arnold Rosé, and two children reside." In the public mind, the names Rosé and Příhoda remained inextricably linked.

In the 1950s Příhoda moved to Austria, where he taught at the Vienna State Academy and continued to concertize. The Czechs finally made peace with their famous native son, allowing him to play again in Czechoslovakia. Upon his return to Prague, on 30 May 1956 during the annual Spring Festival, crowds gathered in the street to hail him, and he received a thirty-minute ovation before playing a single note in Smetana Hall. So overwhelming was the reception that Příhoda left the stage trembling with emotion. When he reappeared, he gave a dazzling concert that was carried over Czech radio.

In July 1960, a month before his sixtieth birthday, Příhoda died in Vienna of heart failure. Forty years after Alma's death, a member of his family who wished to remain anonymous said loyally of Příhoda: "Along with his artistic successes, he had in his life so much sorrow and bitterness for such a noble character. That he should have been guilty of the death of Frau Alma, eight or ten years after the divorce, is an improbable hypothesis."

In January 1946, Arnold resolved not to return to Vienna. Four days later he received notice that his Austrian pension had been restored and the Vienna Philharmonic wished to reinstate him as concertmaster. He wrote to Alfred that he could not reconsider, adding: "I am so agitated that music is impossible. . . . Alma's death has finished me completely, and broken my heart." A severe heart attack on 7 February 1946 did not deter Arnold from relaying an unsubstantiated claim from Vienna that fifty-six Nazis remained in the Vienna Philharmonic, as opposed to six in the Berlin Philharmonic.

On 11 February 1946, Marye Staercke again wrote from Holland, thanking Alfred and Maria for parcels they had sent to her family and describing Alma's tribulations in France. She reported that Alma had been able to write to her Dutch friends with some regularity and acknowledged receipt of every package she received at Drancy, whether through official channels or through the "organization." Marye wrote: "I know from people who were in Drancy with your sister that she was a tower of strength and courage and a great help to many others. Her letters to us, too, were full of spirit and unwavering hope and courage. At least she went down with all colors flying—and not in despair as we were at first led to believe."

Marye added her own comments on the Anders poem: "An elegy . . . wholly poetical fiction, but still a tribute to the marvelous impression that Alma must have made on people who knew her but slightly."

Further news from Vienna came through the aging Buxbaum, who traveled across London to visit Arnold regularly. Willi Silberstein, a Viennese relative of Arnold's, had been shot as he tried to flee across the border; Viennese violinist Viktor Robitsek, his wife, and the Tyrolean oboeist Max Starkmann had died in camps in Poland. Rosé's nemesis and successor, Philharmonic concertmaster Franz Mairecker, had been pensioned. Arnold mentioned the number of former Nazis still in the orchestra and concluded charitably for the sake of his beloved Philharmonic, "They should stay [and not be dismissed] so that the orchestra can survive [a sentiment also expressed by Wilhelm Furtwängler]. But I'm glad my job is finished. Enough!" To Alfred he wrote, "Standing in front of me—nothing. No hope." Comparing himself to blossoms renewed every year, he said, "Only the human being doesn't grow any more."

On 16 April 1946, Dr. Fuchs cabled Alfred that his father had passed the American embassy medical examination for immigration to the United States. Two weeks later, Leila Pirani returned to England from Canada and cabled Alfred: "KINGSLEY AND I SAW PROFESSOR CONDITION MUCH WORSE THAN REALIZED VERY WEAK STRONGLY URGENTLY ADVISE AGAINST UNDERTAKING JOURNEY SPECIALIST CONSIDERS DANGEROUS COMFORTABLE FUCHS COULD YOU VISIT IF NOT TAKE RESPONSIBILITY FOR JOURNEY."[12]

By 26 May 1946, Arnold was so weak he could hardly write. "Can do nothing—not play violin—no energy—*fertig* [finished]." He found the energy to report that Toscanini would appear in London the following month for nine concerts and that Leo Slezak had died in Germany.

Arnold wrote his final letter on 21 July 1946. He had his U.S. visa, he said. "All I need is patience. Leila has been told everything."

In August German-born soprano Elisabeth Schumann, who had emigrated to London from Austria in 1938, was invited back to Vienna to perform. Seeking to clarify her feelings, she visited her old friend Arnold. Her son, Gerd Puritz, wrote of the encounter:

> It was August 6 when Elisabeth drove out of Central London to Blackheath to see the old, sick [Arnold]. . . . How ill he looked! His wonderful beard and head of white hair had all but disintegrated.
>
> Vienna—the name brought only the faintest flicker of memory to his eyes. His brother, Eduard, was uppermost in his mind—where he was, whether he was still alive, had he perhaps died just like . . . ? He could not say the name, but Elisabeth knew it just the same—Alma, his daughter. That beautiful, talented young violinist with whom [her son] had fallen in love twenty-five years ago in Bad Ischl, had died in a concentration camp.[13]

On Sunday, 25 August 1946, Arnold died quietly in his sleep. After a memorial service attended by a few surviving friends, his body was cremated and buried temporarily in England. Five years later, his ashes were taken to Vienna for burial beside Justine in Grinzing, near the grave of Gustav Mahler.

Memorials went out over the airwaves from London and New York. "Londoner's Diary" in the *Daily Telegraph* reported Arnold's death with the note that at the height of the Blitz, the old lion had taken his Stradivarius to an air raid shelter and entertained. The music world remembered that Arnold Rosé, through his teachers, had represented the last living link with Beethoven. In January 1947, Bruno Walter gave the eulogy at a concert in Chelsea Town Hall in memory of his friend.

IN MID-JUNE 1946, Marye Staercke reported to Alfred that a Dutch lawyer had found a survivor of the orchestra, the accordionist Flora, who testified that Alma had not committed suicide. The following August, Marye wrote that she had met Flora, whose account was to be trusted.

As civilian mobility increased, the international music community remained embroiled in disputes over artists who had performed for the Nazis. When Bruno Walter appeared with the Vienna Philharmonic in the eastern United States in 1946, Alfred attended the performance. Afterwards he went to the conductor's dressing room to censure the man he had called "Uncle Bruno."

"But you must forgive," Walter told Alfred.

"I cannot forgive," said Alfred. For him, the wounds of Nazism never healed.

Bassoonist Hugo Burghauser, for nineteen years the president of the Vienna Philharmonic, described a scene in 1947 when the Philharmonic was invited to play in London. In the furor that arose over inviting an orchestra that was banned in every other capital of Europe, Prime Minister Clement Attlee rose in the British House of Commons to answer critics: "At our request, we have been told that Bruno Walter and Rudolf Bing are the responsible personalities for this concert. Since they are both refugees from Hitler's Third Reich, we see no cause to be better represented than by those two people."[14]

When the Vienna Philharmonic appeared in London, Friedrich Buxbaum returned to the orchestra, eager to play again under the beloved Walter. At the first rehearsal he was welcomed back to his place at the head of the cello section in the orchestra. After the tune-up, recalled Burghauser, Buxbaum stood up: "Dear friends," he began: "I'm so happy to be invited to be with you again. I heard you tuning. It's wonderful—*ganz Judenrein* [completely free of Jews]."[15] The response, said Burghauser, was "deadly quiet."

IT WAS Fania Fénelon who eventually preserved the memory of Alma and the Auschwitz-Birkenau women's orchestra. In the early 1970s, Fania, a Parisienne, had the idea that the camp orchestra should be the subject of a book. She gathered together Anita Lasker-Wallfisch, Violette Jacquet Silberstein,

Hélène Scheps, and Fanny Korenblum Birkenwald. Writer Marcelle Routier was present as they held their first reunion nearly thirty years after Alma's death. Routier, who became Fania's collaborator, found the story so fantastic that she frequently called Anita in London for confirmation of aspects of orchestra life too bizarre to be believed. As the book progressed, Fania made one visit to Poland, where she interviewed an old friend in the orchestra, Ewa Stojowska, but declined to see other orchestra survivors living in Cracow.

Fania's book was published in 1976 in France as *Sursis pour l'orchestre;* English and German translations subsequently appeared under the titles *Playing for Time* and *Das Mädchenorchester in Auschwitz.* Dramatically the account was riveting, but as a factual record it was immediately challenged by many survivors and their families in both Eastern and Western Europe. The book was revised for a second edition and some historical inaccuracies were remedied, yet controversy continued to swirl around it. It is not uncommon for books on the Nazi terrors to arouse heated debate, yet reactions to Fania's book were extreme. Anita spoke for many of the survivors when she wrote: "It is a pity that Fania created such a misleading impression about the camp orchestra when she wrote her memoirs which were subsequently made into the film. For reasons best known to herself, she indulged in the most preposterous distortions of the truth about practically everyone who took part in this 'drama.'"[16]

Helena Dunicz-Niwińska wrote from Poland that Fania's book should be read as a novel rather than an eyewitness account, an opinion shared by Hélène Scheps, Zofia, and others. Fania herself said the book was not intended as a "documentary." Violette, in a 1992 interview, flatly pronounced the book "*Mist*"—garbage or worse.[17]

Fania's book became the basis of a screenplay written by Arthur Miller for the 1980 CBS film *Playing for Time,* in which Vanessa Redgrave played the part of Fania and Jane Alexander played Alma. (Fania, who was petite, protested the casting of Redgrave, criticizing the actress's heroic proportions as well as her association with Palestinian causes, despite the fact that Fania's own book belittles the Zionist views of fellow orchestra members.) Within a few years, millions around the world became aware of Alma Rosé and her concentration camp orchestra.

When Jane Alexander took the role of the orchestra leader, she set about to learn all she could about the historical Alma. For her portrayal, she won an Emmy award as best actress in a supporting role in a television drama. Because Fania's tale was her main source, however, her portrait of Alma was distorted. As Anita protested in the London Sunday *Times* when the film was shown on British television:

> In the film Fania Fénelon emerges as the moral force who bravely defied the Germans and held members of the orchestra together, while the conductor, Alma Rosé, is depicted as a weak woman who imposed a

cruel discipline on the orchestra from fear of the Nazis and who was heavily dependent upon gaining Fénelon's approval.

"It just wasn't like that," [said Anita]; "Fania was pleasant and talented, but she was not as forceful as Alma, who helped us to survive. She was the key figure, a woman of immense strength and dignity who commanded the respect of everyone."[18]

Lurid and deprecatory descriptions in Fania's book have struck many survivors as fanciful and even wildly invented. Describing the orchestra women's reaction to a visit from Mengele, Fania said that they wet their lips, "remembering. . . . Under the gaze of this man one felt oneself become a woman again."[19] Such comments were absurd and offensive to many former orchestra members. Fania's dislike for certain Polish prisoners, Czechs, Slovaks, Germans, and other German-speakers, colored the pages of her memoir. Causing pain that endures to this day, she described her fellow prisoners in cutting ways as "a female mountain," a "fat cow," a "bitch" without human traits. Perhaps aware that her assertions were untenable, she renamed some of the orchestra players to "protect" them. The thinly disguised pseudonyms further confuse fact and fiction.

Most particularly, almost every survivor of the orchestra has challenged Fania's characterization of Alma, who was portrayed as cold and imperious. In Fania's book, Alma was an inaccessible "goddess" for whom only music and cleanliness counted, a tyrant who saw the orchestra women as a "musical infantry, to be slapped and driven as the will took her," and a pathetic woman who had never known love.

Among the most derogatory distortions of Alma's attitudes was Fania's depiction of her near-hysteria as the orchestra prepared the program for a visit to Birkenau by "Reichsführer Heinrich Himmler," the SS chief.[20] In fact, Himmler never visited Birkenau after 17–18 July 1942, when the camp was a massive construction project and women prisoners were still housed in the *Stammlager.*[21] The highest-ranking SS official to visit Auschwitz-Birkenau during Alma's—or Fania's—time at the camp was Adolf Eichmann, chief of SS Jewish Affairs, who in February 1944 toured the Birkenau family camp and briefly visited the Music Block (see Chapter 21).

Dispute over whether Alma was really promised her freedom—a chance to perform outside the camp as an emissary of Birkenau sent to entertain the troops of the Third Reich—can scarcely be settled this many years after the events. Fania's claim is conceivable but unlikely, say many credible witnesses and survivors. In any case, Alma's fate was sealed within the camp. She led the Birkenau women's orchestra for the last time on 2 April 1944 and died a few days later. Fania died on 23 December 1983, Alma's survivor by almost forty years.

Epilogue: Memories of Alma

Who was to know that Alma's voice, through her violin, would continue to be heard in one of the world's great opera houses. In the confusion of age and ill health, Arnold never told the full story of the day Alma's 1757 Guadagnini was delivered to him. The most likely of several accounts was that Marie Anne Tellegen sent it to Arnold through the Red Cross; at least that is what he told his quartet colleague violinist Max Jekel.[1] The story is supported by Leonard Jongkees' testimony that he turned the instrument over to his mentor and medical colleague Dr. J. J. Groen, a member of the quartet Alma led in Utrecht. When it became public knowledge that Alma would not return, Dr. Groen, in turn, delivered the instrument to Marie Anne Tellegen, the executor of Alma's estate. The concertmaster of the Utrecht Symphony Orchestra, J. J. Oellers, pleaded with Groen to find a way to keep the violin in Holland, to help restore the country's plundered artistic estate. But Miss Tellegen insisted on returning the violin to Arnold. After a short time, Arnold sold it to a wealthy hotelier identified merely as Gough, who had taken violin lessons from Arnold in England.

In 1947, the summer after Arnold's death, Felix Eyle went to England to visit his wife's parents, who were none other than Dr. and Mrs. Moriz Tischler. By this time the Tischlers had moved from Ashtead to Wimbledon. During Arnold's exile, Dr. Tischler had become an intimate friend and musical partner. Eyle himself was no stranger to the Rosés: in 1920 and 1921 he and Alma had been fellow students at the Vienna State Academy of Music, and Eyle also studied with Arnold. After he moved to the United States in 1928, Eyle traveled to Vienna regularly, never failing to call at Pyrkergasse.

One Saturday morning in Wimbledon while Eyle was engaged in his daily practicing, the telephone rang, and his mother-in-law answered. It was Stella Fuchs. According to Eyle:

> Mrs. Fuchs told my mother-in-law, Anna Tischler, that Mr. Gough had decided to stop playing the violin. [Alma's] violin, he said, was too important an instrument for an amateur such as himself. He told Mrs. Fuchs to sell the violin and keep whatever she would receive over the £700 he had paid Professor Rosé for it.
>
> The famous Hill family violin shop, Mrs. Fuchs said, had refused to try to sell it because there was no certification with it. The only evidence of its identity was the certificate of insurance. Ardent music lover that she was, Mrs. Fuchs knew little or nothing about violins and their value, nor where to turn, but she knew a violin played by the Rosés must have value. She telephoned Mrs. Tischler for help: "Your son-in-law is a violinist. Could you write or speak to him about it?"
>
> "He's here right now," said my mother-in-law.
>
> I knew the instrument. I knew that Professor Rosé had bought it on one of his tours [in 1924]. It was a phenomenal instrument that was also fantastically beautiful to look at.
>
> I went over to Mrs. Fuchs'. The violin was the jewel I expected it to be. I played it, and it was as I expected. I made a down payment and agreed to pay the balance later when I could make arrangements with the bank in the United States. I was playing a Guarnerius Andrée at the time but wanted a very big sound, because I was about to join the Metropolitan Opera.[2]

When Eyle's brother-in-law, Peter Terry (the former Peter Tischler), came to the United States after completing studies at Cambridge, he delivered the instrument. Said Eyle: "I had some repairs made, added a few features it didn't have, and had it recertified with new papers. What I paid for it is immaterial, but it is well worth more than $100,000 in the 1980s. The sound is so heavenly, so gorgeous and powerful, that it goes through anything."

Eyle christened the instrument the "Alma Guadagnini." In his hands, its special strains sounded at the Metropolitan under the general managership of Sir Rudolf Bing, who had heard the instrument many times before in Vienna. Coincidentally, the former president of the Vienna Philharmonic, bassoonist Hugo Burghauser, played in the woodwind section of the orchestra at the same time.

Eyle believed for many years that the instrument had been at Auschwitz with Alma. He even heard that it had been found in a "cloakroom" at the camp. In the decade after the war, so little was known of life in the camps that the story seemed to make sense.

In 1969, the Viennese commission for culture, education, and school administration named a street after Alma, as a martyr of the Nazi regime. The formal documents note only that she was a violinist who died between 1940 and 1945; the fact that she died a prisoner and conductor of the women's orchestra in the Auschwitz-Birkenau extermination camp is not publicly recorded. The street name became official on 3 December 1969, a month to the day after what would have been Alma's sixty-third birthday.

A sign with white lettering on a dark blue background stands high to announce Alma Rosé–Gasse. For thousands of commuters from the satellite city of Per Albin Hanssen-Siedlung Ost in the tenth district, the sign is a farewell in the morning and a welcome home in the evening.

Strolling with a new generation along Alma Rosé–Gasse, one looks in vain for traces of Alma. Yet on a quiet, sunny afternoon in late May, thoughts of her are easily revived.

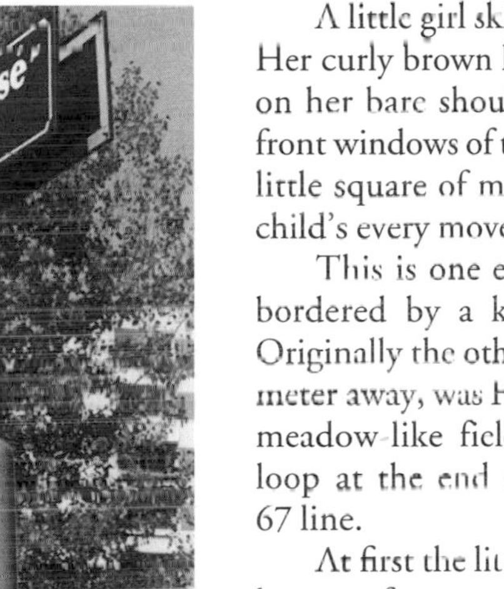

A little girl skips across a sandy play pit. Her curly brown hair sparkles as it bounces on her bare shoulders. The shining storefront windows of the shops surrounding this little square of modern Vienna mirror the child's every move.

This is one end of Alma Rosé–Gasse, bordered by a kindergarten and school. Originally the other end, almost half a kilometer away, was Franz Koci Strasse, across a meadow-like field from the turn-around loop at the end of the Strassenbahn No. 67 line.

At first the little girl is alone. She makes her own fun, running from one playground attraction to another as her parents enjoy their afternoon *Jause* of coffee and cake at an outdoor café table.

She will be tall and just a little chunky. She is erect and agile as she dances around the pool of sand or dashes under the evergreens. She glows as she turns now and then to seek her parents' approving smiles.

This little girl has rosy apple-cheeks. Alma too had apple-cheeks, brushed by dark curls.

For a while she has worn a bathing suit to absorb the bright sunshine. When a cool breeze rises, she disappears into the café with her mother, to emerge in a blue print frock with a skirt that swirls as she darts around the tiny park.

As school ends for the day, the square fills with children. A group of boys crowd into the candy store. The little girl stands on the fringes, half hidden. From the shop, the older boys emerge, surrounding the one who could afford the most sweets. She listens to their banter and comes a little closer, only to realize she is unwelcome.

Her parents call. She returns to the sand pit alone, climbing again over the play equipment, but her heart has gone from her solitary play.

For years an optician's shop in the square has advertised its wares "in Alma Rosé–Gasse," but not even the employees of the shop know who Alma Rosé was. Some think she was a poet, since the five neighboring streets in this planned city were named after writers and poets who perished between 1938 and 1945. Their names, too, are little remembered in Vienna today: Adolf Unger, a writer who died in 1942 at Auschwitz; Moritz Seeler, a poet (also an avant-garde stage director and theater manager) who died in the Riga ghetto or at Auschwitz between 1942 and 1945; Herbert Csur, a martyred poet; Eugenie (Jenny) Fink, a poet deported in 1942 who died in a Nazi camp; and Arnold Holm, also known as Emil Arnoldi, a writer killed in a pogrom in Vienna after the Anschluss.

A poster in an apothecary shop in the square announces a performance in the Per Albin Hanssen–Siedlung Ost community center: *Die Fledermaus* by Johann Strauss. With this exception, the square bears no mark of waltzing Vienna.

The parked cars of commuters line the street, polished with Austrian pride; the only city sound is an occasional delivery van. A few women stroll with young children and baby carriages in the afternoon sun. The quiet suburban scene is a far cry from the Vienna Alma knew in life—the bustling, glamorous Ringstrasse she toured in her Aero convertible with the Rosés' black dog Arno sniffing the excitement in the air and police waving her through intersections.

Vienna's official remembrance of Alma received a fitting postscript in September 1982, when the city's Gemeinderatsausschuss für Kultur und Bürgerdienst decided to extend Alma Rosé–Gasse some two hundred meters beyond Franz Koci Strasse to the Ostbahn Fontanastrasse. No longer would it be necessary for city-bound tram riders walking to the turn-around loop of Tram 67 to cross the field where Alma Rosé–Gasse once ended. Now Alma's memorial led to the heart of Old Vienna.

Notes

CHAPTER 1: MUSICAL ROYALTY: THE BACKGROUND

Epigraph: Pirani 1962.

1. Letter from Bruno Walter to Alfred Rosé, 17 July 1945, now in the Mahler-Rosé Collection, the Gustav Mahler–Alfred Rosé Room, the Music Library, the University of Western Ontario, London, Canada, henceforth cited as the Mahler-Rosé Collection.
2. Zweig 1944, 21.
3. Franz Lehár (1870–1948), a prolific Austrian composer, was originally from Hungary.
4. Graf 1969, 72–73.
5. Otto Mahler, the talented youngest surviving brother, committed suicide in 1895 at the age of twenty-two. Alois, seven years younger than Gustav, was more aloof from the family and reputedly became involved in shady financial dealings. He managed the office of a candy company in Vienna then moved to the United States, where he became a baker and real estate broker. He died in 1931 in Chicago.
6. Ferruccio Busoni (1866–1924), a German-Italian composer and pianist, lived in Vienna in the 1880s, where he knew Brahms and Karl Goldmark.
7. Adrian Boult, "Arnold Rosé and the Vienna Philharmonic," *Music and Letters*, vol. 32, no. 33 (July 1951): 257. Boult first made this statement in London in 1930.
8. As a refugee in England, Arnold would reform the ensemble; thus the Rosé Quartet was a performing ensemble for over sixty years. Violinist Albert Bachrich and violist Hugo von Steiner later joined the quartet, with Reinhold Hummer on cello. The best-known group, who performed together during the first two decades of the 1900s, were Rosé as first violinist; Paul Fischer, second violinist; Anton Ruzitska, violist; and Friedrich Buxbaum, cellist. Anton Walter replaced Buxbaum on the cello in 1921. Later Buxbaum rejoined the ensemble, and Max Handl became the violist.
9. Emma Mahler Rosé died in 1933 in Weimar. Eduard would die in 1942 in the Theresienstadt (Terezín) ghetto. Ernest Rosé became an actor. During the Second

World War, he directed German-language broadcasts to Austria on the "Voice of America." He emigrated to the United States in 1939 and died in Washington, D.C., in 1988. Wolfgang, a student of Austrian pianist and composer Artur Schnabel, became an eminent pianist. After following his brother to North America, he became an accompanist for the renowned Russian bass Alexander Kipnis, among other singers and instrumentalists. Wolfgang died during a visit to Austria in 1977. His widow subsequently lived in New York with Alma Mahler-Werfel.

10. Information from Ernest Rosé derives from a weekend of interviews in Washington, D.C., in 1987, the year before his death.
11. Although perhaps apocryphal, this was an oft-repeated Rosé family story.
12. Arnold Rosé's numerous awards are recorded in the Mahler-Rosé Collection.
13. Paul Bechert was Viennese correspondent for the *Musical Courier,* published in New York.
14. Described by Julius Korngold in his foreword to *Das Rosé-Quartett: Fünfzig Jahre Kammermusik in Wien (Arnold Rosé gewidmet, von Verehrern seiner Kunst),* a seventy-four-page pamphlet published in Vienna in 1933 in celebration of Arnold Rosé's seventieth birthday. The commemorative booklet lists a number of programs of the quartet's musical seasons in Vienna from 22 January 1883 through April 1932 and includes a two-page list of premiere performances.
15. The Mahler-Rosé Collection contains numerous letters from the early years of the twentieth century in which young composers request Rosé Quartet performances of their works.
16. Natalie Bauer-Lechner (1858–1921), a violist with the Soldat-Röger Quartet and a friend and admirer of Gustav Mahler's, filled many notebooks with accounts of Gustav's life and work. After his marriage in 1902, she disappeared from both his life and Justine's. Her memoirs, published in English in 1980 as *Recollections of Gustav Mahler,* have provided biographers of the Mahlers and the Rosés with valuable details.
17. This is the Rosé family version of events, as recalled by Alfred and Maria Rosé. Bruno Walter concurred: "Justine would not have left her brother alone," he wrote in a contemporary letter announcing Gustav's engagement (Walter 1959, 52).
18. The Secessionist arts movement was conceived at the home of Berta Szeps Zuckerkandl. Among its members were painters Gustav Klimt, Oskar Kokoschka, and Egon Schiele; writers Hugo von Hofmannsthal and Arthur Schnitzler; musicians Artur Bodanzky and Alexander von Zemlinsky; theater designer Alfred Roller; and music critic Max Graf. Arnold Schoenberg later joined the avant-garde group.
19. De La Grange 1995, 462.
20. Walter 1959, 52.
21. In her diaries and reminiscences, published many years later, Alma Mahler wrote that Justine opposed her marriage to Gustav, but letters in the Mahler-Rosé Collection belie this claim. In a letter to Justine written in Berlin on 10 December 1901, Gustav seemed undecided about marriage and reaffirmed his strong bond with his sister: "Whatever happens, you and I will remain close to each other for life. . . . Please, have a close look at Alma, with your feminine and more objective eye. Your opinion will be most important to me. Greetings and kisses—your Gustav." (The Mahler-Rosé Collection holds a photocopy of this letter; translation by Reinhard G. Pauly.)
22. Thus Alma Mahler asserts in *Gustav Mahler: Memories and Letters* (Mahler 1976, 33). Justine's official death certificate, issued in 1938, gives the date of the Rosé

marriage as 21 March 1902; Vienna's registry office records the same date. In any case, both couples wed in March 1902.

23. Marie Gutheil-Schoder (1874–1935), a soprano favored by Gustav Mahler, became a stage director and remained a close friend to the Mahler-Rosé family.
24. Three of Schoenberg's letters still reside in the Mahler-Rosé Collection; the remainder have been deposited in other library collections. The Mahler-Rosé championing of Arnold Schoenberg is well documented by Mahler biographers Blaukopf, De La Grange, and Gartenberg. So warm and mutually admiring were relations between Rosé and Schoenberg that in the late 1920s and early 1930s Rosé sent his son Alfred to Berlin to study composition with Schoenberg.
25. Friedrich Buxbaum's son Walter (who took the name Paul Walters) recalled his father's accounts in an interview in Vienna in 1985. Walters, a follower of Albert Schweitzer, died three years later.
26. As a French Army intelligence officer, Picquart worked twelve years to clear the name of Captain Dreyfus, a Jewish officer wrongly convicted of passing military secrets to the Germans. Later Picquart served as French minister of war under Clemenceau. The music-loving Picquart visited the Rosé home whenever he was in Vienna (see Zuckerkandl 1939, 185, and letters in the Mahler-Rosé Collection).
27. Walter describes the sustaining role of his Viennese friendships in his autobiography, *Theme and Variations* (Walter 1946, 145–156).
28. De La Grange 1995, 3 n.
29. See De La Grange 1995, 6–7.
30. Note from Anton (Toni) Schittenhelm to Arnold Rosé, 16 May 1906.
31. Discouragement was a recurring theme in Mahler's letters to Justine. In April 1892, for example, he wrote: "Dearest Justi: After great efforts, my new scores (five of them) are finally here, in clean copies. Now once more I'll start peddling them among my esteemed colleagues. But—since they are even more unusual than my earlier works and display a very sophisticated kind of humor (something that only very unusual people can appreciate)—I'll probably end up adding them to the others. What an inspiring prospect, to write a whole library that will end up only in my desk drawer!" (Letter in the Mahler-Rosé Collection; translation by Reinhard G. Pauly.)
32. Events concerning the directorship are variously described by Mahler biographers Kurt Blaukopf, Henry-Louis de La Grange, Egon Gartenberg, and Donald Mitchell.
33. In "recent times," Mahler once said, only Shakespeare, Beethoven, and Wagner among millions of poets and composers were geniuses of the "most sublime and most universal kind" (Bauer-Lechner 1980, 30).
34. Quoted in De La Grange 1974, 390.
35. Justine Mahler to Ernestine Löhr, 2 December 1896.
36. Justine Mahler to Ernestine Löhr, 18 February 1897.
37. De La Grange 1974, 411 and 905.
38. This and subsequent quotations from Hugo Burghauser derive from an interview in New York in 1984. Burghauser emigrated to the United States after the Anschluss.
39. Walter 1946, 176–177.
40. See the chapter "Years of Study and Suffering in Vienna" in Toland 1976, 29–51.
41. Bruno Walter testified: "I shall never forget the sublime beauty of [Rosé's] violin solo in the third act of *Tristan*. It made me realize for the first time how inspiring

an individual sound could be detaching itself impressively and eloquently from the warm *tutti* of the violins." (Walter 1946, 160–161.)

42. Zweig 1943, 57–58.
43. Schnabel 1963, 30. Austrian pianist Artur Schnabel (1882–1951), virtuoso performer and composer, emigrated to the U.S. in 1939 and became a naturalized American.
44. Saerchinger 1957, 38–39.

CHAPTER 2: A FINE MUSICAL NURSERY

Epigraph: Selma Halban-Kurz, Vienna Opera soprano, writing in Alma's autograph book in 1917.

1. Pirani 1962. A copy of Leila Doubleday Pirani's unpublished memoir is available in the Mahler-Rosé Collection, provided by her daughter, Gina Alexander, and her son, Felix Pirani. This and subsequent excerpts are reprinted with their kind permission.
2. Pirani 1962.
3. Leo Slezak (1873–1946), romantic and dramatic tenor, was engaged by Mahler for the Vienna Opera in 1901. A favorite of Toscanini's who starred in Wagner, Tchaikovsky, and Verdi operas for more than twenty years in Europe and at New York's Metropolitan, Slezak also had careers as a much-recorded lieder singer and in his retirement as the "comic uncle" in German and Austrian films. (He starred in the movie *G'schichten aus'm Wienerwald,* in which Arnold Rosé appeared as a conductor.) Throughout the Second World War, Slezak lived at Rottach-Egern am Tegernsee in Bavaria, having sold homes in Vienna and Berlin. He wrote six books, including his 1964 memoir *Wann geht der nächste Schwan* (What Time Is the Next Swan?)—a title recalling his loudly whispered comment in a Vienna Opera performance of *Lohengrin* when the swan that was to take him offstage left too soon. A seventh book, *Mein lieber Bub* (My Dear Boy), published in 1966, consisted of excerpts from letters he wrote to his son, Walter, who was in the United States and did not see them until after his father's death. The letters document the years in which father and son were separated.
4. Ludwig Karpath (1866–1936) wrote a popular book of recipes favored by musical celebrities.
5. In 1983 the only vestiges of the Rosés at Pyrkergasse 23 were a memorial plaque at the entrance commemorating the building as the former home of Arnold Rosé and an aging glass-holder in the bathroom on the second floor. The large apartment had been divided in two, with one apartment on each floor, and the spiral staircase was gone.
6. In *A Knight at the Opera,* Sir Rudolf Bing mentions Justine's hospitality: see Bing 1981, 88.
7. This and subsequent comments by Vienna Philharmonic archivist Otto Strasser derive from interviews in Vienna in 1981 and 1985.
8. Interview with Alan Hetherington in Norwich, England, in 1985. Dorothy Beswick Hetherington, Alan's mother, had died many years before.
9. Schnitzler 1992, 114. Arthur Schnitzler (1862–1931) studied medicine and psychiatry before he took up writing and was known for creating fictional characters of unusual psychological depth.

10. Guido Adler (1855–1941), Austrian pioneer in musicology, taught in Prague and Vienna and was a longtime friend of Mahler's.
11. Pirani 1962.
12. Mahler 1976, 181–182.
13. Pirani 1962. During the Second World War, as a refugee in England, Arnold gave the death mask to Anna Mahler, who enshrined it in her garden.
14. This and subsequent quotations from Anna Mahler derive from an interview in Spoleto, Italy, in 1983.
15. Alma Mahler to Justine Rosé; undated letter in the Mahler-Rosé Collection.
16. See Mahler 1976, 36.
17. Kokoschka 1974, 29.
18. In *The Bride of the Wind* (1992), Susanne Keegan traces the romantic life of Alma Mahler (later Alma Mahler Werfel) in greater detail, and more accurately, than Mahler-Werfel herself in her published memoirs. Keegan devotes twenty pages to the love affair with Kokoschka.
19. Although she was married to Gustav for less than a decade before his death, Alma Mahler-Werfel thrived on his legacy for another half-century. Ever the collector of celebrity admirers, she died in 1964 in New York.
20. In 1984 Dory's son, Alan Hetherington, now living in Norwich, England, found this postcard and others quoted below among his mother's memorabilia.
21. Eleanor Rosé, the daughter of Arnold's brother Alexander Rosé, remained close to Alma and Alfred. In the thirties and early forties she lived in Paris with her daughter, also named Eleanor but called "Farouel" to avoid confusion. The young Eleanor, an artist, took this nickname as her signature: as a painter living in Brittany, she became known as Eleanor Farouel. Eleanor Rosé later moved to London, where she died in 1992 at the age of ninety-eight. Her recollections throughout the present book derive from interviews in London in 1977 and 1981 and from letters and conversations between 1976 and 1992.
22. *Der Morgen,* 12 December 1927; the unnamed critic was commenting on the Viennese premiere of Alfred Rosé's string quartet.
23. Interview with Walter Strauss, Berkeley, 1982.
24. Interview with Anita Ast in Vienna, 1985. Ast, born in 1905, became the well-known leader of her own quartet in Vienna and often played on RAVAG, Vienna radio.
25. Telephone interview with Carl Bamberger in New York, 1984. Author of *The Conductor's Art* (published in 1965 by McGraw Hill in New York and reissued in 1989 by Columbia University Press), Bamberger died in 1985.
26. Telephone interview with Willy Amtmann, former concertmaster of the Ottawa Philharmonic, in Ottawa, Canada, in 1980. Erica Morini (1904–1995) made her professional debut at age twelve at the Leipzig Gewandhaus with the Berlin Philharmonic under Arthur Nikisch, who had to tune her instrument for her.
27. Telephone interview with Erica Morini conducted with the assistance of Maria C. Rosé in 1982. Subsequent reminiscences of Erica Morini derive from this interview, a second interview with Richard Newman, and correspondence.
28. See Chapter 7 for an account of Gretl Slezak's later career. Gretl, probably born in 1903 (although she gave her birth date as 1907), was slightly older than her two friends.

CHAPTER 3: WAR

Epigraph: Franz Werfel, from the poem "Secret," 1917.

1. Zweig 1943, 24.
2. Zweig 1943, 24.
3. Canetti 1979, 90–91.
4. Canetti 1979, 117.
5. Canetti 1979, 119.
6. Mann 1979, 332 and 337.
7. Otakar Ševčík (1852–1934) led orchestras in Vienna and Salzburg and taught in Vienna, Prague, and Kiev. His most notable female student for the international audience was Erica Morini.
8. Gustav Mahler to Natalie Bauer-Lechner in November 1900; from *Gustav Mahler, Erinnerungen von Natalie Bauer-Lechner,* ed. Herbert Killian (Hamburg: Wagner, 1984), 176 ff.; translated for and quoted in De La Grange 1995, 307 n.
9. Telephone interview with Margit Pessl Cartwright, Northampton, Massachusetts, 1985. Margit's sister Yella, a harpsichordist, played for the New York debut of the Trapp Family Singers after their flight to the United States and became the ensemble's accompanist. Margit, a flautist, married Richard Cartwright (former husband of the Viennese opera star Gertrude Foerstel) and later emigrated to the United States.
10. Interview with Kurt Herbert Adler, San Francisco, 1985. Vienna-born Adler (1905–1988) made his conducting debut in 1925 and assisted Toscanini at Salzburg in 1936. In 1943 he joined the San Francisco Opera, where he became artistic director and later general manager.
11. Interview with Walter Strauss, Berkeley, 1982.
12. Both autograph books are now in private hands, gifts made by Maria Rosé. Photocopies of important pages and a synopsis of entries are available in the Mahler-Rosé Collection.
13. Lotte Lehmann (1888–1976), among the leading lyric-dramatic sopranos of the era, was a stalwart friend of the Rosé family. Alfred Rosé later coached Lehmann for the role of the Marschallin in Richard Strauss's *Der Rosenkavalier,* an opera in which she sang all three major female roles.
14. Mahler had recommended Pfitzner's work to Rosé, and the quartet gave the Viennese premieres of several Pfitzner compositions.
15. The Hungarian-born Molnar created *Liliom,* which served as the basis for the Rodgers and Hammerstein musical *Carousel.*
16. "Secret" first appeared in a volume of Werfel's poetry entitled *Judgment Day.*
17. Elisabeth Schumann (1888–1952), German soprano, joined Richard Strauss at the Vienna Opera in 1919. An active recitalist, she was noted for her renditions of songs by Schubert and Schumann.
18. Puritz 1993, 126–127. Gerd was the son of Elisabeth Schumann's first husband, Walther Puritz. Reprinted with the kind permission of Joy Puritz.
19. This and subsequent quotations from Rudy Karter derive from a 1984 letter from Rio de Janeiro in which Karter described his relationship with Alma. The Karter family spent the summers of 1919–1924 in Mitterach am Attersee.
20. Pirani 1962.
21. Franz Schalk (1863–1931), the Vienna-born conductor, studied under Bruckner at the Vienna Conservatory and devoted almost thirty years to the Vienna Opera,

from 1900 as a conductor under Mahler, between 1918 and 1924 as codirector with Richard Strauss, then as sole director until 1929.

22. Letter of 1 November 1922 from Puccini to Julius Korngold, quoted in Carroll 1997, 381.
23. Vienna's famed Redoutensaal in the Hofburg was described by an earlier visitor, Count de la Garde, as "an enormously long hall in which six hundred people could be seated. The walls were covered with the finest Gobelin tapestries. Above these were long mirrors reflecting and counter-reflecting all the formal elegance made dazzling by the brilliance of the crystal chandeliers." (Quoted in Gartenberg 1968, 146.)
24. The aircraft in the photograph was identified with the aid of John Stroud's *European Transport Aircraft Since 1910*, published by Putnam in London
25. Paul Wittgenstein (1887–1961), Austrian pianist, was the brother of philosopher Ludwig Wittgenstein and the son of wealthy businessman Karl Wittgenstein, a close friend of Brahms' and a supporter of Mahler's. On 21 October 1930, Wittgenstein joined the Rosé Quartet in Vienna for the first performance of Erich Korngold's Suite for two violins, cello, and piano for the left hand, opus 23 (Carroll 1997, 211).

CHAPTER 4: DOUBLE-EDGED SWORD

Epigraph: Gustav Mahler to Bruno Walter, from Bruno Walter, "Mahlers Weg: Ein Erinnerungsblatt," *Der Merker* 3:5 (March 1912), 166; translated for and quoted in De La Grange 1995, 368.

1. Adolf Busch (1891–1952), German violinist and composer, cofounded the highly regarded Busch Quartet. In 1939 Busch emigrated to the United States, where in 1950 he founded the Marlboro School of Music in Vermont.
2. Unidentified clipping in the Mahler-Rosé Collection.
3. Paul Bechert, *Musical Courier*, 13 January 1927.
4. "Arnold Rosé and the Rosé String Quartet," a two compact disc release by Biddulph Recordings (LAB 056-057), includes the Bach Adagio from the Sonata in G minor with Arnold Rosé; the Bach Double Violin Concerto with Arnold and Alma Rosé; and Beethoven's String Quartets no. 4 in C minor, opus 18; no. 10 in E-flat (the "Harp"), opus 74; and no. 14 in C sharp minor, opus 131. These legendary interpretations were remastered from Czech and German recordings of 1927 and 1928 in the personal collection of Raymond Glaspole. Further information is available from Peter Biddulph Violins, 35 St. George Street, Hanover Square, London W1R 9FA, England.

    The seventh in an eight-compact-disc release featuring the music of Váša Příhoda (POL-1007-2) is soon to be released by Podium Legenda. This recording also includes Arnold and Alma Rosé playing the Bach Double Violin Concerto. Information is available from Wolfgang Wendel, Schwetzinger Strasse 98, D-76139 Karlsruhe, Germany.
5. Joseph Hellmesberger the Elder (1828–1893), Austrian violinist and conductor, directed the Vienna Conservatory. A member of a prominent musical family, he also founded and led the Hellmesberger Quartet.
6. The comments of Dea Gombrich were reported by Tully Potter in "The Last Flowering of Old Vienna," *The Strad* 105 (March 1994), and repeated in his liner notes for the Biddulph recording (see note 4 above).

7. Undated clipping from the *Musical Courier* in the Mahler-Rosé Collection.
8. Hubert Marischka (1882–1970), with his brother Ernst, was active in Viennese operetta over several decades beginning in the early 1900s. A singer, actor, director, and impresario, he was immensely popular with the public. After World War II, he became known as a filmmaker.
9. Paul Bechert, *Musical Courier;* undated clipping in the Mahler-Rosé Collection.
10. Undated clipping from the *Musical Courier* in the Mahler-Rosé Collection.
11. Berlin-born Oskar Fried (1871–1941) earned a reputation as a composer as well as a conductor specializing in Mahler's works.
12. Artur Bodanzky (1877–1939), Austrian conductor, assisted Mahler at the Vienna Opera in 1903 and rapidly made his name in the concert halls of Central Europe, England, and the United States, where he made his debut in 1915. His later career centered at the Metropolitan Opera in New York.
13. Interview with Elisabeth Joner Fellmann in Badenweiler, Germany, in 1982. Fellmann's son ran the luxurious hotel in later years.
14. Interview with Elisabeth Marum Lunau, New York, 1981.
15. Interview with Theo Bakker, The Hague, 1985.
16. Eleanor Rosé recalled Justine's attitude toward Příhoda.
17. Bing 1981, 88.
18. Interview with Rudolf Bing in New York, 1983. Born in Vienna in 1902, Bing died in New York in September 1997. His Viennese contacts led to management positions at the Darmstadt Opera and the Municipal Opera in Berlin. Bing helped to found both the Glyndebourne Festival in England and the Edinburgh Festival in Scotland. Between 1950 and 1972, he was general manager of the Metropolitan Opera in New York.
19. Canetti 1982, 244–245.
20. Felix Weingartner (1863–1942), Austrian composer and conductor, was among the foremost classical conductors of his time. He wrote several symphonies and operas that were widely performed in Germany and Austria.
21. The tour was announced in "Rosé Quartet of Vienna to Appear," *Musical Courier,* 21 October 1927.
22. John Alden Carpenter (1876–1951), who studied with the composer John Knowles Paine at Harvard, wrote songs and orchestral music as well as chamber music. He is best remembered for his 1924 *Skyscrapers,* written for Diaghilev.
23. Over the following seventy-five years, Coolidge Auditorium has been the site of more than two thousand concerts, including performances by every major chamber music group of the twentieth century.
24. Erich Wolfgang Korngold (1897–1957), the son of Viennese music critic Julius Korngold (1860–1945), was a child prodigy who became a prolific composer. After 1934 he worked in Hollywood, where he wrote several outstanding film scores.
25. Anna Mahler's marriage to Ernst Křenek, which followed a brief early marriage to Rupert Koller, began in Berlin when Anna was an art student and lasted almost three years, until 1929. Křenek (1900–1991), born in Vienna, composed in a dazzling variety of genres. In 1938, the year he was featured as a "degenerate" artist in the Nazis' spring exhibition at Düsseldorf, he emigrated to the United States, where his chief interest became the techniques of serial music.
26. Alban Berg (1885–1935) was born and died in Vienna. He began his studies with Schoenberg in 1904 and became one of the foremost adventurers in the realm of

atonal music. His close associate in the early years, Anton Webern (1883–1945), also born in Vienna, adhered more rigorously to Schoenberg's example, composing a small body of work based on the twelve-note method. Webern would survive World War II only to be shot the evening of 15 September 1945 by an American military policeman as he stood outside a friend's house in darkness smoking a cigar.

27. Alma Mahler was married to Walter Gropius from 1915 to 1920. In 1917 she met Werfel and began an affair that would lead to marriage in 1929, a few weeks before her fiftieth birthday.
28. With his wife Fritzi Massary (1882–1969), an operetta star, comic actor Max Pallenberg (1877–1934) fled Germany for Switzerland in 1933. Pallenberg died in an airplane crash a year later. Massary performed in London and Vienna until she retired to Hollywood in 1938. There she joined a community of exiled German intellectuals that included Thomas Mann, Bruno Walter, Alma Mahler-Werfel, and Franz Werfel.
29. Max Reinhardt (1873–1943), Austrian actor, director, and producer, achieved great success as a theater manager after 1902. In 1940 Reinhardt became a U.S. citizen.
30. The pen-and-ink cookbook, with recipes from the Mahler family, Anna Moll, Alma Mahler-Werfel, Ludwig Karpath, and other Rosé family familiars, now resides in the Mahler-Rosé Collection.
31. The Mahler-Rosé Collection includes three exquisite pillow covers from Alma's wedding trousseau.
32. The Příhoda villa no longer exists. Information about Alma's and Váša's life at Zariby derives primarily from the memories of Maria Rosé, who visited as a young bride, and from interviews with the former housekeeper of the villa, Pani Sklenárová, and with the tailor of the young Příhoda, conducted in 1983 by a relative of Příhoda's second wife, Premsyl "Tom" Dolezal.
33. Gérard Kantarjian was a young Egyptian Příhoda took as a student after the Second World War on the basis of an audition in Cairo. Kantarjian's family gave up everything in Egypt to allow their son to study with Příhoda in Rapallo. In his lessons, Kantarjian reported, Příhoda accompanied students in a most fantastic way. He mastered all the progressions, chords, and harmonies. "He . . . could pluck the strings like no one else I ever heard. He treated the steel strings of his violin as though he were taming them, tried not to change them any more than was absolutely necessary, constantly testing them with his powerful fingers. . . . He was generous to others with talent. He encouraged me by saying: 'I am so glad you're not playing like I do, and are developing your own style.'" Kantarjian, who became concertmaster of the Toronto Symphony Orchestra and played with the Rembrandt Trio, recalled his lessons with Příhoda in a 1986 interview.
34. Eventually Příhoda himself amassed a valuable collection of instruments, including a 1710 Stradivarius (the "Camposelice") that he sold to the Czech government shortly before his death in 1960. Josef Suk later played the instrument.
35. Pirani 1962.

CHAPTER 5: WALTZING

Epigraph: Ingeborg Tonneyck-Müller, interviewed in Amsterdam, 1983.

1. This and the following reviews of Alma's November 1931 Regensburg perform-

ance are quoted in translation from four unidentified, undated German-language clippings preserved in the Mahler-Rosé Collection.

2. Severyn Barbag, *Chopin,* published in Poland, 1932. This and other Polish reports were discovered through Helena Dunicz-Niwińska's research in Cracow.
3. This and subsequent quotations derive from an interview with Anny Kux Poláková in Bratislava in 1979, conducted by telephone by Maria C. Rosé; a letter from Anny to Gerhard Wuensch, a Viennese composer on the faculty of the University of Western Ontario, dated 19 May 1982; and a personal interview with Richard Newman in 1982 in the company of Anny's husband, Eduard Polak.
4. Early in 1932 Alfred had returned to Vienna from Berlin to escape Nazi pressures. (Bruno Walter would leave Berlin the following year.) During this period Berlin's Jewish performing community in theater and music, suddenly "under political suspicion," fled to Vienna in droves. They took with them a phenomenon of the times, the small cabarets called *kleine Bühnen* (small stages) that had sprouted across Germany.
5. This and subsequent quotations from Michal Karin derive from an interview in Bratislava, Czechoslovakia, in 1985. Karin had been one of Příhoda's accompanists as well as a conductor of considerable stature in and around Bratislava.
6. Max Rostal (1905–1991), Austrian-born violinist and longtime Rosé family friend, studied with Arnold Rosé in Vienna and with Carl Flesch in Berlin. Rostal left Germany for London, where he toured as a soloist and taught violin from 1944 to 1958.
7. Telephone interview with Caroline Rostal in Switzerland in 1986.
8. This and subsequent quotations from Ingeborg Tonneyck-Müller derive from an interview in Amsterdam in 1983.
9. Folk quartet music became the favorite of Emperor Franz Josef. Years later in Vienna, these musical groups were still known as "schrammel quartets."
10. This and subsequent quotations from Lisl Anders Ullman derive from an interview in Pörtschach, Austria, in 1983.
11. Davidowicz 1975, 173 and 189.
12. Davidowicz 1975, 174.
13. The only surviving autograph full score of *Das klagende Lied* remained in Alfred's possession until the 1960s, when he sold it to the Osborn Collection at Yale University. It has since been the model for numerous recorded and concert performances.
14. Oskar Morawetz, who became one of Canada's most frequently performed composers, was forced to leave his studies when the Nazis took over in Austria. He recalls with some irony that the Nazi informer against him was a student of his, and was blind.
15. *Illustrowanny Kurier Codzienny,* 3 February 1935.
16. Dr. Apte, *Nowy Przegląd,* 7 February 1935.

CHAPTER 6: BLOOD AND HONOR

Epigraph: Bruno Frank, German poet, writing in Alma's autograph book on 15 August 1927.

1. Quoted from Baynes 1942, 731–732.
2. Shirer 1959, 233.
3. Ernest later left Vienna for an engagement with the Jewish Community theater in

Cologne. Such ghettoized companies, supposedly serving the cultural life of a separate and subject Jewish community, were allowed to exist for a time.

4. "Argentine Editor Traces His Path from the Ukraine Via Germany: Interview with Peter Gorlinsky by Paul Schwarz," *Rheinischer Merkur / Christ und Welt,* Bonn (30 August 1991); reproduced in English in the *German Tribune,* no. 1484 (15 September 1991).
5. Walter Slezak (1902–1983) became an internationally recognized actor and singer of stage and screen. In 1955 he won a Tony award for the male lead in *Fanny;* in 1957 he performed in *The Gypsy Baron* at the Metropolitan Opera. Active in Hollywood between 1941 and 1972, Slezak appeared in more than three dozen films. He played character roles in such classics as *Abbott and Costello in the Foreign Legion* (1950), *Bedtime for Bonzo* (1951), and *Treasure Island,* with Orson Welles (1972). In *Once Upon a Honeymoon* (1942) and *Lifeboat* (1944), he portrayed sinister Nazis. Slezak committed suicide at his home on Long Island, New York, on 22 April 1983.

CHAPTER 7: ANSCHLUSS

Epigraph: Seneca, *The Happy Life,* first century A.D. From *The Stoic Philosophy of Seneca,* trans. Moses Hadas (New York: Norton, 1958), 239.

1. This and subsequent quotations from Thomas Salzer derive from a 1983 letter from Salzer to Richard Newman and an interview in Vienna in 1985.
2. See Molden 1979, 27–28.
3. Quoted in the *Musical Courier,* 1 May 1938.
4. Graf 1969, 248.
5. After World War II Strauss remained preoccupied with his own material well-being. Reinhard G. Pauly, who was in Salzburg at the end of the war when Strauss was in Berchtesgaden, remembers that a U.S. Army sergeant was sent to interview him. Strauss, who had "played along fully with what the Nazi government wanted, . . . mostly wanted to find out how his foreign royalties were coming along!" (Letter from Reinhard G. Pauly to Karen Kirtley, 11 August 1997.)
6. Levi 1994, 75 and 81. Chapter 3 of Levi's scholarly *Music in the Third Reich* provides an overview of Nazi anti-Semitism as applied to German cultural life and particularly to music; see pages 39–81. Another useful study of music in Nazi Germany is Michael H. Kater's 1997 *The Twisted Muse: Musicians and Their Music in the Third Reich.* Chapter 3, "Persecuted and Exiled Jewish and Anti-Nazi Musicians," traces the fate of numerous musicians.
7. Letter from Louis Meijer to Alfred Rosé, 10 July 1938. The Meijer encounter with Stokowski and Greta Garbo coincides with the time they parted ways, according to Antoni Gronowicz in his 1990 biography *Garbo* (New York: Simon and Schuster), 349–358.
8. Walter would try and fail to get a Monaco passport. Later he became a French citizen and went on to a major conducting career in the U.S. and abroad.
9. Among the best-known films of Margarete Slezak (1903?–1953) were *Darby* and *The Veiled Maja.* After World War II she was in Elia Kazan's *Man on a Tightrope.*
10. Margarete Slezak's 1953 autobiography, *Der Apfel fällt nicht weit vom Stamm,* tells of her first meetings with Hitler and describes how, when she pleaded on behalf of Jewish family friend Max Taussig, Hermann Goering cautioned her to leave the Jewish question alone. She died the year her book was published. Leo Sle-

zak's *Mein lieber Bub* mentions many of Gretl's wartime activities, including her attempt to save Taussig. Her relationship with Hitler was mentioned in the 10 November 1942 issue of the New York–published *PIC* magazine in Eugene Tillinger's illustrated article "Wives of Nazi Hangmen Fight for Social Supremacy," which dissected the rivalry among the wives of Nazi officials in Berlin and the competition for "first lady" status while Eva Braun, Hitler's longtime mistress, was in Berchtesgaden. From this article: "Pretty Margarete Slezak was an early Hitler favorite and is now popular with Nazi party leaders who like to revel at her luxurious Berlin mansion on Kurfürstendam."

11. Hanfstängl 1970, 285.
12. Riefenstahl 1993, 181.
13. Both paintings appear in the German edition of Billy F. Price's 1984 *Adolf Hitler: The Unknown Artist,* published in 1985 as *Adolf Hitler als Maler und Zeichner* (plates 600 and 601, page 225). Price records Margarete's handwritten note proposing the paintings for display: "I offer you for exhibition both these pictures that the Führer painted from photographs of me. The Führer was and is a dear and good friend. 2 March 1936. Gretl Slezak." Rudolf Hess determined that because the paintings were personal gifts, they were not suitable for exhibit.
14. Telephone interview with Felix Eyle, December 1983. Eyle would later acquire Alma's 1757 Guadagnini violin: see "Epilogue: Memories of Alma."

CHAPTER 8: BLACK WEDNESDAY

Epigraph: Wilhelm Backhaus, German pianist, writing in Alma's autograph book on 23 November 1928.

1. Bruno Walter to Arnold Rosé, autumn 1938.
2. Mauthausen, a camp for men, would have the distinction of being the German concentration camp (a category that excluded the Eastern extermination camps) with the largest number of officially recorded executions: over thirty-five thousand in six and a half years of operation.
3. Davidowicz 1975, 104–105.
4. Presser 1969, 345.
5. Alma and Franz Werfel reached safety in California in 1940; Werfel died five years later. Also in 1940, Anna settled in London, where she married the Russian-Jewish conductor Anatole Fistoulari. Fistoulari was Anna's fourth husband. Her fifth and last would be Albrecht Josef.
6. Carl Flesch (1873–1944), Hungarian-born violinist, began his concert career in 1894 and settled after 1908 in Berlin, where he became a chamber music player of international reputation. His career later took him to London and Holland. A superb diagnostician, he published several method books.
7. Willem Mengelberg (1871–1951), born in the Netherlands, studied in Utrecht and Cologne and spent four years in Lucerne. In 1895 he returned to Holland to become conductor of the Amsterdam Concertgebouw, a position he held throughout World War II. He was a champion of Mahler's symphonies until they were banned by the Nazis. After the war Mengelberg was barred from concert work in the Netherlands because he had conducted in Germany during the Nazi years. His plight aroused international debate; he died in exile in Switzerland. Mengelberg, also a composer, was known for his vigorous interpretations of Mahler and Strauss and also for his free approach to other composers' markings.

8. Pirani 1962.
9. Manina's return to the Rosé household was a dangerous act of loyalty, for it was against the race laws for a non-Jew to work in a home classified as Jewish.
10. Quoted in Shirer 1959, 423.
11. When Anny Kux Poláková and her husband moved to Bratislava, Anny turned her Walzermädeln archive, including the orchestra's account books, over to Alma. During the war Michal Karin protected these materials, hiding them on his property in Bratislava. What remains of the archive is now preserved in the Mahler-Rosé Collection.
12. Letter from Alma Rosé to Nina Maxwell, 22 October 1938; Vienna Philharmonic Archives.
13. Molden 1979, 59.
14. Mengelberg's recommendation is preserved in Alma's file at the War History Documentation Center in Amsterdam.
15. Wilhelm Backhaus (1884–1969) studied at Leipzig then became a pupil of Eugen d'Albert. Backhaus was admired above all for his mastery of the Beethoven repertory. Under the Nazis he was connected to the Prussian cultural ministry together with Furtwängler and Georg Kulenkampff; later he moved to Switzerland in opposition to the Nazi regime. His offensive behavior on the occasion described may have been due to his awareness of German agents operating in England at the time of Alma's visit.
16. Sir Adrian Boult (1889–1983), the English conductor, was music director of the City of Birmingham Symphony Orchestra from 1924 to 1930. He was associated with the Proms from 1942 to 1950 and served as principal conductor of the London Symphony Orchestra from 1951 to 1957. On the occasion of his ninetieth birthday in 1979, Sir Adrian acknowledged congratulations from the Vienna Philharmonic and wrote that one of his precious possessions was a document bearing the signatures of a hundred members of the Vienna Philharmonic, including that of "Professor Rosé," commemorating his engagement with the orchestra in 1933. A few weeks before he died in 1983, Sir Adrian wrote to Richard Newman that he remembered the charm and the musical gifts of both Arnold and Alma.
17. Pirani 1962.

CHAPTER 9: ANOTHER BLOW

Epigraph: Seneca, first century A.D. From *The Stoic Philosophy of Seneca,* trans. Moses Hadas (New York: Norton, 1958), 44.

1. In fact, Wolfgang Rosé would remain in Germany until summer 1941. Ernest was already in the United States when Wolfgang emigrated.
2. Pirani 1962. As Leila knew, Alma was eight years older than Heini.
3. Bronisław Huberman, a contributor to the Rosé Fund, founded the Palestine Symphony Orchestra (later the Israeli Philharmonic) to provide employment for Jewish musicians fleeing Nazi Germany.
4. Heini Salzer died of cancer in 1968.
5. Heini did not have to fear conscription into the Wehrmacht: he was exempted from military service as a result of congenital kidney trouble. Thomas did serve in the German army, mostly in Holland, until he became ill and had to be hospitalized.
6. In retrospect it appears that Heini might have been safe in Britain until after Dunkirk, in late May 1940, when the British army made a miraculous evacuation

from continental Europe in the face of the advancing German army. Only then did the British begin to pay serious attention to the internment of so-called enemy aliens living in their midst.

CHAPTER 10: THE NEED TO SACRIFICE

Epigraph: Arnold Rosé to Alfred Rosé, August 1939.

1. Jan Masaryk, son of the founder of the former Czechoslovak Republic and foreign minister of the Czech government in exile, may have helped Alma in her quest. Marcia Davenport, author of the 1967 *Too Strong for Fantasy* (extensive memoirs covering the period when Alma and her family were most active), commented in a letter to Richard Newman of 5 February 1985: "I have no personal knowledge that Jan Masaryk was of assistance to [Alma Rosé]. But he was quick and usually unfailing in his response to people trapped in the Nazi (and later Communist) grinders of their epochs."
2. Dame Myra Hess (1890–1965) made her debut as a pianist in London in 1907 and her U.S. debut in 1922. In appreciation of the historic recital series she arranged at the National Gallery during the war years, she was made a Dame Commander of the Order of the British Empire. The quartet's participation in the concert series led to a continuing friendship between Rosé and Dame Myra. In January 1941, acknowledging a gift of flowers and a treasured item of Mozart memorabilia, Dame Myra Hess wrote to Arnold: "When I listened to you in Vienna, Berlin, and Amsterdam, I little thought that I would have the honor of playing with you. This profound musical experience has meant so much to me, and in this world of sorrow the value of any happy event has an added significance."
3. Pianist Walter Robert, who had fled Vienna, became a pianist and teacher in the United States, based at the University of Indiana.

CHAPTER 11: REBIRTH

Epigraph: Winston Churchill, speech delivered in the House of Commons on 4 June 1940.

1. Interview with Louis Meijer in Amsterdam, 1983.
2. A doctrinaire Nazi, Seyss-Inquart brought a passion for music and art as well as abundant terror to his rule until almost the end of the war. With others of Hitler's proconsuls, he was tried at Nuremberg in 1945–46 and hanged.
3. Alma did not know that Lisl had left Arnold because Lisl's mother needed her assistance, and a second cousin of Arnold's named Malchen had taken her place.
4. Interview with Eugenia and Eugene Meth in Staffa, Ontario, Canada, 1981.
5. From later letters it appears that Alma's benefactress was a Frau Ashkenazy, who may have been a sister of Meta Lissauer, another elderly friend and patron in Holland.
6. Telephone interview with Camilla Youssef in Amsterdam, 1983.
7. The young Gutheil is said to have committed suicide in Switzerland.
8. Alma did not know that Johannes Schmutzer had managed to get his family out of Greece to Egypt. There he joined the British army, served as a commissioned officer, and worked as an interpreter for the remainder of the war.
9. "Sara" was the middle name assigned to all Jewish women by Nazi order, as the middle name "Israel" was assigned to all men.

10. This letter too is on deposit in the War History Documentation Center in Amsterdam.
11. Interview with Antonia Bakker-Boelen in The Hague, 1985.
12. According to the late Dr. Ferdinand Eckhardt, interviewed in London, Canada, in 1989, even Nazi officers in mufti (civilian dress) attended Dutch house concerts.
13. After the war, with the Nieuw Ensemble and various solo musicians, Ed Spanjaard conducted works composed in the Theresienstadt ghetto by Hans Krasa, a performance now available on compact disc.
14. Johan Wagenaar (1862–1941), a well-known teacher and cathedral organist in Utrecht, directed the Conservatory of The Hague for nearly two decades, from 1919 to 1937.
15. Interview with Dr. Jaab Spanjaard in Haarlem, the Netherlands, 1985. He and his brother—both survivors of the war—were spared from arrest when their mother, with the help of a cooperative official in The Hague, was able to change their birth registrations. She filed affidavits reporting that her sons had been fathered by a non-Jew, and the purported father offered verification. The Nazis later "got rid of" the Dutch official who had demonstrated "double loyalties."
16. This remark and the following quotations derive from an interview with Mrs. Millie E. Prins-Marczak conducted by Corinne Vandervelden in Bilthoven, the Netherlands, in 1984.
17. This and subsequent quotations from Dr. J. J. (Jaab) Henkemans derive from an interview in the Netherlands in 1985 and from correspondence with Richard Newman between 1985 and 1987.
18. Alma's informal excursion into music therapy anticipated by almost two decades a major turn in her brother's career. Through links with the music therapy pioneer Theodor Reik, Alfred became Canada's first accredited music therapist.

CHAPTER 12: MUSICAL FORTRESS

Epigraph: Alma Rosé, May 1941.

1. In fact, Flesch did not leave Holland until late summer 1943.
2. The letter from Carl Flesch, dated 9 February 1941, is preserved in the War History Documentation Center in Amsterdam.
3. Violinist and teacher Lorand Fenyves commented in an interview of March 1997 that current editions of the work give alternative fingerings, reflecting various approaches to the difficult opening passage of the "Kreutzer."
4. This and subsequent quotations derive from an interview with Rutger Schoute and his wife in Bilthoven, the Netherlands, in 1983.
5. As a young man, Alfred published numerous poems under the pseudonym "Wolfgang Hauser," thirteen of which are now in the Mahler-Rosé Collection.
6. E. Huizinga, American Medical Association, *Archives of Otolaryngology,* vol. 100 (December 1974), 409–410.
7. Quotations from Dr. Leonard B. W. Jongkees derive from a series of telephone interviews and correspondence with Richard Newman between 1978 and 1997.
8. Jongkees' long career included many firsts for Holland. He was chief editor of the *Dutch Journal of Medicine,* a member of the board of the Royal Dutch Academy of Science, and founder of the vestibular department at the Wilhemina Huis, University of Amsterdam.

9. This and subsequent quotations from Marye Staercke derive from an interview in Amsterdam in 1983 and from correspondence with Alfred Rosé following World War II and with Richard Newman between 1983 and 1993. Marye spoke and wrote excellent English.
10. Arrested later in 1941, James H. Simon was deported to the Theresienstadt ghetto, where he contributed to the active musical program and gave lecture recitals on his specialty, the music of the Romantic composers. Later he was sent to Auschwitz, where he perished.
11. Branching out from contacts in the Dutch church, Marie Anne Tellegen built a network of international contacts that included W. A. Visser't Hooft, the general secretary of the World Council of Churches in Geneva. Eventually, maintaining contact through clandestine radio, she worked with Prince Bernhardt, prince consort in exile, to coordinate the activities of the many Dutch resistance groups. After the Allied victory when Queen Wilhelmina returned to Holland, Miss Tellegen became the director of her cabinet, principal secretary to the powerful queen.
12. Marie Anne Tellegen to Arnold Rosé, 15 October 1945. Miss Tellegen spoke and wrote flawless English.
13. Lotte Meijer, remembering the painful years of separation in an interview in Amsterdam in 1983, said she was sometimes able to watch her baby at play or with the other children in the Gentile family. On occasion she even managed to hug him and bathe him, but she never let him know she was his mother, lest he call out to her and put himself and his hosts at risk. The Meijers were reunited with their son on the evening of the German surrender, 8 May 1945.
14. Julius Röntgen (1855–1932), born in Leipzig, lived from 1877 to 1925 in Amsterdam, where he taught piano and directed the Conservatory. The elder Julius had four sons who also became notable musicians.
15. Interview with Annemarie de Boer-Röntgen, herself a talented pianist, in Amsterdam in 1988.
16. Alfred's major work *Triptychon* remains unplayed except for the premiere of the Adagio movement, which the London (Canada) Symphony Orchestra performed in 1975.
17. In 1949 the Anna Mahler bust of Rosé was placed in the foyer of the Vienna State Opera along with Alma Mahler-Werfel's original Rodin bust of Mahler.

CHAPTER 13: COUNCIL OF WAR

Epigraph: Bruno Walter, "Mahlers Weg: Ein Erinnerungsblatt," *Der Merker* 3:5 (March 1912), 166; translated for and quoted in De La Grange 1995, 368.

1. This and subsequent quotations derive from an interview with Géza Frid and his wife in the Netherlands conducted by Corinne Vandervelden in 1984.
2. Géza Frid (1904–1989), born in Hungary, studied between 1912 and 1924 at the Budapest Academy. He spent most of his working life in Holland.
3. Heydrich's words are quoted in translation in Shirer 1959, 965–966.
4. Records show that a "Van Raaltje"—perhaps the Albert van Raaltje who led the Jewish Symphony Orchestra—played in one of the camp orchestras at Auschwitz.
5. Ironically, it was Leonard Jongkees who recalled the words of Alma's proposed bridegroom.
6. Telephone interview with Carel van Leeuwen Boomkamp in Amsterdam in 1983. The eminent cellist has since died.

7. Henk Badings (1907–1987), a prolific Dutch composer, faced accusations of "cultural collaboration" with the Germans after the war and was barred for two years from resuming his professional activities.
8. Ernst Jünger, a literary giant who died in 1998 at the age of 102, published both World War I and World War II diaries. The latter, published in 1949, was titled *Strahlungen;* see pp. 125–126.
9. Illustrator Abraham Smit, who was a member of the Dutch resistance, termed the Dutch stance "accelerated passive resistance."
10. Several hundred pages of Colonel Lang's reports to German military authorities offer detailed information about occupied Holland and the temper of Hollanders as seen from Lang's command post in Utrecht. This documentary account, which includes reports from section commanders, is in the Bundesarchiv (Militärarchiv), Wiesentalstrasse 10, Freiburg im Breisgau, Germany. Irmgard Cayre, of Majadahonda, Spain, supplied English translations.
11. Annemarie Selinko (1914–1986), Viennese-born journalist, married Erling Kristiansen in 1938 and was active in the Danish underground. In 1943 she was arrested, but she and her husband escaped to Sweden in an open fishing boat. She later wrote the best-selling *Désirée,* which was translated into nine languages and became a movie with Jean Simmons in the title role. The book was dedicated to the memory of Liselotte Röder.
12. Interview with Fryke Oostenbrug, originally from Friesland, in London, Canada, in 1986.
13. Letters from Alma Rosé to Anny Kux Poláková in Bratislava were provided by Mrs. Poláková in 1981. A year later, she died of multiple sclerosis.
14. This account of distinctions made between Catholic-baptized and Protestant-baptized Jews was reported by Dr. Louis de Jong, former director of the War History Documentation Center in Amsterdam.
15. The scene is described by historian Jacob Presser in his 1969 *The Destruction of the Dutch Jews,* originally a study commissioned by the Netherlands State Institute for War Documentation (Rijksinstituut voor Oorlogsdocumentatie) in Amsterdam under the direction of Dr. Louis de Jong.
16. Editorial in the Dutch newspaper *De Waarheid,* 7 August 1942.
17. This document was translated by Abraham Smit. As Smit explained, although such precisions may seem trivial today, "in those days it was of vital importance for records to be correct because the Germans used the official Dutch records in The Hague and were fanatics about correct paperwork, forms, passes, identification, and so on."
18. Frank 1991, diary entries of 9 October 1942 (p. 54) and 19 November 1942 (p. 72).
19. Anny herself was living with her parents in hiding in the garden house of Michal Karin, who was also protecting four Jewish members of the Bratislava Radio Orchestra, which he conducted. Professor Karin later remarked that Anny's efforts to help Alma from afar were loyal but naive.

CHAPTER 14: FLIGHT

Epigraph: Charles Baudelaire, *Intimate Journals.*

1. Marie Anne Tellegen to Arnold Rosé, 15 October 1945.
2. The building now houses the War History Documentation Center.

3. This and subsequent quotations from "Martin" derive from two interviews in The Hague in 1985 and letters to Richard Newman in 1986.
4. Interview in French conducted by Jean Newman with Alberic Bernard Guillemin and Raymond Pallot, French resistance fighters during World War II, in Francheville, France, in 1989.
5. Jean-Paul Gay's recollections are drawn from correspondence with Richard Newman between 1982 and 1991 and personal interviews with William Bush in 1986 and Newman in 1989. Supporting Gay's account of his family's resistance efforts is a certificate in Gay's possession signed by Georges Picard, a highly decorated officer of the French gendarmerie, which reads as follows: "I, the undersigned, . . . certify having made the acquaintance in 1942 of GAY, Jean-Paul, residing at 57 Rue de la Préfecture in Dijon, who agreed, at my request, to shelter and feed charitably on several occasions escaped prisoners as they waited until I led them across the demarcation line. I know that M. GAY himself was actively involved with the [refugees'] passage of this line."
6. A community organization of the Strasbourg Jewish population reports several Hemmendinger families in Strasbourg, but no record of Hems, Heyms, or Hayems. The name Hayem, however, is not uncommon, and it must be remembered that those in flight frequently disguised their names.
7. This datebook has been treasured since 1944 by a member of Alma's Birkenau camp orchestra, Hilde Grünbaum Zimche, now a citizen of Israel.
8. Tikhonoff's house at 9 Avenue Villeneuve has been razed for new construction, and the street has been renamed Maréchal Delatte de Tassigny.
9. Gay described the restaurant as it was at the time. Today the ground floor contains shops and boutiques, and the balcony and upper floors house offices.
10. The neighborhood café with a few tables still exists in Dijon, on a corner facing Place des Cordeliers, where six important streets meet.
11. Jean-Paul Gay was later involved in the rescue of one of Britain's top female agents, who had been arrested and tortured, subjected to ice-water baths and forced to run in freezing temperatures in the prison courtyard with the toes cut out of her shoes. The agent recuperated briefly in the Gay home before escaping. After March 1943, Gay himself smuggled refugees through the "red" zones to Switzerland. After the liberation, Gay was employed by the military security service, which gave him the opportunity to examine numerous dossiers and to refresh wartime memories.
12. "Klaus Barbie: Le 'Boucher de Lyon' était à Dijon en 1942," *Le Bien public* (10 February 1983), Dijon, France. This article deals with Gottlieb Fuchs, "Le Renard" (The Fox), interpreter for the German police at the Dijon train station, whose services Barbie used.
13. Barbie was tried and convicted of crimes against humanity in 1989.
14. John Weidner to Richard Newman, 1 July 1986. On 25 May 1978, the State of Israel awarded John Weidner the Righteous Gentile Medal for his work in the Dutch–Paris Underground. Herbert Ford tells Weidner's story in his 1966 *Flee the Captor.*

CHAPTER 15: ENTER ALOIS BRUNNER

Epigraph: Anonymous Anglo-Saxon saying.

1. This entry was probably made by a French prisoner-clerk. Drancy intake docu-

ments have been deposited by Serge Klarsfeld, president of the Association of Sons and Daughters of Deported French Jews, in the YIVO Center for Jewish Research in New York.

2. During the war Farouel joined the Maquis (the rural resistance) and Eleanor found "essential work" in Paris, translating for the Germans. When useful information passed through her mother's hands, Farouel relayed it to comrades in the underground. In one close call, the Gestapo raided Eleanor's living quarters. Fortunately they missed incriminating files hidden in a closet.
3. Marye Staercke to Alfred Rosé, 1946.
4. Interview with Pietronella d'Aquin Boot in The Hague, 1985. Mme Boot, a young woman when Miss Tellegen entrusted her with Alma's documents, is now the veteran of many years in the foreign service of Dutch firms, the Dutch government, and the European Economic Community.
5. Was Suzanne Tikhonoff, who may have been interned at Drancy before her "release" in April, among the friends who helped Alma to recover? This is one explanation that has been advanced for the listing of her name and address in Alma's datebook.
6. Wellers 1973.
7. The Klarsfelds reported that after the war, Brunner lived in Damascus for many years under the name of Georg Fischer. He has been reported in South America.
8. Wellers 1973.
9. At Auschwitz as elsewhere, the inmates themselves maintained camp operations, and many internees were hired out as slave labor to companies that sustained the German war effort by manufacturing armaments, vehicles, fuel, and synthetic rubber.
10. Telephone interview with Henry Bulawko, Paris, 1985, conducted with the aid of Canadian cultural attaché Chantal Darcy and Karen Domanski.
11. This document was deposited by Serge Klarsfeld in the YIVO Center for Jewish Research in New York.

CHAPTER 16: INSTANT NIGHTMARE

Epigraphs: Buber is quoted in Lifton 1986, 381; Thilo is quoted in SS Dr. H. H. Kremer's Auschwitz diary, translated by Richard and Clara Winston for Schnabel 1958, 111.

1. Survivor figures for Convoy 57 derive from records gathered by Serge and Beate Klarsfeld and deposited in the YIVO Center for Jewish Research, New York.
2. The cargo list was supplied by the Auschwitz Museum.
3. Bulawko 1980. Translated and reprinted with the kind permission of Henry Bulawko. Bulawko later became president of the Jewish Deportees of France.
4. Danuta Czech reports these figures in her massive documentary diary of the camp, *Auschwitz Chronicle,* first published in Poland in 1964 as *Hefte von Auschwitz.* An abbreviated first American edition is available as Czech 1990.
5. Poem by Wojciech Gniatczyński (1924–1985), a clarinetist in the *Stammlager* men's orchestra; translation from the Polish by Florian Smieja.
6. Levi 1961, 22.
7. Czech 1990.
8. The prostitutes, all non-Jews, had their own brothel in Block 24 of the main

Auschwitz camp and were at one point part of an "incentive" program to increase work productivity.

9. Lifton 1986, 17.
10. Dr. Adélaïde Hautval was sent to Ravensbrück a month after Alma arrived at Auschwitz.
11. Although Dr. Rohde was a relatively sympathetic SS doctor according to many witnesses, on 1 June 1946, following the Struthof-Natzweiler War Crimes Trial, he was hanged for his participation in the execution by injection 6 July 1944 of four women arrested for spying. Three of the women were members of the British Women's Transport Service who had operated behind German lines. One of them, British Diana Rowden, section officer, W.A.A.F., was a courier operating in the Dijon area who was denounced on 18 November 1943.
12. This and subsequent quotations from Magda Hellinger Blau derive from correspondence with Richard Newman in 1983. Mrs. Blau lives in Australia and remains in touch with many fellow Auschwitz survivors.
13. This and subsequent quotations from Ima van Esso Spanjaard derive from an interview in Haarlem, the Netherlands, in 1983. Ima was then married to Dr. Jaab Spanjaard, Alma's four-hand piano partner in Utrecht and the brother of Ed Spanjaard, Alma's host in Utrecht until she moved to the Staerckes'. Dr. Spanjaard, who became an eminent psychiatrist and neurologist, died during heart surgery a few years later.
14. Alma's confidante, Regina (Rivka) Kupferberg Bacia, was her personal orderly at Auschwitz-Birkenau. Regina exchanged letters and drawings with Richard Newman between 1985 and 1995.
15. Recollections of Helen "Zippy" Spitzer Tichauer derive from numerous interviews conducted in person and by telephone between 1988 and 1999. After the war, Zippy married Dr. Erwin Tichauer, an official of the International Labor Office under the United Nations, a member of the New York University medical faculty, and a scientist known for his work as a forensic investigator. Dr. Tichauer—also a survivor of Auschwitz, where he worked in a coal mine—died in 1996.
16. Although Alma did not play a Stradivarius at Auschwitz, as rumor sometimes had it, many reports indicate that her instrument was of a high caliber.
17. Mila Potasinski survived Auschwitz and had a successful postwar career in Jewish theater with her husband. She later moved to Australia, where she was reunited with Magda Hellinger Blau, whom she credited with saving her life in Block 10.

CHAPTER 17: MANDEL'S MASCOTS

Epigraph: Dr. Ella Lingens-Reiner, in Lingens-Reiner 1948, 87.

1. Fénelon 1977, 225–228.
2. Bischoff's report is cited in Czech 1964.
3. Although Wolf received a six-year sentence in the Auschwitz war crimes trials in Poland in 1948, he has been mentioned as one of the few SS serving as a *Blockführer,* or barrack warden, who showed sensitivity to the inmates' plight.
4. Laks 1989, 70. Laks, born in Warsaw and educated at the Paris Conservatory, was deported in 1941. Sent to Auschwitz in July 1942, he bore the prisoner number 49543. Much of his work as a composer was lost during his long internment. He died in Paris in 1983.

5. See Lifton 1986, 464–465.
6. Lifton 1986, 423.
7. See Lifton 1986, 374–378.
8. Lifton 1986, 447.
9. Quoted in Lifton 1986, 375–376.
10. Hans Münch, quoted in "Mengele's Henchman—and Proud of It," Edinburgh *Sunday Telegraph,* 29 November 1998.
11. Both Zofia Czajkowska and Stefania Baruch survived the war and returned to Tarnów to live with their families. Czajkowska died in April 1978; Stefania Baruch is also deceased.
12. This and subsequent quotations from Zofia Cykowiak derive from an interview in Cracow in 1985 and from a deposition on file at the Auschwitz Museum.
13. Maria Moś-Wdowik's statement, on record at the Auschwitz Museum, was translated from the Polish by Professor Reuel Wilson of the University of Western Ontario, Canada. Subsequent quotations from Moś-Wdowik derive from the same source.
14. Miraculously, Hélène Scheps found her parents after the war.
15. This and subsequent quotations from Hélène Scheps derive from an interview in Brussels in 1985.
16. This and subsequent quotations from Yvette Assael derive from a telephone interview in 1983. The three Assael siblings survived Auschwitz. Yvette, whose married name is Lennon, now lives in New Jersey. Her sister Lily, briefly the teacher of pianist Murray Perahia, died in New York in 1989. Their brother Michael, who lives in New York, performed for many years with the LaSalle Quartet. Henry Meyer, another Auschwitz survivor and professor at the University of Cincinnati, is a founder of the quartet.
17. This and subsequent quotations from Sylvia Wagenberg Calif derive from an interview on Kol Israel, Israel Radio, Jerusalem, during the 1981 Gathering of Holocaust survivors. Also interviewed were Hilde Grünbaum Zimche and Rachela Olevsky Zelmanowitz. Subsequent quotations from Sylvia, Hilde, and Rachela derive from a German transcript of the discussion, which was broadcast in Hebrew; the English translation is original to this volume. Hilde and the late Lilli Kopecky, general secretary of the Public Committee in Israel of Survivors of Auschwitz and Other Extermination Camps, kindly alerted Richard Newman to the important interview. Sylvia and her sister Karla survived the camp to live in Israel, as did Hilde and Rachela (who died in 1989).
18. Among the earliest of the camp inmates, tattooed 6873, Czajkowska suffered from one of the many chronic ailments that afflicted Auschwitz prisoners. Poor health eventually forced her to relinquish the blockowa position as well.
19. Interview with Helena Dunicz-Niwińska in Cracow, 1985.
20. Lota "Tante" Kröner died in a typhus epidemic in 1945 after her removal to Bergen-Belsen.
21. This and subsequent quotations from Violette Jacquet Silberstein derive from correspondence with Richard Newman between 1981 and 1985 and from an interview in Paris in 1984 conducted by Canadian violinists Scott and Lara St. John. During this interview, Mrs. Silberstein's daughter and granddaughters came into the room, and she remarked: "These are my gifts from Alma."
22. This and subsequent quotations from Margot Anzenbacher Větrovcová, an orchestra survivor who married a prominent Czech stage personality after the war,

are translated from the Czech by Sandford Goldstein. They first appeared in Větrovcová 1979, 129–137. In 1992 Margot was still living in Czechoslovakia but was seriously ill.

23. This and subsequent quotations from Marie-Claude Vaillant-Couturier derive from her testimony at the Trial of Major War Criminals in Nuremberg on 28 January 1946. Vaillant-Couturier, the wife of Pierre Villon, was a photojournalist and a member of the French resistance. Arrested in 1942, she was sent to Auschwitz-Birkenau, where she worked in the Revier with Dr. Hautval. In August 1944 she was transferred to Ravensbrück, where she again worked with Dr. Hautval. At war's end, the two women were among a small group of former prisoners who stayed on as camp administrators, helping to care for the thousands of men and women abandoned by the SS until the camp could be evacuated.
24. This and subsequent quotes from Eugenia Marchiewicz derive from an interview in Canada in 1981. Marchiewicz, a Polish survivor of Auschwitz, died of cancer the next year.
25. This and subsequent quotations derive from a series of interviews with Helena Dunicz-Niwińska in Auschwitz and Cracow, Poland, in 1985; personal correspondence with Richard Newman between 1985 and 1998; and Dunicz-Niwińska's 1996 article "Truth and Fantasy—*Pro Memoria,*" published by the Auschwitz Museum. After the war Helena settled in Cracow, where she worked as a music editor and translated several books on violin music.
26. Charred bread was one of the cures for dysentery attempted in Auschwitz-Birkenau in the absence of charcoal, which is known to adsorb toxins and is still used in Europe in liquid form as a digestive aid.
27. This and subsequent quotations from Flora Schrijver Jacobs derive from interviews in Amsterdam in 1983 and 1985. Flora returned to Holland after the war, married, and had two daughters. Now a fashionable grandmother, she credits Alma with saving her life.
28. This and subsequent quotations from Anita Lasker-Wallfisch derive from a series of interviews and correspondence with Richard Newman between 1979 and 1997; her 1996 memoir, *Inherit the Truth: 1939–1945;* and a BBC 4 interview that aired in August 1996. Anita emigrated to England in 1946 and was a founding member of the English Chamber Orchestra in 1949. She played with the ensemble for half a century, touring extensively. Her late husband, Peter Wallfisch, was a well-known musicologist and pianist. Their son Raphael is a cellist of international distinction.
29. Eric Williams, who wrote of his escape in the 1949 *The Wooden Horse,* used papers prepared by the Lasker sisters.
30. This and subsequent quotations from Henry Meyer derive from a telephone interview in 1992 and a personal meeting in Cincinnati in 1995. Meyer, a professor of violin at the University of Cincinnati, founded the LaSalle Quartet, which included Michael Assael.
31. This and subsequent quotations from Regina (Rivka) Kupferberg Bacia derive from correspondence with Richard Newman between 1985 and 1995. Regina survived the camp to live in Israel.
32. Czech 1964.

CHAPTER 18: THE MUSIC BLOCK

Epigraphs: Arendt 1971, 495; Delbo 1997, xii.

1. Lingens-Reiner 1948, 26.
2. In her 1981 *Return to Auschwitz,* Kitty Felix Hart describes her work on the prisoner staff of Kanada. The size of the Birkenau treasure can be judged by the fact that Kanada consisted of thirty buildings. Completed in December 1943, the complex had a stock comparable to that of a modern department store.
3. Laks 1989, 100.
4. Wiesel 1982, 33–34.
5. Interview with Ella Lingens-Reiner in Vienna, 1983.
6. Lasker-Wallfisch 1996, 76.
7. Frankl 1984, 28 and 40.
8. Fénelon 1977, 53.
9. Lingens-Reiner 1948, 87.
10. Lasker-Wallfisch 1996, 76.
11. Esther Loewy Bejarano was transferred to Ravensbrück when she was officially classified a "half-Jew." Today Mrs. Bejarano lives in Hamburg, her base over many years of touring as a performance artist reflecting on the Holocaust.
12. Alma could not have known that Eduard Rosé died at Theresienstadt on 21 January 1942, before inhabitants of the ghetto were removed to Auschwitz and shortly before his eighty-fourth birthday.
13. Kazimierz Smoleń has reported that in 1943, children of "Aryan" origin born in the camp could be registered and allowed to stay with the "unofficial consent" of the SS, although very few survived (Smoleń 1995, 63).
14. By war's end, 75 percent of the 140,000 Jews who remained in Holland after the Nazi invasion of May 1940 had died in Nazi camps.

CHAPTER 19: ESCAPE INTO EXCELLENCE

Epigraph: Frankl 1984, 75.

1. Interview with Fanny Korenblum Birkenwald in Brussels, 1986. Fanny returned to Belgium after the war and opened a restaurant. She died of cancer in August 1992.
2. Anita Lasker-Wallfisch, interviewed by Sue Lawley on BBC 4's Desert Island Disks, August 1996.
3. This and subsequent quotations from Manca Švalbová derive from interviews in 1983 and 1985 in her native Bratislava, conducted with the aid of interpreter Luba Pavlovicova-Bakova. After the war Dr. Švalbová became a prominent pediatrician. Her memoir, *Vyhasnuté oci* (Extinguished Eyes), devotes a chapter to Alma. Although the memoir was not published until 1964, it was written in 1947 when memories of Auschwitz were fresh. Dr. Hermann Langbein, a member of the Auschwitz underground who became the foremost Viennese authority on the Holocaust, translated the chapter on Alma and other passages from the memoir into German under the title *Erloschene Augen;* these pages can be found in the archives of the Austrian Documentation Center of the Resistance in Vienna but remain unpublished. Fred Ullman, the late husband of Lisl Anders (a singer with the Wiener Walzermädeln), supplied the English translation.

4. Considering the volume of the collection, it is surprising that no trace of the scores prepared for the women's orchestra can be found in the Auschwitz Museum.
5. Franz von Suppé, the nephew of Donizetti, was a popular composer of operetta who brought the Italian style to Viennese musical theater.
6. An extended list of the orchestra's repertoire and possible repertoire (the latter drawn from unverified statements by contemporary witnesses and including music played by the men's orchestra in the main camp) appears in Knapp 1996, 78–81. Gabriele Knapp's study is a dissertation written for Berlin University. Between April 1992 and January 1993, the author interviewed seven former orchestra members, asking two main questions: How could they tolerate having to perform in the camp? What role did music play in their lives after 1945? Pseudonyms are used throughout the report, some directly borrowed from Fénelon. Knapp's primary informants were Eva Steiner Adam, Esther Loewy Bejarano, Zofia Cykowiak, Helena Dunicz-Niwińska, Anita Lasker-Wallfisch, Hélène Scheps, and Violette Jacquet Silberstein. All have contributed substantially to the present volume.
7. Laks 1989, 101.
8. Laks 1989, 100–101.
9. Fénelon 1977, 209 and 80.
10. Knapp 1996, 281.
11. This and subsequent quotations from Ella Lingens-Reiner derive from an interview in Vienna in 1983.
12. This and subsequent quotations from Kitty Felix Hart derive from an interview in Birmingham, England, in 1981.
13. Telephone interview with Alicia Rehl in New Jersey, 1996.
14. Fénelon 1977, 104.
15. Interview with Ewa Stojowska in Cracow, 1985. The former singer, music librarian, and music copyist died in 1996. Helena Dunicz-Niwińska supplied the translation.
16. Among others, a Jewish nurse in the Revier, Viennese Grete Glas-Larsson, heard SS Dr. Mengele whistling tunes from the Verdi opera as he made his selections. Glas-Larsson, interviewed in Vienna in 1983, became close to Alma at the camp.
17. Anita Lasker-Wallfisch, interviewed by Sue Lawley, BBC 4's Desert Island Disks, August 1996.
18. Fénelon 1977, 180.
19. Eva Steiner Adam, interviewed in 1985 in Munich, was a gifted singer taken into the Music Block shortly after Alma's death. Her prisoner number was A-17139; she knew she would survive, she said, when the digits on her forearm totaled 21. Eva was the only member of the orchestra whose mother was with her in the Music Block, where she also worked as a copyist.
20. Laks 1989, 117.
21. Quoted in Laks 1989, 117.
22. Delbo 1968.
23. Recollections of Romana Duraczowa, quoted in Laks 1989, 116.
24. See, for instance, Fénelon 1977, 241.
25. At the end of World War II the survivors of the camp orchestra were so scattered that it would be years before they told their story, much less attempted to reestablish communication among themselves.
26. Fénelon 1977, 37–38.
27. Otto Strasser to Richard Newman, 1981.

28. Kolneder 1998, 536. German conductors had the reputation of being dictatorial, as did Toscanini, George Szell, and many others of wide repute.
29. Reported in Knapp 1996, 211.
30. Fénelon 1977, 55 and 70.
31. See also Czech 1964.
32. Knapp 1996, 72. Translation by Reinhard G. Pauly.
33. As a native Hungarian, Carl Flesch was allowed to return to Hungary. Once there, with a Hungarian passport and an invitation to teach in Switzerland, he was able to flee. Shortly afterwards the great violinist died of a heart attack.

CHAPTER 20: THE ORCHESTRA GIRLS

Epigraphs: Testimony of Helen "Zippy" Spitzer Tichauer and Dr. Ena Weiss Hronsky.

1. This and subsequent quotations from Grete Glas-Larsson derive from an interview in Vienna in 1983.
2. Telephone interview with Lily Assael in 1981.
3. Many women recall Danuta (Danka) Kollakowa's fine piano playing. After the war she graduated from the Warsaw Music Academy and served as pianist in the Polish Mazowsze dance company. Danka died over two decades ago.
4. Švalbová 1964, chapter 1.
5. Danuta Czech (1964) also reported these selections.
6. Wiesel 1982, 32.
7. Ruth Elias describes life inside the Czech Jewish family camp in her 1998 *Triumph of Hope: From Theresienstadt and Auschwitz to Israel,* 111–115.
8. Czech 1964.
9. Szmaglewska 1947, 265 and 273.
10. See, for example, Elias 1998, 154.
11. Many times since 1945, international teams of investigators, with sound reproduction equipment placed on the site of the former Music Block and listening equipment on the railway sidings opposite, have sought to understand how arriving deportees could report hearing music when they were in the trains.
12. Millu 1991, 46–47.

CHAPTER 21: FRAU ALMA

Epigraph: Švalbová 1964.

1. Mala Zimetbaum was in love with a prisoner in the men's camp, Edek Galinski, a member of the Polish resistance. Together, she and Edek planned to escape and tell the outside world what was happening at Auschwitz. Once they exposed the Nazis' atrocities, they believed, the Allies or the Christians of the world would storm the camps and set the prisoners free. The escape attempt, which took place after Alma's death, ended in disaster. Mala and Edek were recaptured after a single night of freedom. They were paraded back to Birkenau, tortured, and publicly executed. Mala became a legend, cheating her hangman by slashing her wrists and slapping the face of an SS with her bloodied hand. The Auschwitz camp museum still displays interlaced locks of their hair, a tribute to their love and courage.
2. Translation by Fred Ullman. Zofia Cykowiak and Helena Dunicz-Niwińska identified the artist in a 1985 interview in Cracow, Poland.

3. Frau Schmidt was mistakenly identified as an SS woman in the film *Playing for Time* and as the head of Kanada in Fania's written account of the orchestra.
4. Pawełczyńska 1979.
5. The sheet music of the Marischka version, arranged by Melichar and published in 1934 by Hans Sikorski of Hamburg, is currently available through Beboton-Verlag of Berlin and Hamburg.
6. Mrs. Muguette Myers of Quebec supplied the French lyrics to "Tristesse" in a letter to Richard Newman of 1991. For her the song became a symbol of beauty and hope when in September 1939, at the age of six, she was evacuated with her schoolmates from Paris to Sens. One night after dark as the children lay on straw mattresses on the floor of the school gymnasium, a young girl named Rachel sang this song. Afterwards the children called for Rachel to sing it every night, sometimes three and four times. "That voice soothed us and made us forget where we were," wrote Mrs. Myers.
7. J. Hamelle published these French and English lyrics to "Tristesse" (Grief) in Paris in 1930 in an arrangement by F. Litvinne for mezzo-soprano or baritone and piano.
8. Ruth Bassin survived the war and lived for many years in New York, where she died in 1989.
9. Danuta Czech (1964), quoting H. G. Adler's *Theresienstadt, 1941–1945,* reports that "Edelstein together with his family and a group of co-workers" was shot and killed in crematorium III in Birkenau on 20 June 1944. The camp resistance noted that fifty persons were executed in the group.
10. Yahil 1990, 525; Troller 1991, 166.
11. Adler 1960, 573.
12. Czech 1964.

CHAPTER 22: DEATH IN THE REVIER

Epigraph: Quoted in Lasker-Wallfisch 1996, 154.

1. Fénelon 1977, 204.
2. Interview with Wanda Marossányi and Anna Polarczyk-Schiller in Cracow, 1985.
3. Indeed, in January 1945 it was the Soviets who liberated Auschwitz-Birkenau and found the remnants of the prisoner population left behind by the fleeing Germans.
4. See Lingens-Reiner 1948, 145.
5. Dr. Hronsky now lives in Adelaide, Australia.
6. A photographic copy of the order signed by Mengele, and the results of the analysis by the SS Hygiene Institute in the Auschwitz camp, were provided by the Auschwitz-Birkenau State Museum at the request of Dr. Arthur Hudson of the research department of University Hospital, London, Canada.
7. Czech 1964.
8. The War History Museum in Amsterdam erroneously lists the date of Alma's death as July 1944. Documents in the Auschwitz Museum correctly give the date as 5 April 1944.
9. Fénelon 1977, 208.
10. A search was conducted under the direction of Professors Anna Urban and Zdzislaw Marek at the request of violinist Helena Dunicz-Niwińska.
11. Letter from Marye Staercke to Alfred Rosé, 1946.
12. Interview with Wanda Marossányi, Cracow, 1985.

13. Fénelon 1977, 210.
14. Hans Münch to Richard Newman, 1984. In 1944 during the monumental influx of Hungarian Jews, Münch was told he was expected to take part in selections. In his words, as recounted in Sereny 1995, 465–468: "I took the night train to Berlin that very evening [and told the department head that it] was against my ethical principles and that I refused. He said he, too, had children and would have refused, that certainly I didn't have to, and he telephoned Bär (with Kramer a commandant) then and there and told him so." Sereny further reports that "at the end of the war forty Auschwitz doctors were arrested by the Russians and handed over to the Poles. The trial in Cracow ended December 22, 1947, with twenty-three sentenced to death, six to life imprisonment and ten to prison for between three and fifteen years. Münch alone was acquitted. Nineteen former prisoners testified in his favor." At the same war crimes trial, Maria Mandel was sentenced to be hanged.
15. Interview with Dr. Jaab Spanjaard in Haarlem, the Netherlands, 1983.
16. Laks 1989, 102.
17. Fénelon 1977, 211.
18. In his 1964 book *I Cannot Forgive,* Vrba described his escape and his attempts to tell the world what was going on at Auschwitz-Birkenau.
19. Tedeschi 1992, 59.
20. Interview with Halina Czajkowska Robinson of London, Canada, 1998. Mrs. Robinson is the daughter of Polish war hero and chief of military intelligence, Warsaw, in the Polish Underground Army (A.K.) during the German occupation, Colonel Czeslaw Karol Czajkowski (1885–1998). Colonel Czakowski, a survivor of Auschwitz and Dachau, emigrated to Canada with his wife and daughter in 1951.
21. Josef Kramer, along with Irma Grese and others who ran Bergen Belsen (Hössler was executed later), was tried and hanged in October 1945.
22. Lily Mathé, a violinist who had played around the world with a Gypsy boys' band, arrived in the Hungarian transports of May 1944. After the war she married a British officer she had met at Bergen-Belsen and lived in London, where she performed as a Gypsy violinist in a restaurant. She died in 1993.

CHAPTER 23: REVERBERATIONS

Epigraph: Frankl 1984, 19.

1. Telephone interview with Peter Terry (formerly Peter Tischler), a resident of New Jersey, in 1983.
2. Rudolf Bing to Alfred Rosé, 18 October 1948.
3. With the help of her sculptor friend Paul Peschke, whom she later married, Susanne Schmutzer saved her Jewish mother from arrest many times.
4. "Nachruf" is translated for this volume by Reinhard G. Pauly.
5. Contacted in 1988, Anders said that he had not included "Nachruf" in his volume of collected poems, and forty-three years after he wrote it, he had forgotten his sources.
6. Arnold's 1718 Stradivarius would pass through several hands in the next decades. Most recently Robert Mann, retired violinist of the renowned Juilliard Quartet, gave the violin to his son and pupil, violinist Nicholas Mann, who plays it as a member of the Mendelssohn Quartet.
7. Lasker-Wallfisch 1996, 86.
8. Quoted in Gill 1988, 405.

9. The letters exchanged by Feinstein and Morini are preserved in the New York Public Library for the Performing Arts.
10. Vratislavský 1970.
11. Interview with Ralph Aldrich, 1990. In frequent consultations with Richard Newman between 1990 and 1998, Aldrich, a violist and authority on stringed instruments, provided information on music studies in Vienna.
12. By this time Leila and her husband Max Pirani, who had received an appointment at the Western Ontario Conservatory of Music in London, Canada, had encouraged Dr. Harvey Robb of the conservatory to hire Alfred as leader of a summer opera workshop on the campus of the University of Western Ontario. Thus Alfred was committed in North America for the six weeks of the summer school. The following year his workshop became part of the year-round conservatory program. Alfred and Maria later moved to London, Canada, where the opera workshop still thrives. Alfred became a professor on the music faculty while carrying on his work in music therapy. He died in 1975, aware of an impending tribute: three weeks after his death, the university awarded him an honorary doctorate of music.
13. Puritz 1993, 274–275. Reprinted with the kind permission of Joy Puritz.
14. Interview with Hugo Burghauser in New York, 1984.
15. Reinhard G. Pauly notes that this was a bitter pun, since *rein* also means "in tune." In 1948, when the Vienna orchestra again appeared in London, Buxbaum dropped dead of a heart attack on the street as he ran for a bus to attend a rehearsal.
16. Lasker-Wallfisch 1996, 84.
17. Quoted in Knapp 1996, 279.
18. Sunday *Times*, London, England, 11 January 1980.
19. Fénelon 1977, 159.
20. Fénelon 1977, 177–193.
21. In *Menschen in Auschwitz*, Hermann Langbein reports that Reichsführer Heinrich Himmler visited Auschwitz-Birkenau the second and last time on 17–18 July 1942, to view a demonstration gassing. Józef Garliński's account in *Fighting Auschwitz* coincides.

EPILOGUE: MEMORIES OF ALMA

1. Telephone interview with Max Jekel in London, 1981. Jekel, a member of the Royal Opera House orchestra in Covent Garden, played second violin in the reconstituted Rosé Quartet for many National Gallery concerts.
2. This and the subsequent quotation from Felix Eyle derive from a telephone interview in 1983. Eyle emigrated from Vienna in 1928. For several years he was associated with the Cleveland Symphony Orchestra and headed the violin department at the Cleveland Institute of Music. In 1947 he became concertmaster of the Metropolitan Opera Orchestra; later he served as the orchestra's manager. Upon his retirement in 1970, Eyle took a teaching position at Colgate University in Hamilton, New York, where he contributed to the university's musical life over the next decade. Eyle died in 1988. In his memory his widow, Elisabeth Tischler Eyle, established the Felix Eyle Memorial Prize, a scholarship fund for outstanding violin students. In 1998 Nicolas Eyle, his son, still owned the "Alma Guadagnini," with its satin-lined red velvet cover decoratively embroidered with the initials "AR."

Interviews and Major Sources

Unless otherwise specified, the interviews listed below were conducted by Richard Newman in person, often preceded and followed by correspondence. The names of orchestra survivors appear in boldface type.

Eva Steiner Adam, Munich, 1985
Kurt Herbert Adler, San Francisco, 1985
Ralph Aldrich, London, Canada, 1990
Willy Amtmann, Ottawa, Canada, 1980 (telephone interview)
Lily Assael, New York, 1981 (telephone interview and correspondence)
Anita Ast, Vienna, 1985
Regina (Rivka) Kupferberg Bacia, 1985–95 (correspondence from Israel and Holland)
Theo Bakker, The Hague, 1985
Antonia Bakker-Boelen, The Hague, 1985
Carl Bamberger, New York, 1984 (telephone interview)
Esther Loewy Bejarano, Hamburg, 1985 (telephone interview)
Sir Rudolf Bing, New York, 1983
Fanny Korenblum Birkenwald, Brussels, 1986
Magda Hellinger Blau, Australia, 1983 (correspondence)
Sir Adrian Boult, England, 1983 (correspondence)
Henry Bulawko, Paris, 1985 (telephone interview conducted with the aid of Canadian cultural attaché Chantal Darcy and Karen Domanski)
Hugo Burghauser, New York, 1984
Margit Pessl Cartwright, Northampton, Mass., 1985 (telephone interview and correspondence)
Zofia Cykowiak, Cracow, 1985

Pietronella d'Aquin Boot, The Hague, 1985
Annemarie de Boer-Röntgen, Amsterdam, 1988–94 (interview in 1988 and correspondence)
Helena Dunicz-Niwińska, Auschwitz and Cracow, 1981–98 (interviews in 1985 and correspondence)
Ferdinand Eckhardt, London, Canada, 1989
Felix Eyle, Hamilton, New York, 1983–88 (telephone interview and correspondence)
Eleanor Farouel, 1992 (correspondence)
Elisabeth Joner Fellmann, Badenweiler, Germany, 1982
Géza Frid and Mrs. Frid, the Netherlands, 1984 (interview by Corinne Vandervelden)
Jean-Paul Gay, Dijon, 1982–91 (interview by William Bush in 1986, interview by Richard Newman in 1989, and correspondence)
Grete Glas-Larsson, Vienna, 1983
Alberic Bernard Guillemin, Francheville, France, 1989 (interview by Jean Newman)
Kitty Felix Hart, Birmingham, England, 1981
J. J. (Jaab) Henkemans, the Netherlands, 1985–87 (interview in 1985 and correspondence)
Alan Hetherington, Norwich, England, 1985 (interview by Alice Linden)
Flora Schrijver Jacobs, Amsterdam, 1983 and 1985
Max Jekel, London, 1981 (telephone interview)
Leonard B. W. Jongkees, Utrecht, 1978–97 (telephone interviews and correspondence)
Gérard Kantarjian, Toronto, 1986
Michal Karin, Bratislava, 1985
Rudy Karter, Rio de Janeiro, 1984 (correspondence)
Greta Kraus, Toronto, 1995
Ota Kraus, Prague, 1995
Szymon Laks, Paris, 1982 (correspondence)
Hermann Langbein, Vienna, 1981 and 1984 (personal interviews and correspondence)
Anita Lasker-Wallfisch, London and Vienna, 1979–97 (interviews and correspondence)
Yvette Assael Lennon, New Jersey, 1983 (telephone interview)
Ella Lingens-Reiner, Vienna, 1983
Elisabeth Marum Lunau, New York, 1981
Anna Mahler, Spoleto, Italy, 1983
Eugenia Marchiewicz, Canada, 1981
Viktor Marischka, Vienna, 1987 (correspondence)
Wanda Marossányi, Cracow, 1985
"Martin," The Hague, 1985–86 (interviews and correspondence)

Lotte and Louis Meijer, Amsterdam, 1979–85 (interviews and correspondence)
Eugene and Eugenia Meth, Staffa, Ontario, Canada, 1981
Henry Meyer, Cincinnati, Ohio, 1992 and 1995 (telephone and personal interviews)
Erica Morini, New York, 1982 and 1983 (telephone interview by Maria C. Rosé, personal interview by Richard Newman, and correspondence)
Charlotte Obermeyer-Groen, Utrecht, 1985
Fryke Oostenbrug, London, Canada, 1986
Raymond Pallot, Francheville, France, 1989 (interview by Jean Newman)
Paul Peschke, Vienna, 1983
Leila Doubleday Pirani, London, 1977–1981 (correspondence and interview in 1981)
Anny Kux Poláková, Bratislava, 1979 and 1982 (telephone interview by Maria C. Rosé, correspondence with Gerhard Wuensch, and personal interview by Richard Newman)
Billy F. Price, Houston, 1982
Millie E. Prins-Marczak (Millie Spanjaard), Bilthoven, the Netherlands, 1984 (interview by Corinne Vandervelden)
Alicia Rehl, New Jersey, 1996 (telephone interview)
Halina Cjakowski Robinson, London, Canada, 1980 and 1998
Eleanor Rosé, London, 1976–92 (interviews in 1977 and 1981 and correspondence)
Ernest Rosé, Washington, D.C., 1987
Maria Caroline Rosé, 1972–99 (numerous personal interviews)
Caroline Rostal, Switzerland, 1986 (telephone interview)
Thomas Salzer, Vienna, 1983 and 1985 (correspondence and interview)
Hélène Scheps, Brussels, 1972–98 (interview in 1985 and correspondence)
Rutger Schoute and Mrs. Schoute, Bilthoven, the Netherlands, 1983
Violette Jacquet Silberstein, Paris, 1981–85 (correspondence and interview in 1984 by Scott and Lara St. John)
Pani Sklenárová, Prague, 1983 (interview by Premsyl "Tom" Dolezal)
Ima van Esso Spanjaard, Haarlem, the Netherlands, 1983
Jaab Spanjaard, Haarlem, the Netherlands, 1983
Marye Staercke, Amsterdam, 1983–93 (interview in 1983 and correspondence)
Ewa Stojowska, Cracow, 1985
Otto Strasser, Vienna, 1981 and 1985
Walter Strauss and Mrs. Strauss, Berkeley, 1982
Manca "Dr. Mancy" Švalbová, Bratislava, 1983 and 1985
Henry Swoboda, Switzerland, 1987 (interview by Hanna Spencer)
Peter Terry (formerly Peter Tischler), New Jersey, 1983 (telephone interview and correspondence)
Erwin Tichauer, New York, 1988–95 (personal interview in 1983, numerous telephone interviews, and correspondence)

Helen "Zippy" Spitzer Tichauer, New York, 1988–99 (personal interview in 1983, numerous telephone interviews, and correspondence)
Ingeborg Tonneyck-Müller, Amsterdam, 1983
Lisl Anders Ullman, Pörtschach, Austria, 1983
Carel van Leeuwen Boomkamp, Amsterdam, 1983 (telephone interview)
Paul Walters (formerly Walter Buxbaum), Vienna, 1985
John Weidner, California, 1986 (correspondence)
Camilla Youssef, Amsterdam, 1983 (telephone interview)
Hilde Grünbaum Zimche, 1882–85 (correspondence from Israel)

Depositions on file at the Auschwitz Museum provided firsthand memoirs of
Zofia Cykowiak
Maria Moś-Wdowik
Helga Schiessel

The transcript (in English translation) of a 1981 Kol Israel interview provided testimonies of
Sylvia Wagenberg Calif
Rachela Olevsky Zelmanowitz
Hilde Grünbaum Zimche

Other major sources were the published memoirs of two orchestra members:
Fania Fénelon (*Playing for Time,* 1977)
Anita Lasker-Wallfisch (*Inherit the Truth,* 1996)

The authors and publisher wish to acknowledge the great help they have received from Maria Rosé and the Mahler-Rosé family archive she deposited with the University of Western Ontario in London, Canada. Most of the illustrations reprinted in this volume, as well as the letters and documents quoted, belonged to Mrs. Rosé. She died in London on 3 May 1999, as this book went to press.

Maria Rosé in her home on Cheapside Street, London, Ontario, in the 1980s. On the wall hangs an etching of the Rosé Quartet by Stössel, a pupil of Ferdinand Schmutzer. On the mantel at left is the famed 1909 Rodin bust of Mahler, and at center a photograph of Alfred Rosé in 1974, the year before his death. Photograph © Walter Curtin RCA, Toronto, Canada.

Bibliography

Adelsberger, Lucie. 1995. *Auschwitz: A Doctor's Story.* Trans. Susan Ray. Boston: Northeastern University Press. First published in German as *Auschwitz: Ein Tatsachenbericht.*

Adler, H. G. 1960. *Theresienstadt, 1941–1945.* Tübingen: J. C. B. Mohr (Paul Siebeck).

Adler, H. G., Hermann Langbein, and Ella Lingens-Reiner. 1962. *Auschwitz: Zeugnisse und Berichte.* Frankfurt: Europäische Verlagsanstalt.

Annas, George J., and Michael A. Grodin, eds. 1922. *The Nazi Doctors and the Nuremberg Code: Human Rights and Human Experimentation.* New York: Oxford University Press.

Arendt, Hannah. 1971. "On Responsibility for Evil," in *Crimes of War: A Legal, Political-Documentary, and Psychological Inquiry into the Responsibility of Leaders, Citizens, and Soldiers for Criminal Acts in Wars.* Ed. Richard A. Falk, Gabriel Kolko, and Robert J. Lifton. New York: Random House.

Aron, Robert. 1969. *Histoire de l'Épuration: des prisons clandestines aux tribunaux d'exception,* September 1944–June 1949. Les Grandes Études Contemporaines. Paris: Fayard.

Barea, Ilsa. 1966. *Vienna: Legend and Reality.* London: Secker and Warburg.

Bauer-Lechner, Natalie. 1980. *Recollections of Gustav Mahler.* London: Cambridge University Press. Ed. Peter Franklin. Trans. Dika Newlin. First published in German in 1923 as *Erinnerungen an Gustav Mahler.*

Baynes, Norman H., ed. and trans. 1942. *The Speeches of Adolf Hitler: April 1922–August 1939,* 2 vols. London: Oxford University Press.

Bazin, Jean François. 1984. *La Libération de Dijon.* Saint-Seine-l'Abbaye: Michaut.

Beattie, John. 1984. *Klaus Barbie: His Life and Career.* London: Methuen.

Berkley, George E. 1993. *Hitler's Gift: The Story of Theresienstadt.* Boston: Branden Books.

Bing, Sir Rudolf. 1981. *A Knight at the Opera.* New York: G. P. Putnam's Sons.

Blaukopf, Kurt, and Herta Blaukopf. 1992. *Die Wiener Philharmoniker: Welt des Orchesters—Orchester der Welt.* Vienna: Löcker Verlag.

———, eds. 1992. *Mahler: His Life, Work and World.* London: Thames & Hudson.

Botz, Gerhard. 1988. *Nationalsozialismus in Wien: Machtübernahme und Herrschaftssicherung,* 3rd rev. ed. Buchloe, Germany: Obermayer. Earlier editions appeared as *Wien, vom "Anschluss" zum Krieg.*

Bower, Tom. 1984. *Klaus Barbie: The "Butcher of Lyon."* New York: Pantheon.

Boyer, John W. 1981. *Political Radicalism in Late Imperial Vienna: Origins of the Christian Social Movement, 1848–1897.* Chicago: University of Chicago Press.

Brook-Shepherd, Gordon. 1963. *The Anschluss.* Philadelphia: J. B. Lippincott.

———. 1969. *The Last Habsburg.* New York: Weybright and Talley.

Bulawko, Henry. 1980. *Les Jeux de la mort et de l'espoir.* "Convoi du 18 juillet 1943." Paris: Amicale des Déportés d'Auschwitz et des Camps de Haute-Silésie. First published in 1954; reissued in 1993 by Critères, Éditions Montorgueil, Paris.

Canetti, Elias. 1979. *The Tongue Set Free: Remembrance of a European Childhood.* Trans. Joachim Neugroschel. New York: Seabury Press. First published in German in 1977 as *Die gerettete Zunge.*

———. 1982. *The Torch in My Ear.* Trans. Joachim Neugroschel. New York: Farrar, Straus and Giroux. First published in German in 1980 as *Die Fackel im Ohr: Lebensgeschichte, 1921–1931.*

———. 1986. *The Play of the Eyes.* Trans. Ralph Manheim. New York: Farrar, Straus and Giroux. First published in German in 1985 as *Das Augenspiel.*

Carroll, Brendan G. 1997. *The Last Prodigy: A Biography of Erich Wolfgang Korngold.* Portland, Ore.: Amadeus Press.

Carsten, F. L. 1977. *Fascist Movements in Austria: From Schönerer to Hitler.* London: Sage.

Centre de Documentation Juive Contemporaine. 1947. *La Persécution des Juifs en France et dans les autres pays de l'ouest.* Paris: Éditions du Centre.

Chambard, Claude. 1976. *The Maquis: A History of the French Resistance Movement.* Trans. Elaine P. Halperin. Indianapolis: Bobbs-Merrill.

Clary-Aldringen, Alfons. 1978. *A European Past: Memoirs by Price Clary.* Trans. Ewald Osers. New York: St. Martin's Press. First published in German as *Geschichten eines alten Österreichers.*

Combs, William L. 1986. *The Voice of the SS: A History of the SS Journal "Das Schwarze Korps."* New York: Peter Lang.

Czarnecki, Joseph P. 1989. *Last Traces: The Lost Art of Auschwitz.* New York: Atheneum.

Czech, Danuta. 1964. *Hefte von Auschwitz.* Vol. 7, *Kalendarium der Ereignisse im Konzentrationslager Auschwitz-Birkenau.* Auschwitz: Państwowe Muzeum.

———. 1990. *Auschwitz Chronicle, 1939–1945,* first American ed. New York: H. Holt. First published by the Auschwitz Museum as *Kalendarz wydarzeń w obozie koncentracyjnym Oświęcim-Brzezinka, 1939–1945,* to be found in the *Zeszyty Oświęcimskie* (Auschwitz Notebooks), nos. 2–7, Auschwitz, 1959–1964.

———. 1994. "The Auschwitz Prisoner Administration" in Yisrael Gutman and Michael Berenbaum, eds. *Anatomy of the Auschwitz Death Camp.* Bloomington: Indiana University Press, in association with the United States Holocaust Memorial Museum, Washington, D.C.

Czerniakow, Adam. 1979. *The Warsaw Diary of Adam Czerniakow: Prelude to Doom.* Ed. Raul Hilberg, Stanislaw Staron, and Josef Kermisz. Trans. Stanislaw Staron and staff of Yad Vashem. New York: Stein and Day. First published in Polish as *Dzienn ik getta warszawskiego.*

Dabringhaus, Erhard. 1984. *Klaus Barbie.* Washington: Acropolis Books.

Dank, Milton. 1974. *The French Against the French: Collaboration and Resistance.* Philadelphia: J. B. Lippincott.

Das Rosé-Quartett: Fünfzig Jahre Kammermusik in Wien (Arnold Rosé gewidmet, von Verehrern seiner Kunst). 1933. Foreword by Julius Korngold. Privately published in Vienna to commemorate Arnold Rosé's seventieth birthday.

Davenport, Marcia. 1967. *Too Strong for Fantasy.* New York: Scribner.

Davidowicz, Lucy S. 1975. *The War Against the Jews, 1933–1945.* New York: Holt, Rinehart and Winston.

Davidson, Eugene. 1966. *The Trial of the Germans: An Account of the Twenty-two Defendants Before the International Military Tribunal at Nuremberg.* New York: Macmillan.

De Jong, Louis. 1990. *The Netherlands and Nazi Germany.* The Erasmus Lectures. Cambridge, Mass.: Harvard University Press.

De La Grange, Henry-Louis. 1973. *Mahler,* vol. 1. Garden City, N.Y.: Doubleday.

———. 1995. *Gustav Mahler: The Years of Challenge (1897–1904).* New York: Oxford University Press. First published in French between 1979 and 1984 in three volumes.

Delbo, Charlotte. 1968. *None of Us Will Return.* Trans. John Githens. New York: Grove. First published in French in 1965 as *Aucun de nous ne reviendra.*

———. 1990. *Days and Memory.* Trans. Rosette Lamont. Marlboro, Vt.: Marlboro Press. First published in French as *Mémoire et les jours.*

———. 1995. *Auschwitz and After.* Trans. Rosette Lamont. New Haven, Conn.: Yale University Press. First published in French as *Auschwitz et après.*

———. 1997. *Convoy to Auschwitz: Women of the French Resistance.* Trans. Carol Cosman. Boston: Northeastern University Press. First published in French in 1965 as *Convoi du 24 janvier.*

Dietrich, Margaret, ed. 1976. *Das Burgtheater und sein Publikum.* Vienna: Verlag der Österreichischen Akademie der Wissenschaft.

Dolmetsch, Carl R. 1992. *"Our Famous Guest": Mark Twain in Vienna.* Athens, Ga.: University of Georgia Press.

Drewniak, Bogusław. 1983. *Das Theater im NS-Staat: Szenarium deutscher Zeitgeschichte, 1933–1945.* Düsseldorf: Droste.

Dunicz-Niwińska, Helena. 1996. "Truth and Fantasy—*Pro Memoria.*" State Museum of Auschwitz Birkenau / Państwowe Muzeum Bulletin 3–4 (January).

Dwork, Deborah, and Robert Jan Van Pelt. 1996. *Auschwitz, 1270 to the Present.* New York: Norton.

Elias, Ruth. 1998. *Triumph of Hope: From Theresienstadt and Auschwitz to Israel.* Trans. Margot Bettauer Dembo. New York: John Wiley & Sons, in association with the United States Holocaust Museum, Washington, D.C. First published in German in 1988 as *Die Hoffnung erhielt mich am Leben.*

Falk, Richard A., Gabriel Kolko, Robert Jay Lifton, eds. 1971. *Crimes of War: A Legal, Political-Documentary, and Psychological Inquiry into the Responsibility of Leaders, Citizens, and Soldiers for Criminal Acts in Wars.* New York: Random House.

Feig, Konnilyn G. 1981. *Hitler's Death Camps: The Sanity of Madness.* New York: Holmes & Meier.

Fénelon, Fania, with Marcelle Routier. 1977. *Playing for Time.* Trans. Judith Landry. New York: Atheneum. First published in French in 1976 as *Sursis pour l'orchestre.*

Fischer, Ernst. 1970. *Erinnerungen und Reflexionen.* Hamburg: Rowohlt.

Ford, Herbert. 1966. *Flee the Captor.* Nashville, Tenn.: Southern Publishing Association.

Fraenkel, Josef, ed. 1967. *The Jews of Austria: Essays on Their Life, History and Destruction.* London: Vallentine, Mitchell.

Francis, Mark. 1985. *The Viennese Enlightenment.* London: Croom Helm.

Frank, Anne. 1991. *The Diary of a Young Girl.* Ed. Otto H. Frank and Mirjam Pressler. Trans. Susan Massotty. New York: Doubleday. First published in Dutch in 1947.

Frankl, Viktor E. 1984. *Man's Search for Meaning,* 3rd ed. Trans. Ilse Lasch. New York: Simon & Schuster. First published in German in 1946 as *Ein Psychologe erlebt das Konzentrationslager.*

Friedman, Philip. 1981. *Roads to Extinction: Essays on the Holocaust.* Ed. Ada June Friedman. New York: Conference of Jewish Studies.

Funder, Friedrich. 1963. *From Empire to Republic.* Trans. Barbara Waldstein. New York: A. Unger.

Gainham, Sarah. 1979. *The Habsburg Twilight: Tales from Vienna.* New York: Atheneum.

Garliński, Józef. 1975. *Fighting Auschwitz: The Resistance Movement in the Concentration Camp.* New York: Holmes & Meier. First published in Polish in 1974 as *Oświęcim walczacy.*

Gartenberg, Egon. 1968. *Vienna–Its Musical Heritage.* University Park: Pennsylvania State University Press.

———. 1978. *Mahler: The Man and His Music.* New York: Schirmer Books.

Gay, Peter. 1978. *Freud, Jews and Other Germans: Masters and Victims in Modernist Culture.* New York: Oxford University Press.

Gehl, Jürgen. 1963. *Austria, Germany, and the Anschluss, 1931–1938.* London: Oxford University Press.

Gilbert, Martin. 1978. *The Holocaust: Maps and Photographs.* London: Board of Deputies of British Jews.

———. 1979. *Final Journey: The Fate of the Jews in Nazi Europe.* New York: Mayflower Books.

———. 1981. *Auschwitz and the Allies.* New York: Holt, Rinehart and Winston.

———. 1986. *The Holocaust: A History of the Jews of Europe During the Second World War.* New York: Holt, Rinehart and Winston.

———. 1993. *Atlas of the Holocaust.* New York: William Morrow. First published in London in 1982.

———. 1997. *Holocaust Journey: Travelling in Search of the Past.* New York: Columbia University Press.

Gill, Anton. 1988. *The Journey Back from Hell: An Oral History: Conversations with Concentration Camp Survivors,* first U.S. ed. New York: William Morrow.

Goldner, Franz. 1977. *Die österreichische Emigration, 1938–1945,* 2nd enlarged ed. Vienna: Herold. Also published in English in 1979 as *Austrian Emigration, 1938–1945.*

Gradenwitz, Peter. 1996. *The Music of Israel: From the Biblical Era to Modern Times,* 2nd ed. Portland, Ore.: Amadeus Press. First published in 1949 in New York as *The Music of Israel: Its Rise and Growth Through 5000 Years.*

Graf, Max. 1969. *Legend of a Musical City: The Story of Vienna.* New York: Greenwood Press. First published in 1945 in New York by Philosophical Library.

Gregor, Joseph. 1933. *Weltgeschichte des Theaters.* Zurich: Phaidon.

Gregor, Neil. 1998. *Daimler-Benz in the Third Reich.* New Haven, Conn.: Yale University Press.

Gulick, Charles A. 1948. *Austria: From Habsburg to Hitler.* Vol. 1, *Labor's Workshop of Democracy.* Berkeley: University of California Press.

Gutman, Yisrael, and Michael Berenbaum, eds. 1994. *Anatomy of the Auschwitz Death Camp.* Bloomington: Indiana University Press, in association with the United States Holocaust Memorial Museum, Washington, D.C.

Halasz, Nicholas. 1955. *Captain Dreyfus: The Story of a Mass Hysteria.* New York: Simon & Schuster.

Hanfstängl, Ernst. 1970. *15 Jahre mit Hitler.* Munich: Piper.

Hart, Kitty. 1974. *I Am Alive.* London: Century.

———. 1982. *Return to Auschwitz: The Remarkable Story of a Girl Who Survived the Holocaust.* New York: Atheneum.

Hartman, Geoffrey H. 1986. *Bitburg in Moral and Political Perspective.* Bloomington: Indiana University Press.

———, ed. 1994. *Holocaust Remembrance: The Shapes of Memory.* Cambridge, Mass.: Blackwell.

Heideking, Jürgen. 1996. *American Intelligence and the German Resistance to Hitler: A Documentary History.* Boulder, Colo.: Westview Press.

Hilberg, Raul. 1985. *The Destruction of the European Jews,* rev. ed., 3 vols. New York: Holmes & Meier.

———. 1992. *Perpetrators, Victims, Bystanders: The Jewish Catastrophe, 1933–1945.* New York: HarperCollins.

Hill, Mavis. 1965. *Auschwitz in England.* New York: Stein and Day.

Hillesum, Etty. 1983. *An Interrupted Life: The Diaries of Etty Hillesum, 1941–43.* Trans. Arnold J. Pomerans. New York: Pantheon. First published in Dutch in 1981 as *Het verstoorde leven.*

———. 1986. *Letters from Westerbork.* Trans. Arnold J. Pomerans. New York: Pantheon. First published in Dutch in 1981 as *Het denkende hart van de barak.*

Hitler, Adolf. 1939. *Mein Kampf,* annotated ed. New York: Reynal & Hitchcock.

Hofmann, Paul. 1988. *The Viennese: Splendor, Twilight, and Exile.* New York: Anchor Press.

Höss, Rudolf. 1992. *Death Dealer: The Memoirs of the SS Kommandant at Auschwitz.* Ed. Steven Paskuly. Trans. Andrew Pollinger. Buffalo, N.Y.: Prometheus Books. First published in Polish in 1956 as *Wspomnienia komendanta obozu oświęcimskiego.*

Iggers, Wilma Abeles. 1967. *Karl Kraus: A Viennese Critic of the Twentieth Century.* The Hague: Martinus Nijhoff.

International Auschwitz Committee. 1986. *Nazi Medicine: Doctors, Victims and Medicine in Auschwitz.* New York: Howard Fertig.

Irving, David. 1987. *Hess: The Missing Years, 1941–1945.* London: Macmillan.

Jewish Community Relations Council / Anti-Defamation League of Minnesota and the Dakotas. 1990. *Witnesses to the Holocaust: An Oral History.* Ed. Rhoda G. Lewin. New York: Twayne Publishers.

Kann, Robert A. 1965. *A Study in Austrian Intellectual History: From Late Baroque to Romanticism.* London: Thames & Hudson.

Kaplan, Gilbert, ed. 1995. *The Mahler Album.* New York: The Kaplan Foundation.

Kater, Michael H. 1997. *The Twisted Muse: Musicians and Their Music in the Third Reich.* New York: Oxford University Press.

Keegan, Susanne. 1992. *The Bride of the Wind: The Life of Alma Mahler-Werfel.* First American edition. New York: Viking.

Kershaw, Ian. 1999. *Hitler. 1889–1936: Hubris.* New York: W. W. Norton.

Keyserlingk, Robert H. 1988. *Austria in World War II: An Anglo-American Dilemma.* Kingston, Montreal: McGill–Queen's University Press.

Kielar, Wieslaw. 1980. *Anus Mundi: 1,500 Days in Auschwitz/Birkenau.* Trans. Susanne Flatauer. New York: Times Books. First published in Polish in 1972.

Kieser, Egbert. 1997. *Hitler on the Doorstep: Operation "Sea Lion": The German Plan to Invade Britain, 1940.* Trans. Helmut Bögler. Annapolis, Md.: Naval Institute Press. First published in German in 1987.

Klarsfeld, Beate. 1975. *Wherever They May Be!* Trans. Monroe Stearns and Natalie Gerardi. New York: Vanguard. First published in French in 1972 as *Partout où ils seront.*

Klarsfeld, Serge. 1978. *Collection of 2,000 Documents of German Authorities Concerning the Persecution of the Jewish Population in France: 1940–1944.* Photocopies deposited in the YIVO Institute for Jewish Research, New York. Originally published in French in 1978 as *Recueil de 2000 documents des dossiers des autorités allemandes concernant la persécution de la population juive en France: 1940–1944,* 8 vols.

Klarsfeld, Serge, ed. 1978. *The Holocaust and the Neo-Nazi Mythomania.* Trans. Barbara Rucci. New York: The Beate Klarsfeld Foundation.

Klodziński, Stanisław. 1961–1985. Various papers submitted to *Przegląd Lekarskiego.* Cracow: Drukarnia Narodowa.

Klusacek, Christine, Herbert Seiner, and Kurt Stimmer, eds. 1971. *Dokumentation zur österreichischen Zeitgeschichte, 1938–1945.* Vienna: Jugend und Volk.

Knapp, Gabriele. 1996. *Das Frauenorchester in Auschwitz: musikalische Zwangsarbeit und ihre Bewältigung.* Hamburg: Von Bockel.

Kokoschka, Oskar. 1974. *My Life.* Trans. David Britt. London: Thames & Hudson.

Kolneder, Walter. 1998. *The Amadeus Book of the Violin: Construction, History, and Music.* Ed. and trans. Reinhard G. Pauly. Portland, Ore.: Amadeus Press.

Kraus, Karl. 1974. *The Last Days of Mankind.* Ed. Frederick Ungar. Trans. Alexander Gode and Ellen Wright. New York: Frederick Ungar. First published in German in 1922 as *Die letzten Tage der Menschheit.*

———. 1976a. *In These Great Times: A Karl Kraus Reader.* Ed. Harry Zohn. Trans. Joseph Fabry, Max Knight, Karl F. Ross, and Harry Zohn. Montreal: Engendra Press.

———. 1976b. *Selected Aphorisms.* Ed. and trans. Harry Zohn. Montreal: Engendra Press.

———. 1977. *No Compromise: Selected Writings of Karl Kraus.* Ed. Frederick Ungar. New York: Frederick Ungar.

Kraus, Ota Benjamin, and Erich Kulka. 1966. *The Death Factory: Documents on Auschwitz.* New York: Pergamon. First published in Czech in 1966 as *Útěk z tábora smrti.*

Křenek, Ernst. 1966. *Exploring Music.* Trans. Margaret Shenfield and Geoffrey Skelton. London: Calder & Boyars. First published in German in 1958 as *Zur Sprache gebracht.*

Kulka, Erich. 1986. *Escape from Auschwitz.* South Hadley, Mass.: Begin and Garvey.

Laks, Szymon. 1989. *Music of Another World.* Trans. Chester A. Kisiel. Evanston, Ill.: Northwestern University Press. First published in French in 1948 as *Musiques d'un autre monde.*

Lang, Berel, ed. 1988. *Writing and the Holocaust.* New York: Holmes & Meier.

Langbein, Hermann. 1980. *Menschen in Auschwitz.* Frankfurt: Ullstein.

———. 1994. *Against All Hope: Resistance in the Nazi Concentration Camps, 1938–1945.* Trans. Harry Zohn. New York: Paragon House. First published in German in 1980 as *—nicht wie die Schafe zur Schlachtbank.*

Langbein, Hermann, Robert Karl, and Ludwig Mulka. 1965. *Der Auschwitz-Prozess: Eine Dokumentation,* 2 vols. Vienna: Europa.

Lasker-Wallfisch, Anita. 1996. *Inherit the Truth: 1939–1945.* London: Giles de la Mare.

Lennhoff, Eugene. 1938. *The Last Five Hours of Austria.* New York: Frederick A. Stokes.

Levi, Erik. 1994. *Music in the Third Reich.* New York: St. Martin's Press.

Levi, Primo. 1961. *Survival in Auschwitz.* Trans. Stuart Woolf. New York: Collier. First published in Italian in 1958 as *Se questo è un uomo* and in English in 1958 as *If This Is a Man.*

Lifton, Robert Jay. 1986. *The Nazi Doctors: Medical Killing and the Psychology of Genocide.* New York: Basic Books.

Lingens-Reiner, Ella. 1948. *Prisoners of Fear.* London: Victor Gollancz.

Littlejohn, David. 1972. *The Patriotic Traitors: A History of Collaboration in German-Occupied Europe, 1940–45.* Garden City, N.Y.: Doubleday.

Loewenstein, Karl. 1939. *Hitler's Germany: The Nazi Background to War.* New York: Macmillan.

Lorant, Stefan. 1974. *Sieg Heil! (Hail to Victory): An Illustrated History of Germany from Bismarck to Hitler.* New York: W. W. Norton.

Luža, Radomír. 1975. *Austro-German Relations in the Anschluss Era.* Princeton, N.J.: Princeton University Press.

Mahler, Alma. 1976. *Gustav Mahler: Memories and Letters,* 3rd ed. Ed. Donald Mitchell. Trans. Basil Creighton. Seattle: University of Washington Press. First published in German in 1940 as *Gustav Mahler: Erinnerungen und Briefe.* First English edition published in New York by Viking.

Mahler-Werfel, Alma. 1999. *Diaries: 1898–1902.* Selected and trans. Antony Beaumont. Ithaca, N.Y.: Cornell University Press. First published in Germany, ed. and trans. Antony Beaumont and Susanne Rode-Breymann.

Mann, Thomas. 1979. *Tagebücher, 1918–1921.* Frankfurt: S. Fischer.

Marek, George R. 1974. *The Eagles Die: Franz Joseph, Elisabeth, and Their Austria.* London: Hart-Davis, MacGibbon.

Marrus, Michael Robert. 1987. *The Holocaust in History.* Hanover, N.H.: Brandeis University Press / University Press of New England.

———. 1989. *The Victims of the Holocaust.* Westport, Conn.: Meckler.

Marrus, Michael Robert, and Robert O. Paxton. 1981. *Vichy France and the Jews.* New York: Basic Books.

Mayer, Arno J. 1988. *Why Did the Heavens Not Darken? The "Final Solution" in History.* New York: Pantheon.

McCagg, William O., Jr. 1989. *A History of Habsburg Jews, 1670–1918.* Bloomington: Indiana University Press.

Mendelsohn, John, ed. 1982. *The Holocaust: Selected Documents in Eighteen Volumes.* Vol. 9, *Liquidation Through Labor.* New York: Garland.

Michalik, Krystyna. 1967. *A History of KL-Auschwitz.* Ed. Kazimierz Smoleń. Translated from the Polish. Auschwitz: Państwowe Muzeum.

Micheels, Louis J. 1989. *Doctor #117641: A Holocaust Memoir.* New Haven, Conn.: Yale University Press.

Millu, Liana. 1991. *Smoke Over Birkenau.* Trans. Lynne Sharon Schwartz. Philadelphia: Jewish Publication Society. First published in Italian in 1986 as *Il fumo di Birkenau.*

Mitcham, Samuel W., Jr., and Gene Mueller. 1992. *Hitler's Commanders.* Lanham, Md.: Scarborough House.

Molden, Fritz. 1979. *Exploding Star: A Young Austrian Against Hitler.* Trans. Peter and Betty Ross. New York: Morrow. First published in German in 1976 as *Fepolinski und Waschlapski auf dem berstenden Stern.*

Morgan, Ted. 1990. *An Uncertain Hour: The French, the Germans, the Jews, the Klaus Barbie Trial, and the City of Lyon, 1940–1945.* New York: Arbor House / William Morrow.

Morton, Frederic. 1979. *A Nervous Splendor: Vienna 1888/1889.* Boston: Little, Brown.

Müller, Filip, with Helmut Freitag. 1979. *Auschwitz Inferno: The Testimony of a Sonderkommando.* Ed. and trans. Susanne Flatauer. London: Routledge and Kegan Paul.

Murphy, Brendan. 1983. *The Butcher of Lyon: The Story of Infamous Nazi Klaus Barbie.* New York: Empire.

Nahon, Marco. 1989. *Birkenau: The Camp of Death.* Ed. Steven Bowman. Trans. from the original French typescript by Jacqueline Havaux Bowers. Tuscaloosa: University of Alabama Press.

Neuman, H. J. 1970. *Arthur Seyss-Inquart.* Graz, Austria: Verlag Styria.

Nielsen, Erika, ed. 1982. *Focus on Vienna 1900: Change and Continuity in Literature, Music, Art and Intellectual History.* Vol. 4, Houston German Studies Series, ed. Edward R. Haymes. Munich: Wilhelm Fink

Nomberg-Przytyk, Sara. 1985. *Auschwitz: True Tales from a Grotesque Land.* Ed. Eli Pfefferkorn and David H. Hirsch. Trans. Rosalyn Hirsch. Chapel Hill: University of North Carolina Press. Translated from an unpublished Polish manuscript.

Nyiszli, Miklós. 1993. *Auschwitz: A Doctor's Eyewitness Account.* Trans. from the Hungarian by Tibère Kremer and Richard Seaver. New York: Arcade Publishing. First published ca. 1960 in New York by F. Fell.

Overesch, Manfred. 1982. *Chronik deutscher Zeitgeschichte.* Vols. 1 and 2, *Das Dritte Reich: 1933–45.* Düsseldorf: Droste.

Pawełczyńska, Anna. 1979. *Values and Violence in Auschwitz: A Sociological Analysis.* Ed. and trans. Catherine Leach. Berkeley: University of California Press. First published in Polish as *Wartosci a przemoc.*

Perl, Gisella. 1979. *I Was a Doctor in Auschwitz.* New York: Arno.

Phillips, Raymond, ed. 1949. *Trial of Josef Kramer and Forty-four Others (The Belsen Trial).* London: William Hodge.

Pirani, Leila Doubleday. 1962. *Letter to My Grandchildren.* Unpublished manuscript in two volumes. Copy housed in the Mahler-Rosé Room, Music Library, University of Western Ontario, London, Canada.

Posner, Gerald L., and John Ware. 1986. *Mengele: The Complete Story.* New York: McGraw-Hill.

Prawy, Marcel. 1970. *The Vienna Opera.* New York: Praeger.

Prégardier, Elisabeth, and Anne Mohr. 1994. *Elf Frauen. Leben in Wahrheit: Margita Schwalbová: Eine Ärztin berichtet aus Auschwitz-Birkenau 1942–1945.* Annweiler: Plöger Verlag.

Presser, Jacob. 1969. *The Destruction of the Dutch Jews.* Trans. Arnold Pomerans. New York: E. P. Dutton.

Price, Billy F. 1984. *Adolf Hitler: The Unknown Artist.* Houston, Texas: Billy F. Price. Published in German in 1983 as *Adolf Hitler als Maler und Zeichner.*

Puritz, Gerd. 1993. *Elisabeth Schumann: A Biography.* Ed. and trans. Joy Puritz. London: A. Deutsch. Reprinted, with corrections, 1996 by Grant & Cutler Ltd., London.

Riefenstahl, Leni. 1993. *Leni Riefenstahl: A Memoir.* New York: St. Martin's Press. First published in German in 1987 as *Memoiren.*

Rittner, Carol, and John K. Roth, eds. 1993. *Different Voices: Women and the Holocaust.* New York: Paragon House.

Rose, Leesha. 1978. *The Tulips Are Red.* South Brunswick, N.J.: A. S. Barnes.

Royal Institute of International Affairs. 1943. *Chronology of Principal Events.* No. 10, "1 April to 30 June 1943." London: Chatham House.

Saerchinger, César. 1957. *Artur Schnabel: A Biography.* New York: Dodd, Mead.

Salzer, Thomas F. 1966. *Ueberreuter: Carl Ueberreuter Druck und Verlag: 100 Jahre in Besitz der Famillie Salzer.* Vienna: Ueberreuter.

Schloss, Eva, with Evelyn Julia Kent. 1988. *Eva's Story: A Survivor's Tale.* New York: St. Martin's Press.

Schnabel, Artur. 1963. *My Life and Music.* New York: St. Martin's Press.

Schnabel, Ernst. 1958. *Anne Frank: A Portrait in Courage.* Trans. Richard and Clara Winston. New York: Harcourt, Brace & World. First published in German in 1958 as *Anne Frank: Spur Eines Kindes.*

Schnitzler, Arthur. 1970. *My Youth in Vienna.* Trans. Catherine Hutter. New York: Holt, Rinehart and Winston. First published in German as *Jugend in Wien.*

———. 1992. *The Road into the Open.* Trans. Roger Byers. Berkeley: University of California Press. First published in German in 1908 as *Der Weg ins Freie.*

Schorske, Carl E. 1979. *Fin-de-siècle Vienna: Politics and Culture.* New York: Knopf.

Sedgwick, Henry Dwight. 1939. *Vienna: The Biography of a Bygone City.* Indianapolis: Bobbs-Merrill.

Sereny, Gitta. 1995. *Albert Speer: His Battle with Truth.* New York: Knopf.

Shirer, William L. 1990. *The Rise and Fall of the Third Reich: A History of Nazi Germany,* 30th anniversary ed. New York: Touchstone. First published in 1960 in New York by Simon & Schuster.

Simbrunner, Peter. 1987. *Wiener Strassennamen von A bis Z.* Vienna: Ueberreuter.

Slezak, Leo. 1948. *Mein Lebensmärchen.* Munich: Piper.

———.1966. *Mein lieber Bub: Briefe eines besorgten Vaters.* Munich: Piper.

Slezak, Margarete. 1953. *Der Apfel fällt nicht weit vom Stamm.* Munich: Piper.

Slezak, Walter. 1962. *What Time's the Next Swan?* New York: Doubleday.

Smith, Joan Allen. 1986. *Schoenberg and His Circle: A Viennese Portrait.* New York: Schirmer Books.

Smoleń, Kazimierz. 1995. *Auschwitz, 1940–1945.* Trans. Krystyna Michalik. Albuquerque, N.M.: Route 66 Publishing. First published in Polish in 1978 as *Oświęcim, 1940–1945.*

Spiel, Hilde. 1987. *Vienna's Golden Years (1866 to 1938).* London: Weidenfeld and Nicolson.

Strasser, Otto. 1978. *Otto Strasser: Und dafür wird man noch bezahlt. (Mein Leben mit den Wiener Philharmonikern).* Munich: Deutscher Taschenbuch Verlag.

Švalbová, Manca. 1964. *Vyhasnuté oči.* Bratislava: Osveta.

Świebocka, Teresa, ed. 1993. *Auschwitz: A History in Photographs.* 1993. English ed. by Jonathan Webber and Connie Wilsack. Bloomington: Indiana University Press, in association with the Auschwitz-Birkenau State Museum, Oświęcim. First published in Polish in 1990 as *Auschwitz: Zbrodnia przeciwko ludzkości.*

Syberberg, Hans Jürgen. 1982. *Hitler: A Film from Germany.* Trans. Joachim Neugroschel. New York: Farrar, Straus and Giroux. First published in German in 1978 as *Hitler, ein Film aus Deutschland.*

Szmaglewska, Seweryna. 1947. *Smoke Over Birkenau.* Trans. Jadwiga Rynas. New York: Henry Holt. First published in Polish on 1945 as *Dymy nad Birkenau.*

Tedeschi, Giuliana. 1992. *There Is a Place on Earth: A Woman in Birkenau.* Trans. Tim Parks. New York: Pantheon. First published in Italian in 1988 as *C'è un punto della terra.*

Timms, Edward. 1986. *Karl Kraus, Apocalyptic Satirist: Culture and Catastrophe in Habsburg Vienna.* New Haven, Conn: Yale University Press.

Toland, John. 1976. *Adolf Hitler.* Garden City, N.Y.: Doubleday.

Troller, Norbert. 1991. *Theresienstadt: Hitler's Gift to the Jews.* Ed. Joel Shatzky. Trans. Susan E. Cernyak-Spatz. Chapel Hill: University of North Carolina Press.

Umbreit, Hans. 1968. *Der Militärbefehlshaber in Frankreich.* Boppard am Rhein: H. Boldt.

Větrovcová, Margot. 1979. "Ctyri Roky" (Four years), in *Bojovali Jsme a Zvitezili* (We Fought and We Won). Ed. Nakladateistvi Svoboda. Trans. Sandford Goldstein. Publication no. 4406. Prague.

Vratislavský, Jan. 1970. *Váša Příhoda.* Prague-Bratislava. Editio Supraphon.

Vrba, Rudolf, and Alan Bestic. 1964. *I Cannot Forgive.* New York: Bantam.

Wagner, Dieter, and Gerhard Tomkowitz. 1971. *Anschluss: The Week Hitler Seized Vienna.* Trans. Geoffrey Strachan. New York: St. Martin's Press.

Waissenberger, Robert, ed. 1984. *Vienna, 1890–1920.* New York: Rizzoli. First published in German in 1984 as *Wien, 1890–1920.*

Walter, Bruno. 1946. *Theme and Variations.* Trans. James A. Galston. New York: Knopf. Original German manuscript first published in 1947 as *Thema und Variationen: Erinnerungen und Gedanken.*

———. 1959. *Letters, 1894–1962.* Trans. supervised by Lotte Walter Lindt. New York: Knopf. Original German manuscript first published in 1969 as *Briefe, 1894–1962.*

Webb, Anthony M., ed. 1949. *Trial of Wolfgang Zeuss, Magnus Wochner, Emil Meier, Peter Straub, Fritz Hartjenstein, Franz Berg, Werner Rohde, Emil*

Bruttel, Kurt Aus Dem Bruch and Harberg (The Natzweiler Trial). London: William Hodge.

Weinzierl, Erika. 1975. *Öesterreich: Zeitgeschichte in Bildern, 1918–1975.* Innsbruck: Tyrolia.

Weinzierl, Erika, and Kurt Skalnik. 1983. *Österreich: Geschichte der Ersten Republik.* Graz, Austria: Styria.

Wellers, Georges. 1973. *L'Étoile jaune à l'heure de Vichy.* Paris: Fayard.

Weyers, Wolfgang. 1998. *Death of Medicine in Nazi Germany.* Ed. A. Bernard Ackerman. Philadelphia: Ardor Scribendi.

Wiesel, Elie. 1982. *Night,* 25th anniversary ed. Trans. Stella Rodway. New York: Bantam. First published in French in 1958 as *La Nuit;* first American ed., 1960.

Williams, Elvet. 1975. *Arbeitskommando.* London: Victor Gollancz.

Williams, Eric. 1979. *The Wooden Horse,* rev. ed. London: Collins.

Wistrich, Robert. 1982. *Who's Who in Nazi Germany.* London: Weidenfeld and Nicolson.

Wulf, Josef. 1964. *Theater und Film im Dritten Reich: Eine Dokumentation.* Gütersloh: Sigbert Mohn.

Yad Vashem. 1957–. *Studies on the European Jewish Catastrophe and Resistance.* Jerusalem: Yad Vashem Remembrance Authority. Published irregularly beginning in 1957.

———. 1981. *Documents of the Holocaust.* Ed. Yitzak Arad, Yisrael Gutman, Abraham Margaliot. Jerusalem: Ktav.

Yahil, Leni. 1990. *The Holocaust: The Fate of European Jewry.* Trans. Ina Friedman and Haya Galai. New York: Oxford University Press. First Hebrew edition published in 1987 as *Sho 'ah.*

YIVO Colloquium. 1972. *Imposed Jewish Governing Bodies Under Nazi Rule.* New York: YIVO Institute for Jewish Research.

Zuckerkandl, Berta. 1939. *My Life and History.* Trans. John Sommerfield. New York: Knopf.

Zweig, Stefan. 1943. *The World of Yesterday: An Autobiography.* New York: Viking. Published in German in 1982 as *Die Welt von Gestern.*

Żywulska, Krystyna. 1951. *I Came Back.* New York: Roy Publishers. First published in Polish in 1951 as *Przeżytam Oświęcim.*

HOLOCAUST RESOURCES ON THE WORLD WIDE WEB

Cybrary of the Holocaust (http://www.remember.org)

"Hopesite" by Victoria Holocaust Remembrance and Education Society (http://veritas.nizkor.org/~hopesite)

Museum of Tolerance Online Multimedia Learning Center (http://motlc.wiesenthal.com)

Simon Wiesenthal Center (http://www.wiesenthal.com)
The Sydney Jewish Museum of the Holocaust and Australian Jewish History (http://www.join.org.au/sydjmus)
U.S. Holocaust Memorial Museum (http://www.ushmm.org)
Yad Vashem, Israel (http://www.yad-vashem.org.il)
YIVO Institute for Jewish Research (http://www.baruch.cuny.edu/yivo/Holocaust.html)

The Mahler-Rosé Family

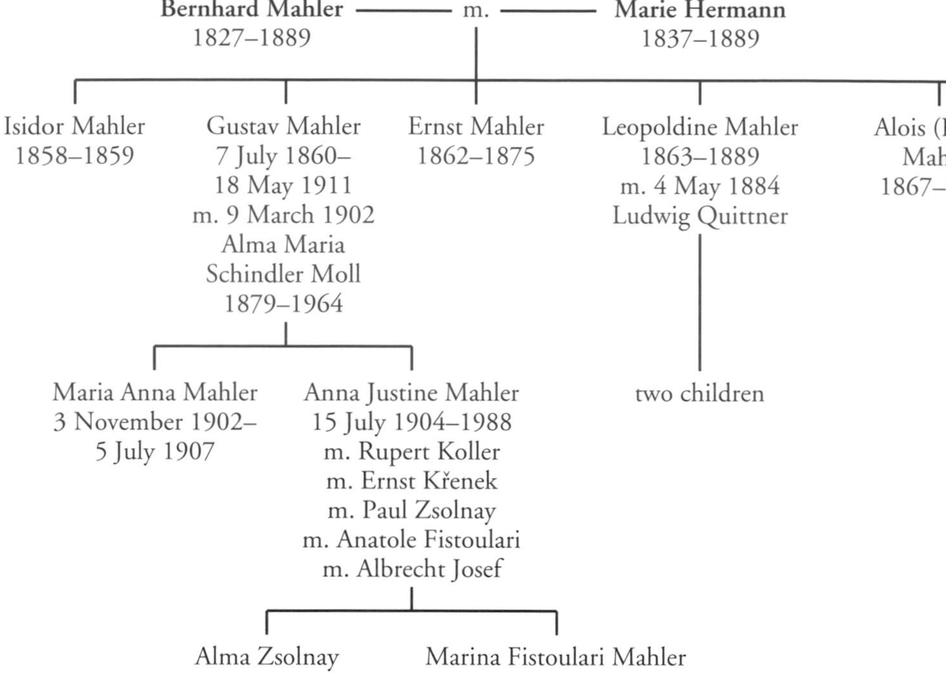

Bernhard Mahler 1827–1889
m.
Marie Hermann 1837–1889
Isidor Mahler 1858–1859
Gustav Mahler 7 July 1860– 18 May 1911 m. 9 March 1902 Alma Maria Schindler Moll 1879–1964
Ernst Mahler 1862–1875
Leopoldine Mahler 1863–1889 m. 4 May 1884 Ludwig Quittner
Maria Anna Mahler 3 November 1902– 5 July 1907
Anna Justine Mahler 15 July 1904–1988 m. Rupert Koller m. Ernst Křenek m. Paul Zsolnay m. Anatole Fistoulari m. Albrecht Josef
two children
Alma Zsolnay
Marina Fistoulari Mahler

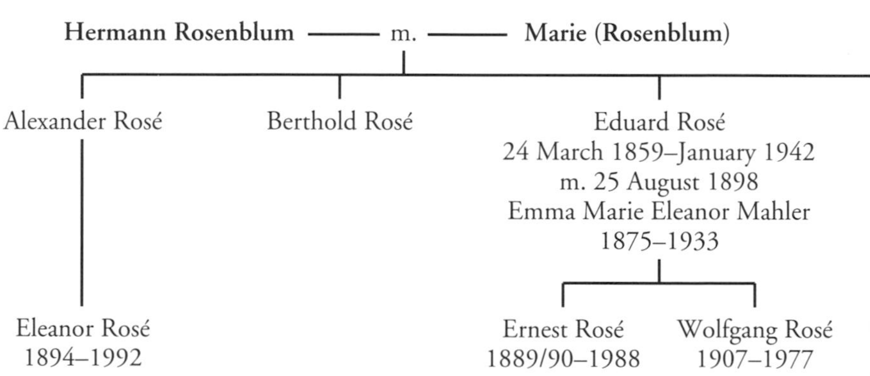

Hermann Rosenblum
m.
Marie (Rosenblum)
Alexander Rosé
Berthold Rosé
Eduard Rosé 24 March 1859–January 1942 m. 25 August 1898 Emma Marie Eleanor Mahler 1875–1933
Eleanor Rosé 1894–1992
Ernest Rosé 1889/90–1988
Wolfgang Rosé 1907–1977

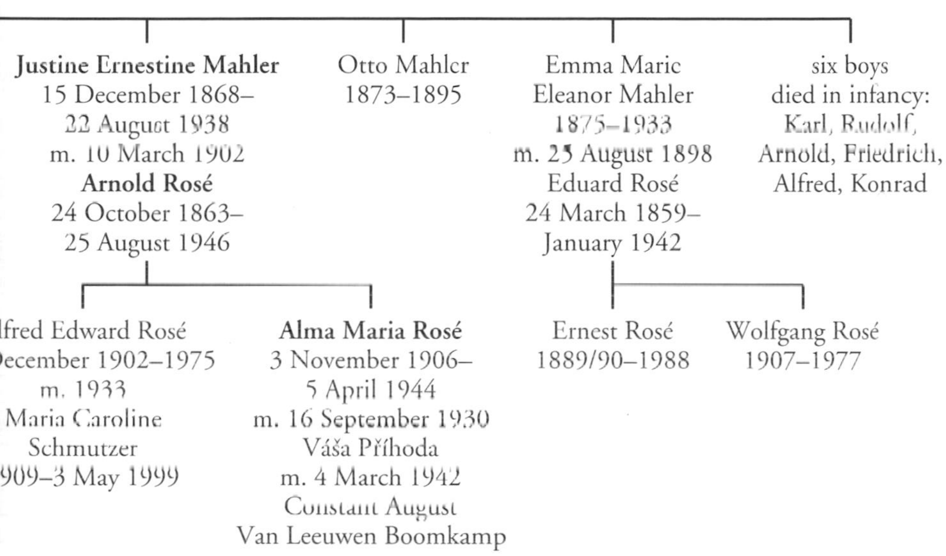

Arnold Rosé
24 October 1863–25 August 1946
m. 10 March 1902
Justine Ernestine Mahler
15 December 1868–22 August 1938

Alfred Edward Rosé
11 December 1902–1975
m. 1933
Maria Caroline Schmutzer
1909–3 May 1999

Alma Maria Rosé
3 November 1906–5 April 1944
m. 16 September 1930
Váša Příhoda
m. 4 March 1942
Constant August Van Leeuwen Boomkamp

The Women's Orchestra of Auschwitz-Birkenau

ALPHABETICAL LIST BY GIVEN NAME

The following list is a combined effort, the result of research by interviews and written communications with survivors in Israel, England, Belgium, France, Holland, Australia, Germany, Poland, the former Czechoslovakia, and the United States. (Inquiries to the former Soviet Union failed to reveal the full names of several Russian and Ukrainian members of the women's orchestra.) The record remains incomplete. Further information will be appreciated and incorporated into future editions of this book.

The list includes members of the orchestra throughout its existence, from its founding in April 1943 until the evacuation of Jewish players to Bergen-Belsen in October 1944. Maiden names precede married names except in the case of orchestra members who have shown a preference for hyphenated forms. Alternate spellings appear in parentheses. Pseudonyms used in Fénelon 1977 and Knapp 1996 are not to be confused with the actual names listed here.

Name	*Nationality*	*No.*	*Role(s) in Music Block*	*Block Member*
Ala (Alla) Gres	Russia		pianist, music copyist	Dec 43–Oct 44
Alma Rosé (Jewish) (d. Apr 44)	Austria	50381	conductor/kapo, violinist and pianist	Aug 43–Apr 44
Anita Lasker-Wallfisch (Jewish)	Germany	69388	cellist	Oct 43–Oct 44

Name	*Nationality*	*No.*	*Role(s) in Music Block*	*Block Member*
Bronia: *see* Pronia (Bronia)				
Claire (half-Jewish) (d. after 45)	France		singer	Jan 44–Oct 44
Danuta (Danka) Kollakowa (d. after 45)	Poland	6831	percussionist, pianist, music copyist	Apr 43–Oct 44
Dorys (Jewish) (d. Nov 43)	Germany		singer	Aug 43–Nov 43
Else Felstein (Jewish) (d. 1964)	Belgium		violinist, music copyist	May 43–Oct 44
Emmy (Jewish)	Switzerland		singer	Sep 43–Oct 44
Esther Loewy Bejarano (half-Jewish)	Germany	41948	recorder (& piccolo?) player, guitarist, accordionist	May 43–Oct 43 (moved)
Eva Steiner Adam (Jewish)	Transylvania	A-17139	singer, music copyist	May 44–Oct 44
Ewa Stojowska (d. 1996)	Poland	64098	singer, music librarian, music copyist	Nov 43–Oct 44
Fania Fénelon (half-Jewish) (d. Dec 83)	France	74862	singer, orchestrator	Jan 44–Oct 44
Fanny Korenblum Birkenwald (Jewish) (d. Aug 92)	Belgium		mandolinist, singer	Jun 43–Oct 44
Flora Schrijver Jacobs (Jewish)	Holland	61278	accordionist	Aug 43–Oct 44
Founia (Funja)	Poland		head of kitchen	May 44–Oct 44
Helen "Zippy" Spitzer Tichauer (Jewish)	Czechoslovakia	2286	mandolinist	Apr 43–Oct 44
Helena Dunicz-Niwińska	Poland	64118	violinist, concert mistress	Oct 43–Oct 44
Hélène Rounder (Jewish) (d. after 80)	France		violinist	Sep 43–Oct 44
Hélène Scheps (Jewish)	Belgium		violinist, concert mistress	Aug 43–Oct 44
Helga (Elga or Olga?) Schiessel (Jewish) (d. after 45)	Germany		percussionist	Aug 43–Oct 44

Name	*Nationality*	*No.*	*Role(s) in Music Block*	*Block Member*
Henryka Czapla	Poland		violinist	Jun 43–Sep 43 (moved)
Henryka Gałązka	Poland		violinist	May 43–Aug 43 (moved)
Hilde Grünbaum Zimche (Jewish)	Germany		percussionist, music copyist	May 43–Oct 44
Ibi	Hungary		violinist	Oct 44
Irena Łagowska (d. after 45)	Poland	49995	violinist	Jul 43–Oct 44
Irena Walaszczyk Wachowicz (d. Dec 85)	Poland	43575	mandolinist, block caretaker	Apr 43–Oct 44
Jadwiga (Wisia/Wisha) Zatorska (d. Jan 81)	Poland	36243	violinist	Apr 43–Oct 44
Julie Stroumsa Menache (Jewish) (d. 1987)	Greece		violinist	Sep 43–Oct 44
Karla Wagenberg Hyman (Jewish) (sister of Sylvia)	Germany		recorder & piccolo player	Apr 43–Oct 44
Kazimiera Małys Kowalczyk	Poland	48295	mandolinist, music copyist	Jun 43–Oct 44
Lily Assael (Jewish) (sister of Yvette) (d. 1989)	Greece		accordionist, music copyist	May 43–Oct 44
Lily Mathé (Jewish) (d. 1993)	Hungary		violinist	May 44–Oct 44
Lota (Lola) "Tante" Kröner (Jewish) (sister of Maria) (d. 1945)	Germany		flutist	Jul 43–Oct 44
Lotte Berran (Jewish) (d. after 80)	Austria		violinist	May 44–Oct 44
Lotte Lebedová (Jewish) (d. after 60)	Czecho-slovakia		guitarist, singer	Jul 43–Oct 44
Margot Anzenbacher Větrovcová (Jewish)	Czecho-slovakia		guitarist, music copyist, interpreter	Aug 43–Oct 44
Maria	Russia		block senior	Jan 44–Oct 44
Maria Bielicka (d. after 45)	Poland		singer	May 44–Oct 44

Name	*Nationality*	*No.*	*Role(s) in Music Block*	*Block Member*
Maria Kröner (Jewish) (sister of Lota) (d. Aug 43)	Germany		cellist	Jul 43–Aug 43
Maria Langenfeld-Hnydowa	Poland	42873	violinist, block caretaker	May 43–Oct 44
Maria Moś-Wdowik (d. Jun 94)	Poland	6111	mandolinist, music copyist	Apr 43–Oct 44
Masza (Masha) (Jewish) (d. Dec 43)	Poland		mandolinist	Jun 43–Dec 43
Olga	Ukraine		mandolinist	Jun 43–Oct 44
Pronia (Bronia)	Ukraine		guitarist	May 43–Oct 44
Rachela Olevsky Zelmanowitz (Jewish) (also spelled Olewski) (d. 1989)	Poland		mandolinist	Jun 43–Oct 44
Regina (Rivka) Kupferberg Bacia (Jewish)	Poland	51095	music copyist, block worker	Aug 43–Oct 44
Ruth Bassin (Jewish) (d. 1989)	Germany	41883	piccolo player	Apr 43–Oct 44
Sonya Winogradowa	Russia		pianist, music copyist, conductor/kapo	Dec 43–Oct 44
Stefania Baruch (d. after 45)	Poland	6874	guitarist, mandolinist, block caretaker	Apr 43–Oct 44
(Madame) Steiner (mother of Eva)	Transylvania		violinist, kitchen helper	Mar 44–Oct 44
Sylvia Wagenberg Calif (Jewish) (sister of Karla)	Germany		recorder player	Apr 43–Oct 44
Szura	Ukraine		guitarist	May 43–Oct 44
"Tante" Kröner: *see* Lota (Lola) "Tante" Kröner				
Violette Jacquet Silberstein (Jewish)	France	51937	violinist, singer	Sep 43–Oct 44
Yvette Assael Lennon (Jewish) (sister of Lily Assael)	Greece		double bassist	May 43–Oct 44
"Zippy": *see* Helen "Zippy" Spitzer Tichauer				

Name	*Nationality*	*No.*	*Role(s) in Music Block*	*Block Member*
Zofia Cykowiak	Poland	44327	violinist, music copyist	May 43–Oct 44
Zofia Czajkowska (also spelled Cjakowska, Tschajkovska, Tchaikowska) (d. Apr 78)	Poland	6873	conductor/kapo, block senior	Apr 43–Oct 44

MUSICIANS OF THE ORCHESTRA BY INSTRUMENT APRIL 1943–OCTOBER 1944

Conductors

Zofia Czajkowska (April 1943–August 1943)
Alma Rosé (August 1943–April 1944)
Sonya Winogradowa (April 1944–October 1944)

Violin

Alma Rosé
Else Felstein
Helena Dunicz-Niwińska
Hélène Rounder
Hélène Scheps
Henryka Czapla
Henryka Gałązka
Irena Łagowska
Jadwiga Zatorska
Julie Stroumsa Menache
Lily Mathé
Lotte Berran
Maria Langenfeld-Hnydowa
(Madame) Steiner
Violette Jacquet Silberstein
Zofia Cykowiak

Mandolin

Fanny Korenblum Birkenwald
Helen "Zippy" Spitzer Tichauer
Irena Walaszczyk Wachowicz
Kazimiera Małys Kowalczyk
Maria Moś-Wdowik
Masza
Olga
Rachela Olevsky Zelmanowitz
Stefania Baruch

Guitar

Esther Loewy Bejarano
Lotte Lebedová
Margot Anzenbacher Větrovcová
Pronia
Stefania Baruch
Szura

Cello

Anita Lasker-Wallfisch
Maria Kröner

Double Bass
Yvette Assael Lennon

Flute
Lota "Tante" Kröner

Recorder/Piccolo
Esther Loewy Bejarano
Karla Wagenberg Hyman
Ruth Bassin
Sylvia Wagenberg Calif

Accordion
Esther Loewy Bejarano
Flora Schrijver Jacobs
Lily Assael

Percussion
Danuta Kollakowa
Helga Schiessel
Hilde Grünbaum Zimche

Piano (Rehearsal Only)
Ala Gres
Danuta Kollakowa
Alma Rosé
Sonya Winogradowa

Singers
Claire
Dorys
Emmy
Eva Steiner Adam
Ewa Stojowska
Fania Fénelon
Fanny Korenblum Birkenwald
Lotte Lebedová
Maria Bielicka
Violette Jacquet Silberstein

Music Copyists
Ala Gres
Danuta Kollakowa
Else Felstein
Eva Steiner Adam
Ewa Stojowska
Hilde Grünbaum Zimche
Kazimiera Małys Kowalczyk
Lily Assael
Margot Anzenbacher Větrovcová
Maria Moś-Wdowik
Regina (Rivka) Kupferberg Bacia
Sonya Winogradowa
Zofia Cykowiak

Camp Glossary

Appell Muster and roll call; prisoners were known by numbers tattooed on their left forearms.

Arbeitskommando Work detail.

Aufseherin Overseer.

Auschwitz I Main camp: see *Stammlager.*

Auschwitz II Adjunct camp: see *Birkenau.*

Aussenarbeit Work outside the camp.

Aussenkommando Heavy work kommando or detail; see also *Kommando.*

Bekleidungskammer Laundry and clothing storeroom at Birkenau.

Birkenau Literally, "birch grove" or "birch meadow." Adjunct camp, also known as Auschwitz II, established August 1942 three kilometers from Auschwitz I, the main camp.

Block Barrack for housing prisoners or camp establishment with a distinct purpose, such as the laundry block or the music block.

Block 10 See *Experimental Block.*

Block 11 Punishment block in the main camp, which included an underground bunker with isolation cells.

Block 12 The Music Block, which housed the orchestra.

Block 25 Holding barrack for women selected for the gas chamber.

Blockälteste Block senior or warden, also known as the *Blockowa.*

Blockführer, Blockführerin SS block wardens.

Blockführersstube Nazi or SS headquarters outside the camp.

Blockowa Block senior or warden, also known as the *Blockälteste.*

Blocksperre Literally, "block sealed": general prisoner confinement, called during in-camp selections. Prisoners remained in their barracks until the process was completed.

Buna A synthetic rubber needed for the German war effort. The I. G. Farben synthetic oil and rubber plants near Auschwitz, which used prisoner labor, were called "the Buna"; they were also known as Monowitz and Auschwitz III.

Experimental Block Block 10 at Auschwitz, the barrack for women used in medical experiments, housing approximately four hundred women prisoners and sixty-five prisoner-nurses. This was the only women's barrack at Auschwitz I except for a brothel.

Familienlager Family camp. Jews deported from the Theresienstadt ghetto and Gypsies (Sinti and Roma) lived in special areas at Birkenau as families until their liquidation in 1944.

FKZ (Frauenkonzentrationslager) Women's concentration camp.

Functionary SS-appointed prisoner who enforced SS orders; see also *Kapo*. Prisoner-functionaries wore a special armband.

GU (Gesondert Untergebracht) Literally, "separated accommodation": an order for extermination.

Häftling Prisoner.

Hauptscharführer SS rank equivalent to senior sergeant.

Hauptsturmführer SS rank equivalent to captain.

Judenrein Purified of Jews, Jew-free.

Kanada Installation of some thirty-five buildings where new arrivals' confiscated possessions were sorted, stored, and sent to Germany or redistributed in the camp.

Kapo SS-appointed leader or head, a prisoner-functionary charged with enforcing SS orders. Kapos at Auschwitz Birkenau had special privileges and were often abusive to prisoners in their command.

Karteihäftlinge Prisoners "with a file"—prostitutes, common criminals, and others with criminal records, a privileged group who could not be selected for the gas chambers in case they should be called to testify or to face further charges in court.

Kommando Work detail. Prisoners were assigned to kommandos for forced labor both outside and inside the camp.

KZ (Konzentrationslager) Concentration camp.

Lagerführer, Lagerführerin Camp commandants, male and female.

Lagerkapelle Camp band or orchestra.

Läuferin Messenger.

Leichenkommando Body detail; a work party that collected and disposed of corpses.

Leichenwagen Hearse; at Auschwitz-Birkenau, the body wagon that transported naked corpses to the crematorium.

Mischlinge Hybrid; a person of mixed Jewish and "Aryan" ancestry. *Mischlinge* of the first degree had two Jewish grandparents; *Mischlinge* of the second degree, only one. Under certain circumstances the *Mischlinge* could be granted exemptions from Nazi policy.

Muselmann Literally, "Moslem": inmate who had given up; a spiritless, despairing prisoner too emaciated and weak to respond to surroundings.

Oberaufseherin Senior overseer (Inspector-General).

Obergruppenführer SS rank equivalent to general.

Oberscharführer SS rank equivalent to quartermaster-sergeant or technical sergeant.

Obersturmbannführer SS rank equivalent to lieutenant-colonel.

Obersturmführer SS rank equivalent to first lieutenant.

Quarantine Blocks Areas of the women's and men's camps at Birkenau, consisting of numerous barracks, where arriving prisoners were registered, shaved, tattooed, and temporarily housed.

Rapportführerin A female administrator.

Rassenschande Literally, racial tainting by miscegenation; disgrace or crime. A Nazi term referring to sexual contact between Jews and "Aryans," which was prohibited by law.

Reichsführer SS commander-in-chief in Berlin (Heinrich Himmler).

Reichsmark (RM) German mark, a monetary unit in use from November 1924 until 1948, having a value equivalent to 0.238 of a U.S. dollar.

Revier Medical center; the blocks that made up the women's hospital at Birkenau.

Sauna Bath or delousing house, a block with overhead showers that doubled as a concert hall.

Scharführer SS rank equivalent to staff sergeant.

Schreibstube Camp office.

SA (Sturmabteilung) Literally, "assault division": elite para-military corps of the Nazi party.

SB (Sonderbehandlung) Literally, "special treatment": a euphemism for extermination.

SD (Sicherheitsdienst) SS Security Service.

Selektionen The "selection" process by which Nazi camp doctors determined which prisoners would work and which would go to the gas chambers.

Sonderkommando Literally, "special command": prisoner labor squad assigned to work in the gas chambers.

Stammlager Main or parent camp. Auschwitz I (established June 1940) was the parent concentration camp. Birkenau, or Auschwitz II, was established in August 1942 as an adjunct camp and equipped for mass murder.

Strafkommando Punishment detail.

Stubenälteste Block maintenance worker or caretaker, also known as the *Stubowa.*

Stubowa Block maintenance worker or caretaker, also known as the *Stubenälteste.*

Sturmbannführer SS rank equivalent to major.

Triangles Prisoner identification badges. Red signified a political prisoner;

green a criminal; black an "asocial"; purple a Jehovah's Witness; pink a homosexual; brown a Gypsy; yellow, doubled to form a six-point star, a Jew.

Unterscharführer SS rank equivalent to corporal.

Zählappell Roll call.

Zyklon B Poisonous gas made from hydrogen cyanide crystals used in the gas chambers for mass killing. The gas was originally intended for use as a disinfectant and pest control.

Index

The names of orchestra members appear in boldface type. Page numbers in italics refer to illustrations.